# QUEER BLUES

*This book is dedicated to the family we lost at Club Q,*
*Colorado Springs on 19 November 2022.*
*'Melt the guns' – Andy Partridge*

# QUEER BLUES

## THE HIDDEN FIGURES OF EARLY BLUES MUSIC

## DARRYL W. BULLOCK

**OMNIBUS PRESS**

London / New York / Paris / Sydney / Copenhagen / Berlin / Madrid / Tokyo

Copyright © 2023 Omnibus Press
(A division of the Wise Music Group
14–15 Berners Street, London, W1T 3LJ)

Cover designed by Amazing15
Cover images © Alamy
Picture research by the author

ISBN 978-1-9131-7252-7

Darryl W. Bullock hereby asserts his right to be identified as the author
of this work in accordance with Sections 77 to 78 of the Copyright,
Designs and Patents Act 1988.

A catalogue record for this book is available from the British Library.

Typeset by Evolution Design & Digital Ltd (Kent)
Printed in The Czech Republic

www.omnibuspress.com

# Contents

# CONTENTS

# The Songs

15 – Ma Rainey – Prove It On Me Blues (Gertrude Rainey), 1928

16 – Sloppy Henry – Say I Do It (Wayman Henry), 1928

17 – Bessie Brown – 'He Just Don't Appeal to Me' (Porter Grainger), 1929

18 – Bertha Idaho – 'Down on Pennsylvania Avenue' (Tom Delaney), 1929

19 – Mary Dixon – 'All Around Mama' (Henry Cole), 1929

20 – Tampa Red's Hokum Jug Band, vocal chorus by Frankie Half Pint Jaxon – 'My Daddy Rocks Me (With One Steady Roll)' (J. Berni Barbour), 1929

21 – The Hokum Boys – 'Somebody's Been Using That Thing' (Al Miller), 1929

22 – Speckled Red – 'Dirty Dozen' (Rufus Perryman), 1929

23 – Tampa Red and his Hokum Jug Band, vocal chorus by Frankie Half-Pint Jaxon – 'I Wonder Where My Easy Rider's Gone' (Shelton Brooks), 1929

24 – Meade Lux Lewis, vocal Geo Hannah – 'Freakish Blues' (Hannah), 1930

25 – Meade Lux Lewis, vocal Geo Hannah – 'The Boy in the Boat' (Hannah), 1930

26 – Rufus and Ben Quillian – 'It's Dirty but Good' (no author credit), 1930

27 – Blind Blake – 'Righteous Blues' (Arthur Blake), 1930

28 – Billy Banks and His Orchestra – 'Oh! Peter (You're So Nice)' (Herb Wiedoeft/Gene Rose/ Jesse Stafford), 1932

29 – Billy Banks' Rhythmakers – 'Mean Old Bed Bug Blues' (Jack Wood), 1932

30 – Kokomo Arnold – 'Sissy Man Blues' (James Arnold), 1935

31 – Bessie Jackson – 'B.D. Woman's Blues' (Bessie Jackson), 1935

32 – Monette Moore – 'Two Old Maids in a Folding Bed' (Monette Moore), 1936

33 – The Harlem Hamfats – 'The Garbage Man' (Herb Morand), 1936

34 – Robert Johnson – 'I'm a Steady Rollin' Man' (Robert Johnson), 1937

35 – Louis Powell with The Jazz Wizzards – 'Sissy' (Irving Kahal/Louis Panico/Jack Fascinato), 1938

# Introduction

*'You just don't make the blues out of air but out of the corner of your head where everything has been put away.'*[1] – Jelly Roll Morton

The 1920s and 30s saw the release of hundreds of raunchy, bawdy blues recordings, packed with innuendo and sexual imagery, from both male and female singers. These songs – with their tales of handymen, jelly rolls, suggestive fruit and bowls full of sugar – were primarily aimed at a knowing, heterosexual audience, but from the very beginning, the blues has had a close connection with the LGBTQ community, and the book that you are holding is chiefly concerned with the history of queer blues, with the LGBTQ composers and entertainers of the same period, and the wonderfully outlandish, life-affirming songs they performed and recorded. Having said that, although critics like to put things in neat little boxes, musicians rarely restrict themselves to one style, and over the course of the next few hundred pages we shall also dip in and out of the development of queer jazz music over the same period, looking at how both genres cross-pollenated with each other. During the early years of jazz and blues, artists moved seamlessly from one side of the divide to the other, and performers, composers and critics seldom differentiated between the two. The types of popular music we now recognise as jazz and blues were born within a few years of each other, and both came from the same roots, via poor, self-taught musicians with a story to tell. It is significant that the first recognisable jazz record released, in 1917, was an instrumental – issued by the Original Dixieland 'Jass' Band – called 'Livery Stable Blues', and that two years earlier Gordon Seagrove wrote a column for the *Chicago Tribune* titled 'Blues is Jazz, and Jazz is Blues'.[2]

The story of the beginnings of jazz, like that of the blues, is steeped in misinformation. Some written and oral histories will tell you that a blind Black boy named Stale Bread invented jazz, on the streets of New Orleans in the 1890s... only Stale Bread (real name Emile Lacoume) was not Black and not blind, at least not at the point in his life when he supposedly gave birth to jazz. Born in Passage de la Bourse, a small street in the French Quarter of New Orleans, better known as Exchange Alley, the decidedly Caucasian amateur boxer and newspaper seller would lose most of his sight not long after his 15th birthday in 1900 (the loss caused by his eyes becoming infected after he accidentally rubbed pepper into them: despite attempts by doctors to restore his vision (and a futile visit to a faith healer in 1920) he would remain virtually blind for the rest of his life), but when he and several friends formed the Razzy Dazzy Spasm Band five years earlier – some utilising the same kind of homemade instruments that would later find popularity with jug bands and skiffle artists – he was fully sighted. Even then, he did not invent jazz: Stale Bread (he earned the nickname stealing loaves from a local bakery to feed his penniless band members) was influenced by the ragtime piano he heard coming from houses of ill-repute as he sold his newspapers. The word 'jazz' (or jass, as it was first known) had not even been coined then. Some say that 'jazz' comes from 'jism', or that 'jass' was a slang word used in the vice district of New Orleans, and it is therefore appropriate that many songs in the blues and jazz oeuvres deal with sex and sexuality. Stale Bread called his style of music 'hot'. 'I don't care what it is,' he said, when asked about the origins of the word, 'if you don't put hot spots into it, it's not worth the paper it's printed on.'[3] Whatever you choose to call it, the Razzy Dazzy Spasm Band is credited with being history's first recognisable jazz band. Discovering the first identifiable blues singer is a harder task.

\*

There is a long history of so-called 'dirty blues' recordings, and a longer history still of blues songs that celebrate sex. Before Mamie Smith recorded what we now think of as the first 'proper' blues record, even before the first published song with blues in the title appeared in sheet music stores or on piano rolls, musicians were performing raunchy songs containing double entendres, slang and dialect words to represent male and female anatomy and the panoply of sex acts. Sadly, because the majority of early music historians, field recorders and archivists were white, middle-class folk whose agenda was the documentation of morally uplifting songs that fitted their clean, Christian idea of what folk songs were, many of the more obscene blues and jazz songs that were being performed in bawdy houses, bars and bordellos around the southern states have been lost forever. Luckily, we still have those that were recorded. 'People forget that there was a far more liberal attitude at that time, before the conservativism of the 1950s and 60s,' explains civil rights activist and musician Chris Houston-Lock. 'Because a lot of these artists were Black, they were not being censored. They were so off the mainstream that the authorities didn't bother.'[4]

Today we're becoming more used to women using music to express their sexuality, and although it is still shocking, we barely bat an eyelid when an artist such as Nicki Minaj disses fellow rapper Young Thug and accuses him of being a clothes-stealing cross-dresser in her song 'Barbie Dreams', but it is nothing new. Bessie Smith, Ma Rainey and the other classic blues stars were singing songs that were just as provocative; in fact, if you consider that they were performing these songs a century ago, before anyone had laid the groundwork, at a time when women were oppressed and Black women doubly so, while working in an industry that was run primarily by white men, then you begin to see that their lyrics were more shocking than anything Cardi B and Megan Thee Stallion dreamt up in 'Wet Ass Pussy'.

It is not difficult to find LGBTQ references or lyrics in blues songs. In this book I will highlight around three dozen recordings whose lyrics clearly demonstrate at least a passing connection to the lesbian, gay, bisexual, transgender or queer experience, but proving the sexuality or even gender identity of the artists or musicians involved is more problematic. In the early days of both jazz and blues, and of vaudeville and music hall, women often travelled together, shared rooms, even shared beds and slept together, but that alone does not automatically make them lesbian or bisexual. After all, who would waste their time questioning the heterosexuality of Stan Laurel or Oliver Hardy, even though they were often seen sharing a bed in their movies? There were many reasons that female artists shared a bed while they were on the road, from saving money to providing companionship, keeping warm at a time when there was no such thing as central heating, and offering security against male aggressors. In those dark years of segregation, Black artists often found it impossible to access hotel rooms and were forced to bunk up together in whatever boarding houses would offer them shelter from the weather. The LGBTQ community has for decades claimed as its own musicians about who little or nothing is known about their private lives, extrapolating whole histories from no more than gossip and rumour. But through their words, the careful use and understanding of the language of the day, and the stories told by their peers, we are able to build a more accurate picture of at least some of these important and influential lives.

Known variously as 'Vaudeville Blues' or 'Classic Female Blues', the early urban blues style popularised by Ma Rainey, Alberta Hunter and so on is a product of both the cotton field and the church, of travelling tent shows, of brothels and bars. The earliest exponents of this 12-bar, three-lines-to-a-verse form (with, more often than not, the second line a repeat or adaptation of the first) including Rainey and her protégé Bessie Smith learned their art in front of a paying audience, in shows where, as well as performing these increasingly fashionable and popular numbers, they had to sing ballads, minstrel songs, the latest jazz hits, ragtime standards and just about anything their audience required. These shows were advertised as 'refined', and suitable for the whole family: the dirty blues or queer blues songs that many of these artists would later perform and record would have no place here. Those were reserved for private audiences, and it would be a few years yet before anyone would dare record any of them.

There was an honesty about the blues, a candour missing from the other popular songs of the day. Blues writers were penning songs about their own lives, and singers imbued their performances with a frankness that audiences had not heard before. People wrote about, and sang about, their own experiences; it is hardly surprising that they would sing about their own sexuality with such authenticity.

Although you can easily trace its roots back through the work songs sung in the cotton fields by enslaved men, women and children of African descent, and further still to the storytelling tradition of folk songs, trying to define 'The Blues' is a fiendishly difficult job. William Christopher Handy and Gertrude Pridgett, the press-anointed 'father' and 'mother' of the blues respectively, told similar tales about how – in the early years of the 20th century – they discovered and helped give birth to what, for the past hundred or so years, we have called 'The Blues', but you can trace the birth of some of the earliest blues standards back to the mid-1800s, through vaudeville performances and music hall songs and to the immense popularity of the blackface minstrels. Reach back further and you soon discover recognisable elements in church hymns. It is folk music in its truest form: music of the people, for the people, by the people, from a time when there was no such thing as mass entertainment. There was no radio, no cinema and no recorded music of any type. Outside of church, most people had one option, and that was to entertain themselves, and the music they created was akin to storytelling; it mirrored their lives, work and relationships. Songs were not written down but passed from one generation to the next as part of an oral tradition, and those that repeated them were not passive consumers, simply repeating something they knew, but would adapt these songs to reflect their own experiences. Certainly by the time Mamie Smith came to record, the 'sorrowful' songs that both W. C. Handy and Ma Rainey claimed to have first heard almost two decades earlier had been augmented by elements of jazz, ragtime, vaudeville and folk.

Rather fittingly for a bandleader, composer and multi-instrumentalist, W. C. Handy often changed his tune about how he first came into contact with this new and exciting music. One story he told claimed that he first heard the blues sometime around 1903 when, half asleep and waiting for a long-delayed train in the town of Tutwiler, Mississippi, fate sat down by his side. 'A lean, loose-jointed Negro had commenced plunking a guitar,' he would write in his 1941 autobiography, *Father of the Blues.*

'His clothes were rags; his feet peeped out of his shoes. His face had on it some of the sadness of the ages.'[5] This unnamed, sad-faced, ragged man was using a knife as a primitive bottleneck, singing a few repetitive lines about his travels. Handy – a peripatetic musician who two years earlier had been leading both the Twin City Colored Orchestra and the Agricultural and Mechanical College Band of Normal, Alabama, as well as playing cornet in Mahara's Minstrels – claimed that the tune, and the doleful lyrics, stayed with him and he soon began to introduce similar themes into his compositions.

That was one version, but it has about as much truth in it as a Disney-animated fairy tale. Jelly Roll Morton, a man who for years would claim that he invented jazz, stated that he was writing blues numbers before Handy had ever copyrighted a song and that blues musicians were commonplace in New Orleans in the early years of the first decade of the 20th century, yet even he did not go as far as to claim to have invented the blues, insisting that the honour belonged to a local woman, Mary 'Mamie' Desdunes. Handy would also recount another, perhaps more believable explanation of how he first became aware of the blues, which he initially revealed more than a decade and a half before he incorporated both tales into the *Father of the Blues*. Handy, the son and grandson of Methodist ministers whose family had wanted him to join them in the church, told an interviewer for Baltimore-based Black news weekly the *Afro-American*:

> In the south they have community affairs called 'script dances'. The promoter hires a hall, engages an orchestra, generally Negroes, and retains the profits. My band was engaged for one of these dances in Cleveland, Mississippi, sometime between 1905 and 1910. During the evening some local colored talent came into the hall. They were three men, and requested that they be permitted to put on a number for the occasion. They had a mandolin, guitar and bass violin. They played from memory and their music was a low, mournful tune. That was the beginning of the blues.[6]

That same story was also recounted, by Handy, to folk-song archivist Dorothy Scarborough and her assistant, Ola Lee Gullage, for the 1925 book *On the Trail of Negro Folk-Songs*. Although none of this itinerant trio was mentioned by name, years later, the leader of that band was identified as Prince Albert McCoy. Handy happily basked in the nickname 'The Father of the Blues'; perhaps McCoy should therefore be recognised as the genre's grandfather.

Ms Pridgett, who in 1904 would marry and become 'Ma' Rainey, told blues scholar John Wesley Work III that she had first stumbled upon the blues around a year before Handy's earliest recollection, making that claim more than a decade before he published his autobiography. In her tale she heard this strange new music 'in 1902 in a small town in Missouri where she was appearing with a show under a tent'. Ma claimed that she overheard, 'A girl from town who came to the tent one morning and began to sing about the "man" who left her. The song was so strange and poignant that it attracted much attention. "Ma" Rainey became so interested that she learned the song from the visitor, and used it soon after in her "act" as an encore. The song elicited such response from the audience that it won a special place in her act. Many times she was asked what kind of song it was, and one day she replied, in a moment of inspiration, "It's the Blues".'[7] A wildly inaccurate puff piece that appeared in Black newspaper the *Afro-American* during her week-long appearance in Baltimore in 1926, claimed that Ma had 'been singing the blue numbers for 30 years'.[8]

The truth, unsurprisingly, is a lot more complicated. But let us go back a couple of years, to the end of the 19th century, and begin our story there.

# 1

# Leaving the South

*'Mr. Chappelle... carries with him his three private cars and fifty people, performers, artists, canvas men, drivers, etc. In towns that contain no opera house or where the use of opera houses are refused to colored people, Mr. Chappelle erects his own canvas tent, which will accommodate from twelve to fourteen hundred people. He carries his own teams and wagons and light rigs, very much on the order of the Barnum and Bailey circus.'* [1]

In January 1900, Patrick Henry 'Pat' Chappelle, an African American from Jacksonville, Florida, and his business partner R. S. Donaldson, announced their intention to form 'a company of Negro comedians.' [2] The pair declared that their company would 'travel in its own private car [railway carriage] and give entertainments in every town of any importance in this and other states.' [3] Chappelle was one of the best-known and most successful Black entrepreneurs in the region. His venues catered to both Black and white audiences, but the entertainment provided was exclusively Black, including male impersonator Miss Jessie Thomas, comedian Arthur 'Happy' Howe, plus 'cake walkers' (a dance that had begun on plantations), 'coon shouters' (minstrel singers) and 'buck and wing' dancers, the latter a style of tap dancing derived from clog dances and jigs.

The former banjo player and pianist opened his first business, a saloon and pool hall, in Jacksonville in 1894, which quickly expanded to include a small concert venue, the Excelsior Hall, the South's first Black-owned theatre. Soon after he – along with support from various brothers and cousins, and with financing from Donaldson – was also acting as manager and director of Fort Brooke's Buckingham Theatre. A true visionary, Chappelle saw that, by working together instead of against each other, Black artists and entrepreneurs could avoid being shut out of show business by a system geared towards more powerful, better organised white acts and management. 'Colored people in the theatrical business are .the same as they are in any other business. They do not "pull together",' he told the *Colored American* newspaper. 'The white performers are organizing to fight the Negro... the time is coming fast when he will have to look only to the colored manager for engagements, as the white performer is closing every door against him. The colored managers are also to blame, for they too ought to organize as it seems that the whites do not want to see any colored manager carry on business successfully.'[4] Despite Chappelle's warning, it would take almost two decades for Black American entrepreneurs to assemble their own successful touring circuit.

Black entertainment was still very much in its infancy. Following the Emancipation Proclamation, issued on 1 January 1863 by President Abraham Lincoln, small numbers of African Americans in some southern states began to taste a limited amount of freedom, but it was not until 18 December 1865 that the 13th Amendment was adopted as part of the United States Constitution, officially abolishing slavery and freeing more than 100,000 enslaved people. Earlier that same year the first Black minstrel troupe, Brooker's Georgia Minstrels, was formed. Advertised as 'The only Negro troupe in the United States'[5] – prior to their formation minstrel shows had predominantly featured white performers in blackface – in its early days the act often had to perform under armed guard, for fear that anti-abolitionists would attempt to drag the former slaves off the stage and attack them.

The American theatre was going through a period of incredible, and swift, change, and not everyone liked what they saw. In April 1900 British-born actor and director Olga Nethersole was hauled into court in

New York on a charge of violating public decency after she attempted to stage a play titled *Sapho*, based on the book by French novelist Alphonse Daudet, at Wallack's Theatre. After a sensational trial which made headlines worldwide, Miss Nethersole and *Sapho* were found not guilty of bringing immorality and disrepute to the stage, and the play – which had very little to do with the true story of the famed Lesbian poet – was allowed to continue.

By the time that Chappelle and Donaldson commissioned – from Philadelphia-based writer Frank Dumont – a two-act musical comedy, nominally set in the Philippines, called *A Rabbit's Foot* for their new touring company, Black vaudeville had become firmly established. Sissieretta Jones, known as Black Patti (after the Italian opera singer Adelina Patti) had been touring theatres with her own Troubadours – which included pioneering Black entertainers Salem Tutt Whitney and his brother J. Homer Tutt – since 1896, and others soon followed. Vaudeville revues like the Black Patti Troubadours would include singers, comedians, speciality acts, dancers and even female impersonators, such as Andrew Tribble, who toured the States extensively from the turn of the century until his death in 1935, playing dowdy characters including Lily White, Sis Hopkins, and Ophelia Snow, a character that he introduced in early Black musical *The Shoo-Fly Regiment* in 1906, and that he would later revisit on stage with lesbian blues singer Clara Smith in New York in 1929.

Appearing in blackface (lighter-skinned Black performers were often required to blacken up, especially if they were playing comedic roles), Tribble's portrayal of silly, flighty girls (known as 'wench characters', and distinctly different from the busty, blowsy mammy) came directly from minstrelsy. These comedy roles were not intended to fool audiences into believing that they were indeed watching a woman perform, but as he progressed and honed his craft, Tribble gained a reputation for the accuracy of his imitations and the quality of his wardrobe. He would soon become known as the 'Black Eltinge', a reference to Julian Eltinge, the most famous female impersonator in America at the time, who began his own stage career about the same time that Tribble first popped on a skirt. Eltinge was the gold standard of female impersonators: theatre-goers were used to seeing men and women caricatured by the opposite sex, but he was one of the first to present himself on stage as if he *were* a woman, and he was regarded as having 'raised female impersonation into the sphere of art'.[6] We cannot be sure that Tribble was either homosexual or bisexual: he married and had a son, although that in itself proves nothing, and LGBTQ historians have a tendency to claim anyone outside of the binary norm as their own, but we do know that Eltinge, who was homosexual, held Tribble in great regard, recognising him 'as a real genius'.[7]

Born in Richmond, Kentucky in 1879, Tribble shared his name with an illustrious ancestor, a white Baptist minister and close friend of Thomas Jefferson, and was probably the result of the elder Andrew Tribble having had sex with a Black servant. As a child he was appearing, along with his brother Amos, as part of the Original Pickaninny Band, a troupe of child actors, singers and dancers who toured the South in the 1890s. In 1893 Tribble and the Original Pickaninny Band were added to a revue called *In Old Kentucky*. 'The little darkies under twelve years of age composing the band are an entertaining feature of the performance,'[8] and were the Menudo of their day, with members being swapped out whenever they grew too tall or began to look older than a pre-teen. With his slight build and feminine look, Tribble may have lasted longer than many of his contemporaries. In April 1894 the show landed in New York, and it would continue to tour for the rest of the year, the elaborate musical becoming one of the biggest box-office hits of the era. Perhaps unsurprisingly, there were soon other so-called Original Pickaninny Bands touring the States, including a troupe that was added to the annual revue, *The Passing Show*, in December 1894, and another that was part of the 1895 show *The South Before the War*, which saw the directors of *In Old Kentucky* rebrand their star act 'The only genuine and original Picaninny Brass Band'.

When he became too tall for the Original Pickaninny Band, Tribble retired from the stage for a period. After attempting to become a jockey (no doubt influenced by appearing in *In Old Kentucky*, which featured a racing scene with live horses on stage), he married, and he and his wife, an actor named Bessie, would have one son, Atwood. Horse racing was clearly not his forte, for around 1904 he went back on stage as an adult performer, playing comic roles. He and Bessie joined the stock company of the Pekin Theatre in Chicago, and in 1906 he appeared at the recently refurbished Pekin as part of the cast of a musical comedy entitled *The Man From 'Bam*. It was around this time that he began to make a name for his comedy female characters and, while appearing at the Pekin in a revue called *Two African Princes*, he was poached by comedians Bob Cole and J. Rosamond Johnson. From August 1906 he was appearing in *The Shoo-Fly Regiment* with the Cole and Johnson company. The show opened in Washington on 21 August and went on to become one of the first all-Black revues to play on Broadway. It seems that, while Tribble was off becoming a star, Bessie and Atwood remained in Chicago; they would not reunite, but neither Tribble nor his wife would seek a divorce.

On 24 December 1908 prominent African American newspaper, the *New York Age*, featured a short interview with Tribble, then appearing in Cole and Johnson's *The Red Moon*, under the title 'Well Known Character Comedian'.

I never go on the stage unless I try to do my best. That, somehow, has always been my motto, and I have been well paid for sticking to it. One night to a very small audience I was doing my best, not dreaming of anyone watching me but the manager. I was surprised to learn that among the few in the audience were Cole and Johnson. I was also told that they liked my work very much. They sent for me and gave me plenty of encouraging talk and pictured a beautiful future for me. Well, as all the other big stars had told me the same thing, I paid but little attention to it.

One day I received a letter bearing the postmark London, England. It was from Cole and Johnson, who were then in London. They reminded me of our agreement. My contract soon arrived. I had no idea what they had planned to do with me, but to make a long story short, they gave me the part of 'Ophelia' [in] the 'Shoo-Fly Regiment'... Now I am 'Miss Lily White' in 'The Red Moon'.

Cole and Johnson were former members of Black Patti's Troubadours. A decade earlier the duo had produced *A Trip to Coontown*, the first musical performed, directed and produced by Black Americans, and they made their London debut in July 1905, billed as 'The biggest Negro turn in America',[9] returning in both 1906 and 1907. Tribble was a huge hit in *The Red Moon*, as the washerwoman Lily White, and Cole and Johnson wanted Tribble to rejoin the cast when the show was restaged in New York in August 1909, but they could not agree terms with Tribble's manager, and his part was played first by John Jackson and later by Rebecca Delk. Tribble instead joined S. H. Dudley's Smart Set, first appearing, in September 1909, in *His Honor, the Barber*. When this show closed, Tribble played dates on his own, and with Joe Jordan at Brighton Beach, Brooklyn.

After a few months on tour, in September 1910 Tribble once again joined S. H. Dudley's Smart Set touring minstrels for a revival of *His Honor, the Barber*. 'Andrew Tribble, a Washington favorite, plays "Babe Johnson" [the lead character's girlfriend] with a naturalness that stamps him as the best impersonator of female comedy roles in the business, and the house was in a constant roar all the time he was on the stage. His costumes were up to date, and his "hobble skirt" was a wonder to behold. Mr. Tribble was given a big "hand" nightly.'[10] As part of the Smart Set, Tribble continued to attract favourable reviews. 'Andrew Tribble, as Babe Johnson is one of the laughing hits of the show,' one of many similar critics enthused. 'Each year Mr. Tribble is seen to better advantage in the character he plays, and he has been such an attentive student in his line of work that now he is recognized as a female impersonator of no little ability.'[11] Cole and Johnson were struggling after making losses on tour, and Bob Cole committed suicide in 1911, drowning himself in a Catskills creek while suffering from depression. Tribble, however, went from strength to strength, appearing on Broadway that same year, and being advertised as 'The colored Eltinge'. He would rarely be out of work. Tribble was just one of dozens of men donning dresses to make a living at that time, such as C. Adam La Rose, who appeared on stage in drag, playing a melophone (a French instrument related to the accordion) as part of A. G. Allen's Big Minstrels band, as well as performing speciality songs solo.

\*

Acts like the Black Patti Troubadours, the Original Pickaninny Band and the Smart Set were only able to play in venues that catered for Black audiences, or that were run by Black managers, and they were few and far between. When his calls for Black managers to band together in a supportive trade organisation fell on deaf ears, Pat Chappelle looked for the solution elsewhere. He had seen the massive tent revival churches touring the South, and the white-run circuses that had pitched up around the region for years. His show would not need to rely on the largess of sympathetic venue owners, he reasoned. A Rabbit's Foot would invest in its own tent.

The idea of purchasing a tent was a stroke of genius: it meant that the show would be able to play anywhere. Every city, and most small towns, had a theatre or community hall, but not all of them would welcome Black performers. With their own tent, Chappelle's company could perform wherever they could find, or rent, a vacant lot. A Rabbit's Foot would take his crew of some forty singers, musicians, comedians and high-wire balancers to theatres around the South and as far away as New York, and give a permanent name to his troupe: the Rabbit Foot Company. In November, Chappelle took on the running of the Bijou Theatre in Tampa, Florida, and the troupe set up home there for the winter.

This was something of a turnaround in fortunes for Chappelle: two years previously he had been so badly beaten by soldiers following an incident in his bar that he narrowly escaped with his life. The beating came after Chappelle was accused of having drugged several Black soldiers who had spent the day drinking at his bar, slipping 'knock-out drops' into their beer. He had almost certainly been set up by other businessmen, jealous of his success and of his influence. Chappelle had become a vocal critic of the area's Black leaders, who he accused of lining their own pockets while others went in need: 'It is not what the white man does [to] the colored people of the South,' he wrote in a letter printed in the Colored American, 'All the dirty work is done to [the] Negro by some of the supposed leaders of his own race.'[12]

By the summer of 1901, and now equipped with a tent that could seat up to 1,200 people, P. H. Chappelle's Rabbit Foot Company – which Chappelle himself called 'one of the greatest Negro shows of the age'[13]

– was touring throughout the southern states; his business partner, Donaldson, elected to stay in Tampa and look after the Mascotte Theatre. With their newly acquired canvas, and usually playing a different town or city every night apart from Sunday, the original two-act musical would quickly mutate into something more akin to a revue, with speciality acts, dancers and singers doing their thing with scant regard to any overarching script. In the early days, with the twin evils of racism and segregation to deal with, subterfuge was called for, and as far as certain newspapers were concerned, the message was that 'this company is under white management.'[14] This deception worked; the Rabbit Foot Company quickly established itself as the South's premier, Black-run attraction, and Chappelle invested in his own train carriages (one of which was named Pocahontas), equipped with beds, a fully working kitchen and space to rehearse.

Chappelle told reporters that the train carriages were a necessity as 'in no town in the state is there any hotel large enough to hold the entire company'.[15] That is not strictly true. There were plenty of hotels that could accommodate the company, however none were willing: Chappelle may have been one of the most successful businesspeople in the region, but no white-owned or run lodging house would take his acts. In towns where the show's crew could find accommodation – often in small boarding houses run by former actors – the average wage for those lowest on the bill would be eaten up by the weekly cost of a bed, a hot meal and laundry. Rail transport was also segregated at that time; owning your own carriages solved the problem of dozens of musicians, performers and crew having to fight for the limited space available to Black travellers on regularly scheduled trains, as well as providing sleeping, eating and rehearsal quarters.

Owning and operating their own railway carriages may have offered a solution to the difficulties of trying to arrange transportation, food and lodgings for anything up to 100 Black performers, crew members, management, and their instruments, animals and props, but travelling in these often rickety and run-down cars brought about its own problems. In August 1908, after a performance in Charlotte, North Carolina, seven members of the company and crew, including singer Isaiah Grant and cook Willie Moran, were badly burned after a fire broke out whilst the train was in motion. A skittish horse kicked over a can of gasoline which quickly spread to where Moran was preparing breakfast. Two horses died in the fire and a third member of the crew, George Connolly, was almost kicked to death by the animals as they struggled for freedom from the flames. A similar accident, in Florida in December 1910, saw no major casualties but the loss of the company's $5,000 sleeping car.

'A traveling show composed entirely of colored people,'[16] the Rabbit Foot Company was a sell-out wherever it appeared: Chappelle organised daily street parades to ensure that everyone knew that his troupe was in town (a brilliant advertising ruse that was quickly adopted by other touring companies), and their annual tour became the stuff of legend. Life on the road was tough: touring annually from August until mid-February the following year, the troupe often faced hostility from whites in the towns they played, and were occasionally pelted with rotten vegetables, had bricks and other missiles thrown at the tent during performances and on at least one occasion had the guy ropes securing the canvas in place cut. The threat of a racist attack was ever present, and when the locals in Gonzales, Texas created such a fuss that the show could not begin, performers were forced to hide from a barrage of eggs in their railway carriages. The police failed to step in and Chappelle, who had paid for a license to perform in the town, sued the local council for failing to look after his performers. Pat Chappelle was not afraid to stand up to the those who saw him as an uppity Negro, and would happily take companies who refused to provide services to him and his company to court, including railway companies who declined to transport his carriages or insisted on attaching them to goods, rather than passenger, trains. However, he was a businessman, not a philanthropist, and he saw no need to cosset his company: when, in June 1904, comedian 'Happy' Howe became homesick and jumped ship at Wilmington, North Carolina, taking his trunk, stage costume and props with him, Chappelle had an arrest warrant issued and had Howe thrown into jail.

## 2

# Ma Rainey Gets the Blues

*'Pornography is such an organic part of [the work song's]*
*structure that it cannot be excised without destroying*
*the point of the songs.'*[1] – Gates Thomas

In late 1906 comedian and award-winning cake walk dancer Will Rainey brought his young bride into the Rabbit Foot fold. Gertrude Pridgett had married Will Rainey in Muscogee County, Georgia on 2 February 1904. The new Mr and Mrs Rainey moved in with Gertrude's mother, into an already overcrowded home at 804 Ninth Street, Columbus City, Georgia, and for a while tried to make it on their own, playing several dates as the Alabama Fun Makers (or Funmakers) Company, until Will brought his woman out to Florida to meet with Mr Chappelle. While playing as the Fun Makers, the couple were billed as William and Gertrude Rainey – their more famous nicknames yet to be bestowed. Will's big song was 'Let Him Without Sin Cast the First Stone', while Gertrude's hit was a comedy song, now lost to the mists of time, called 'I'll Be Back in a Minute, And I'll Do the Same for You'.

Ma and Pa Rainey, as the couple soon came to be known, stayed with the troupe until the close of the season and swiftly became the Rabbit Foot Company's leading attraction, advertised as the 'assassinators of the blues'*, an epithet used by a number of other acts, including 'famous novelty entertainers'[2] Stanford and Darlington, Black vocal duo Kelly and Davis, actor Francis Pierlot, and comedian Don Carney. Among the songs Ma performed with the Rabbit Foot at this time were 'The Man in the Moon' and 'Miss Jane', while Will joined her in a duet, 'I've Said My last Farewell'.[3]

Jazz clarinettist Norman Mason was a part of the Rabbit Foot orchestra, and he recalled those days in an interview with Blues archivist Paul Oliver:

Minstrel shows was very interesting and I played with the Rabbit Foot Minstrels for quite a few years. I could properly start to talk about the Rabbit Foot with the band. This feller Joe White was the drummer and Real Mark Chainey was the violinist in the orchestra and Archie Blue was the bass drummer and I played trumpet. Now for the blues singers we had Ida Cox sing, we had Lizzie Miles. Also Mamie – Mamie Smith, and speakin' of Chippie Hill and of course, Ma Rainey... The show traveled around on a car; we had a Pullman car – one side we used for keepin' the members of the show and the other side for the canvas. We had the canvasmen to put up the tents and we ate on the car and we traveled by railroad. We made short jumps mostly during the week because of the fact that we played quite a few small towns. Caught the cotton crop down in Mississippi in the fall and we'd go out and catch the tobacco crop in North and South Carolina in the spring you see. We also traveled out in West Virginia where we played the coal mines, up in the hollers there... I like the blues because it do express the feelings of people and when we used to play around through Mississippi in those cotton sections of the country we had the people with us! They hadn't much outlet for their enjoyment and they get together in those honkytonks and you should hear them. That's where they let out their suppressed

---

\* 'blues' is used here in relation to feeling blue. The word had not yet been associated with blues music.

11

desires, and the more suppressed they are the better the blues they put out, seems to me.[4]

Ma's powerful voice and sense of comic timing soon set her apart from her fellow performers, including slack-line walker Mack Allen, contortionist Delamon Miles and acrobats the Watts Brothers, and when the Rabbit Foot Company closed for the season in February 1907, Will and Gertrude set out on their own, forming a small troupe they named Will Rainey's Plantation Show and joining a travelling street fair company known as the No Name Show to play dates in Georgia. Ma's first mention in the national press appeared in trade magazine *Billboard* in March 1907, where it was reported that 'Miss Gertrude Rainey, the Plantation star, is winning new laurels with every performance,'[5] not that surprising considering that the show mentioned took place in her hometown of Columbus.

Ma really was something special, as piano player and composer Thomas 'Georgia Tom' Dorsey, who first got the blues bug as a pre-teen, hanging around backstage at Atlanta's fabled '81' Theatre, recalled: 'Ma... packed 'em in. ...I traveled with her almost four years... She was a natural drawing card.'[6] However Gertrude Pridgett's early years are steeped in mystery, not helped by court reporters, census takers and church ministers' inability to spell her name correctly (she appears as Gertrude Pritchard in the marriage register, and several writers have insisted that her middle names were Malissa Nix, when that was, in fact, the married name of one of her sisters), or by contemporary newspaper reporters happy to embellish the facts or too lazy to check the wild claims made by her own press releases. She was born in September 1882 (if you believe the 1900 census), in 1884 (if you prefer to believe the census of 1910), or on 20 November 1892, according to her death certificate. Other sources will tell you that she first entered the world on 26 April 1886, and when not treading the boards she worked as a washerwoman. Will had been born in 1876, making him somewhere between six and sixteen years older than his bride... although the 1910 census has them both the same age.

Although she first trod the boards as a dancer and singer in the amateur revue *A Bunch of Blackberries*, at the Springer Opera House in

Columbus (according to her brother, Thomas Pridgett Junior, in a letter written in 1940),[7] in either 1898 or 1900, the eldest daughter of Thomas and Ella Pridgett (née Ella Allen) was first and foremost a vaudeville and minstrel singer, and is said to have inherited her fondness for the stage from her maternal grandmother, who also performed on stage following her emancipation. Unlike W. C. Handy, whose claim on the blues was a moveable feast, Ma would always state that she first heard the blues in 1902, when 'she heard a girl who was hanging around the tent sing a "strange and poignant" song about how her man had left her. The entertainers in the troupe had never heard anything quite like it before, and Rainey decided to work it into her act. The response she got from rural black audiences was overwhelming, so she began looking for similar songs as she travelled.'[8] One press report has her singing the blues from the age of three, but Ma would often repeat the tale of a heartbroken young woman hanging around the tent show, as she did to folklorist John Work.

Despite this being Ma's preferred origin story, the legend does not quite ring true, as it would be another few years before Gertrude would join a tent show, but whenever (or if ever) this mythical event took place, one thing is certain: Rainey understood what these songs meant to an audience – 'The blues ain't nothing but the easy going heart disease,' she once explained. 'In short, it is the cry of a lover who has been mistreated.'[9] By late 1909 the press were starting to take notice: 'Gertrude Rainey always brings down the house when she renders a late and up-to-date coon song.'[10] In the years before the word 'blues' became common, the singers of these types of songs were often called 'coon shouters' or 'moaners', and the songs that they sang were invariably referred to as 'coon songs'. Ma was a moaner of the old school, and it was her delivery that turned that material she sang 'blue'.

With no children of their own, Gertrude and Will adopted a boy, named Daniel: their fellow performers joked that the only conceivable way Gertrude and Will would have progeny would be by adoption, as Ma made no attempt to hide her sexual preference, much to her husband's chagrin. Danny Rainey soon became an integral part of his adoptive parents' musical comedy act, and was billed as 'The world's greatest juvenile stepper'.[11] Life under canvas was hard: the Rabbit Foot shows

13

occasionally descended into violent near-riots, both from within the audience and from outside the tent as jealous show promoters, racist gangs and drunk locals were refused entrance. 'Of course on the Rabbit Foots we had some really famous blues singers and entertainers,' Norman Mason told Paul Oliver,

> Like Butterbeans and Susie... And Ida Cox of course. Her husband also came to the Foots and played a while with the band, but Ida, she was really what they call a 'coon shouter'. Oh, she could really sing the blues you know. Of course she left the show and went into Tom Anderson's out in New Orleans and sang there for several years before she went out on the vaudeville circuit. I guess Ma Rainey was the most famous. Because Ma Rainey was quite a character or legend in America here, in that she had such an outstanding voice for the blues, and she sang songs like the 'Florida Blues' and the 'Kansas City Blues' and the 'Jelly Roll Blues'. She sang songs then that would sound as up-to-date as if it were played right now. During that time people didn't dress like they do now. In that people then used to have more clothes on and she used to have those real long dresses sometimes with a high neck, well, like you would call it – like the Gay Nineties. But she had one of those voices you never forget – particularly for singing the blues.[12]

While Chappelle, the Raineys and the rest of the Rabbit Foot Company were taking their show to just about anyone who would have them, Ma Rainey's chief challenger for the title of parent of the blues was swiftly making a reputation for himself in the fledgling music industry. In 1907, while living in Memphis, W. C. Handy met a young man named Harry Pace, chief cashier of a Black-owned financial company, the Solvent Savings Bank. That meeting was a fortuitous one: Pace had a great head for business, and he was also a keen singer and amateur lyric writer. The pair quickly became friends, writing and publishing their first song together, 'In the Cotton Fields of Dixie', that same year. They quickly followed up this initial success by establishing their own publishing house, the Pace and Handy Music Company, although Pace

14

continued to work in finance, moving to Atlanta, to take on the role of secretary and treasurer of the Standard Life Insurance Company, and leaving Handy to look after their affairs in Memphis. Not long afterwards, Handy wrote the song that formed the genesis of his first big hit, 'The Memphis Blues'.

Published in September 1912, 'The Memphis Blues' has gone down in history as the first song with 'blues' in the title to have been published... but, like many of the legends that surround the birth of the blues, this is simply not true. 'The Memphis Blues' was an instrumental, and a rag at that, and did not have lyrics until George A. Norton added them a year later. Handy's tune, its author claimed, had been adapted from his earlier song 'Mr. Crump', an election campaign song Handy had written for a local politician, although 'Stack' Mangham, a member of Handy's band, would later reveal that the tune was based on one Handy had heard at a dance in Cleveland, Mississippi around 1903. A short piece that appeared just two months after Handy copyrighted the song, in Nashville newspaper *The Tennessean*, stated that, 'The song was composed by an old Negro years ago, and at the time the tune was so ragged that nobody could get it on paper. The old Negro was finally taken to Memphis and he explained the tune as best he could to the producers, who finally put it together into one of the niftiest pieces of music ever turned out.'[13] Handy, it should be said, would refute the notion that any part of 'The Memphis Blues' had come from any source other than his own creativity, telling music critic Abbe Niles that, 'I did not obtain the idea from a Florida Negro... But wrote what I felt.'[14] 'Stack' Mangham's version of events may conflict with those of the song's official author, but it has a striking similarity to Handy's own recollection of how he first encountered the blues, as recorded in the 1925 article for the *Afro-American*.

'The Memphis Blues' may have been awarded the laurels, but it was not the first. Six months earlier, in March 1912, Hart Wand published the tune 'Dallas Blues' (although this time lyrics would not be added until 1918), and in August Franklin 'Baby' Seals, proprietor of the Bijou Theatre in Greenwood, Mississippi who, two years before, had composed a song titled 'Shake, Rattle and Roll' (an entirely different song to the rock 'n' roll standard), published the ragtime

15

piano tune 'Baby Seals Blues', which he quickly followed with another song, 'Sing Them Blues', which Seals was performing on stage – and selling copies of the sheet music – by the beginning of October. Seals's blues songs were a sensation, and although he would accuse other artists, including the Raineys, of stealing his best material, his clever marketing (as well as selling sheet music at his shows, he also took out display ads in *The Freeman*) soon paid off: before the year was out singers including Earl Burton were featuring 'Baby Seals Blues' in their act. Sadly Seals – a former vaudeville star and outspoken critic of theatre owners who refused to treat Black and white talent equally – had the misfortune to die early (on 29 December 1915), denying him the opportunity to claim the title of 'Father of the Blues'. Four years before all of these songs were published, in 1908, Sicilian-born musician Antonio Maggio wrote and published 'I Got the Blues'. Although 'I Got the Blues' was, like 'Baby Seals Blues' and 'The Memphis Blues', a piano rag, and other songs were already being performed that included blues motifs, notes and lyrical subjects, it was the first song published to incorporate a recognisable 12-bar blues section.

Maggio, a stocky, self-confessed anarchist with a fiery temper, had become notorious in Kansas for having predicted the assassination of President McKinley some six months before the event itself took place, telling fellow musicians that he was a member of an Italian anarchists' society intent on curtailing the careers of McKinley, Kaiser Wilhelm II and Emperor Franz Joseph of Austria. A disciple of anarchist and homosexual rights advocate Emma Goldman – who toured the States delivering a series of lectures, one of which was called 'The Indeterminate Sex: A Study of Homosexuality' – Maggio was arrested while playing piano in a saloon in New Mexico. Charged with conspiracy to murder, he was moved from a cell in Silver City to Albuquerque after an attempted lynching. Maggio spent six months in prison, awaiting trial, but was released in April 1902 after the case against him was dismissed.

Like Handy and Rainey, Maggio claimed not to have invented the blues, but to have heard it from another musician, as he recalled in 1955:

I took the ferry boat from New Orleans across the Mississippi...
On my way up the levee, I heard an elderly Negro with a guitar
playing three notes. He kept repeating the notes for a long time.
I didn't think anything with only three notes could have a title so
to satisfy my curiosity I asked what was the name of the piece. He
replied, 'I got the blues.' I went home. Having this on my mind, I
wrote 'I Got the Blues,' making the three notes dominating most
of the time. The same night our five-piece orchestra played at
[Fabacher's] restaurant (in New Orleans) 'I Got the Blues', which
was composed with the purpose of a musical caricature, and to
my astonishment became our most popular request number. In a
very short time all the Negroes in New Orleans with street organs
were playing the Blues.[15]

Ferdinand 'Jelly Roll' Morton, a man who was just as adept as W. C.
Handy at self-aggrandisement, was indignant with Handy's claim to
be the 'Father of the Blues', telling readers of *Downbeat* magazine
that he had first heard the blues back in New Orleans, where Mamie
Desdunes, a neighbour of his grandmother, first introduced him to the
genre. Mamie had lost two fingers on her right hand in 1893, after
falling under the wheels of a moving train she was attempting to board,
but the injury did not stop her learning how to play piano, nor from
performing at several brothels in the city's Storyville district. According
to Morton, Mamie had composed and was performing a song in a blues
style, which Morton later adapted as 'Mamie's Blues', in the late 1890s,
around the same time that Stale Bread Lacoume and his Razzy Dazzy
Spasm Band were being chased off street corners by the local police.
Clearly a colourful character, Mamie was arrested in 1898 and charged
with assault with a dangerous weapon. A part-time sex worker, she
was known to have played piano at Lulu White's house, a bordello
where Morton's friend Tony Jackson also played regularly. If Morton's
tale is true, and it was later backed up by other musicians who had
passed through New Orleans and had either met or played with Mamie
Desdunes, then it is clear that sex and the blues were intertwined
from the very beginning: in the red-light district of Storyville (given
the nickname as a backhanded compliment to city councilman Sidney

Story), women would shelter in doorways, using their song as a calling card.

Two years before Handy, Maggio, Seals and Wand published their first 'blues' songs, on 16 April 1910 female impersonator and blackface ventriloquist Johnnie Woods, hailed as 'The greatest ventriloquist in either race',[16] made history. In a review of his performance, *The Freeman* noted that, as part of the act, Woods appeared to get his doll, Henry, intoxicated and that 'he uses the "blues" for little Henry in this drunken act'.[17] This is not only the first ever use of the term 'blues' (in the sense of blues music, as opposed to a general feeling of melancholy) in print, but it also establishes the involvement of queer artists at its very birth: more than eleven decades on, we do not know if Woods was LGBTQ, but in appearing on stage in drag, providing the voice of a male dummy, he certainly has a place in the wider queer community.

Pat Chappelle became ill in 1911, and retired his show, taking his wife to Europe in the hope that the climate would better suit his health. It did not. The couple rented a flat in Charing Cross Road, in the heart of London, staying for the coronation of King George V on 22 June, before making 'a tour of the continent, visiting Paris, Berlin, Venice, Milan, Florence, Rome and Naples'.[18] Chappelle's plan was to 'sail for America about July 22, as we hope to be home about the first week of August to prepare for the opening of the Rabbit Foot Company in September'.[19] Once the pair were back in the States they returned to Jacksonville, where Chappelle resumed his position as one of the town's wealthiest and most prominent landowners: a pretty impressive feat for a Black man in Florida – or in fact in any part of the United States – at that time. Adverts ran in the trade papers and the Black press for performers, musicians and crew to join the Rabbit Foot Company, but in spite of his best intentions Pat Chappelle was in no condition to join them on the road.

The Rabbit Foot Company had been running out of steam for some time before Chappelle took his enforced retirement, attracting poor reviews and receiving diminishing returns. The Raineys left and once again attempted to organise their own show, but it was exhausting. Will and Gertrude both appeared on the bill solo and as a double act (alongside several of Chappelle's former crowd pleasers including 'Happy' Howe), organised travel, dealt with the bills and paid the wages. They soon gave up running their own business, and decided instead to concentrate on working the slowly evolving circuit of Black-owned and run vaudeville theatres instead.

Following Chappelle's death – from tuberculosis – on 21 October 1911, the Rabbit Foot Company was sold by his widow Rosa to Fred Wolcott, a white entrepreneur from Michigan who had previously run a small minstrel company of his own. Wolcott set about expanding the business, taking his troupe to northern cities where new Black communities were beginning to establish themselves. Ma and Pa would occasionally rejoin the troupe when it suited them, but they would never return to performing exclusively under canvas. Part of Wolcott's plan for expansion was to advertise the Rabbit Foot revue as a minstrel show, something Chappelle had vehemently fought against doing. Right or wrong, changing their name to the Rabbit Foot Minstrels worked, and Wolcott brought a new life to the show, although the series of serious accidents that had plagued Chappelle continued: Wolcott himself received serious injuries in September 1914 after he mysteriously and, apparently, voluntarily walked out of his carriage while the train was crossing a bridge at 1 a.m. Had he, half asleep, assumed the train had stopped, or was his 'accident' the result of a fight with a disgruntled employee? Two months earlier he had contacted police to swear out an arrest warrant for Louis Coles – leader of a troupe of 'eccentric dancers' – after, he claimed, Coles robbed him of a cornet and three suits, worth $115.

There is an oft-repeated legend that tells of how Gertrude Rainey, at around the same time as Wolcott took over the running of the Rabbit Foot troupe, in awe of young Bessie's abilities, hired two of her husband Will's less salubrious friends and had them bundle Smith up in a burlap sack, abducting her off the street corner where she sang for nickels and dimes while her brother, Andrew, danced. These two fellows are supposed to have brought her, kicking and screaming, to Ma's train carriage and dumped her at the feet of the star, where a benign Ma convinced the young and untrained singer to join her and her troupe on the road.

19

Jack Gee the man who, in 1923, would become Bessie's second husband and erstwhile manager, insisted that the story was true. It was not; in fact, by the time that Ma is supposed to have Bessie join her on tour, the younger woman had already been performing for the paying public for several years... and on a number of occasions had played on the same bill as Ma and Pa Rainey. 'I remember one time when we were in Augusta, Georgia,' her sister-in-law Maude Faggins told Bessie's biographer, the late jazz historian and radio presenter Chris Albertson, 'Bessie and Ma Rainey sat down and had a good laugh about how people was making up stories of Ma taking Bessie from her home, and Ma's mother used to get the biggest laugh out of the kidnapping story whenever we visited her in Macon. Actually, Ma and Bessie got along fine, but Ma never taught Bessie how to sing. She was more like a mother to her.'[20]

A second origin story has Ma in the audience of a children's choir's performance in Chattanooga, with Ma's attention drawn to the fine, full voice of one of the girls, a 13-year-old Bessie, who she immediately offered a job. A third tale has Bessie joining a tent show in 1912: some years earlier Bessie's oldest brother, Clarence, had landed a job as a dancer with a travelling show owned by Moses Stokes. After several years of her constantly badgering him to make an introduction, when she was in her teens he arranged for his young sister to meet with Stokes's managers when the show pulled in to the Smiths' home town. The show was not looking for a singer; they already had a star blues shouter, one 'Madame' Gertrude Rainey, so instead Bessie was offered a role as a dancer, which she willingly accepted.

That is the official line, promulgated by Bessie's brother Clarence and taken as gospel by writers ever since. Only, of course, like so many of the tall tales that surround the birth of the blues and the careers of these women, this colourful story does not stand close scrutiny. Both Bessie and Clarence would have known Moses Stokes; for years he was the manager of Roosevelt Park, a leisure resort in their home town of Chattanooga, owned by a consortium of local Black businessmen and used exclusively by the town's Black residents. He was also a landowner, property developer and at one point stood for election to the local constabulary. But he does not appear to have run his own touring company. It is possible, of course, that Clarence had arranged for Bessie to audition for a show being put on at Roosevelt Park. Whatever the truth of the matter, if she did join Moses Stokes's company in 1912 (and, if she did, she would not remain with the Stokes show for long, as her ambition was to sing, not to be a hoofer), she did not do so fresh off the streets; she had been performing, under her own name and in front of a paying audience, for at least three years.

The men in Bessie's life were constantly trying to insert themselves into her story, or to exaggerate their importance. There can be no doubt that Clarence was a major influence on his younger sister, and she repaid that favour later by having him join her touring show, but it seems unlikely that he was in any way involved with her debut in front of an audience or with her initial meeting with the great Ma Rainey. In fact, Bessie and the Raineys had first encountered each other at least two years earlier, and during the summer of 1910 were working together – not just on the same bill but as part of the same act.

# 3

# The Truth About
# Ma and Bessie

*'After many years of appearing in theatres of the south, Ma Rainey went to New York – astounding and bewildering the northerners with what they called "queer music". She left, and they still did not understand.'*[1]

An orphan before she hit double figures – her mother Laura had died in April 1903, ten days before Bessie's ninth birthday and around three years after the death of her husband, William – Bessie and her four youngest siblings were raised in a tenement apartment in the Tannery Flats neighbourhood of Chattanooga, Tennessee, by their sister Viola, who was fourteen years older than Bessie. Family life was tough: Viola, who also had her own young daughter, Laura, to take care of, was a strict disciplinarian who regularly beat Bessie and locked her in the outhouse for hours on end, although she and their sister Tennie were often in trouble themselves, both arrested on more than one occasion for selling liquor without a license. Despite this, Bessie had strong ties to her family; once she started making money she began to send regular payments to Viola to help with the upkeep of the family home, and after her marriage to Jack Gee she insisted that the family move out to Philadelphia to live closer to her and her new husband.

In a 1969 interview Cora 'Lovie' Austin, who would become one of the most important blues and jazz musicians of the classic period, playing with everyone from Ma and Bessie to Louis Armstrong, told William Russell a much more believable tale concerning Bessie's first encounter with Ma Rainey. Like Bessie, Lovie was raised in Chattanooga, and the two girls were close. 'Bessie Smith lived right next door to me. She was raised in my mother's house. We were raised together... The way Bessie learned how to sing. Ma and Pa Rainey... They used to come there with the carnival. They'd have it in a vacant lot. Bessie and I used to sit out there, back of the carnival 'cause we couldn't go in. We'd sit out there. Ma would sing "oh, these dogs of mine..." [Ma's own composition, 'Those Dogs of Mine (Famous Cornfield Blues)', which she would eventually record in February 1924] and she would imitate Ma Rainey's singing. That's the way she learned how to sing.'[2]

Bessie Smith made her first billed appearance in 1909 at Atlanta's Arcade Theatre, better known as the '81' due to its occupying number 81 Decatur Street; prior to this she had appeared at amateur nights hosted by Chattanooga's Ivory Theatre and, she would later claim, had even won an award for roller skating. The following August, aged just 16, she was back at the 81, this time – according to a news report in Indianapolis-based Black weekly *The Freeman* – sharing a bill with Ma and Pa Rainey (which means that neither Ma and Pa nor Bessie could have been on tour with Pat Chappelle and his Rabbit Foot Company that season). Thomas Dorsey, who had just turned 11 himself, saw first-hand how the working relationship developed between Ma and Bessie, as he would later tell Ma's biographer, Sandra Lieb: 'When I worked at that theater in Atlanta, Ma taught Bessie Smith. Ma was comin' to this theater singin', she and Pa Rainey, when I was a boy in Atlanta, workin' there at that theater.... And she's the ma of all of 'em. She taught Bessie Smith, Butterbeans and Susie, a lot of those black actors who came along in that day. That's why they called her Ma.'[3]

Bessie and the Raineys played at the 81 for six weeks during July and August 1910, with *The Freeman* noting that they presented 'a strong trio... Bess Smith a favorite Tennessee coon shouter; Gertrude Rainey is still holding her own and setting the town wild with her singing. W. M. Rainey... Introduces his act by entering the club in an airship.' The report ended with the announcement that: 'W. M. Rainey and his wife would like to hear from all of their friends.'[4] The same report revealed that the trio were about to spend a further six weeks at the Pekin Theatre on South Fourth Street in Memphis, Tennessee. The 81 was a venue that Bessie would return to several times over the years: despite its sale to a white owner, C. P. Bailey in 1911, it would continue to cater exclusively for a Black audience and, around 1916, it would convert into a picture house (although it would continue to show vaudeville acts between screenings and at weekends), again exclusively for Black patrons.

Tracking Bessie's early career is complicated by the fact that there was another Bessie Smith appearing on stages throughout the South at the very same time. Born in Pennsylvania in 1890, Bessie Mae Smith appeared in a company called The Crackerjacks, took part in Wild West shows alongside cowboy star Tom Mix, and toured as Bessie Smith and Company before marrying Vasilios Caramessinis, adopting her husband's surname, and forming a duo known as the Musical Greeks. Luckily there are plenty of reports in the Black press to help plot our Bessie's timeline.

The trio of Ma and Pa Rainey and Bessie Smith opened at the Pekin in a blaze of glory, 'making good at every performance',[5] according to *The Freeman*, however, Bessie left Memphis under a cloud, vaguely alluded to by a piece the following week in the same newspaper, which claimed to have received 'a note of warning concerning Bessie Smith' from the Pekin, advising other theatre managers to 'cancel engagements with her... Managers don't have to keep disturbers of the peace. And if she is all said of her she won't need anyone to help her out of employment, since her own actions, according to information, would stop her.'[6] Whatever Bessie had been up to, and whatever the anonymous letter-writer had hoped to achieve by having her blackballed, is unknown. The wording of the article is unusual, and although it avoids any detail of her misdemeanours, the suggestion is that Bessie was more trouble than she was worth. Had she spurned the advances of the Pekin's manager, or simply refused to toe the line in the chorus? She would not be the only performer chastised through the pages of *The Freeman* for disturbing the peace, a thinly veiled allusion to being a handful when drunk. Bessie was known to be a heavy drinker, with a taste for illicit booze rather than the shop-bought variety, and was unashamedly bisexual: had her offstage activities aroused the displeasure of management or her co-workers? The editors of *The Freeman* enjoined Bessie to write back and put the record straight, but even if she had seen the letter, the virtually illiterate singer would not have been able to send back a reply. *The Freeman*, like other newspapers and magazines that catered for those in show business, ran a mail-box service for performers: letters sent to Bessie via the newspaper went uncollected for months on end.

Undoubtedly the Raineys would not have been happy: they had been guaranteed twenty weeks' work, covering pretty much all of the summer and autumn months, with their six-week residency at the 81 followed by six weeks at the Pekin, four at the Globe in Jacksonville before returning to the 81 for a final four weeks. Working in theatres was a great improvement on the months they had spent on the road with a tent show, and neither Ma nor Pa wanted that to end. With dates as a trio to fulfil, the Raineys had no option but to replace Bessie, which they did with blues singer Laura Smith, fresh from a nine-month engagement at the Savoy in Memphis, who stayed with them for the next three months. Laura proved a popular addition to the show, but it was Ma and Pa who were making a name for themselves, as is obvious from the notices they were receiving: 'Rainey and Rainey are still cleaning up in the comedy sketches. Gertrude always makes good.'[7] After Laura Smith left, the duo carried on, working at Langman's Theatre in Mobile, Alabama before finishing off the year with three weeks at the Belmont in Pensacola, Florida. While in Florida, William became ill, and Ma temporarily became a solo act, but he seems to have recovered a little by Christmas, when Gertrude's sister Malissa came to visit. On 2 January, and still billed as Rainey and Rainey, they began a four-week engagement at the Globe Theatre, in Jacksonville, Florida, Malissa Nix accompanying them for the first week of their stay. From there the couple went on to the Dixie Theatre in Charlotte, North Carolina.

Whatever she had or had not done, Bessie and Ma would remain friends for the rest of their lives. After leaving the Raineys, Bessie continued to work steadily, swapping places with Laura Smith at the Savoy where she was noted for being 'quite the dancer' and was 'receiving encores nightly'.[8] She stayed at the Savoy for a while, dancing, singing and even appearing as a character called 'The Adventuress' in a western drama, 'The Girl From Dixie', all the while becoming 'quite a favorite with our audiences'.[9] In February 1911 she was playing in Mobile, Alabama as part of Fred Barrasso's Strollers, and being hailed as 'The girl with educated feet, and a great coon shouter,'[10] and within weeks she was being acclaimed as 'our star' by the management of the American Theatre in Jackson, Mississippi, where it was noted that she was 'sending [audiences] away screaming with "Lovey Joe",'[11] a ragtime song written by Eubie Blake, that had been a big hit for Fanny Brice in Florenz Ziegfeld's *Follies of 1910*, which had also starred the African American superstar Bert Williams. Around the same time the Raineys, once again expanded to a trio and appearing in theatres in North Carolina and Virginia, were being hailed as the 'talk of the town', with Ma 'taking from five to six encores every night'.[12] The newspaper report does not name the third member of the troupe, only referring to him or her as 'their little Pick' or picaninny, slang for a Black child. This may be the first reference to their adopted son, Danny Rainey, performing as part of the family act, although for several months in 1911 the Raineys were playing alongside juvenile hoofer Bishop Brown, and in April 1912 the third member of the Rainey Trio was named by *The Freeman* as Kid Bishop, clearly the same boy. That same issue of *The Freeman* noted that Ma, like Bessie, was making a hit of singing ragtime standards: 'When Gertrude Rainey sings 'Dreamy Rag' and 'Barber Shop Chord' and Wm. Rainey put on that song 'Woman, Pay Me Now', the house came down.'[13]

In April 1911, the Raineys – again with Bishop Brown and others – were playing the Wizard Theatre in Norfolk, Virginia, and by the beginning of May, Ma and Pa were appearing as half of an act dubbed The Rainey's Big Musical Comedy Four at the Lyric, in Newport News, Virginia, alongside the Marshall Sisters, formerly of the Smart Set's second company. Virginia liked the Raineys: after three successful weeks the quartet moved to the American Theatre in Petersburg, then on to the Globe Theatre in Richmond before returning to Newport

News for the entire summer: 'The Raineys are here and have been for seventeen weeks and are going as big as ever. Mr. and Mrs. Rainey open their act with a very lovely song, 'How Would You Like to Marry Me' and Mr. Rainey gets away singing one of E. B. Dudley's latest successes, 'I Ain't Nobody's Fool'. Mrs. Gertrude Rainey comes back with 'Steamboat Bill', taking from five to six encores each night.'[14] As late as November, the Raineys were still wowing them in Newport News, although by that point the Marshall Sisters had moved on, replaced by husband and wife act The Porters. This same quartet moved on to Washington, D.C., opening at the Blue Mouse Theatre on 6 November, but within a fortnight the two couples had parted ways: the Porters moved on to Louisville and the Raineys, now listed as the Rainey Trio (presumably with either young Danny or Kid Bishop as the third member of the troupe), were off first to Washington's newly opened, white-owned but Black-run Howard Theatre, then to Philadelphia and, finally, New York, where they would play the Lincoln Theatre right up until Christmas.

For a significant part of 1911, while the Raineys were wowing them in Virginia, Bessie's name is all but absent from the pages of *The Freeman*. She turns up in August, playing at the Pekin in Savannah, Georgia (playing the soubrette in the E. Deb Levi Trio) before heading off to Tampa, Florida in the middle of the month, and does not appear again until October, when she is listed as performing on the opening night of the Bijou Theatre in Bessemer, Alabama. The newspaper's entertainment pages relied heavily on managers, venue owners and the artists themselves writing in to keep the paper's section editors abreast of their comings and goings, and Bessie was not one for writing letters. It is also possible that she continued working in and around Florida with the E. Deb Levi Trio and that the paper simply chose not to cover those dates – *The Freeman* tended to concentrate on acts touring the southern and central states, and usually gave no more than a cursory coverage to cities such as New York and Washington D.C., or the western states. It's highly unlikely that she would have taken several months off work unless she were either ill or pregnant, but it is more than possible that she had taken on a role as dancer or singer (or both) with another act. Wherever she disappeared to, she had not been lazy: on 1 December, comedian, singer and roller-skate dancer Wayne Burton wrote to *The Freeman*, informing the newspaper's readers that Bessie was appearing with his 'standing room only' show in Birmingham, Alabama. 'Bessie Smith gets the hands in singing "Southern Gal",'[15] he boasted, and soon afterwards Bessie formed a double act with Burton, who had spent most of 1911 building up a name for himself as a solo artist after leaving the family trio to go it alone.

In February 1912, while filling dates without Burton, audiences in Louisville, Kentucky were going wild for 'The girl with the big voice', with reviews of her appearance at the town's Lyre Theater calling her 'undoubtedly the best coon shouter ever seen in this house'. So great was the response that 'she was compelled to refuse her encores',[16] if only to let the next act on the stage, and by her second week at the theatre her status had been elevated; no longer was she simply the best singer seen in that particular venue, she was now 'undoubtedly the greatest coon shouter of her race', a woman who 'knows how to put her songs over the footlights in a way that makes her audience scream with delight'.[17] By 8 April the couple were reunited and appearing as Burton and Smith – the 'boy with the insane feet' and the 'girl with the ragtime voice' – at the Auditorium, Philadelphia. During his solo part of the act 'That Boy Burton', as he had been billed prior to teaming up with Bessie, sang 'Plant a Watermelon on My Grave', the same song that Will Rainey featured in his act. By the summer Bessie had built quite a name for herself, as was mentioned in a report from Kentucky's *Lexington Leader*: 'Bessie Smith is no stranger to Lexington crowds, as she has appeared here several times before, and has made an enviable reputation all over Southland as a "coon shouter".'[18]

If Bessie did join her brother and the Raineys in the Moses Stokes troupe, as Clarence told it, it was unlikely to have been in 1912. While Bessie was enjoying a successful tour of the eastern states, Ma and Pa were also making good. Throughout January and into February 1912 they proved a huge success at the Globe Theatre, in Jacksonville, Florida, spending several weeks sharing a bill with their old friends Porter and Porter. At this point in her career, despite her later assertion that she had been including blues numbers since 1902, Ma's solo repertoire consisted mainly of 'coon' and ragtime songs, with titles

28

such as 'Play That Mikell Rag', 'The Barber Shop Chord' (a big hit for Bert Williams, the biggest Black star of the day) and, according to contemporary reports, the 'audience would not let her go until she sang'[19] her showstopping closer, 'That Dying Rag', Irving Berlin's latest hit. She and Will also appeared alongside other artists on the bill, in one-act comedies, including 'The Old Kentucky Home'. Burton and Smith spent much of late spring and early summer in the east, playing in Washington D.C. (again at the Blue Mouse) and Philadelphia (at the Auditorium, alongside three other Black duos and a white singer luxuriating in the rather pompous soubriquet Madame Dekora), while at the same time the Raineys were playing to packed-out theatres including the Airdome and the Lyric in Rome, Georgia. Will Rainey took on the management of the Lyric for the season, and founded his own W. M. Rainey Stock Company, keeping himself and Gertrude in work for the next six months.

Burton and Smith saw the summer out playing Chicago (opening at the Monogram on 17 June), then Cincinnati, Indianapolis, Lexington and Louisville. Usually billed as openers for the main act, the pair were soon recognised as, 'a very lively turn. Miss Smith has a strong voice, sings a good number and makes a very attractive appearance, while Mr Burton is a funny comedian and gets away with a freak lot of eccentric dancing,'[20] although not all critics agreed with this appraisal. 'Burton and Smith would have a good act by making several changes,' sniped Lester Walton in the New York Age. 'In the first place, the male member unnecessarily takes up valuable time trying to crack jokes which no one can see with a telescope. With more singing by the young woman and more dancing by her partner they would attract favorable attention in the East.'[21] They spent eight weeks in Nashville in August and September, leaving very little time for Bessie to do anything else, although while the pair were there something happened between them that caused Wayne Burton to split from Bessie, albeit temporarily, and go solo. There is no report on what caused the split, but it is more than likely that either Wayne or Bessie were simply filling a prior obligation as a solo performer. By the end of November the duo were reunited, working in St Louis under the name Burton and Burton, although there is absolutely no evidence to suggest that

Bessie and Wayne were ever legally entwined, and elsewhere as 'Buzzin and Burton', 'Buzzin' being Wayne Burton's nickname and Bessie retaining the conceit that she was either Burton's sister or wife. The Christmas issue of *The Freeman* carried a photograph of the pair, part of a full-page advertisement taken out by Atlanta theatre operator L. D. Joel.

Clarence Smith's story about Bessie and the Raineys joining up with Moses Stokes in 1912 simply cannot be true. With the Raineys running the Lyric in Rome (where Gertrude's big hit was a song titled 'That Baboon Baby Dance', which opens with the line 'Oh honey, won't you listen here? I'm lonesome and I'm feeling queer'), and Bessie busy with (or without) Wayne Burton, there was no opportunity for the two women to be with the same touring company at the same time. However, if they had shared a stage that year then there can be little doubt that Bessie would have been transfixed by the new and improved Ma Rainey. Gertrude's stints as a solo artist during her husband's bouts of ill health had taught her that she was more than capable of holding an audience without having to rely on the talents of a comedian alongside her on stage, and she was now taking a more prominent role in the act. For the sake of bookings, the couple played down the fact that William Rainey was suffering from tuberculosis, and although he continued to perform he was incapable of sustaining the lead in the family business. Soon reviewers were singling her out as 'a great coon shouter', the same critic noting that Ma 'caught the house from the go and kept them with her. One could sit all night and hear her sing "the Dying Rag".' However, he also dismissed the ailing Will Rainey as someone who 'should retire from the stage for good'.[22] Unlike Bessie, who had ignored *The Freeman*'s slight on her own abilities, Gertrude came out fighting: the following week the newspaper printed 'Mrs. Rainey's Letter of Protest', penned by an indignant Ma while at the Globe in Jacksonville.

In regard to the knock in last week's FREEMAN, concerning W.M. Rainey, this is from Mrs. Rainey. To my brothers and sisters in the profession, I think there should be some boosting instead of knocking, as this knock was put in by his enemies.

I appreciate the compliment for myself, but as for him retiring, he is doing good for a performer that has been on the sick list for three years.

As I was with him when he was well and able to work for me, now I am going to stick by him while he is sick: and either the stage or the washtub suits me.

Wherever we have played, we were not run out for knocking, and always played return dates. You, Mr Knocker, would have made some noise by getting under one corner of the globe and turning it over. You haven't made any as yet.

Regards to all friends, especially the knocker of the Rainey team.

Mrs. W. M. Rainey[23]

The Raineys' prospects continued to improve. Instead of moving from place to place every few days they could now expect to remain at one venue for four weeks or more. In the two years or so since Ma and Bessie last worked together, Ma had matured into the consummate performer, in shimmering gowns festooned in bugle beads, and gold jewellery – including her famous necklace, fashioned from gold coins. The previous winter Gertrude and Will, along with several of the other members of the Rabbit Foot troupe, had taken a residency at the Southern Theatre in Wilmington, North Carolina, and the gas lights at the foot of the stage must have sent rays around the room as they reflected off every inch of her. Short and stout, Gertrude Rainey was never going to be the prettiest girl on stage, so instead she made sure that she looked like the most sophisticated, with feathers woven into her horsehair wigs, and the tent show and theatre crowds lapped it up. When she threw back her head to sing, those same lights reflected off her mouthful of gold teeth, and the sound that emanated from her was a powerful, sorrowful moan: the blues.

Gertrude Rainey was seen as 'dicty', the kind of woman Alberta Hunter would later describe as 'someone who thought God made her and threw the pattern away'.[24] She may have been dumpy but she was always dressed to the nines – when not on stage she favoured old-fashioned, full-length silk dresses with high necklines – and she affected airs and graces that some saw as pretentious. At that time some upwardly mobile Black women were using creams to bleach their skin whiter (African American women with a lighter complexion were at an advantage when it came to finding work) and products to straighten their hair, and although Ma preferred to have light-skinned girls in her chorus, she never attempted to hide her own dark skin or her wild hair. People who knew her often spoke about her sweet nature and generosity, and it was said that if you landed a role in Ma's band the first thing she would present you with was a sparkling new instrument. Married and with an adopted son, and with a decade of experience as a performer behind her, when travelling she would become the troupe's de facto mother, always ready to dispense advice and to comfort those suffering from the blues themselves. No one ever said that about Bessie. Bessie may have been a tremendous singer, but she was coarse, she drank like a man, and her upbringing had made her wary of getting too close to anyone. Later in life Ma gained a reputation for being tight with money and for occasionally acting like a diva, but women in the music industry have always been exploited by the men around them: the years Ma spent touring the country in tent shows and flea-pit theatres taught her how to look after herself. Bessie, occasionally wilful and aggressive, usually had a man around to take care of business.

'Ma Rainey was a tremendous figure,' the poet Sterling Allen Brown would later recall. 'She wouldn't have to sing any words: she would moan, and the audience would moan with her. She had them in the palm of her hand. I heard Bessie Smith also, but Ma Rainey was the greatest mistress of an audience. Bessie was the greatest blues singer, but Ma really *knew* these people; she was a person of the folk; she was very simple and direct.' Brown, who had gone to visit Rainey with folklorist John Work, told blues historian Paul Oliver that Ma's wandering eye was not confined to the ladies: 'She liked these young musicians, and in comes John Work and I – we were young to her. We were something sent down, and she didn't know which one to choose... We just wanted to talk, but she was interested in other things. She was that direct.'[25]

Within a few months of their fabled yet non-existent 1912 association, the two women are supposed to have crossed paths again, this time when Bessie and the Raineys were employed, independently of each other, by another touring tent show. But again, this long-accepted timeline does not hold up to scrutiny: during 1913 Ma and Pa were touring as The Rainey Trio, playing the Pekin in Cincinnati in June and the Gem Theatre in Lexington, Kentucky that August, where it was reported that, 'The Raineys are handling an entirely new line of stage work and making quite a name for themselves,'[26] on a bill with Stevens the ventriloquist, two short silent movies and a couple of local singers. Bessie was also working: in 1913 she was once again employed at the 81 in Atlanta, but even if the two women were not sharing the limelight in the same tent show, Bessie's path would continue to cross that of Ma Rainey. A decade or so younger than Ma (Gertrude's natal details may be shrouded in mystery, but there is no confusion whatsoever over Bessie's birth, 15 April 1894), the untrained Bessie learned stagecraft from watching Ma. The two women became firm friends and, it has been suggested, lovers. 'I believe she was courtin' Bessie,' guitarist Sam Chatmon, who as a young man played in Ma's revue, told biographer Sandra Lieb in a 1975 interview. 'The way they'd talk... I believe there was somethin' goin' on wrong... [Bessie] said, "Me and Ma Rainey had plenty of big times together." I'd talk to [Ma] and she'd say, her and Bessie had big times... She was actin' so funny, I believe one or the other of them was the man, the other one was the girl... I believe Ma Rainey was the one, was cuttin' up like the man... If Bessie'd be 'round, if she'd get to talkin' to another man, she'd [Ma] run up. She didn't want no man to talk with her.'[27]

There is a tale that, while performing in a tent show in New Orleans in 1914, Ma quite literally made the earth move. She was performing the song 'Limehouse Blues', '...and when she came to the words, "look what a hole I'm in," the stage collapsed.'[28] It's a great story, but again it is simply not true. Not only does the 'Limehouse Blues' not contain that particular line, the song was not written until 1930, but she was appearing under canvas at that time, so it is perfectly possible that the stage did indeed collapse under Ma's stomping feet, but that she was performing an entirely different song. In early 1914 Ma and Pa were working in Florida, as part of a troupe led by female impersonator Little Jimmie Cox, but they soon left to join the cast of Tolliver's Smart

33

Set. The Raineys were not with the Rabbit Foot folk during their fall 1914 season, and were not mentioned in dispatches from that tour that appeared in *The Freeman*, but it seems that, for at least part of the time, they were accompanied by Bessie Smith. Could this have been the fabled tent show of 1912 that Clarence had both Ma and Bessie performing in, or the show of 1913 that many have claimed the pair appeared in together?

Based in Osawatomie, Kansas, and led by Black comedian Alexander Tolliver (previously a member of the Dixie Fashion Plate Minstrels and, along with his brother Jesse and sister Mabel, a member of roller-skating dancers the Tolliver Trio), the outfit was known variously as Tolliver's Smart Set Minstrels, Tolliver's Original Smart Set Company, Tolliver's Big Show and, it has been reported by other authors, Tolliver's Circus and Musical Extravaganza. Just to confuse the issue there was a second outfit, headed by brothers Salem Tutt Whitney and J. Homer Tutt, that styled itself the Smart Set and that would later rename itself the 'Smarter Set'. While with what was then billed as 'The largest colored show in America', Ma's status continued to grow: the Raineys were once again using the mantle 'The assassinators of the blues', and her solo spot became the highlight of the travelling tent show, where for a ten cent admission price you could not only see Ma, Pa, Danny and Bessie, but Peg Lightfoot (born Edward Rogers in Memphis in 1895), the troupe's amazing one-legged dancer. African American singer, dancer and comedian Artie Belle McGinty, who toured with Ma as part of Tolliver's troupe, said that 'She had a heart as big as this house.'[29]

Although Tolliver's was famous for having 'The best talent of the colored race… Carrying over 80 people and two cars of special scenery', advertising for the Smart Set would appear that had Ma top of the bill as 'The original Ma Raniey [*sic*], the great "Blues" singer,' and by late 1915 she was being written about in newspapers as being the star of the show, dubbed 'Madam Rainey, famous singer of the "BLUES".'[30] Will Rainey smarted at the realisation that his wife, the woman he had brought into show business, had surpassed him in fame (his name does not appear at all on those same advertisements), and it must have been a huge blow to his masculinity to discover that not only could the couple not have children of their own, but Gertrude made no secret of the fact that she was more attracted to several of the girls in the chorus than she was to her own husband. Ma may have claimed, in that earlier letter to *The Freeman*, that 'I am going to stick by him', but going back under canvas as part of Tolliver's Smart Set would have bruised her ego, despite the fact that by now she was being singled out as a solo star, the only artist named on the Smart Set handbills littering the streets of every city they played in. Will and Gertrude may not have had the most rewarding relationship, but for the majority of their marriage he had kept her away from tent shows and found work in the safer, more financially rewarding and less peripatetic world of vaudeville theatres; Ma had no intention of taking a step backwards, but over the next few years as well as appearing in vaudeville theatres and picture houses she would also join tent shows between bookings to supplement her income: she took a job with the New Orleans-based Eph Williams, who ran the Silas Green Minstrels and made a number of friends among New Orleans's nascent jazz fraternity.

Ma and Pa Rainey separated in 1916: throughout their time with Tolliver, Pa dipped in and out of the act – possibly due to his ongoing health issues. In September 1915 Ma was playing as part of a new double act, Rainey and Lovejoy, and in March 1916, during a month-long residency in New Orleans, Pa was again nowhere to be seen, with Ma credited as the sole 'assassinator of the blues'[31] with the show. The two of them appeared together in reports about Tolliver's troupe (now dubbed Tolliver's Big Show) in April and again in August, but they seem to have parted not long afterwards. Before the year was out Pa had vanished for good, and Ma was being highlighted as a solo singer, performing songs such as 'Lonesome Melody', 'Morning, Noon and Night', 'I'll Be Gone' and 'Down Home Blues' – the same song that Ethel Waters would have a hit with in 1921. Danny stayed with Ma and continued to perform with her for at least the next decade. One story, from 1926, stated that she had adopted seven children (she had not), and owned 'a three story apartment on Grand Boulevard, Chicago, assessed by the taxman at $36,000'.[32]

While with the Tolliver outfit Ma had become friends with Susie Edwards, the young wife of comedian Jodie Edwards, himself part of the team of Lightfoot and Edwards with Peg Lightfoot, the one-legged dancer. Ma appeared in a one-act drama with several other members of the cast, including the Edwardses, and it was suggested that the two women would form their own comedy team. They did not: Ma continued to perform solo, and Jodie and his new bride would become famous in their own right, as Butterbeans and Susie. Butterbeans and Susie would often share a bill with Ma, and in 1926 Black newspaper the *Afro-American* would erroneously claim that she had actually adopted the pair.

While with Tolliver, Ma first met fellow blues singer Clara Smith. She had been with the show for a period in 1915 – about the same time that Ma was working as Rainey and Lovejoy – and briefly joined them again in 1916. It was unusual for two blues singers to appear on the same programme, personal and professional jealousy would often lead to trouble backstage, and there can be no doubt that both women would have been eager to attract the attentions of some of the prettier girls in the chorus, but Ma's status was well established. She had nothing to fear from any incomer, no matter how talented she was, and there are no reports of any bad feeling between the two women.

In 1914 Bessie met pianist and songwriter Perry Bradford, in Atlanta. Bradford – who at one point fronted his own Black vaudeville company, Bradford's Chicken Trust and who would go on to write 'Crazy Blues', the first truly authentic blues record – recalled that this meeting took place while Bessie was performing at the city's Douglass Theatre as one half of Buzzin' and Burton, although by March 1914 (when playing at the new Circle Theatre in Philadelphia) their act was billed as Burton and Smith. Bradford did meet Bessie in Atlanta, but it was while he was performing as part of the husband and wife team Bradford and Bradford at the city's Majestic Theater in July that year. Bessie was on the same bill, singing in a trio with a male dancer, Dinah Scott and a pudgy comic known as Fat Child. The trio did not last long, and she was soon appearing as a solo act once more. Actor and theatre manager Leigh Whipper recalled seeing Bessie perform at the 81 sometime around 1913, although if his statement about her performing 'Weary Blues' is correct then it was more likely to have been after 1915, as that song (penned by Artie Matthews, who was working out of the Princess Theatre in St Louis) was not written until that year, and did not become a hit until 1916, when released on piano roll and as sheet music.

By the summer of 1916 it had become commonplace for theatrical revues to advertise a blues singer as part of their featured line-up. Bessie and Burton had split permanently, with Wayne Burton teaming up with a succession of mediocre female singers over the next few years. Every touring show worth its salt added a blues singer to its roster, each one claiming to be 'the original' or 'the best', appearing side by side with the other marvels of the day, a troupe of dancing girls, a Jewish comedian, and any number of speciality acts. Bessie had elected not to join the Tolliver line-up for the 1915–16 season, possibly because she knew that they had no room for two blues divas, and instead joined another touring company, the Florida Blossoms, although it seems as if Bessie and a Pa-less Ma were with Tolliver again the following year (for at least part of the 1916–17 season), as Ma struggled to manage her career without her husband. In early 1919 Ma attempted to set up her own travelling show, advertising in the New Orleans press for 'colored girls to travel with Smart Co. tent show',[33] rather cheekily trading off the reputation of the Smart Set. At some point she paired up with entertainer Billy Hughes, who would act – on and off – as a business partner-cum-manager, and it was speculated that their pair had exchanged marriage vows. Although it has often been suggested that Ma married for a second time, it was not to Hughes, despite a *Billboard* report that Ma and Billy had indeed married, had already divorced some time before July 1921 but had plans to remarry that year while Ma was playing in Wichita Falls, Texas. The truth is that when Will Rainey died, on 28 June 1919, he and Gertrude were still officially married, and at the end of the year, the far-from-grieving Ma received a nice Christmas bonus: a $300 insurance pay-out from her late husband's lodge, the Knights of Pythias.

# 4

# Alberta, Tony and the Grizzly Bear

*'It matters not what others think about it, dancing is some form of social degradation. That it has its extenuating and mitigating circumstances but while it is offered as a social exercise and a thriller for the blues it has opened the door to many marauding hell for the youth of all of the races.'* [1] – Dr M. A. Majors

In the early years of the 20th century the Great Migration, as it became known, saw 1.5 million Blacks leave the South and move north, an exodus that would continue over the course of the next few decades. America had been undergoing a massive change, with a rapid increase in industrialisation leading to major growth – and demand for workers – in northern cities. People of all ethnicities were leaving rural districts for the promise of better pay and conditions elsewhere. A further boost came in 1917: as the war effort ramped up, more men were being sent off to fight in Europe, which left more industrial jobs vacant.

In the years immediately before America's entrance into the First World War (in April 1917), xenophobia was rife: European migrants were characterised as potential spies, jobs that had traditionally been filled by immigrants went begging, and the factories of the great cities of the

North were increasingly turning to the African American community to occupy those roles. Labour agents went south in search of fit and healthy Black men: many African Americans were still working in the same cotton fields that their ancestors had slaved in, paid a pittance or forced into one-sided sharecropper deals where the families of their former masters always came off best, but a crisis in the cotton industry, brought on initially by overproduction and declining demand and then exacerbated by the devastation wrought by boll weevil infestation was forcing many of them off the land permanently. Encouraged by Black-owned newspapers in Chicago and Memphis, before long the Great Migration was underway.

In the first six months of 1923 alone, according to the national Industrial Conference Board, more than 100,000 southern folk moved northwards. At that time, it was noted that:

> The flow seems to be gathering in volume. As these newcomers, who are deserting agriculture for industry in locations hundreds of miles away from their traditional American homeland, come into contact with northern ideas, atmosphere and the larger measure of freedom accorded their race in these parts, letters to friends left behind are likely to keep the movement in being for some time... Reasons for the latest swelling of this migratory tide are not far to seek. Social and economic pressure in the South, and the sudden industrial suction in the North, has loosed the flood.[2]

Although it would slow to a trickle after the arrival of the Great Depression, a second wave took place from 1940 in response to the outbreak of the Second World War. It is reckoned that as many as 6 million Black Americans had migrated from the South to various parts of the country by 1970.

Lured by the promise of work, schooling and better living conditions, everyone had their own reason for leaving, but for the vast majority this was a chance to escape extreme poverty and discrimination. Although slavery was formally abolished in December 1865, the heinous Jim Crow laws had allowed many states to legally enforce racial segregation, denying Black men and women the right to vote and forcing them into ghettoes. To be allowed to vote you had to undergo a literacy test, and these were stacked against emancipated slaves and their descendants, whose access to schools and libraries was severely restricted. Racially motivated mob violence was rife, white supremacist groups such as the Ku Klux Klan (who, despite being officially dormant until reactivated following the success of D. W. Griffith's film *Birth of a Nation* in 1915, still held out in small pockets around the South) struck terror into the Black and Jewish communities, and public lynchings became a regular occurrence, with gangs of vigilantes – some headed by court officials and officers of the law – murdering hundreds, possibly thousands of men, women and children. According to contemporary reports, 3,436 people – an average of two a week – were lynched in the United States between 1889 and 1922; figures from the National Association for the Advancement of Colored People (NAACP) confirm that 4,743 lynchings occurred in the US between 1882 and 1968, and around 72 per cent of the victims were Black.[3] It seemed that the South did not want Black families, unless they conducted themselves in exactly the same way that their enslaved ancestors had. With workers leaving the land in droves, business owners paid preachers to tour the southern states, telling people that they would be no better off in the North, yet, 'in spite of concerted efforts to discourage this new exodus, the railroad stations of St Louis, Columbus, Cincinnati and Richmond are daily clogged with dark newcomers... Catching the first trains for points farther North.'[4]

But, as well as job security and the promise of financial independence, moving to a city offered something else, too: the chance to meet other people with whom you could identify. For many LGBTQ people (at the time labelled 'queer', 'sissies', 'pansies', or worse) relocation brought with it their first opportunity to find their own community, their own support networks. For the very first time, many Black LGBTQ people were able to socialise – and form lasting relationships – with their own kind.

The rapidly expanding and increasingly industrialised cities in the North needed an endless supply of workers. It must have been attractive, yet many would have been shocked to discover that the cities they had dreamed of moving to in search of a better life were just as segregated as the places they had left. The Chicago of the 1910s was

40

a city divided, bisected by the Chicago River into a north and a south side, each run by criminal gangs, but also into Black and white sections, with the vast majority of the 500,000 African Americans who migrated there ending up in the south side of the city, an area that soon became known as Bronzeville. Property was cheap, but often owned by white landlords who refused to spend money on improving what amounted to little more than slum dwellings. The city also had its own artists' enclave, Towertown (named after the water tower, the only structure in the area to survive the devastating fire of 1871), an added attraction for writers, poets, painters, sculptors and LGBTQ people... although, as a rule, the queer residents of Towertown were white.

In his book *Studies in the Psychology of Sex Volume Two: Sexual Inversion*, British writer and physician Henry Havelock Ellis quoted from an American correspondent who wrote to him about the lives of homosexual men in the US during the early years of the 20th century:

The world of sexual inverts is, indeed, a large one in any American city, and it is a community distinctly organised – words, customs, traditions of its own; and every city has its numerous meeting places: certain churches where inverts congregate; certain cafés well known for the inverted character of their patrons; certain streets where, at night, every fifth man is an invert. The inverts have their own 'clubs', with nightly meetings. These 'clubs' are, really, dance-halls, attached to saloons, and presided over by the proprietor of the saloon, himself almost invariably an invert, as are all the waiters and musicians. The frequenters of these places are male sexual inverts (usually ranging from 17 to 30 years of age); sightseers find no difficulty in gaining entrance; truly, they are welcomed for the drinks they buy for the company – and other reasons.[5]

Havelock Ellis's unnamed correspondent went on to describe a scene that would still be recognisable a century later:

Singing and dancing turns by certain favorite performers are the features of these gatherings, with much gossip and drinking at the small tables ranged along the four walls of the room. The habitues of these places are, generally, inverts of the most pronounced type, i.e., the completely feminine in voice and manners, with the characteristic hip motion in their walk; though I have never seen any approach to feminine dress there, doubtless the desire for it is not wanting and only police regulations relegate it to other occasions and places. You will rightly infer that the police know of these places and endure their existence for a consideration; it is not unusual for the inquiring stranger to be directed there by a policeman.[6]

Towertown's Dill Pickle Club – which in its early years was presided over by anarchist and physician Ben Reitman and hosted talks from German homosexual rights pioneer Magnus Hirschfeld – began hosting drag balls in 1916, where men dressed as women, women dressed as men and same-sex couples could hide in plain sight; Hirschfeld would later recall how, on an earlier trip to Chicago, he 'was introduced to a Negro girl on Clark Street who turned out to be a male prostitute'. Queer Black performers were regularly seen on stage in the district's clubs and bars, but despite laws banning discrimination in public places and in schools the city would remain, for the most part, segregated. This did not stop white thrill-seekers mixing with Black queer people in Chicago's 'black and tan' night spots.

The 1910s saw a massive expansion in vice in the South Side, especially in the area known as 'the Loop', where many trans sex workers would ply their trade in the hotels, cafés, bars and brothels. Chief of Police John McWeeny set out to rid the Loop of the scourge of 'male perverts [who] make up like women and call each other women's names',[7] for in Chicago, as was true of most towns and cities in the States, anyone seen in public dressed as the opposite sex was committing a crime, charged with vagrancy and either heavily fined or imprisoned. The offence of vagrancy included a clause that covered anyone who had 'his face painted, discolored, covered or concealed, or being otherwise disguised, in a manner calculated to prevent his being identified'. Although not specifically an anti-LGBTQ law – sex workers and their pimps were also classed as vagrants – police around the country would continue to use this as an excuse to arrest anyone suspected of being LGBTQ for decades to follow.

Although the population of Chicago swelled massively during the middle of the decade, many musicians had already made the move to the city's South Side, enticed by this dilapidated, bohemian area full of clubs and cafés where ragtime, blues and jazz could be heard twenty-four hours a day. Music publishers set up offices in the city, and travelling performers – including Ma Rainey and Bessie Smith – would decamp to the city for weeks on end in search of the latest hot material: many of the tunes that the two women sang in the early years of the decade, including Ma's big hit 'That Baboon Baby Dance' and Bessie's showstopper 'My Ever Loving Southern Gal', were published in Chicago.

Naturally, LGBTQ people made up a significant number of the African Americans who migrated to the South Side, and LGBTQ-run (and LGBTQ-friendly) businesses soon followed. Following the lead of the Dill Pickle Club, masquerade balls quickly became part of the city's entertainment offering, with the opportunity for men to don their finest frills and for women to put on their fanciest tuxedos. These balls were also racially integrated, affording a rare opportunity for people from both sides of the divide to mingle. Chicago had a number of cafés, restaurants and cabarets, the infamous 'black and tans', where people of all races – and all sexualities – mixed openly, much to the disgust of the local police force, religious reformers and certain press outlets. In an exposé by the *Chicago Tribune*, it was reported that:

> The Pekin, a notorious 'black and tan' rendezvous which should have been suppressed years ago, operates night and day – as the 'Pekin' at 2700 South State Street until 1 a.m., and then as the Beaux Arts club, directly upstairs, until daylight. The races dance and drink together there, and one of my informers states a white woman was beaten without mercy by a colored man in the Pekin the other night and none attempted to interfere... The police, though they know that gambling and 'black and tan' cabarets and other disorderly resorts where the races indiscriminately mix are in flagrant operation, do nothing because they fear the influence of politicians.[8]

Police captain Max Nootbaar made his feelings clear when he told a court that, 'No place is respectable where young white girls are allowed to drink and dance with Negro men. I maintain that no white woman is respectable who goes to places like the "Onion café", for example. I would shoot my wife or daughter if I found them in such places.'[9] In 1914 the Onion café had been the venue for a shoot-out that resulted in the death of a police officer, sergeant Stanley J. Birns, whose men – three of whom were also injured – were attempting to stem the uncontrolled spread of vice in the district. A crusading group of Christian women who toured the area under police escort 'found the cabarets unspeakably demoralizing. In the Elite we saw young white boys associating with colored girls. The air was vile.'[10] Earlier that evening the same group of women had been disturbed by a scene they had witnessed in Otto's Place, where 'an elderly man... was caressing Irene, the cabareter in the black dress, and Irene was exhibiting intense emotion by eating peanuts.'[11]

Blues singer Alberta Hunter moved to Chicago in the summer of 1911, shortly after her 16th birthday: years later, she would claim to have been much younger, telling reporters that, 'I was about nine or 10 I guess... I ran away from home but it wasn't because I was mistreated. Girls got $10 a week singing in Chicago. I ran away from home to get some of that money.'[12] Born in Memphis in April 1895, she had been a weak and sickly child, brought up by a single mother after her father abandoned her and her elder sister, the exotically named La Tosca. Alberta's mother, Laura, worked as a maid at a local, white-run bordello. Alberta grew up in the thrall of W. C. Handy, whose band – in their matching regalia – could often be seen marching on the streets of Memphis, or be heard in the clubs on Beale Street, the same street where Alberta lived with her mother and sister for a time.

Beale Street felt safe: Tennessee began enacting the Jim Crow laws in 1866, enforcing segregation, but on Beale Street Black Americans could congregate, shop, eat, drink, and play music. Beale Street may have felt like a haven, but Alberta herself was not safe; she would later recall that at least two of the older men in her life molested her while she was still a child. When her mother remarried – and had a child

44

with her second husband – Alberta felt even more isolated. She started getting into trouble, becoming obstinate and difficult at home and fighting with La Tosca. By the time she was 15 she had made up her mind that she was going to strike out on her own, and was singing the one song she knew by heart in any venue on Beale Street that would have her. Not long afterwards she resolved to leave Memphis for good, and when a friend offered her a free train ticket to Chicago, she was off.

After a year of trying to find work as a singer in Chicago, she began performing at Dago Frank's bordello, on the corners of Archer and South State streets in 1912. State Street was vibrant and bustling, with the tramlines of the Chicago City Railway running down the centre, and had recently seen an influx of gamblers, prostitutes, pimps and thieves thanks to attempts by the local authorities to clean up the Levee, Chicago's notorious red-light district. But it was nowhere near as 'safe' as Beale Street had been: racial tensions ran high, and violence against the Black residents of the area was commonplace. The smallest excuse could start a race riot, as it had in January 1910 when a Black patron was ejected from the Folly Theatre on South State Street after an argument with an usher and, within minutes, an armed mob of white men and boys had amassed which attacked an entirely innocent man simply because he had the same colour skin. The mob was only prevented from lynching him by a quick-thinking police officer, who picked up the injured man and ran up the street with him in his arms.

The manager of Dago Frank's had tried putting Alberta off working there – she was small, looked much younger than her age and Dago Frank himself had already been in trouble for employing underage girls in his houses – but she persisted. 'Roy, the manager, wanted to put me out, but Bruce, the piano player, said to keep me,' she recalled.[13] The girls who did business at Dago Frank's took pity on her, bought her clothes and allowed her to sing the songs that she knew – her repertoire having doubled to two tunes by the addition of a new number, 'All Night Long'. Soon she was earning $10 a week: almost twice what she had previously earned, cleaning tables and peeling potatoes in a boarding house. When Alberta was not singing, she was hanging around other less-than-salubrious saloons, listening to other singers and adding their songs to her burgeoning catalogue.

Bruce was 'the worst piano player you ever heard in your life'[14] according to Alberta, but he was soon replaced by a new arrival, Tony Jackson, and Alberta and Tony became quite the draw. Born in New Orleans, Jackson was a self-taught pianist and songwriter, whose mother worked as a washerwoman and whose father was a labourer. He was also homosexual; Alberta was a lesbian, although she mostly kept that quiet, but each recognised a kindred spirit. When asked about why she was not interested in men, she would brush such questions aside, occasionally mentioning those who had abused her back in Memphis. There was no subtlety about Jackson: he was out, proud, and not afraid to let people know that he liked men. Tony, who suffered with epilepsy, was a brilliant pianist who could play any tune by ear, but he was also a heavy drinker and often in trouble. In the few photos that exist of Tony he invariably has the right-hand side of his face turned to the camera, that's because in May 1915 he was involved in a fight in Rock Island, Illinois, which left him with blood streaming from a four-inch razor gash in his left cheek. The wound was sustained following a drinking session with a man named George Brown in a Black-run bar on First Avenue called the Blue Goose, notorious locally for having been at the centre of a prostitution scandal a decade earlier, regularly used by working girls to 'roll' their customers (steal from, usually after getting them drunk), and no stranger to the occasional knife or gun battle. Although Tony reported the incident to the police, pointedly 'The police know of no Negro by that name [Brown] and were unable to arrest any one who answered the description.'[15]

That may be because Tony preferred white boys to those of his own race, and was often in the company of male prostitutes and hustlers, one of whom he became so close to that he wrote a song for him, 'Pretty Baby', while still living in New Orleans and playing piano at Frank Early's My Place Saloon, one of less than a handful of original buildings still standing today in what was once Storyville. Early was a petty criminal and drug peddler who had gone legit – on the surface at least – and there's little doubt that his Storyville tavern was a front for his nefarious activities. At that time the Storyville section of New Orleans was a hive of LGBTQ activity: brothel owner Nell Kimball later wrote about a wild party she witnessed on Baronne

Street, at an establishment run by a local character known as Miss Big Nellie:

> It was a hell of queen's ball at two in the morning. Most of the gowns were off, and some of the most respectable people you ever saw were playing at soixante-neuf on the staircase, and a daisy chain was going full blast in the parlor... Some of the lavender group used to come to my house; those were the bi-sexual ones. Later the joke was that they were AC and DC like the electric currents. Sometimes a John wanted a boy and girl together for his pleasuring, but I didn't cater to such tastes. I ran a good old-fashioned whorehouse and they knew what I had to offer, and if they didn't like it, they could go elsewhere. I'll say this, there were plenty of places in New Orleans they could get what they wanted.[16]

Alberta would be the first person, apart from Tony of course, to sing 'Pretty Baby' in public. 'Tony was just marvellous,' she would later recall. 'A fine musician, spectacular, but still soft. He could write a song in two minutes and was one of the greatest accompanists I've ever listened to. Tony was always jolly, but he had bad teeth, just terrible! He had mixed grey hair and always had a drink on the piano – always! It was only beer, but he drank plenty of that. Tony wrote "Pretty Baby", which he dedicated to a tall, skinny fellow...'[17]

Although Tony was primarily a ragtime pianist, in the Scott Joplin tradition ('that was all we knew in those days,' Lovie Austin recalled), he could play – and sing – pretty much anything, as his friend Ferdinand 'Jelly Roll' Morton recalled: 'Tony Jackson was maybe the best entertainer the world has ever seen. He enjoyed playing all classes of music in the style they was supposed to be played in, from blues to opera,'[18] and 'Pretty Baby' was written to be played in a slow blues style. In an unpublished interview recorded in 1959, Tony's friend and fellow pianist Glover Compton, who first met Jackson when both were employed at the Cosmopolitan Club, in New Orleans' French Quarter in 1904, was able to recall some of the words Jackson – and later Alberta Hunter – performed for audiences:

You may talk about your jelly roll, but none of that compares
With my baby, my pretty baby
She's a tall, dark yellow girl, with big brown eyes and curly hair
I call her baby, my pretty baby
Maybe not today, but there will come a time
When you will hear those church bells chime
Kings and queens may reign supreme, but none of them outshine
This pretty baby of mine.[19]

Tony would never record the song, but it reached great heights after he sold the rights to songwriters Egbert Van Alstyne and Gus Kahn, who remodelled the song, creating a pop standard that would give singers from Fanny Brice to Dean Martin a hit. It has often been suggested that Tony was easily duped out of the rights to his song, however he received co-writer credit and its success would lead to a number of his other compositions being issued as sheet music, piano rolls and – occasionally – recordings. Outside of the tune to the chorus, little of Tony's original song remained in this updated version anyway, and nothing of the lyric as Jackson first conceived it, which featured the author singing the praises of his boyfriend's manhood.

In Storyville, Tony had been recognised as the finest player of the age. Even Jelly Roll admitted as much, which was quite something for a man who usually claimed as much of the limelight for himself as he could get away with. 'Tony was real dark and not a bit good-looking, but he had a beautiful disposition,' Morton explained. 'He was the outstanding favorite of New Orleans...'[20] Said his friend Clarence Williams, 'At that time, everybody followed the great Tony Jackson. We all copied him. He was so original and a great instrumentalist. I know I copied Tony, and Jelly Roll too... Tony Jackson was certainly the greatest piano player and singer in New Orleans. He was on the order of how [Nat] King Cole is now, only much better. About Tony, you know he was an effeminate man – you know.'[21]

Jackson had started playing in Black whorehouses, but had quickly progressed to white establishments, where the money was better and Tony was bestowed with the honorary title 'professor', in recognition of his status among the local musicians. But although he was doing well in New Orleans, around 1911 or 1912 he decided to move – along with around half of his family including two sisters, a brother-in-law and three of their children – to Chicago. According to Morton, it was more than the music that Jackson was attracted to:

> Tony Jackson was no doubt the favourite... And he was the favourite among all. He had such a beautiful voice, such a marvellous range. His range on a blues tune would be just exactly like a blues singer, on an opera tune would be just exactly as an opera singer, and he was always one of the first with the latest tunes. He went to Chicago and was the favourite there. He was very much instrumental in me going to Chicago, very much to my regret because there was much more money in New Orleans than there was in Chicago. But Tony Jackson liked the freedom that was there. Tony happened to be one of these gentlemen that's called, a lot of people call them a lady or a sissy or something like that. But he was very good and very much admired.[22]

It was certainly easier to be 'different' in Chicago: Bronzeville was hip and bohemian, with Black artists, writers and musicians of all sexual persuasions filling the cafés, bars and nightclubs. Pianist and composer Lovie Austin moved to Chicago in 1913, and spent a lot of time with Tony and his crowd, including Jelly Roll Morton (who she transcribed music for) and Alberta Hunter. 'I was working at the Monogram, on 35th [Street]... I knew Tony very well,' she told interviewer William Russell. Talking about how other artists would steal his music, she recalled that, 'Irving Berlin stole a couple of pieces. Irving Berlin did himself. Tony worked right next door to me, at a little one of those beer joints, and Irving used to come out here, sit for hours, and listen to Tony. "Pretty Baby", and all that stuff.'[23] 'The white shows used to come in from New York and everybody was down there to see us work,' Alberta told author Chris Albertson in 1976. 'The stars, the chorus girls, Al Jolson, Sophie Tucker, everybody. One night I was doing "A Good Man Is Hard to Find" and they handed me a little note from Sophie Tucker. She wanted that song, and that's how they were, always trying to get something out of us, always trying to pick up on our little tricks.

49

And what could we do? Only thing we could do was do those numbers even better – which we did!'[24]

His venue may have been doing well, but it was not a good time for people like Dago Frank Lewis: with the campaign underway to clean up vice in Chicago, especially in the part of the South Side known as the Levee, his businesses were under constant scrutiny and his name was frequently in the press. In 1910 a local law was passed that forbade men from owning brothels in the city (it was perfectly legitimate for such houses to be owned and operated by women), and the following year he barely escaped prison after being accused of harbouring underage girls at one of his establishments, the Mint. It was an open secret that his businesses allowed gambling and drinking, and that sex was readily available and easily purchased, but when he brought an outlawed dance, the Grizzly Bear, to the city he was in real trouble.

The Grizzly Bear scandalised polite society. In St Louis, Missouri, the chief of police issued a ban, prohibiting public dance halls from allowing such displays of carnality, with its hip swaying, thrusting and hugging moves, and other cities followed suit: in Boston the mayor threatened to revoke the license of any hall that allowed its patrons to dance the Grizzly Bear. Dance halls appointed censors to break couples up if they began to do the Grizzly Bear and other provocative dances of the day, including the Hoochie-Coochie, Walkin' the Dog, and the Texas Tommy. But Dago Frank Lewis, the 'King of the Levee', was a law unto himself.

An imposing man, six feet four inches tall and weighing 200 pounds, Lewis was well-in with the men who ran the police department and looked after the law courts. It is no exaggeration to state that Chicago was just about lawless in the early years of the 20th century: police officers were given no formal training and the court system was overrun with men who could be bought for a few dollars. Despite several attempts to do away with corruption, it was endemic; even the Superintendent of Police, installed by reforming Mayor Fred Busse (in office from 1907–11), announced that certain parts of the city were 'beyond the control of law enforcement'. Lewis was cash-rich and always able to buy himself out of a sticky position, although that is not to say that he did not occasionally run into trouble. He was shot on Christmas Day, 1913, in an altercation with two rookie police officers at the Ivory Hotel, another Lewis-run business that acted as a front for prostitution. The officers, one of whom shot Lewis three times after he had tried to divest the other officer of his gun, clearly did not know that he was under the protection of the Chicago P.D. Luckily for them, and for Dago Frank, the wounds were not serious. Charged with assault with a deadly weapon (namely the gun he had wrested from the police officer), the court found that Lewis was innocent, reprimanding the police instead for their actions. Despite Busse's attempts at cleaning up immorality and crime, many of his colleagues were crooked. State Attorney John E. W. Wayman was often accused of corruption by the editors of Chicago newspaper the *Day Book*, and the publication was seemingly vindicated when Wayman shot himself in April 1913. Mayor Carter Harrison Jr (in office 1911–15) and Chief of Police John McWeeny also bore the brunt of the *Day Book*'s dissatisfaction with the way that the city's vice businesses were allowed to run riot; the pair were regularly hauled over the coals by the editors of the *Day Book* and the *Chicago Tribune* for their failure to close unlicensed premises down.

Alberta left Dago Frank's after a little under two years and went to work for Hugh Hoskins, owner of the Iowa Club at 3161 South State Street. 'It was there I started singing the blues,' she would remember. 'When I sang a blues it was nothing for somebody to give me a $5 bill.'[25] The petty criminals, prostitutes and pimps that hung out at Hoskins's place were far less secretive about their business dealings than the ones she had encountered at Dago Frank's. Fraternisation between performers and audience members was strictly forbidden, and shortly after Alberta went there Hoskins was fined for breaking the so-called 'cabaret ordinance', a local bylaw that banned dancing in restaurants and imposed hefty license fees on every venue where food and drink was provided. Hoskins was forced out of business in March 1916, charged with being unfit to operate saloons, although his license was later restored after 'reputable citizens had interceded'[26] on his behalf. By this time Tony Jackson had found a job at the Elite Café (aka the Elite Number One, another disreputable 'black and tan'), leading

51

a four-piece band, and Alberta would join him there, standing at the piano while he played 'Pretty Baby'. Owner Henry 'Teenan' Jones was another Black business owner constantly at odds with Chicago's authorities. He had run a saloon and gambling den in the Hyde Park area of the city, an almost exclusively white district, and the locals wanted him and his kind out. In late 1907 an operation began to drive the Blacks out of Hyde Park; by enacting a local bylaw that forbade trading on Sundays they were able to deny businesses a substantial portion of their income, and warrants were issued for the arrest of scores of Black men and women. Teenan (identified by the *Chicago Tribune* as a 'police fixer'[27]) moved, taking his business – and his illegal bookmaking operation – to State Street.

From there Alberta went to the Panama Café, where Tony Jackson's friend Glover Compton played piano. She was fast becoming one of the most popular singers in Chicago, and composers would come to the Panama with new songs, assured that if they could persuade her to sing them then they had a sure-fire hit on their hands. It did not take the always-financially savvy Alberta long to wise up to the fact that there was money to be made here, and soon songwriters including Porter Grainger, Maceo Pinkard and even the great W. C. Handy were slipping her a few dollars to encourage her to sing their latest numbers. Alberta would later recall Grainger bringing her a song called 'Michigan Water Tastes Like Sherry Wine', although Jelly Roll Morton would contend that the song had first been performed by Tony Jackson. Copyright in the song was claimed by Clarence Williams (as 'Michigan Water Blues'), a pianist and songwriter who had toured with Handy and also had an office in Chicago. Williams was well known for buying the rights to songs from impoverished musicians and reissuing them under his own name. Williams would not have purchased the song from Grainger, but Tony had form there, selling the rights to 'Pretty Baby' for $45 to Van Alstyne and Kahn, who ended up coining in tens of thousands of dollars.

It was at the Panama one night, sometime in 1916, that Alberta first saw the woman who would become her lover, Lottie Tyler. Lottie was the niece of Bert Williams, the highest-paid Black actor and singer in the US at the time, and Williams would regularly call into the

Panama when he was in town, primarily to check out what new songs were being performed. Lottie and Alberta locked eyes, and both were smitten. Although she was only passing through Chicago, Lottie gave Alberta her card and told her that, 'If you ever want to come to New York, you come to this address.'

The Panama Café had two floors, each with its own piano player and act. The act in residency downstairs, where the audience was predominantly white, was known as the Panama Quartet or the Panama Four, which at various times included Florence Mills, Nettie Compton, Cora Green and bisexual singer Ada 'Bricktop' Smith, and was accompanied by pianist Glover Compton, Nettie's husband. Bricktop (whose full name was Ada Beatrice Queen Victoria Louise Virginia Smith) left in 1917 and the act disbanded, although Mills would band together with two more singers (including Cora Green, a big influence on Bessie Smith) as the Panama Trio the following year, with Tony Jackson as their pianist, before she too was off to solo stardom. Bricktop (named for her freckles and fiery red hair, the product of her grandmother being made pregnant by her Irish American slave master), would eventually move to Paris where she became one of the leading lights of French café society and embarked on an affair with dancer Josephine Baker. Florence Mills would become a huge star, play in Europe, but would sadly be dead at 31, following complications from appendix surgery.

Problems continued to dog Dago Frank Lewis. In September 1916 his summer home, in Fox Lake, was completely destroyed by fire. Firefighters and volunteers battled the blaze for fifteen hours, but the cottage and its contents were razed to the ground. The following year the Panama Café was closed by police after a man was shot there, and Alberta went to work at the Dreamland Café, recently taken over by Black businessman Bill Bottoms, where she was paid an unprecedented $150 a week.

The next couple of years were a whirlwind: within twelve months she had become the star attraction of the Dreamland Café, on South State Street, part of the South Side's Stroll, and by June 1918 Alberta was appearing on stage at the Lyceum, which had opened as a vaudeville house in 1908. It was there that Alberta would introduce several songs that would go on to be blues and jazz standards, including 'A Good Man is Hard to Find', and a 'comedy fox-trot'[28] composed by her friend Porter Grainger entitled "Tain't Nobody's Biz-ness If I Do', both later recorded by Bessie Smith. The Dreamland had a massive, and expensive, makeover in late 1920, reopening on 5 November with Alberta once again the star attraction. She was also closely associated with Shelton Brooks, appearing in no less than three of the Canadian-born, African American composer's revues in the second half of 1920 alone: Brooks's musical comedy, *Canary Cottage*, opened at the Avenue Theatre on 31st Street and Indiana Avenue in Chicago's South Side on 23 August 1920, with Alberta featured singing a new song, 'Wake Me Up with the Blues'. Two weeks later she was appearing in another new Brooks-penned musical, *Miss Nobody from Starland*, at the same theatre with much of the same cast. A week later (19 September) Alberta was appearing in another Brooks musical, *September Morn*. After that closed, the entire cast were off on a short tour, taking *Canary Cottage* to Philadelphia and then Harlem.

Bill Bottoms had given Black Chicago a venue worthy of Broadway, and boasted that the Dreamland Café was now the:

> prettiest cabaret in the country. In the large dome in the center of the ceiling hangs a beautiful bunch of green foliage, in which blaze red, white and blue incandescent electric lights. On the outer edge of the dome are several dozen incandescent lights, with the initial D. Hanging from the ceiling there are four lights covered with shades, hand painted. These are the artistic wonder of Dreamland. Gold decorations is the color scheme and on the floor is a new Brussels carpet. In the center is a glass flooring, five feet square under which brilliant lights burn with stunning effect. On each table is an electric shade. The new addition is the balcony which can be reached at the four corners of the room. At the west end is the special balcony for the New Orleans Jazz Band under the direction of Professor Joe Oliver.[29]

Joe 'King' Oliver was just one of the many jazz and blues stars Bottoms would employ; over the next few years Louis Armstrong,

Sidney Bechet, Cab Calloway and dozens of others would appear at the Dreamland Café. It was reported that Alberta's performance at the Dreamland on 5 November, where she featured a new W. C. Handy song, 'Loveless Love', drew so many tips from the audience that she would be able 'to purchase a sealskin coat for the winter'. She might have let that success go to her head, for a month later she was arrested at the Dreamland after remonstrating with a policeman who had attempted to break up dancers for 'shimmying too violently'.[30]

# 5

# Porter Grainger

*'The opinion is still widely prevalent that music is for women and effeminate men, says Henry T. Finck, veteran music critic of the* New York Evening Post.*'*[1]

In November 1920 the *Chicago Whip* reported on the plight of Sherman Robinson, of Wabash Avenue, who was the 'complainant in one of the most peculiar divorce cases to yet be heard in Chicago, when last week he asked for complete divorce from his wife, Ida May Robinson, on the grounds that she had forsaken him to run away with another woman'. Robinson told the court that the pair had married in 1910, and that he had 'lived with his wife in marital peace and harmony until September 1916, when she left him without any cause with a girl she had formerly known in Paducah, Ky',[2] and moved into a rented room on State Street with her girlfriend. Inevitably, the judge granted Robinson his decree.

It seems that Ida May found Chicago a reasonably safe place for a queer woman to live, but according to Lovie Austin, it was time for Alberta Hunter to move on to pastures new. 'She was in Chicago, and I sent her away to New York,' she told William Russell. 'She went off with a show.'[3] It was a good time to move on. Alberta's star had risen about as far as could be expected locally, and anyway, her once-safe haven was becoming ever more violent: in August 1920 two police officers were shot and killed at the Beaux Arts Club, the notorious 'black and tan' attached to the Pekin Theatre, in a row over a bootleg booze protection racket. She had also upset the boyfriend of another singer, Mae Alix who, it seems, was none too happy about Alberta making moves on what he considered to be his territory.

It would not be a permanent move; not yet anyway, and for the next couple of years Alberta would split her time between New York and Chicago. Alberta was no stranger to New York. Two years earlier, in July 1919, she had turned up unannounced at the home of the entertainer Bert Williams, dog-eared visiting card in hand, and rapped on the front door. Mr Williams was less than impressed. 'I didn't know you had to meet people formally,' she said. 'I didn't know you had to at least walk in and say, "Good morning," graciously. You don't go knocking on the door and say, "Lottie here?"'[4] She did not stay in New York long, in fact she was back in Chicago before 27 July, the day when the city's worst race riot broke out, which followed the death of Eugene Williams, a Black youth murdered by whites at Chicago's 29th Street beach. Although the beach was not officially segregated, whites and Blacks stuck to their own parts of the pleasure ground, and when Williams – on a raft – crossed the invisible line between the two a gang of white youths began pelting him with stones. Williams fell from his raft and, unable to surface through the barrage of rocks, drowned. The resulting five days of riots saw 38 dead, more than 500 injured and thousands of properties razed to the ground. The Chicago race riots followed similar riots in other cities that summer, including in Washington and St Louis, where tensions between Black and white residents had been building for some time, much of it brought about by the massive influx of southern Blacks to the area, and their forced ghettoisation.

Alberta returned to the Big Apple in December, to spend New Year with Lottie at her apartment, at 109 West 139th Street. Earlier in the year Alberta had married a former soldier named Willard Townsend, but the couple had already parted by the time she went looking for Lottie again. Being Bert Williams's niece meant that Lottie (born Charlotte in Illinois in 1887) had an immediate entrée to all of the best parties and events; she and her aunt (also called Charlotte) often appeared together at socials, bridge parties, musicales and dances, and Lottie was on occasion asked to join fundraising and organising committees. Alberta would later report that Lottie had never held a job down for very long (at various points in her life she had been a ladies' travelling companion, a dancer and had worked in a pool hall), but after the deaths of her uncle and (later) her aunt she was left with an annual income that provided enough money to live on. Later still she would assert her claim over the copyrights of several of Bert Williams's hit songs, bringing her regular royalty cheques for the rest of her life.

On 17 January 1920, the Volstead Act was effected, and prohibition gripped the United States. For decades, churches, temperance organisations and doctors had been lobbying for the government to do something about the average American's consumption of alcohol, which many believed to be thoroughly out of control. Voices in support of temperance insisted that the excessive amounts drunk by both men and women were leading to promiscuity, the breakdown of the family, poverty and a huge loss in man hours to alcohol-related illness. The temperance movement was an attempt to halt moral decline, to impose Christian values on American society, and anything that fell outside of those values – which would include any form of sex outside of marriage and anything whatsoever seen to be in favour of LGBTQ emancipation – was fair game for the movement's supporters.

Although the Volstead Act made the manufacture, importation, sale and transport of alcohol illegal, it was not, technically, illegal to drink: many people stockpiled alcohol at home before the law came into effect; cafés, bars, restaurants and clubs just the other side of the Canadian border did a roaring trade from visiting US citizens, and people were able to brew their own fruit wines and ciders at home. Naturally, an illegal market sprang up, selling what booze was available at vastly inflated prices and, once those sources dried up, bootleggers stepped in. It was illegal to make beer and spirits, yet you were perfectly within your rights to sell and purchase the equipment to make either (or both), and soon the bootleggers were producing vast amounts of bathtub gin and whisky. This lucrative business quickly attracted criminals, ready to intimidate, terrorise and even kill to ensure that they retained their share of this vast market.

In north Chicago, Dean O'Banion was beginning to make a name for himself as a thug and petty hood; when prohibition came along he and his gang seized the opportunity to take over the running of that part of town. O'Banion, his second-in-command George 'Bugs' Moran and the rest of the North Side Gang were, for the most part, only interested in the booze and gambling rackets, but south of the river a gang run by Italian immigrant Johnny 'The Fox' Torrio and his newly installed lieutenant Al 'Scarface' Capone, had their sticky fingers in every pie imaginable, from bootleg booze and gambling to local government corruption, gun running, extortion and prostitution.

Also in Chicago at this time was a furiously talented songwriter by the name of Porter Grainger. Grainger is all but forgotten now, but he would become one of the most influential figures in the Harlem Renaissance of the 1920s, a close friend of gay poet Langston Hughes (his 1927 composition 'Hootin' Owl Blues' has lyrics by Hughes based on his poem *Gal's Cry for a Dying Lover*) and of socialite, writer and photographer Carl Van Vechten. Grainger was one of the most important blues and jazz pioneers of the 20th century, writing or co-writing hit songs and blockbuster musicals, and providing the soundtrack for floorshows in some of New York's most prominent nightclubs through the twenties, thirties and forties. For a period before the start of the Second World War, Grainger was one of the biggest names in the African American entertainment industry, with a string of hit shows, hit songs and hit recordings to his name: during the twenties and thirties alone, there were more than 100 recordings of his songs on the market. Grainger was also involved in the birth of calypso music on record, and as pianist and organist for the Reverend J. C. Burnett, in 1926 he played a key role in helping to popularise gospel music, several years before Ma Rainey's accompanist Thomas Dorsey left the blues behind him to become the 'Father of Gospel Music'.

Porter Parrish Grainger (the surname was originally spelled Granger) was born, on 22 October 1891, in the Shake Rag district, a vibrant African American community within Bowling Green, Kentucky, to James T. Granger and Pearl Holmes. Shake Rag had originally been settled by emancipated slaves and their families, and soldiers who had fought for the Union during America's bloody Civil War. Pearl died when her son was just nine years old, and he was raised, along with his sister Ashula (incorrectly named Ursula on the census), some 25 miles away by his grandparents, Patience and Joseph Coleman, who kept a smallholding in Hickory Flat, Kentucky. It was a busy and tightknit household; Porter's uncle and aunt, James and Mattie Covington, were living there at the same time, and he would remain close to his Aunt Mattie for the rest of his life, often referring to her on official documents as his next of kin.

Mattie, his fraternal aunt, was a huge inspiration, and not long after she married James Covington, the pair went back to Bowling Green where, in 1906, they built the Southern Queen Hotel on State Street. The Southern Queen, which also became the family home, was the only boarding house in the Shake Rag district that would provide a room to the Black travellers and performers passing through the town – the only other hotels in Bowling Green were white-owned. Mattie also ran a restaurant, and would make and sell lunches to the students at the nearby State Street High School, where one of her nieces worked as head librarian, long before the town's first Black public school had its own cafeteria. Her entrepreneurial drive would leave a lasting impression on her nephew.

A lyricist, songwriter, piano player, music publisher and bandleader, before becoming a full-time musician Porter supported himself by working as both a labourer and a waiter, first in Kentucky's largest city, Louisville, before moving northwards, to Pittsburgh, a city which had seen huge social and economic growth over the previous four decades, with a booming heavy industry sector. In 1913, while working at the Seventh Avenue Hotel in Pittsburgh, he got his initial break into the entertainment industry, demonstrating the cake walk at a dance competition, part of the first annual ball held by the city's Banner Club, a social group for local Black hotel workers. By the following year he had relocated to Chicago, and was living in an apartment on Wabash Avenue where, despite being homosexual, he married Alies Keith on 7 November 1914. Not long afterwards, Porter decided that a change of name was in order. He added an extra 'i' to the family surname and had begun to use the name 'Grainger' professionally by 1916.

Listing his occupation as 'composer of songs' (on his draft registration card, dated 5 June 1917), Grainger took an office on South State Street in Chicago and published his earliest compositions there in 1917. Very few people thought about songs being recorded, at the time the best way for Grainger to make money from his compositions was to have a 'name' singer feature them in the hope that other singers would then perform them and demand for sheet music would follow. Keen to get his songs performed, Grainger sought out Alberta Hunter, then still singing at the Panama Café. The two would become good friends, their careers continuing to intersect until the mid-forties.

Early success came when he co-authored the humorous musical sketch *On the Puppy's Tail*, which proved a big hit in vaudeville and led to his co-founding the Griffin Music Company Limited, then the largest Black-owned publishing house in the West, with two stores in Chicago including one on South State Street. By that time he had split from Alies and moved in with fellow musician Oliver Brown and his family. Marital upset seemed to work in his favour: in 1919, while still in Chicago, Porter composed the songs 'The Shim-me King's Blues' and 'Brown Skin Soldier Boy', a tribute to the African American men who had fought in the First World War. That Easter, while a member of Chicago's Amateur Minstrels Club, he played piano for a benefit show for a local old folks' home, and for the rest of his life Grainger would give up his time to raise funds and awareness for causes he believed in. Up to two thousand people bought tickets to hear Grainger play his own compositions, including 'It's Back to Chicago for Me', 'The Shim-me King's Blues' and 'Brown Skin Soldier Boy'. The jazz instrumental 'The Shim-me King's Blues' became a sizeable hit, with dance bands across the country playing the tune – although many newspapers confused Porter with Australian-born composer Percy Grainger, whose own career was once again taking off after an eighteen-month stint in the US army. Within a year he would leave Chicago and move to New York: the bright lights of Broadway were calling, and the city's record companies were desperate to get in on the new blues boom. The success of 'Crazy Blues' – selling 75,000 copies in Harlem alone –

convinced New York's record labels that there was a lucrative market among urban Blacks for recordings from jazz and blues singers.

The call to head east could not come at a better time for Grainger. Chicago bars frequented by homosexuals either paid the local police to turn a blind eye, or paid local hoodlums for 'protection'. Some were forced to pay both, and men with his tastes lived their lives in fear of the police and of gangs who actively targeted homosexual men. One such gang was led by a young man who would later write about his life on the streets of the city. Under the penname Clifford R. Shaw, he told of his experiences in two volumes, *The Natural History of a Delinquent Career*, and *The Jack-Roller*. In the latter, Shaw recalled being solicited by homosexuals on several occasions, 'As I'd walk along Madison Street, there'd always be some man to stop me and coax me into having sex relations with him,' and it was experiences such as that which led him into establishing his own extortion racket:

My friend and I used this little scheme to entice men into a room to rob them. That very day a fellow stopped me and asked for a match. I accommodated him, and he started a conversation. He was about eight years my senior, and big and husky. He said he was a foreman in a machine shop, and when I said I was out of work, he promised to get a job for me at his shop. He invited me to supper with him up in his room... He was a kind guy, with a smile and a winning way, so I went up to have supper on his invitation. We ate, and then he edged up close to me and put his arm around me and told me how much I appealed to his passions. He put his hand on my leg and caressed me gently, while he talked softly to me. I had to wait a few minutes for my buddy to come to help put the strong arm on this man. I couldn't do it alone. My buddy had followed us all the time and was only waiting for a chance to come to my rescue. Finally, he came and we sprang into the fellow with fury. He started to grab me and my buddy dealt him a heavy blow. We found thirteen dollars in his pockets. Since he had tried to ensnare me I figured I was justified in relieving him of his thirteen bucks. Besides, was he not a low degenerate, and wouldn't he use the money only to harm himself further?[5]

Luckily for creatives such as Porter Grainger, a new branch of the entertainment industry was about to blossom and, in the early years of blues recording, Grainger would become one of the most popular accompanists, appearing on recordings by most of the great classic blues singers, including Mamie Smith, Bessie Smith, Clara Smith and Victoria Spivey. His association with Mamie Smith began in November 1920, a few months after she signed with Okeh Records, when he played piano on one of her earliest sessions for the company. Their meeting was a fortuitous one, Grainger had only been a resident of New York since April, and it was one that would help him become established as one of the pioneers of the blues on record. By the time that Grainger first sat in on a session with the singer, Smith was enjoying a phenomenal level of fame, one that had never been afforded to a Black female recording artist before.

Over the next twelve months, as he continued to establish his credentials as a jobbing songwriter, Grainger would occasionally join Mamie Smith on the road, and her band, Mamie Smith's Jazz Hounds, would record a hit version of 'The Shim-me King's Blues', released on Okeh in March 1921. To further supplement his income, for a time he acted as manager and musical accompanist on a lecture tour given by Needham Roberts, a Black war hero who had been severely disabled in Germany during the First World War. Roberts, a soldier in the 369th Infantry Regiment, known informally as the Black Rattlers or the Harlem Hellfighters, was one of the first US soldiers to be awarded the Croix de Guerre for his valour, and, in 1996 was posthumously awarded the Purple Heart. The tour gave Grainger plenty of opportunity to plug his latest hit, 'Brown Skin Soldier Boy'.

Up until the late 1910s, the American record industry had been dominated by a handful of labels, including Edison, Columbia, and Victor, by far the biggest of them all. Most of these companies recorded and released what they considered their cultured, white audiences wanted: sentimental songs, opera and classical music and the biggest pop tunes of the day. No one was recording jazz or blues music; few Black artists were making records, and those that were – like Bert Williams, the star of *In Dahomey* – recorded songs that would appeal across the board. When Williams was signed to Columbia in 1906, sheet music sales dwarfed those of records, and few at the top of the industry thought that would change any time soon. Only Caruso sold in the hundreds of thousands.

However, by the end of the decade that was beginning to change. Williams was, by now, an international star: *In Dahomey* had played in England, and Columbia were releasing his records there too. The war helped boost the demand for records in more ways than one: the sale of portable, wind-up gramophones soared dramatically, and the jazz boom that coincided with the end of hostilities increased the need for recordings by dance bands and orchestras. Other companies noticed a gap in the market that the majors were not catering for, and a new breed of record labels emerged. Although the recording process itself was still primitive – singers would stand in front of a horn, with their musicians in the same room, and sing straight into the machine while their essence was captured on a wax cylinder or disc – it was relatively cheap, which allowed plenty of start-up companies to enter the market. Musicians and singers were paid a flat fee, the songwriters might get a royalty if they were lucky, and if a recording sold a couple of thousand copies the company was doing well.

Many of the big tent shows disbanded temporarily when America entered the First World War, but by early 1919 several were back on the road. The Rabbit Foot Minstrels, reformed by Fred Wolcott, gave their first performance at Port Gibson, Mississippi – a few miles from Wolcott's recently acquired plantation, Glen Sade, in May 1919. Life for the travelling show continued to be hard: in May 1920 three members of the crew died when a fire broke out in their sleeping car, but the end of the war presaged massive change in social standards in America, and a seismic shift away from Victorian values. The bohemians embracing the jazz age were rejecting these same mores, challenging the concept of family and investigating radical new ideas around sex and sexuality. To many of these so-called 'bright young things', LGBTQ people were seen not as a threat, but as an exotic, vibrant and exciting part of their brave new world.

The perfectly understandable desire to celebrate life and freedom that followed the end of the war saw more and more women making use of what until then had been men-only spaces. Before the war it was almost unheard of for a woman to be seen drinking in a bar, let along enter one unaccompanied, but by the time the war was over more women were in employment, supporting themselves financially, and becoming politically active. The speakeasies (a term for an unlicensed bar, in use in America since at least 1889; the phrase had already been in use in the British navy for more than a half century, for a private home where alcohol was sold without duty paid) that sprang up immediately following the introduction of prohibition gave women even more opportunity to mix, drink and to enjoy entertainment without being shackled to a man. Although Mona's (or Mona's 440) which opened in San Francisco in the mid-1930s is often cited as the first lesbian bar in the US, women-only and women-friendly spaces existed underground in other cities for years before then. In late 1924 Polish-Jewish émigré Chawa Zloczewer, known variously as Eve Adams, Evelyn Addams and Eva Kotchever, opened her own lesbian space at 129 MacDougal Street in Greenwich Village. Eve's Hangout (also known as Eve Adams' Tearoom) was an unlicensed bar, notorious for having a sign on the door that, according to an article in entertainment trade magazine *Variety*, announced 'Men are admitted, but not welcome'. Described as a woman who 'had effected masculine attire and became a regular at the various resorts catering to "tempermentals"', the following year, Eve published her book *Lesbian Love*. After spending a year in the Blackwell's Island workhouse (where, it has been claimed, she became friends with Mae West) for obscenity and disorderly conduct, Eve was deported from the States to Poland.

Prior to the First World War, New York's chief contribution to the entertainment industry had been live theatre and the new and wildly successful field of cinema, but by the middle of the decade most of the movie makers had moved to California, where taxes were lower and the weather was better. In California you could find venues such as the 606 and the Ninety-Six Club, where on any given night the patrons were 'composed of the "queer" people', where 'members sometimes spent hundreds of dollars on silk gowns, hosiery, etc., in which they dressed... at these "drags" the "queer" people have a good time, but no one could get in without being introduced by a member of good standing.'[6]

A new film community quickly formed in and around Hollywood, which itself was just a half-hour's drive away from Long Beach, where an active LGBTQ social scene was already established. The term was not in use, no one had ever thought that this loose collection of people from all backgrounds, races and social classes might one day form a vibrant, influential and politically active community, but gay men, lesbians, bisexuals, trans and queer-identified people talked about their being in 'the life'... and there were plenty of actors, producers, screenwriters and film technicians, some of whom were openly, flamboyantly, outrageously in 'the life'. 'It is an umbrella term that loosely means "queer" or "gay" but encompasses the truly vast breadth of LGBTQ experiences,'[7] explains author, performer and activist Sarah Kilborne, originator of the stage show *The Lavender Blues: The Story of Queer Music Before World War II*. World-famous drag artist Julian Eltinge made his film debut in 1914, and by 1917 he was a major box-office draw. J. Warren Kerrigan, who lived with his male partner for over thirty years, was a huge star of the silent screen. Lesbian director Dorothy Arzner – the first woman to direct a Hollywood movie – began her career in 1919, and three years later worked on *Blood and Sand*, starring the (it is rumoured) bisexual superstar Rudolph Valentino. Gay British screen star and songwriter Ivor Novello would make his Hollywood debut (for D. W. Griffith) in 1923; he arrived in town the year after gay actor (and later interior designer) William Haines, a man rumoured to have had affairs with Clark Gable and Ramon Novarro (who began his own screen career in 1917), and who would share his home with his lover Jimmy Shields for five decades.

In New York, the nascent film industry had been controlled by Thomas Edison, who headed the Motion Picture Patents Company (MPPC) and was happy to sue anyone he saw as infringing the cartel's closely guarded copyrights. In 1915 the federal court declared that the rules of the MPPC went 'far beyond what was necessary to protect the use of patents or the monopoly which went with them',[8] sounding the death knell for film production in the city. Luckily, at the same time as everyone was running off to Hollywood, the record industry was becoming more firmly established in the Big Apple.

Up until this point there had been no single industry standard for record production. Records and cylinders vied for their own little piece of the market, some gramophones would not play certain types of records (discs were made using either the vertical or lateral cut system), and until 1925 there was no industry-agreed playback speed or size. Record sales were not seen as that important anyway: many companies, such as Brunswick Records which was recording in New York from 1916, saw their record production arm as secondary to their primary business, which was selling record players. But things were changing, demand was increasing and, at the beginning of 1920, they established their own permanent studio and launched their 'new' Brunswick Records, adopting the 'lateral cut' system which was quickly becoming the default for 78 rpm discs. Vocalion had already opened its studios, on West 43rd Street, New York, in 1919. Prior to this, recordings had been made acoustically in the Aeolian Hall. The four-storey building housed a reception room and lounge as well as the recording studio itself. Boasting that, 'The wonderful new system under which Vocalion Records are produced is the last word in the world's knowledge of sound,' the company insisted that, 'The full beauty of the artist's voice – all the overtones, too subtle, too delicate for older systems to record – are caught by the new Vocalion method. The records made under this new system are as superior to all other records as the Vocalion itself surpasses all other phonographs.'[9]

Mamie Smith attended her first recording session, for Victor Records, of Camden, New Jersey, on 10 January 1920, recording a version of Perry Bradford's 'That Thing Called Love'. That went unreleased, but five weeks later she was at Okeh, in New York, to perform the same song alongside another Bradford composition, 'You Can't Keep a Good Man Down'. The record came about by accident, the song having originally been lined up by Okeh's musical director Fred Hager for the popular white stage star Sophie Tucker, but after Tucker fell ill and was unavailable for the session Perry Bradford, a former song and dance man, managed to persuade Hager to use Smith instead. On that session she was backed by the Rega Orchestra, the name used for a fluctuating conglomeration that made up Okeh's house band ('Rega' was a pseudonym used by Fred Hager) and which, at that time, was made up of all-white players, including Frank Banta, the former house pianist with Edison's National Phonograph Company. The disc sold respectably well, certainly more than enough to convince Hager and Okeh that they should bring her back into the studio and, on 10 August 1920, Mamie Smith recorded her second session for the company, another Perry Bradford composition, 'Crazy Blues'.

'Crazy Blues' is often cited as the first blues song to be recorded by a Black vocalist... but it was not. Almost a year earlier, in November 1919 – the same month that he had entranced the Prince of Wales during a visit to Ziegfeld's Follies in New York – Bert Williams, then one of the highest paid recording artists in the world (and the uncle of Alberta Hunter's girlfriend, Lottie Tyler), went into the studio to record the song 'I'm Sorry I Ain't Got It You Could Have It If I Had It Blues' for Columbia. Over the following six months he would record several other sides with blues in the title, including 'Unlucky Blues' in April 1920 and, in May, 'Lonesome Alimony Blues'.

The Bahamian-born Williams, who began his recording career in 1896, was one of the most popular entertainers of the time, touring Great Britain in 1904 and becoming the first Black American to take a lead role on Broadway, when *In Dahomey*, the first full-length musical written, directed and performed by an all-Black cast, made its debut at Oscar Hammerstein's Olympia Theatre. However, like many Black artists at that time, the light-skinned Williams often performed in blackface: he had joined a minstrel company while still a teenager and continued to appear on stage in traditional minstrel garb, and in contemporary advertisements he appeared alongside Columbia's other huge blackface star Al Jolson. He was not happy having to play blacked-up, and even though he was a huge star Williams still faced enormous racism: white actors convened their own union, specifically to protest artists like Williams being given roles in white stage shows, and like other Black performers he was not allowed to use the main entrance to theatres and hotels. On one occasion, when he was refused service in a New York hotel bar and told that he would have to pay fifty dollars for a drink, Williams pulled a roll of $100 bills from his pocket and proceeded to buy a round for everyone in the bar.

Williams may have been the first Black American to record blues songs, but 'Crazy Blues' holds the distinction of being the first blues song recorded by a female African American vocalist, backed entirely by Black musicians, the Jazz Hounds. Mamie Smith had been performing professionally since she was 10 years old, and had been a regular in Harlem's clubs for a few years when Bradford, with an eye on managing her career and potentially getting into the already married Smith's bed, finally persuaded Okeh's Fred Hager that Black audiences would buy something other than the highbrow opera and classical music they were being offered. It was a hard sell. Even though Okeh had already seen success in ethnic markets, shifting thousands of records by Yiddish and European acts, but 'Crazy Blues' was a game changer: selling in its tens of thousands, the disc woke America's record labels up to the fact that there was a ready and hitherto untapped market for authentic Black music. Up until this point, Black Americans had had little opportunity to purchase recordings of their own music by names that they knew; record companies – in part thanks to an aggressive, years-long campaign by the editors of the *Chicago Defender* – had convinced themselves that it was only the newly prosperous, Black middle classes that could afford gramophones and that they were only interested in classical music and religious songs. The blues, replete with scandalous tales of sex, drink and drugs, was considered the Devil's music, at odds with people's deeply held Christian beliefs.

The blues were rough and unsophisticated, and anyway, the last thing this new class of affluent, forward-thinking people wanted was to be reminded of the cotton fields, surely? It was not just the label heads who had decided that Black Americans had something to prove. Booking agents and theatre managers on the Keith theatre circuit – a far more prestigious set-up than the Black-run Theatre Owners Booking Association (T.O.B.A.) – were told to limit the number of blues singers they booked, and to be wary of 'songs with suggestive lines in the lyrics', and performers who 'substitute double-entendre lines of their own composition for those originally written'.[10] The editors of Black newspapers constantly hammered home the message of social uplift, but not everyone who moved northwards wanted to leave their roots behind. For the first time, tens of thousands of Black Americans were earning money, but many of them were missing family and friends. It is no surprise that these people were drawn to the yearning, heartsick sound of the blues, songs that W. C. Handy himself referred to as, 'folk songs... Each one of my blues is based on some old negro song of the south, some folk-song that I heard from my mammy as a child... Some old song that is part of the memories of my childhood and of my race.'[11]

Willie 'The Lion' Smith played piano on that historic session. He later remembered how Mamie stood 'in front of a large megaphone-like horn and really let loose with her fine contralto voice. As I recall, we got twenty-five dollars apiece for the two sides, and we had to wait two months to get our money. In those days it didn't matter how long it took you to get the sides down satisfactorily – the money was the same, regardless of the time, and no royalty deals.'[12]

'Crazy Blues' was an enormous success, but this success did not come without its pitfalls: Perry Bradford was sued by Fred Bowers, who owned the copyright in another song which, he claimed, Bradford had plagiarised for his hit. The song Bowers owned was called 'Broken Hearted Blues', and the songwriter was one Perry Bradford. Bowers was soon joined in his action by another publisher, Max Kortlander, who claimed that Bradford had sold him the rights to another of his songs, 'Wicked Blues', which bore an alarming similarity to 'Crazy Blues'. This was not the first time that Bradford had crossed Kortlander: according to his sworn affidavit, Bradford had previously sold him the rights to 'That Thing Called Love', which Bradford later re-sold to Pace and Handy. With Bradford estimated to earn close on $50,000 from 'Crazy Blues', his previous business partners were now looking to share in his good fortune. In truth, Bradford had gutted some of his earlier compositions for 'Crazy Blues', including a song he called 'Harlem Blues' that Mamie Smith had been performing on stage since 1918 and, as Willie 'The Lion' Smith would later recall, the song was actually based on 'an old bawdy song played in the sporting houses', titled 'Baby, Get That Towel Wet'.

Okeh soon took to advertising their new star as 'The only natural singer of "blues"', claiming that, 'Her songs are true "blues" or products of old negro spirituals. The singing of spirituals is an intuitive art, and Mamie Smith's rich, dramatic voice is inherited from generations of lullaby singers.'[13] But Smith was not a blues singer: she was an all-round entertainer. There were plenty of other blues singers touring the circuit before those first recordings were made, although most of their names are now long forgotten. By late 1915 Ma Rainey was already being advertised as 'The famous singer of the Blues', but although she had many contemporaries, you will seldom hear of Stella Stamper (or of her big song 'If Every Star Was a Little Pickaninny'), Bebe LaPorte, Miss Dot Moore, Thelma Fraley, Ella Brown, Ruby Darby, 'Sugarfoot' Gafney, the 'peppery' Viola Pepper, or 'Happy' Lawson, often advertised as 'the original blues singer',[14] all to a man – or a woman – whiter than white, although many of the men would appear beneath burnt cork – using a mixture of petroleum jelly and burnt, crushed wine bottle corks to create black face paint. It's little wonder then that Mamie Smith, 'The only colored girl that sings for phonograph records',[15] caused such a stir.

In 1921 the Columbia Graphophone Company took over the top eight floors of the twenty-four-storey Gotham National Bank Building in Columbus Circle, New York and opened its offices and recording studios. For years, the only way to make recordings had been for the artists to gather as close as they dared to a large sound-capture horn and perform their material in one take. A way to edit recordings, or to drop in a few notes to cover up a mistake, had yet to be discovered. If a musician missed a cue, or the horn picked up any extraneous noise, the take would have to be abandoned and started again from the top. The acoustic sound gathered by the horn would be transferred, as the artist played or sang, onto a wax master, and this in turn would be used to make shellac copies of the original performance. With no decent, reliable electric microphones available, all of the early blues records would be made this way, which is one of the reasons why companies preferred to offer contracts to singers with a proven track record. Trying to capture a performance from untrained, non-professional singers was simply too risky.

The records that these companies did put out were advertised extensively in the Black press, especially in such newspapers as the *Chicago Defender*, a publication that sold to Black communities far outside of Chicago itself, and which took pains to promote and glamorise those members of the African American community who had taken part in the Great Migration. But many of these advertisements featured crass stereotypes of Black people, minstrel-style cartoon images with watermelon smiles and bulging eyes, or the buxom mammy with her hair hidden under a knotted scarf, and when they appeared alongside advertisements for hair straightening products and skin-whitening creams, rather than promote the idea of Black people as strong and independent, they helped promulgate the impression that those Blacks who had moved northwards were still second-class citizens, and that they had to assimilate to fit into the white world. Grainger himself was confused on the issue: much of his early stage work included work-shy characters and broad, almost blackface performances, yet he would champion Black folk music and wrote almost exclusively for all-Black productions.

At some point in 1921 Bessie Smith, then performing at the Paradise Gardens in Atlantic City, as part of the show assembled by singer and comedian Frankie Jaxon, seems to have auditioned for Columbia: in an advertisement for a performance in Philadelphia that May, she is advertised (alongside her '5 Jazzoway Dandies', referred to elsewhere as her 'Five Jazz Away Dandies',[16] an act she put together for a tour on the Loew's circuit) as having 'hits on Columbia Records'. She did not; in fact, it would be two full years before she would enjoy her first hit for the company, and if she did indeed audition or record for Columbia at that time, no written or recorded evidence has ever surfaced.

# 6

# Ethel Waters and
# Early Harlem

*'I often wonder why we will go down into our jeens* [sic] *and fish out
money enough to pay for the subscription of half dozen Colored papers
and hand it over for a record that grinds out some brand of blues, in
the so-called negro dialect, that has no truth, no poetry nor art in its
construction, and makes a vocal scarecrow of the Colored singer.'*[1]

Like all of the big northern cities, New York proved an irresistible
draw, but LGBTQ people had been descending to the great
metropolis for years before the first wave of the Great Migration hit. In
fact, New York's bars and clubs had been attracting homosexual men
since the late Victorian era, and LGBTQ artists had long been relocating
to the city, some presumably drawn there by the presence of Walt
Whitman, recognised as America's greatest poet, and the gay author
of the distinctly homoerotic collection *Leaves of Grass*, first published
in 1855. However, the bohemians flocking to the salons and saloons of
the Big Apple in the 19th century were almost exclusively Caucasian.

During the late 1850s and early 1860s, Whitman's favourite drinking
den was Pfaff's Restaurant and Lager Bier Saloon (better known as
Pfaff's Beer Cellar) on Broadway, in Manhattan's Greenwich Village.

Then nothing like the great theatre thoroughfare it would later become, Whitman and his lover Fred Vaughan could often be found at Pfaff's, and the poet soon formed his own coterie of handsome young men, which he would refer to as his 'darling, dearest boys'.[2] The cellar bar kept up an air of respectability, and became a home-from-home for many writers and bohemians, drawn by the artistic company, cheap prices and the ready availability of international newspapers (German-born proprietor Charles Ignatius Pfaff had German, Italian, French and English newspapers delivered to the bar, as well as American titles). Unsurprisingly, Pfaff's also attracted hustlers and male prostitutes, although they were not to Whitman's taste. Vaughan and Whitman parted, the younger man was struggling with his sexual identity and had become a heavy drinker, and although Whitman loved Pfaff's it was for the company and the opportunity to express himself freely, not for the alcohol: he would nurse a beer for hours.

Vaughan did what was expected of him, and settled into marriage and family life, while Whitman embarked on a series of one-night stands with coach drivers, plumbers and other tradesmen, which he detailed in his diaries. Civil War began in 1861, and the following year Whitman left New York for Washington, to work as a volunteer nurse. As the fame of his former lover increased, a bitter Vaughan would drift further and further into alcoholism. Even so, the two men would not forget each other, and Vaughan would occasionally visit Whitman after the poet moved to a new home in Camden, New Jersey in 1874 – the house where he would entertain Oscar Wilde and where Whitman would pass away, in March 1892.

Pfaff had closed his Broadway bar more than two decades earlier, in 1870, moving to new premises on 24th Street, but the area remained popular with the LGBTQ clientele. Owned by Frank Stevenson but managed by his brother Tom, The Slide, at 157 Bleecker Street, was a five-minute walk away from Pfaff's, and was a notorious 'fairy resort', where male and trans prostitutes would go in search of trade. The Slide was mentioned in the press as 'morally the lowest in New York', and it was claimed that 'London, Paris or Berlin, with all their iniquity, have nothing to parallel this sink of vice and depravity. Other dives have become notorious on account of their proprietors or the many crimes that have been committed in them, but "The Slide" is notorious chiefly on account of its immoral character.'[3] Referred to in an 1890 guide as 'The lowest and most disgusting place. The place is filled nightly with from 100 to 300 people, most of whom are males... They are addicted to vices which are inhumane and unnatural,' it is no surprise that the bar was identified by police as the 'worst dive' in the city. A reporter from the *Evening World* noted that The Slide 'swarmed with dissolute creatures. Their talk was shocking. Many of the men had painted faces and they called each other by female names.'[4] So bad was its reputation that the authorities closed The Slide down in 1892, although the Black Rabbit, less than a block away at 183 Bleecker Street, was happy to pick up the slack, referred to in a *New York Times* article in October 1900 as so wicked that 'Sodom and Gomorrah would blush for shame at hearing to what depths of vice its habitues had descended.' Just a few blocks away, on Bowery, was the Columbia Hall (known informally as Paresis Hall), a drinking den popular with homosexual and transgender sex workers, with entertainment provided by a pianist who would often accompany raucous songs from the Hall's trans clientele.

New York may have been a magnet for LGBTQ people, but for the most part those able to enjoy the benefits the Big Apple had to offer were white. Racial segregation still existed and would continue to do so long after the passing of the Civil Rights Act in 1964: as recently as June 2021 UCLA's Civil Rights Project reported that 'New York retains its place as the most segregated state for black students, and second most segregated for Latino students.' A century ago, the Black Americans flocking to the city had no option but to find accommodation in predominantly Black areas, such as Greenwich Village and Harlem.

Harlem had originally been developed as an exclusive suburb for the white middle classes but, following the enormous influx of European immigrants to New York in the 19th century (by the middle of the century, a quarter of the city's population was Irish, with thousands of Italians and East Europeans adding to the volatile mix), the area was abandoned by the whites and Harlem became a predominantly African American neighbourhood.

Many would find that the lives they thought they had left behind – of enforced segregation and white-on-Black violence – simply followed them. Although Harlem did not become a Black stronghold until after the end of the First World War, the expanding presence of Black Americans in the area brought ever-present racial tensions to the fore. On Christmas Day 1901, a small riot broke out between whites and Blacks after a group of white youths attacked two Black girls: a white mob drove an angry group of around 100 Blacks back to their tenement homes and continued to bombard them with 'stones and other missiles.' After shots were fired from the tenement windows 'and seeing men fall wounded', the white attackers 'turned and ran, followed by the Negroes, who used knives and clubs freely. At this point a squad of policemen arrived and, with drawn clubs, stopped the rioting.'[5] Three white men were injured, one shot and two stabbed, and thirty-one Black men were arrested. These racial tensions were amplified by the press: 'The north is fast learning to know the "Smart Alek" darkey as he is,'[6] crowed the editor of Virginia's *Clarke Courier*; by the time the story appeared in North Carolina's the *People's Paper*, the number of rioting Blacks had increased ten-fold.

This racial tension was not limited to Harlem. The following day another riot broke out in Childersburg, Alabama, where 'two whites [were] killed and many Negroes wounded'.[7] These skirmishes were nothing new – two months earlier, nine people were killed and many more wounded in a race riot in Balltown, Pennsylvania. Civil unrest had become endemic in America: riots took place in several cities, the Ku Klux Klan were running amok in the South, and in Boston the entire police force went on strike, with a trigger-happy volunteer militia taking over the role for several days. Race riots would continue with alarming frequency, beyond the Black civil rights movement of the 1960s and right up until the present day, but they were not limited to attacks between whites and Blacks: in the racial melting pot of 1920s New York it was not uncommon for fights to break out between Russian and Austrian immigrants, or Italians and Jews, for example.

Due in no small part to the violence and lawlessness, the cost of renting a room or an apartment in Harlem continued to fall, and around 1908 the roots were laid down for the period we now call the Harlem Renaissance. That year a group of Black performers and writers, including singer Bert Williams and the composer J. Rosamond Johnson, formed the Frogs. Initially an organisation for professional artists, membership of the group was soon opened up to include other Black professionals. As the 1910s turned into the 1920s, more and more Black intellectuals, artists and performers settled in the area, many of them drawn there by the opportunity to have their material published in magazines like *The Crisis* – established by W. E. B. DuBois in 1910, the year after he had been one of the founding members of the National Association for the Advancement of Colored People (NAACP). Jamaican political activist and civil rights campaigner Marcus Garvey settled in Harlem in 1916, and soon established an American branch of his Universal Negro Improvement Association (UNIA). He would later become friends with Porter Grainger; Garvey clearly had an effect on Grainger's political development, and he would write and record several pieces related to Garvey; Grainger also composed the music to accompany a comedy, *Brown Sugar*, written by Garvey's first wife, Amy Ashwood Garvey, which featured Fats Waller.

Propelled further by the socialist politics of such publications as *The Messenger*, an African American magazine whose editors questioned Garvey's approach to nationalism and, in the wake of the war, were demanding full social equality for Black people, by February 1920 the *New York Age* was reporting on how:

> The Negro residents of Harlem have much upon which to congratulate themselves... They should be proud of the fact that they are property owners and residents in one of the most eligible sections of the greater city, with all the resources of modern civilization at their command... They have free access to courts, both as petitioners and practitioners, prosecutors and defendants, and equal and exact justice is accorded them. They are represented by men of their own race in the local and state legislative bodies and the ballot box is open for their suffrages.[8]

A 'Negro Literary Renaissance... a group remarkable for its vigor, originality and racial flavor',[9] was well underway.

Hanging around Harlem, and Greenwich Village, was a young woman by the name of Mabel Hampton. Born in Winston-Salem, North Carolina, on 2 May 1902, Mabel was barely 2 years old when her mother died, leaving the infant in the care of her maternal grandmother. When she too passed away just five years later, Mabel was put on a train to New York City, where she went to live with her aunt and uncle; her uncle, although professing to be a minister and a man of God, raped the child. Within a year, Hampton ran away, making her way to New Jersey after buying a bus ticket with a nickel given to her by a woman she met on the street. She was taken in by a Black family; Ellen, the eldest daughter, was lesbian and became a surrogate mother to Mabel, but after she had been there around six months Ellen's father, Mr White, began to make sexual advances too.

In 1921, now living on her own, Hampton was sent to prison for prostitution; she later insisted that she and a girlfriend had been set up, victims of police entrapment because both were lesbians. She was released after serving approximately eighteen months of a three-year sentence in the Bedford Hills Correctional Facility for Women, a notorious women's prison.* Hampton was mortified that people would find out: 'I didn't care anything about them knowing I was a lesbian. I didn't want them to know I was in Bedford Hills... So I just kept quiet and told nobody.'[10] Upon her release, in 1923, she started working at a dress factory before landing a job at the Lafayette Theatre, where she met Gladys Bentley, the Two Ethels and other lesbian and bisexual performers. She became friends with lesbian comedian Jackie 'Moms' Mabley, appearing on stage with her at the Lafayette, and she also worked as a dancer at clubs including the Garden of Joy, with pianist and drag king Gladys Bentley. In a series of taped interviews made between 1978 and 1989, Mabel spoke in great detail about lesbian life in New York during the 1920s and 30s. 'I was in with the show people...

---

* In 1913 a young girl, Elizabeth Trondle, had been sent to Bedford Hills for three years. Her crime: wearing boy's clothes. '"I sent her to the Bedford Reformatory," said Magistrate Nash, "Because I believe she is a moral pervert. No girl would dress in men's clothing unless she is twisted in her moral viewpoint."' – *Brooklyn Daily Eagle*, 3 September 1913.

we'd go to nightclubs and different places. I'd sit there and drink my soda, and we'd talk, you know... you'd go down the steps and go in where they were playing the music. I went to four or five different places [in Harlem], maybe more, and I went down to the Village, to a white place down there where I was treated very nice...'[11]

Tony Jackson died, at his home on Chicago's Wabash Avenue, on 20 April 1921. He had been ill for some time, but he continued to write, penning his last hit, 'I'm Cert'n'y Going to See About That' for a stage production at the city's Monogram Theatre just a few weeks earlier. An epileptic prone to seizures who self-medicated with alcohol, the introduction of prohibition would have forced him to seek illicit booze wherever possible, the quality and strength of which went unregulated. In February, friends worried by the rapid decline in his health had organised a benefit at the Dreamland Café, raising $325 to send Tony to Hot Springs, a spa town where the climate and revitalising waters would surely help him recuperate, but few were surprised when he finally succumbed to cirrhosis of the liver.

His friend Alberta Hunter was conspicuous by her absence at his funeral, but perhaps she had other things on her mind. She was still commuting regularly between Chicago and New York, maintaining a home in the Windy City with Carrie Mae Ward (her local squeeze while Lottie stayed in New York, under the watchful eye of her aunt and uncle) and continuing to pack them in at the Dreamland when, on 17 May 1921, a little over a fortnight after Tony's remains were interred, she entered the offices of the African American-owned Black Swan records in New York and signed a recording contract. Later that same day Alberta took part in her first recording session for the company, laying down four sides for the label. Black Swan had no studio of its own, so Pace rented a small local set-up: 'There was like a hole in the wall, about big enough for a horn to get through. Like the bell of a horn, you know, the big part of a horn. The big part of the horn would come here, where I am, the smaller part of the horn would go to that part. And there were technicians on that side. They could see me and I could see them. You understand? ... and this machine would be cutting the wax as you [were] singing.'[12] Her first disc for Black Swan, the jazz tune 'Bring Back the Joys', coupled with the more blues-flavoured 'How Long, Sweet Daddy, How Long', was issued in September.

In the two years between her first visit to the metropolis, in the summer of 1919, and the day she walked into the offices of Black Swan, Alberta had been steadily working towards making a name for herself, raising herself up from a virtual unknown outside of Chicago to a featured performer in the touring show *Canary Cottage*, which played New York's Lafayette theatre for two weeks in October 1920. But it was landing a recording contract that would make her a star.

Black Swan, which issued its first records in the same month as they signed Alberta, was owned by Harry Herbert Pace and based at West 138th Street, New York. Pace had been W. C. Handy's partner in the Pace and Handy Music Company, which the pair originally established in Memphis but, in July 1918, opened a second office – in truth a desk in a shared office that the pair were forced to pay over the odds for – in Broadway's Gaiety building. The partners had been trying to establish themselves in New York for a while, but Black songwriters were initially wary of getting involved with them, accustomed as they were to being ripped off by publishers, and they struggled with their plans for expansion. Pace elected to remain in the South, overseeing operations there, while Handy – whose success as a songwriter would no doubt open doors – went to New York to try to gain a foothold for the fledgling company. It would not take him long. With the demand for authentic jazz and blues numbers increasing, and with Pace and Handy promising writers a better royalty than they would get from a white publisher, in February 1920, Pace too moved to The City That Never Sleeps to become president of the now-burgeoning business. In his first year in New York, the Pace and Handy Music Company went from strength to strength, and they soon moved to a new suite of rooms on West 46th Street. Then, in January 1921, Pace announced that he and his partner intended to set up their own record company, one 'using exclusively the voices and talent of colored people'.[13]

In retaliation, several white companies, songwriters and record labels told Pace and Handy that they would no longer work with their company, and that no white-owned business would issue songs written or published by them. In mid-February, Pace, who Ethel Waters described as a 'very nice, friendly man and very dignified',[14] resigned from the company, leaving Handy free to work with whomsoever he chose to. A resolute Pace told the press that the 'opposition of the white companies to the entry of a race organization into the phonograph record producing field makes me all the more determined to give the race representation in an entirely new field of business endeavor, and convinces me of the necessity of preserving our race music and preserving for our children the wonderful voices and musical talent that we have in the race. The public wants the kind of records I shall put out and they will get them no matter who objects.'[15]

The Pace Phonograph Company, which claimed to be the 'first enterprise of its kind to be started by a colored corporation',[16] was run entirely by Black Americans and employed only Black musicians and singers.[*] One of the first people Pace approached to join his outfit was Bert Williams, but Williams was already under contract to Columbia. Pace would later claim that Williams had a substantial amount of money invested in Black Swan, and that the entertainer intended to move to the company once his contract with Columbia was up.

Harry Pace set out his modus operandi immediately, taking out full-page advertisements in *The Crisis* and in other Black publications which announced that Black Swan Records 'will give opportunities to our own singers such as they can get from no other companies. Every record you buy means encouragement to some Negro singer and some Negro musician to continue their work and to develop their talent... Every record you buy means employment along new lines to a large number of our talented people, in addition to clerks, stenographers and others... Black Swan Records are the only records using exclusively Negro voices and Negro musicians.'[17]

Amongst its first batch of releases, announced on 5 May 1921, was 'Blind Man Blues' by Katie Crippen, a Philadelphia-born singer who had

---

[*] Black Swan was not the first Black-run record label in the United States, but it was the first to have any measure of success. It was predated by a small mail-order company – Broome Special Phonograph Records – owned and operated by George W. Broome of Medford, Massachusetts.

been performing on the Black vaudeville circuit since at least 1914 and more recently had been making a name for herself in the basement jazz clubs of New York City. 'Black Swan Records are made to meet what we believe is a legitimate and growing demand,' Pace announced. 'There are over twelve million colored people in the United States, and in that number there is hid away a wonderful amount of musical ability... We propose to spare no expense in the search for and developing of the best singers and musicians among this Black Twelve Million.'[18] By the middle of August, Pace was claiming that his company was 'increasing more than thirty percent each month.'[19]

Pace and Black Swan soon felt the wrath of the white-owned companies coming down on them. Columbia dug up recordings they had of artists who had defected to Black Swan and put them out as new releases, advertising the performers as under exclusive contract. Pace, not a man to take things lying down, sued. Columbia had no idea that they were messing with a man who had studied law and who had established his own, highly profitable real estate business.

Alberta was in good company. Also recording at Black Swan that year was Ethel Waters, soon to become 'The highest paid colored phonograph star in the country.'[20] Both women were lesbians, but Alberta liked to keep her life private, and she disliked Ethel being so open about her sexuality.

Waters had been born in Pennsylvania, on Hallowe'en 1896 (in her autobiography, *His Eye is on the Sparrow*, Ethel claimed she was born in 1900). Her mother Louise Anderson, barely a teenager herself, had been the victim of a knifepoint rape by pianist John Waters (an attack, according to Ethel, which had been facilitated by her aunt), and shortly after the birth of her daughter she married a railwayman, Norman Howard. Raised predominantly in Philadelphia by her maternal grandmother, Ethel was a child of the streets, adept at shoplifting, wary of police officers and equally at home with priests or prostitutes. 'I just ran wild as a little girl,' she wrote. 'I was bad, always a leader of the street gang in stealing and general hell-raising. By the time I was seven I knew all about sex and life in the raw. I could outcurse any stevedore and took a sadistic pleasure in shocking people.'[21]

Despite her unfavourable beginnings as soon as she could she decided to adopt her natural father's surname. The Waters family were well-off; perhaps she thought that some of their good fortune would come her way too, but she had no contact with her birth father and instead was forced into an abusive marriage to a man named Merritt Purnsley while she was still only 13. Ethel had known from an early age that she was different from her friends. As they grew older they developed a natural interest in sex, but she was disgusted by the thought of sleeping with a man. 'In crowded slum homes one's sex education begins very early indeed. Mine began when I was about three and sleeping in the same room, often in the same bed, with my aunts and my transient "uncles." I wasn't fully aware of what was going on but resented it. By the time I was seven I was repelled by every aspect of sex.'[22]

Her marriage was a disaster: 'Having seen so much of the ugly side of life as a little girl, I dreaded the sex relationship. Yet I knew that sex had to happen to me as to everyone else. My wedding night, however, couldn't have been nastier or more unpleasant.'[23] She was little more than a servant in her own home, still a child and having to deal with regular beatings from a man ten years older than her, alongside wild accusations from her husband of adultery, a crass attempt to disguise his own infidelity.

Plucking up the courage to leave her husband of less than a year, Ethel moved to Philadelphia where she found work in a hotel. She fantasised about becoming an actor or singer, but had little ambition. However, one evening, when singing at a Hallowe'en party at a basement club known as Jack's Rathskeller in the city's south side, she was spotted by comedy act Braxton and Nugent, who immediately offered her the chance to join their vaudeville troupe. She gave her first professional performance a week later, at the Lincoln Theatre in Baltimore, and the tall, rangy Ethel soon earned the nickname Sweet Mama Stringbean.

Early in her career, Waters played the 91 in Atlanta, officially known as the Royal Theatre and on the same block as the better-known Arcade, or 81 Theatre. Bessie Smith was top of the bill, and she made it clear to the management of the theatre that she wanted no one else singing the blues while she was headlining. 'Bessie was in a pretty good position to dictate to the managers,' Ethel recalled. 'She didn't want anyone else on the bill to sing the blues. I agreed to this. I could depend a lot on my shaking, though I never shimmied vulgarly and only to express myself. And when I went on I sang "I Want to Be Somebody's Baby Doll so I Can Get My Lovin' All the Time." But before I could finish this number the people out front started howling, "Blues! Blues! Come on, Stringbean, we want your blues!" The two-man orchestra struck up Bessie's music and kept it up through three refrains while the audience, feeling cheated, kept yelling, "We want Stringbeans and her blues!"'[24]

When the manager of the 91 told Bessie that the audience was crying out for Ethel to sing the blues an almighty row broke out:

Before the second show the manager went to Bessie's dressing room and told her he was going to revoke the order forbidding me to sing any blues. He said he couldn't have another such rumpus. There was quite a stormy discussion about this, and you could hear Bessie yelling things about 'these Northern bitches.' Now nobody could have taken the place of Bessie Smith. People everywhere loved her shouting with all their hearts and were loyal to her. But they wanted me too. There had been such a tumult at that first show that Bessie agreed that after I took two or three bows for my first song I should, if the crowd still insisted, sing 'St. Louis Blues.' And each audience did insist. I remained courteous and deferential to her, always addressing her as 'Miss Bessie.' I was as crazy about her shouting as everyone else, even though hers was not my style, but I didn't enjoy the conflict. It was just more of the contentiousness I'd known all my life. Besides, I sensed this was the beginning of the uncrowning of her, the great and original Bessie Smith. I've never enjoyed seeing a champ go down, and Bessie was all champ.[25]

Bessie, who used to plant members of her entourage in the audience to throw money on the stage while she was singing, took a shine to Ethel, nicknaming her 'long goody' and telling her, 'you ain't so bad... and you know damn well that you can't sing worth a shit.'[26]

\*

84

In conversations, Ethel Waters was usually a little vague about when she first met Ethel Williams, admitting that she first cast eyes on her when she saw Williams perform in a comedy duo with Rufus Greenlee at New York's Alhambra Theatre. The duo were first booked into the Alhambra in July 1918, around the same time that Waters, who had been booked to sing the blues for a couple of weeks at the Lincoln Theatre, arrived in Harlem. By the early part of 1919 they had already become close. Williams, a dancer, had been out of work since an operation on her leg had affected her confidence, and Waters who had taken a job singing at Edmond's Cellar, a Black nightclub in Harlem, persuaded the owner, Edmond 'Mule' Johnson, to take Williams on too. While working at Johnson's, Waters became friendly with many of the male homosexuals and drag queens that frequented the place, even lending out her dresses to some of them. 'That was the great time of "drags" in Harlem. In these affairs there would be fashion parades for the male queers dressed in women's clothes. Those who came to Edmond's would beg me to let them wear my best gowns for the evening so they could compete for the grand prizes. And they did win many first prizes in my clothes.'[27] This act of largess could prove problematic: 'One night I lent my black velvet dress, trimmed with ermine, to one of these he-she-and-what-is-it types. But he got to fighting with his "husband" at the affair and was locked up in a cell. And with him to jail went my expensive black velvet dress trimmed with ermine. The dress smelled of carbolic acid, the Chanel No. 5 of the cell blocks, for months, and I couldn't wear it. I would not have been much more humiliated if I myself had been thrown into the poky.'[28] 'The Drag Balls... everybody went to those,' dancer Mabel Hampton recalled. 'The women wore pants and the men wore dresses. There were so many of them... you'd get in there and have a nice time!'[29]

By October the Two Ethels were in the cast of the musical revue *Hello, 1919* at the Lafayette Theatre. Waters, Williams and Nina Hunter sang one of the show's big numbers, 'Angelina', and night after night the trio were called upon to perform an encore. In another number Waters was forced to perform in blackface: 'That meant working in burnt cork,' she explained. 'I sang and did a crow-Jane character... I played a sort of blind-date bride whose groom refused to marry her after getting a good look at her face. The white audiences thought I was white, my features being what they are, and at every performance I'd have to take off my gloves to prove I was a spade.'[30] When *Hello, 1919* went on tour, the cast members were often refused accommodation in hotels and guest houses and many – including the Two Ethels – were forced to take rooms in local brothels.

The two women became lovers, and Waters was keen to incorporate Williams in her act whenever possible. Singer and actor Elisabeth Welch recalled that, 'They were known as "The Two Ethels" but I was very young and didn't know about lesbians. It was scandalous for two women to live together. This other Ethel was skinny, and red-haired. She had no personality at all. Ethel Waters was called a bull dyke,* a terrible name.'[31] Their relationship was a tempestuous one: the Two Ethels would think nothing of having a shouting match in public, and this propensity, along with Waters' often vulgar vocabulary, shocked Alberta Hunter, who was no saint herself but who had become increasingly 'dicty' since beginning her relationship with Lottie Tyler and becoming involved with the Bert Williams family. Hunter, who did not drink or smoke and would rarely use curse words, would seldom have a good thing to say about Waters, although she would later admit to admiring her singing, and the animosity went both ways: Alberta gets just one brief mention in Ethel's autobiography.

Ethel recorded her first sides in March 1921, a pair of jazz numbers for the tiny Cardinal Phonograph Company, based on New York's Bleecker Street, 'At the New Jump Steady Ball' and 'The New York Glide'. That disc did not sell, its progress stymied somewhat by the company being sued for copyright infringement by Washington-based phonograph manufacturers the Cardinal Cabinet Company, and Pace quickly stepped in and signed her to his label. Ethel Waters' first disc for the company, 'Down Home Blues' backed with 'Oh Daddy' was in the shops by August and, unlike her debut, her Black Swan recordings

---

* The term 'bull dyke', offensive slang for a butch lesbian, was used throughout the 1920s and 30s, appearing in print as early as 1906, but few can agree on its origin. It may be worth noting that a male wrestler known as Bull Dyke was taking part in bouts around the States in the mid to late 1910s.

would be advertised nationally and sell in their thousands. Alberta's first coupling for the company, 'Bring Back the Joys' and 'How Long, Sweet Daddy, How Long' had originally been planned for release at the same time, but was held over until the following month.

To Alberta, it seemed as if Black Swan were putting all of their energies – and a good deal of their advertising budget – into promoting Ethel Waters, even going as far as to suggest that the company had insisted that Ethel sign a new contact with the company, personally penned by Harry Pace, that forbade her from marrying for at least a year while she 'devote her time largely to singing for Black Swan Records'.[32] Although, in reality, this was little more than a publicity stunt, the company claimed that it had insisted on the clause 'due to the numerous offers for marriage, many of her suitors suggesting that she at once give up her professional life for one of domesticity'.[33] To mollify her, this new contract made Ethel 'The highest salaried colored phonograph star in the country,' a title she would hold until her earnings were surpassed by Bessie Smith.

When promoting Waters' recording of 'Down Home Blues', Pace set out his plans for the company: 'We have a catalog of selections that are bound to have much appeal. Many of the numbers are, and will be, exclusive releases on Black Swan records. While it is true that we will feature to a great extent "blue" numbers of the type that are in current favor, we will also release many numbers of a higher standard, all of which will be chosen for their wide appeal.'[34] It would not be long before Alberta would leave Black Swan to sign with another company, however in January 1922, she played host to Ethel and her girlfriend, as well as several others, including Alberta's own live-in girlfriend Carrie Mae Ward, at their home in Chicago. Waters was in town as part of a Black Swan-promoted tour; Williams accompanied her on the tour – which had begun in Washington the previous October – and appeared on stage as a dancer. By the second week of their engagement Williams had been promoted to second on the bill, alongside her dancing partner Froncel Manly. 'Miss Alberta Hunter, of 4428 Prairie Avenue, entertained last week at dinner in honor of Miss Ethel Waters of the Black Swan Record Company. The other guests present were Miss Ethel Williams, a member of Miss Waters' company, Miss Martha Briscoe,

Miss Marguerite Ricks and Alvin Malone. All voted Miss Hunter a charming hostess,'[35] the *Chicago Defender* reported.

Carrie Mae, who Alberta described as 'a beautiful woman',[36] was conspicuous by her absence in the story, as was any mention of Alberta having recorded for Black Swan herself. Alberta, already unhappy with the promotion that Ethel Waters was getting, would have been none too pleased when she read, in a puff piece printed in the *Chicago Whip* and no doubt penned by someone in the Black Swan office, that her rival 'stands alone when it comes to making records. She has surpassed anybody else who previously have done [sic] this kind of work.'[37]

By the time Waters' show arrived in Chicago, Ethel Williams and Froncel Manly were getting second billing:

Ethel Waters and the Black Swan Troubadours opened [at the Grand] on Monday night to an overflowing house. The presentation was one long to be remembered as the bill was composed of all big time acts... Williams (Ethel Williams) and Manly showed real speed. Miss Williams is a real artist and got over in her dancing specialties; she tied the show in a knot. Her partner, Mr. Manly, ably put over 'Moonlight,' assisted by Mrs. Williams in dance portrayal. Ethel Waters, the race's greatest record star, closed the bill with her famous jazz band. Miss Waters is more than a blues singer. She is a blues artist void of all of the Hokum style, commonly used by most of the entertainers. In her rendition of numbers she shows much dignity and class, although at the same time offering real syncopation. Miss Waters comes on with the shy little smile, that never leaves her face from the time she enters, which shows artistic training and appreciation for a listening audience.

The band is the best seen here at any time. They play that soft penetrating jazz, that goes through one to the bones. There are no nasty discordant effects, commonly used by jazz bands. And this elimination shows that they are real masters of jazz. Miss Waters and her company will be held over next week with an addition of new vaudeville acts, just off the Keith Circuit, in order to accommodate the howling throng once again.[38]

Ethel's Chicago dates were a tremendous success, and Alberta must have been seething at the reviews. While it is true that Ethel would not record anything overtly queer, the suggestion that she was innocent and avoided hokum music was hokum in itself, and her catalogue includes several sexually suggestive songs, such as 'My Handy Man', 'Take Your Black Bottom Outside', 'Shake That Thing', 'Organ Grinder Blues', and the campy 'Hottentot Potentate', which she performed in the 1935 revue *At Home Abroad* and recorded that October in New York, and which was later covered by gay cabaret star Bobby Short.

No longer their number one star, Alberta left Black Swan and signed with the Puritan company which, conveniently for her, had recently opened an office on Chicago's State Street, before moving on to their better-distributed and better-known sister label, Paramount. Waters' two weeks at the Grand may have proved a major success, but at the end of the run four of the musicians jumped ship, refusing to go down South where they feared the all-Black touring party would encounter trouble. Despite the defection, Waters insisted that the tour go on; they quickly hired four replacement musicians and resumed their journey, playing towns and cities in Arkansas, Alabama and Georgia.

The four accompanists who chose not to travel had good reason to fear attacks. They had heard about how, in Mississippi, W. C. Handy and his entire band had been hijacked by a white plantation owner and, after they had witnessed a violent beating, were forced to play at a men-only dance that ended with three black men being murdered. In the middle of their sell-out fortnight at the Grand came the news of the racially motivated murder of jazz pianist Arthur Ford in Oklahoma. Ford had been killed in an ambush near the town Okmulgee, Oklahoma, shot:

> by white assassins, who waylaid the car in which he and his company were driving to Henrietta... As the car containing three men and two women arrived at a secluded section of the highway, three men ran out into the road and began shooting. According to the occupants of the car Ford, who sat in front, ducked and shouted, 'Look out, boys.' ...According to the driver of the death car, Ford slumped over against him shortly after the barrage of

bullets whizzed about their heads, but he thought nothing of it, thinking that he had taken that position in which to hide. Later developments proved that he had been dead for several minutes before his friends knew that they were transporting a corpse. A few weeks ago, Ford exhibited a threatening letter that had been sent him by someone in Henrietta, where he with his orchestra played three times weekly. Henrietta is a small coal-mining town where there has been considerable sentiment always to oppose Negroes stopping in the town overnight. The note said: 'Finish your music tonight, but don't return for more engagements.'[39]

A defiant Ethel insisted on continuing with the tour, telling reporters that 'she felt it her duty to make sacrifice in order that members of her race might hear her sing a style of music which is a product of the Southland',[40] but her bravado was misplaced. In Macon, Georgia, the dead body of a young man – the victim of a lynching – was thrown into the lobby of the theatre shortly before the Black Swan party arrived. As Waters described it many years later, 'They had just removed, say about a half hour before I got there, the remains of a person that had been lynched. A man that had been lynched... and the irony of it was that I stayed with the family of the lynched man. That's where they took in performers. And nothing was said, but oh the grief... and the fear. I'd almost been lynched myself, for cussing out a man in Atlanta, Georgia, so I knew what that fear was.'[41] Soon the *Chicago Whip* was boasting about how Ethel and her company were breaking race barriers, performing in New Orleans to 'overflowing crowds' and broadcasting live over the air to five states (and Mexico) at the behest of a local, white-owned newspaper to 'thousands of radio fans [who] listened to a colored girl sing... Miss Waters, who has broken many records on this trip, adds another star top her laurels by being the first colored girl to sing over the radio.'[42]

As ludicrous as it might seem today, one of the biggest names in the emerging race records field, Gennett Records, owned by the Starr Piano Company, had ties to the Ku Klux Klan. In the early 1920s their Richmond, Indiana studios were used for a series of recordings that appeared on the Klan-owned KKK Records. Featuring a blood-red label emblazoned with a fiery cross, the discs were also pressed by Gennett, and were paid for upfront, which no doubt helped cashflow. The majority of the recordings were made by one or more members of the Famous Logansport Klan Quartet, usually credited on the labels as '100% Americans'. The Quartet – brothers Charles, Less, Jess and William Pollock – were all Klan members and were a popular draw at Klan gatherings.

Gennett, where Porter Grainger would record 'Baa-Baa Blues' and 'Ground Hog Blues' with his own small band, Porter Grainger's Three Jazz Songsters, was also the home of Jelly Roll Morton, of King Oliver's Creole Jazz Band and of other important names in jazz and blues. The company had originally helped with distribution of the Klan releases, and it is possible that they looked upon this as a simple business decision, not one motivated by any political affiliation, but after one of the company's Catholic employees walked out of a 1924 session, the company would no longer act as distributors, and within two years they had discontinued working with the Klan altogether. They were not alone: in 1923 Okeh released 'Ku – the Klucking of the Ku Klux Klan' by the otherwise unknown Billy Frisch. Although the lyrics of the song seem somewhat comedic, KKK-friendly shops – such as the Phono-Record Shop in Arch Avenue, Ohio – happily sold copies alongside their catalogue of Klan-related records, sheet music and piano rolls. Fred J. Kern, the owner of the crusading *Belleville News-Democrat*, claimed that Klan members 'pollute the earth on which they walk because of their Oscar Wildean homo-sexuality', and penned an editorial which claimed that 'by the hung-dog and the holier-than-thou look which they wear on their pious and pasty faces, made that way mostly through homosexual excesses and notorious self-abuse or masturbation, ye shall know the Ku Klux Klan tribe... Oscar Wilde was sent to prison and assigned to the galleys to pay the penalty of the law for indulging in the same form of Phallic worship, which the Ku Klux Klan is covertly and clandestinely trying to substitute for the real Christian love... the fight for the halo of sainthood is won on the borderline of the abnormal psychology, and in the Ku Klux heaven of degeneration and the man-to-man embrace of hooded heroes and emasculated and unsexed eunuchs.'[43]

# 7

# Clara and Josephine

*'She is a sturdy youngster with a winning way and comedy that asserts itself into everything she does... Jolly as she seems to be in her work, the stage romping is serious business with Josephine Baker.'*[1]

Formed in 1920, the Theatre Owners Booking Association (T.O.B.A) was the grand name given to a circuit of vaudeville theatres throughout the States that concentrated primarily on promoting Black artists to Black audiences. Although by using existing theatres and other venues it was a huge step up from Pat Chappelle's touring tent shows, the idea was not exactly new. Pat Chappelle, of the Rabbit Foot Company, had been promoting a similar idea some twenty years earlier, but at that time few were listening.

By 1910 Chicago had ten theatres that only booked Black performers, and the local actors' union were discussing plans to establish a Colored Actors Union for local talent. At the same time, in Memphis, the Barrasso family, owners of the Savoy and Metropolitan theatres, joined forces with fellow Italian immigrant Sam Zerilla, operator of the Pastime Theatre and picture house, partly in an effort to give their Black talent more work. By the following year the Colored Actors Union, based in Washington D.C. with former vaudeville performer Sherman H. Dudley acting as treasurer and general manager, was gaining traction nationwide. Soon Dudley began buying up or leasing theatres to establish his own Black circuit. The same year Fred Barrasso joined forces with L. D. Joel (known as the Theatrical King), giving them control of twenty theatres in the southern states. Dudley opened his own booking agency in 1913, and by the end of the following year he was operating – often in partnership with other Black owners – a circuit of around twenty venues, including those owned by the Barrasso family, which Fred Barrasso's father had taken over after the sudden death of his son in summer 1911.

T.O.B.A. was a direct descendent of Dudley's circuit, initially headed by Milton Starr who, in 1916, had taken over the running of the dilapidated Bijou Theatre in Nashville, installing a screen to show moving pictures and staging plays and vaudeville acts exclusively for Black patrons. At its inception, only a small number of the venues were Black-owned, one of the few being the Lyric Theatre in New Orleans, co-owned by former vaudeville artist manager Clarence Bennett. Not every Black-run venue would join: a smaller operation labelling itself the Managers and Performers Circuit (M&P) set up in direct opposition, but could not muster as much support. In contrast T.O.B.A. grew quickly; in January 1922 they announced that Bennett was to head a new drive to extend the circuit into every state in the union, and on into Mexico, Canada, Puerto Rico and the Bahamas, and soon T.O.B.A. would absorb both Dudley's Southern Consolidated circuit and M&P. By the end of the year the T.O.B.A. circuit would include 115 venues.

With twenty-two companies now producing moving pictures exclusively for Black patrons (Bert Williams had filmed a couple of two-reelers for Biograph featuring all-Black casts in 1916), and more theatres giving space over to screens and projectors, T.O.B.A. would prove an important and regular source of work for many Black performers. For years Black artists had protested about the poor treatment they received from white venue operators: Andrew Tribble had long complained that 'It has been almost impossible for colored performers to get the proper attention and salary from white managers and promotors,' but life on the T.O.B.A. circuit was far from easy. Pay was still poor, and as Tribble pointed out, 'No one in the company gets the proper recognition, either in money or treatment, except the star… [and] Negro performers who have been fortunate enough to be placed at the head of various large shows... seem not to have the courage to make demands upon managers to pay the proper salary or even to command the right sort of treatment for the "unders" who are with them.'[2] It is not surprising that few artists were willing to rock the boat, as many were threatened with recriminations should they defect to another touring circuit, leading to T.O.B.A. earning the nickname 'Tough on Black Actors'. Typically, Ma Rainey awarded T.O.B.A. a slightly more coarse epithet: 'Tough on Black Asses'. Conditions backstage were often intolerable, as Chicago theatre critic Tony Langston reported after a visit to Baltimore. The dressing rooms at the Star were 'in need of everything, including a visit from the Health Department', while the backstage area at the Lincoln was no better than 'a filthy rat hole'.[3]

Some white theatre owners, while happy to make money out of the T.O.B.A. circuit, barely concealed their contempt for the Black performers. Ethel Waters had a run-in with Charles P. Bailey, the white owner and manager of the Arcade Theatre on Decatur Street in Atlanta, better known as the 81. Bailey, who used to run a special midnight show on a Friday night for white patrons at his theatre, is one of the few men known to have bested Bessie Smith, as Ethel Waters later recounted: 'I'd heard what he'd done to Bessie Smith after they'd had an argument. He'd beaten Bessie up, then had her thrown in jail.'[4] Bailey was known for exploiting the Black acts that played at the 81, and for keeping a tight rein on them, so much so that – in Atlanta at least – T.O.B.A. came to stand for 'Take Old Bailey's Advice'. Yet in spite of their altercation, Bessie would continue to work for Bailey throughout the 1920s, performing at several of his white-audiences-only Midnight Frolics.

With blues becoming increasingly big business, Bailey and many other proprietors would run 'whites only' performances, either in Black venues, barring their regular patrons for the night, or in white theatres where the acts pulling the crowds in would usually be refused entrance at the main door. Even after Bessie, Clara and the others became stars, there were many occasions where they had to come in through a side door into a venue or through the kitchen with the rest of the staff. Waters, who described Bailey as 'a Georgia cracker and a sort of self-appointed czar',[5] had to quit town quickly without being paid and leaving half of her stage costumes behind after the pair almost came to blows, following an argument over an untuned piano. Ethel refused to go on unless Bailey found another piano and had it on stage in time for her act. 'Look, you,' he told her, 'No Yankee nigger bitch is telling me how to run my theater.' An angry Ethel spat back, 'No Georgia cracker is telling me how to run my act.'[6] Although he threatened that he would 'kick [her] ass out of here',[7] a new piano duly arrived, however Ethel heard from Bailey's staff that the theatre owner was preparing to have her both physically attacked and arrested, and she skipped town that weekend.

Waters' experience at the hands of Charles Bailey was a momentary setback on her fast-rising career, and when she was brought in to join the cast of a new revue, *Oh! Joy!*, she insisted that her girlfriend, Ethel Williams, came too. Waters was now a star, her first recordings had been hits, and she could command a fee of $125 a week for the show. 'When I planned my routines for *Oh! Joy!* I wanted to make a different kind of entrance than other well-known record singers were using,' she explained. 'They were going in for flash and class, one of their favorite entrances being coming out on the stage through the door of an ornate phonograph,' something both Ma Rainey and Bessie Smith had done.[8] Instead Williams would go on stage and go through an involved pantomime looking for Waters, calling out for 'that partner of mine' and looking behind curtains and even under a rug before Waters would come out on the stage, dressed as a farm girl. 'Are you Ethel Waters?' Williams would ask. 'Well, I ain't Bessie Smith!' she would reply to knowing howls from the audience. Despite having the Two Ethels and Andrew Tribble in the cast of *Oh! Joy!*, the reviews were less than effusive: *Variety* thought that the comedy element of the show was extremely poor, and that Ethel Waters did nothing to deserve her billing as 'The World's Greatest Blues Singer'.

Leaving *Oh! Joy!* after refusing to play under canvas, Ethel and the Black Swan Troubadours, led by Fletcher Henderson, went back out on the road and, naturally, Ethel Williams went too. Waters was well received, but Williams was coming into her own as a comedian and got rave reviews. One newspaper claimed that she was now 'occupying a position of equal importance on the program',[9] having previously stated that she was 'a riot in her dancing specialty'.[10] The extra praise awarded her girlfriend would not have sat well with Waters, although she could take comfort in knowing that she had been admired for her 'stage demeanor' which was 'most pleasing, and her departure from the shouting, hollering sort of blues singers we have been accustomed to hearing was a source of much pleasure to the local music lovers'.[11] Shortly afterwards she was cast in a new, all-Black musical, *Dumb Luck*, alongside her girlfriend Ethel Williams and Alberta Hunter.

Although she would often perform at T.O.B.A. venues, the 'shouting, hollering' Bessie Smith did not rely on the circuit for work: in October and November 1920 she was travelling as part of the Charles Bud Reeves show, touring theatres around Maryland, and the following May she signed with Loew's for a season. Despite not having released a recording, her reputation was so great that Bessie was being advertised throughout the South as 'one of the best "coon shouters" and "blues" singers on the circuit'.[12] Her only real rivals for the affection of her fans were Ma and a singer from South Carolina called Clara Smith – unrelated to Bessie or Mamie – who at that time was both mentor and lover to a brilliant young eccentric dancer who, within a few short years, would become a global superstar: Josephine Baker.

Freda Josephine McDonald was born, in 1906, in St Louis, a city bisected by the Mississippi River and unique in having a foot in two separate states, Missouri and Illinois. Baker grew up in East St Louis (in Illinois) where, in July 1917, race riots broke out, sparked by Black labour being taken on at a local meat packing plant to replace striking white workers. Baker's family fled across the river to the relative security of Missouri, but the two days of rioting left 6,000 African Americans homeless and up to 150 dead. 'It had a terrible effect on me,' Josephine would later insist, stating that, during their flight to safety, she 'saw one of her father's friends [sic] face shot away and pregnant women disembowelled'.[13]

Josephine Baker was only 14, yet had already been married once and was about to marry for a second time (to the man who would give her that surname), when she met Clara Smith. Growing up, Josephine

96

Julian Eltinge, the most famous female impersonator in the world, in the play *Cousin Lucy*, 1915

LEFT: Tony Jackson, composer of 'Pretty Baby', 1916

BOTTOM LEFT: Promotional poster for Bert Williams, issued by Columbia Records, 1919 (Getty Images)

BOTTOM RIGHT: Sheet music for one of Porter Grainger's earliest hits, 1919

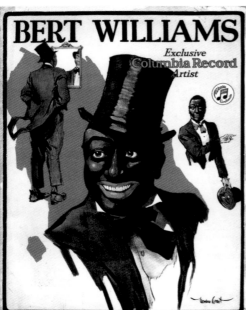

RIGHT: A promotional shot of Eubie Blake (L) and Nobel Sissle, 1920 (Getty Images)

LEFT: Gertrude 'Ma' Rainey with an unidentified member of her show, approx. 1920 (Getty Images)

ABOVE: Ma Rainey with her Five Jazz Hounds, John T Wortham Shows, Breckenridge, Texas 1922 (Basil Clemons Photograph Collection University of Texas at Arlington Libraries)

ABOVE: Ma and her Broadway Strutters, John T Wortham Shows, Breckenridge, Texas 1922 (Basil Clemons Photograph Collection University of Texas at Arlington Libraries)

ABOVE: Bessie often included Alberta's song 'Chirpin' the Blues' in her shows, but despite her image featuring on this sheet music she would not record the number, 1923

ABOVE: Ma Rainey around the time she signed to Paramount Records, 1923 (Getty Images)

ABOVE: One of the few images known to exist of Porter Grainger, approx. 1923

ABOVE: 125th Street Harlem; Hartig and Semon's New Burlesque would later become The Apollo, 1924 (Getty Images)

ABOVE: Douglas Byng in character as The Duchess, mid-1920s (Getty Images)

ABOVE: Josephine Baker in Paris, 1925 (Getty Images)

ABOVE: Bessie on stage in Philadelphia, approx. 1925 (Getty Images)

ABOVE: Mae West on stage in Sex, 1926 (Getty Images)

ABOVE: Josephine Baker poses in an ostrich cart in Paris, 1927 (Getty Images)

had known real poverty; her father, an itinerant percussionist named Eddie Carson, left home when she was a toddler and her mother married another man who gave her two further children but was incapable of holding down a steady job and providing for his family. From an early age, Josephine had been expected to add to the family coffers.

Since she was young, Josephine had yearned to sing and dance, although a childhood injury had almost put paid to those ambitions: she stepped on a rusty nail which caused her leg to become infected. Doctors wanted to amputate, but the tearful child, then just 7 years old, begged them to try and save the limb. Luckily for her the hospital staff were able to drain the poison from her leg and she swiftly recovered. But things at home were not good, and her mother quickly discovered that feeding six mouths was an impossible task with so little money coming in. At the age of 9, Josephine was out in the world, working as a maid for a local widow, Mrs Kaiser.

Josephine's mother had been assured that the widow Kaiser was a kindly woman who would provide Josephine with food, clothing, a bed and schooling, but working for her proved to be torture, quite literally. The girl was beaten regularly, had to share her bed with Mrs Kaiser's dog and on one occasion was scalded so badly – punishment for accidentally breaking some crockery – that the skin on her hands blistered and peeled. After running away from the Kaiser house, Josephine's mother forced her to take on another job, this time with a childless couple called Mason who treated her well... until one night when the man of the house tried to crawl into bed with the terrified child. Unable to afford to keep her, the most sensible thing her mother could think of was to marry her off, but her first marriage, at the age of 13 to a man more than twice her age, ended after she split her husband's head open with a broken beer bottle following a violent row over a faked pregnancy. Yet she persevered, earning her own money by babysitting, waiting tables and doing just about anything to bring in a few cents. Life on the road with someone like the matronly, caring Clara, who read to Josephine and helped with her spelling and diction, must have seemed like heaven after the hell she suffered at the hands of the widow Kaiser, the lecherous Mr Mason and her own violent husband.

Tall and ungainly but with a natural talent for comedy, Josephine managed to land a position as a dancer and comedian with a local trio, the Jones Family Band, who were booked to perform at the Booker T. Washington Theatre in St Louis, as support for dance troupe the Dixie Steppers. The teenager had become close to the Jones's daughter, Doll, and it is more than likely that Doll Jones was Josephine's first same-sex crush. Smith, who would become known as the 'queen of the moaners' following her 1923 recording 'Awful Moanin' Blues', who had recently been engaged to front the Dixie Steppers, took an instant liking to young Josephine and, after she demonstrated her skills while attempting to remove a stain from one of Clara's stage costumes, offered her a job as her dresser. Baker leapt at the chance to leave her difficult family life behind, and before long, the pair became lovers. A few weeks later Josephine made her professional stage debut, appearing as part of a chorus supporting Clara in a skit entitled 'Twenty Minutes in Hell', a comedy piece that had been a stage staple since 1912.

Bob Russell, who managed the company, was none too impressed with these goings-on, as drag artist Booth Marshall later revealed: 'It was Clara who asked Bob Russell to hire Josephine... She had become Clara's protégé, you know, her lady lover as we called it in those days. Bob did not like that kind of hanky-panky, but Clara was a big draw, and anyhow, better a steady date than a fight in every city. Josephine had no real experience, you know, but Bob saw she had potential, and Clara did the rest.'[14] Marshall, who 'performed in drag, as an old mama, big bottom, big breasts, kerchief on my head, wearing big, big shoes and blackface, I was a killer with that number',[15] believed that Russell elected to keep quiet for the sake of his star turn, but as Josephine herself admitted, 'I thought I understood what was bothering Mr. Russell. He felt that his leading lady was monopolizing my time. He wasn't paying me to spend hours in Mama Smith's dressing room improving my penmanship.'[16]

If people thought Ma Rainey was ugly, and Alberta Hunter referred to her as the 'ugliest woman in the business',[17] then they had probably not seen Clara Smith strutting her stuff on stage. Josephine described her as, 'very black, fat and short,' and her costumes and makeup were hardly subtle: 'The red wig that was one of her trademarks was gaily decorated with a bow or paper flowers. Her face was layered with purple powder, her teeth were yellow from pipe tobacco. She favored short, gauzy dresses worn over pink tights and was partial to high-heeled shoes.'[18] Off stage you would scarcely recognise her, dressed more demurely and without the harsh stage make-up, if it were not for the mouthful of crooked yellow teeth, which were invariably clamped around a corn cob pipe. Although she was no relation, she was shamelessly advertised as the 'sister of Bessie Smith',[19] and despite never quite achieving the level of fame that Bessie enjoyed, she would record over 120 songs for Columbia and become the company's second-biggest blues star during her time with them. Coy Herndon, writing in the *Chicago Defender*, stated that: 'Clara Smith is more than a mere blues singer, her voice is a typical blues singing type, combined with a wonderful personality, but she is a comedienne of the highest order. Her blues gained numerous encores and her facial expressions, combined with a distinct personality, caused the audience to ache from laughter.'[20]

Very little has been uncovered about Clara's life before she began her performing career, but by the time she met young Josephine McDonald she had already become a featured attraction on the T.O.B.A. circuit, and she had married a man by the name of William Graham, forming a double act that – like Ma and Pa Rainey – was sidelined as her solo career took off. Clara Smith was almost twice Josephine's age, born in March 1894 in Spartanburg, South Carolina (the 1900 census would suggest that she was born two years earlier, listing her as living with her parents William and Salena and aged 7 years old at the time), but Josephine idolised her, called her 'Mama', and would talk about her importance for the rest of her life. A blues shouter in the Sophie Tucker tradition (Clara would always claim that Tucker had stolen her act, and resented the fact that Tucker had begun her blues career in blackface, advertised as a 'coon shouter'), Smith began performing around 1910: in the summer of 1916 she briefly joined Alex Tolliver's Big Show, singing the blues on the same stage as Ma Rainey; after that she toured for a while with Rainey's juvenile dancer Bishop Brown in Walden's Georgia Minstrels before, in 1919, becoming part of a revue known as Bert Jackson's Girls of Today, singing and playing mammy roles in comedy skits alongside blackface comedian Happy Jim Bonham. By the time she rolled in to St Louis she was a star, one of T.O.B.A.'s biggest pulls. Clara was more than Josephine's lover, she was also her mentor, and through her the younger woman learned the stagecraft that would help make her an international star. Soon Clara and the Dixie Steppers would be off to Memphis, and Josephine was on that train with them.

Josephine's friend, Maude Russell, who first met the rising star when they performed together in Philadelphia in 1921, described life on the road in those days: 'Often we girls would share a room because of the cost. Well, many of us had been kind of abused by producers, directors, leading men – if they liked girls. In those days, men only wanted what they wanted, they didn't care about pleasing a girl. And girls needed tenderness, so we had girl friendships, the famous lady lovers, but lesbians weren't well accepted in show business, they were called bull dykers. I guess we were bisexual, is what you would call it today.'[21] As soon as the Clara Smith tour ended, Josephine went to New York to try out for a role in the new all-Black revue *Shuffle Along*, but was thought to be too young at 15 to join the Broadway cast (and legend has it, too dark skinned and too thin as far as the producers were concerned). However, she was offered a position as a dresser backstage, and when it was discovered that one of the girls in the chorus was pregnant, she stepped in. Her facial mugging was not popular with the rest of the cast, but she was an instant hit with the critics, which led to her being offered a small role when the production went on tour. 'That girl was different from the rest of the girls,' Eubie Blake would later recall. 'She had her way of doing things. She was outlandish. She could out dance anybody in the line, but she gagged it up... And she worked cross-eyed. A lot of rich white people came to see her, especially in New York, Chicago and St Louis. They'd say, "Is that cross-eyed girl in the show?"'[22]

Once she was 16, she was promoted to the Broadway cast, and she soon began an affair with another girl in the chorus, Evelyn Sheppard, known to Josephine and the rest of the cast as Little Shep. By April 1923 she was getting mentioned by name in newspapers, and within a few weeks she was being promoted as a star of the future: 'When the best part of a capacity audience singles out one little girl in the chorus and gives her attention every time she appears, it shows the recognition of qualities such as stars are made of,' the *Philadelphia Inquirer* announced. 'Josephine Baker... knows how to make people laugh and how to sing and dance. Miller and Lyles, Sissle and Blake, producers of this Dixie hit, are so well pleased with her work this season that they have written a better part for her in their new production, "Bandauna Days",* which will be produced on their return from London.'[23] It would not be too long before Josephine became, as Blake described her, the 'highest-paid chorus girl in the world'.[24]

*Shuffle Along* would help make stars of Florence Mills, Paul Robeson and, of course, would help launch the career of Josephine Baker. With music by Eubie Blake and lyrics by Nobel Sissle, and a script by the vaudeville team of Flournoy Miller and Aubrey Lyles, *Shuffle Along* was a sensation, the first genuine, all-Black Broadway hit (*In Dahomey*, which debuted in 1903, was written by Black authors and featured a Black cast, but the show's management team – Hurtig and Seamon – were white). A revue-style comic musical about a mayoral race in an all-Black settlement, Jimtown, it contained the enormous hit song 'I'm Just Wild About Harry', and broke taboos by featuring, for the first time on the US stage, a love story between two Black characters that was not simply played for laughs. The original cast included Gertrude Saunders in the role of Ruth Little, who would record two songs from the show, 'I Am Craving for That Kind of Love' and 'Daddy (Won't You Please Come Home)' for her first Okeh record release, in May 1921. Saunders, who had recently finished touring with the show *Town Topics*, was a hit with audiences, and she explained to the *New York Tribune* what it was about her own artistry that had helped propel her to prominence. 'A dancer should do more than simply frisk gracefully about the stage,' she explained. 'She should be able to give the audience a message, and her dancing should mean something definite. It must either tell them a story or reflect some emotion, happiness, jealousy or anger... The artist dances with her face, her hands and her whole body, not simply

---

*    A spelling error on the part of the newspaper or the reporter: 'Bandana Days' was a song featured in the first act of *Shuffle Along*.

with her feet. As she goes through the various steps her expression and her gestures clearly convey a message to the spectators.'[25] Gertrude, who had spent six years touring the South before making it to New York, could have just as easily been talking about Josephine Baker, and it is possible that young Josephine found the older, more experienced dancer's elucidations illuminating. Lured away with the promise of more money and fame, Saunders left the show and was replaced by rising star Florence Mills, but moving on from such an enormous success so early in her career was a mistake. While Mills became a celebrity almost overnight, Saunders' own progress foundered and, desperate for a comeback, she would soon become a perennial thorn in Bessie Smith's side.

Success breeds imitation, and within two months of its New York debut, *Shuffle Along* was facing competition from a new musical, also in two acts and also starring an all-Black cast. *The Chocolate Brown* featured Mae Crowder in a role reminiscent of the one played by Gertrude Saunders in *Shuffle Along*, alongside female impersonator Andrew Tribble as Aunt Ophelia, the 'funniest character in the show'.[26]

America's women singers, dancers and comedians were reaching new heights at a time when all women were insisting on better treatment, including the right to vote, to equal pay and to manage their own finances. Yet the country's staid newspapers, always frightened of change, dismissed the call for liberation for women in the same way that the majority fought against the emancipation of slaves. The increasing numbers of women on the streets demanding the vote led to editorials on the importance of men controlling their women, and to pastors and priests taking space in newspapers to berate their flocks over the twin scourge of masculine women and feminine men. In Boston the long-standing head of the Catholic Church, Cardinal William O'Connell, stated that 'man should assert his proper authority in the home. Failure to do this leads to a false feminism which, unless it is curbed in time, will have disastrous results for humanity. The women are becoming masculine, if you please, and the men are becoming effeminate. This is disorder.'[27] W. S. Tyler, of the Theosophical Society, suggested that reincarnation was to blame for the apparently sudden increase in mannish women and unmanly men: 'One of the phenomena of the external cycle is the change of sex often experienced in various returns of the soul to earth... What we call "effeminate" men are merely those who, during a recent period of earthly incarnation – probably the one preceding the present one – were feminine in sex. The reverse is true of women who seem masculine in attitude.'[28] It was not unusual for a newspaper publisher to use his editorial column to state, with unquestioned assurance, that feminists were simply militant lesbians, members of a third sex (adopting the title of German author Ernst von Wolzogen's 1914 novel), or extremists that refused to marry, to work for less pay than their male counterparts and to adopt the traditional role of the homemaker.

The media became preoccupied with 'pansies' and 'sissies', with hundreds of column inches given over to articles on how women – the stay at home, non-voting type, naturally – preferred a rootin', tootin', gun slingin', tobacco chewin' he-man over one who enjoyed the occasional manicure. Socialite and author on etiquette Emily Post wrote that 'effeminate men are repulsive, of course. A woman's ideal is naturally of a manly man.'[29] Newspapers and magazines ran articles on how everyone from Sappho, Joan of Arc and Shakespeare through to the 'sophisticated, sensation-hungering flapper symbolizes the third sex'.[30] One reader was so incensed with what he saw on the streets of New York that he wrote to a local newspaper to complain of the 'extremely effeminate' young men 'promenading Broadway leading poodles and other small dogs... What's the world coming to, anyway?'[31] Following the murder of film director William Taylor in 1922, newspapers and gossip magazines were awash with tales of a film industry where sex and drug parties were commonplace, and where effeminate men and masculine women ruled the roost. It was a widely held belief that the world of music was equally corrupt, that music was meant for 'women and effeminate men'.[32] Porter Grainger and his songwriting partner Bob Ricketts, a pair who were always on the lookout for a hook to build a song around, teamed up with W. C. Handy and penned a blues number that satirised the media's obsession, 'Save Your Man and Satisfy Your Soul'. With lyrics that included the lines, 'Men are growing weaker, women growing stronger / So the wise folks say / According to the wise old hounds / The men have had their day,' the song was recorded by Edna Hicks, accompanied by Grainger on piano, and issued by Paramount in late 1923. The public obsession with homosexuality would only increase with the infamous Leopold and Loeb case the following year. When it became known, during their trial, that the teenage murderers were lovers involved in a sado-masochistic gay relationship, homosexuality became big news: American newspapers seemed to become obsessed with stories of homosexual life in prisons, and doctors and psychiatrists were often called upon in court in an attempt to explain away any and all abnormal behaviour as homosexual.

The 'Nosey Sees All, Knows All' gossip column of the *Chicago Whip* was full of tittle-tattle about the city's LGBTQ community, and the anonymous columnist revelled in passing on stories such as one about 'two young "baby male vamps"' he encountered being chased by 'a dusky little maiden as she waved her arms frantically by the fountain on Grand Boulevard and 39th Street at one-thirty Sunday morning... Nosey turned when the first cry was made and saw the two "gentlemen" beating a hasty retreat for fear that the dusky maiden's alarm might by some chance reach the ears of a policeman. The little lady tripped off in the direction of her home and so did Nosey. Who knows where the pale-faced "he-vamps" finally stopped?'[33] The American epidemic was reaching other countries too. In Lisbon, Portuguese police were ordered to arrest any man seen using face powder or other cosmetics on the street.

Nosey's column delighted in tales of effeminate men being turfed out of their lodgings for having committed no greater transgression than to dress in a 'kimono and boudoir cap'[34] and he was positively incandescent with rage at the exploits of Chicago's bohemian set enjoying 'pajama parties', supposedly women-only affairs but often attended by men dressed in women's night attire, wigs and jewellery: 'Husbands gladly give permission for their wives to attend these parties, understanding that only ladies were to be present. Then the terrible news got out that some young society men were there all dolled up in wigs and ladies pajamas... A husband heard about it and called for his wife... he broke that party up causing all of the male "females" to run down the street clad only in their silk pajamas.'[35] When an invite came to a party, Nosey was horrified to find one of the other male guests 'who wore a beautiful pair of ear rings. On his fingers he wore several rings, and a wrist watch adorned his wrist. [Most men would have worn their watch on a chain, tucked into a waistcoat pocket.] Eye glasses with a long flowing silk cord completed his adornment.' But these things were nothing: 'Nosey would not have objected to these decorations had not the gentleman in taking off his hat delicately removed a hat pin. That was the straw that broke Nosey's camel back.'[36]

His opprobrium was not limited to the city's male homosexuals; Chicago's lesbian and bisexual women were also fodder for his column:

Nosey was out on Halowe'en Eve [sic] and what he saw would fill a book. He saw one lady, the mother of six children, out in men's clothes, switching like a bride's train with a cigarette stuck jauntily in the corner of her mouth. He saw young matrons bordering on the danger mark of thirty years running up and down the streets yelling like Comanche Indians. They were attired in keeping with their brains, clown-like. He saw grown up men parading the highways in unspeakable costumes. The evening was a return to the age of foolishness and many fools were in evidence.[37]

It would be more than a decade before local gay hustler Alfred Finnie would establish the annual Finnie's Ball, Chicago's own annual drag party, held in the South Side each Hallowe'en; by the early 1950s Finnie's Ball had grown to attract more than 1,500 people each year and had to move from its original home in an underground bar to the Pershing Ballroom. 'They'd have a big band, maybe about seven or eight pieces in the band, and everybody would be dancing with one another, and they'd be drinking,' drag queen Lorenzo Banyard, who used the name Nancy Kelly, explained to researcher Allen Drexel. 'They had tables like a cabaret, and you'd dance with your friend or you'd dance with someone else's friend. And the lesbians would be there, not too many of them, and they would dance with the queens.'[38]

# 8

# Bessie Makes a Record

*'Wherever blues are sung, there you will hear the name of Bessie Smith, best loved of all the Race's great blues singers. Bessie has the knack of picking the songs you like and the gift of singing them the way you want them sung. Every year this famous "Empress of Blues" tours the country, appearing before packed houses.'[1]*

Despite the media's attempt to root out LGBTQ people, some were finding ways to build their own communities, even their own families, with marriages or blessings between same-sex couples taking place in Black churches in Chicago as early as 1921. In April, gossip columnist Nosey, of the *Chicago Whip*, wrote about an extraordinary scene he had witnessed:

Some people are saying that it is hard to tell the mothers from the daughters on account of the short skirts. That is a mere trifle compared to the delicate task of telling the father from the mother. Nosey tried it and was about to give it up when he detected in the voice of one of the beautifully gowned ladies a huskiness that seemed to mean that the person should have been in masculine attire. Powder, paint, perfume and silk trinkets all went to make this apparition beautiful and Nosey would have fallen for the dress and figure if he had not caught little traits that told him, 'Look out!' The vision kept on its way with Nosey closely following. The two dainty things came to a church and entered to the tune of a wedding march. Nosey was 'surprised', but the ceremony came off and this queer thing in ladies' clothes went through the mock ceremony and came out. The crowd gathered smiled, Nosey smiled. The 'bride' smiled and they all passed on. Nosey too.[2]

Gossip columnists may have tried to convince their readers that there were queer goings-on on every street corner, but the truth is that the majority of LGBTQ people socialised away from the public eye. LGBTQ people lived double lives, with jobs, husbands, wives and families to think of, and although bars and cafés proliferated in major cities, there was still the need to be circumspect. In most of those meeting places it was illegal for same-sex couples to dance together, and even if the venue was under the protection of the mob or the local police, violence – and the very real possibility of being blackmailed – were ever-present concerns. It was much safer to do your partying in private.

It was the time of the infamous 'buffet flats', parties that began in Harlem in the early years of the century, and that quickly spread to other cities. Entrepreneurial women (buffet flats were more commonly operated by women, according to a 1916 exposé on the practice printed on the front page of the *New York Age*)[3] would buy liquor wholesale from a local supplier and then throw a party at their home, providing food and charging people to attend. Often it was hoped that, once the cost of food and drink had been covered, there would be enough left over to pay the rent. But buffet flats were more than simple rent parties: they provided many LGBTQ people opportunity to socialise with their own kind, away from prying eyes.

By 1910 reporters were complaining of the 'many hundreds of vile "buffet flats" contaminating our social life. Liquor is sold there; there is a continuous round of music, mirth and merriment, the seclusion of the flat gives the screen and opportunity for the evil minded; these, together with the comforts of home attached, make this new devil's workshop a place as seductive as it is destructive to the morals of the young.'[4] These illicit drinking parties would invariably feature entertainment, a couple of musicians jamming... and more. Bessie Smith was no stranger to the buffet flat scene: Ruby Smith (born Ruby Walker: she adopted the surname Smith after her aunt Bessie's death) described a visit to a buffet flat in Detroit to Bessie's biographer Chris Albertson: 'A buffet flat is nothing but faggots and bull daggers. Everything, everybody that was in "the life". Buffet means everything goes on. They had a faggot that was so great that people used to come there just to watch him make love to another man. He'd give him a tongue bath and by the time he got to the front of that guy he was shaking like a leaf. People would pay good just to see him do his act.'[5]

In October 1913 the *Chicago Daily News* reported that 'investigators found more than 100 buffet flats and similar resorts with their doors wide open to the public,'[6] and by the following decade, with the introduction of prohibition, this number had increased dramatically. Regular parties took place at the notorious Violet Room, on Chicago's Calumet Avenue, where men and women both had to wear something purple – such as a necktie or a scarf – to get in. Many were run simply to help the residents pay their rent, some were no more than a front for prostitution, but the Violet Room was something else: the lights and decoration were in shades of purple, cigarettes (and, no doubt, reefers) were handed around liberally, and drinks were cheap. LGBTQ people mixed freely with straight Chicagoans, and the place became so popular that it turned out to be impossible to keep it a secret from the authorities.

If you did not have something purple to wear, then perhaps a flower in your buttonhole would do, as Nosey knew:

Every person who wears a certain little rosette in his button hole has a right to enter a certain massive residence on 'Strivers Row' and failure to appear with this insignia means that you will have trouble gaining admission. Nosey was idly watching the snow fall the other night when a gentleman tried to tell the man who answered the door bell that he lived there. The man on the door said, 'Do you love flowers?' The new roomer said, 'Heavens, No!'

"Then you can't come in,' said the doorman as he closed the door. The man left in the snow swore and started down the steps, he stopped and picked up a crushed carnation. Then he returned to the door with the flower in his hand and rang the bell. The same doorman answered and asked the same question. The man said that he liked flowers and the doorman let him in. Nosey now keeps a flower in his pocket all of the time and hopes that the password does not change. The House of Flowers must be interesting.[7]

In November 1921, the Violet Room closed: the woman behind the operation moved to new premises and opened the far more exclusive, and expensive, Gold Room, the 'one spot in the city where you can find almost anything that you want'.[8] On Thanksgiving Day 1922, police broke up a 'women only party' after the 'piercing screams of a woman had penetrated the street' – police told the *Chicago Defender* that they had dealt with many complaints from neighbours, 'as the women who congregated there were of an unusual type'.

According to a short news item that appeared in the *Chicago Defender* on 12 February 1921, Bessie Smith signed her first recording contract not with Columbia, as we have all been led to believe for the last century, but with the small Emerson Phonograph Company in New York. She recorded her first session for Emerson that same month, with the *Defender* telling its readers that, 'One of the greatest of all "Blues" singers is Miss Bessie Smith, who is at present making records with the aid of 6 Jazz musicians for the Emerson Record Company. The first release will be made about March 10.'[9] Sadly that record would not appear, possibly because of the serious financial mess that Victor Emerson was in: having watched his company's profits almost treble year-on-year between 1917 and 1920, he launched ambitious plans for expansion and opened a second recording studio in Los Angeles, overextending the company's finances and forcing it into receivership. At around the same time as the yet-to-surface session for Emerson, Bessie auditioned for Okeh, accompanied by Sidney Bechet, but was turned down because her voice was deemed too rough for records. A few months later Bessie auditioned for Black Swan, but owner Harry Pace found her style 'too nitty-gritty' for his taste: an apocryphal tale has Pace, who had set his sights on quality and class for his label, deciding not to employ Bessie after she spat on the floor of the studio during her test. Despite rumours about other early sessions, in more than 100 years no recordings of Bessie have emerged from this period.

In 1922 Alberta Hunter teamed up with her old friend Lovie Austin, then the in-house piano player for Paramount Records. Lovie, who would also accompany Ma Rainey, was quite the character: three times married and well known for driving her Stutz Bearcat open-top car, with its seats upholstered in leopard-print, at breakneck speed around town. One of the very few Black women to front their own band, Lovie had studied music at the Roger Williams University in Nashville, Tennessee and at Knoxville College before joining the vaudeville circuit.

The pair composed the song 'Down Hearted Blues', which Alberta recorded in July of that year for Paramount. Alberta would later claim that, 'I was less than eleven years old when I started writing "Down Hearted Blues", before I ran away from home,' and, as she would later admit, 'I had no formal training... I cannot read notes. If a melody comes to me I try to remember it and I pay someone who does write music [to] write it down. When I sing a song, I sing it as I feel it.'[10] Lovie wrote the tune, based on Alberta's guide vocal, and the pair shared credit: Alberta, used to being ripped off by other people in the industry, was impressed with Lovie's honesty and the two women would remain friends for the rest of their lives.

The company advertised the disc heavily, boasting of how Alberta had 'captivated thousands with her fascinating melodies', and at the same time claiming that the song, a typical tale of a woman disappointed in love, was 'a favorite down on the plantation and the levees'.[11] The following year, Bessie Smith would cover the song at her first recording session for Columbia, and there were competing versions available from Eva Taylor, Sissle and Blake, W. C. Handy's Orchestra and Edna Hicks, among others. 'Bessie made it after it had been recorded on almost all the labels and even on piano rolls,' Alberta marvelled. 'We thought it was exhausted, but it was Bessie's first record, and it sold

780,000 copies!'[12] Despite being co-author of the massive hit, Alberta would not see a cent in royalties for decades.

Even though it was white-owned, Paramount boasted a black A&R man, J. Mayo Williams, a former professional sportsman who had earned the nickname 'Ink' as one of the National Football League's first Black players. Briefly associated with Black Swan, Williams began working for Paramount, initially as a talent scout, shortly after he moved to Chicago in 1921. By 1924 he was officially the Recording Manager of the joint Paramount-Black Swan race records series, the larger company taking over Black Swan after Pace's company got itself into financial difficulties. Pace attempted to emulate the white-owned companies who, as well as recording and pressing discs, also had their own line in phonographs, but in taking over the failing Remington company to produce his own range of Swanola players he seriously overextended his company financially, and by 1924 was out of business.

Alberta would have shed no tears for Black Swan, but she was not happy about having her career directed by Ink Williams. Ink was unscrupulous: by now he was also heading operations at Chicago Music, the company that published much of Paramount's output and, despite knowing little about music, his name appeared as co-writer on dozens of jazz and blues songs, including Ma Rainey's 'Stack O' Lee Blues' and songs by Ida Cox, Joe Turner and Count Basie, principally because he would buy songs outright from their composers at anything from $20 to $60 a time and grab credit for tidying them up or embellishing them. Alberta would blame him for ripping her off and denying her royalties on her compositions, calling him 'A thief from the day he was conceived.' 'She said I screwed her out of publishing money,'[13] he would candidly admit, adding that it was understood in the industry at the time that one should 'Screw the artist before he screws you,'[14] and he boasted about how many of the artists signed to Paramount earned nothing in royalties from the discs they sold, yet as the first African American executive at a white-owned recording company he wielded huge influence.

In September 1923 Paramount opened what was intended to be a temporary studio in Chicago. Lovie, 'The only girl pianist of the race to play for records,'[15] came too, to accompany singers including Ida

111

Cox and Monette Moore and, of course, Alberta Hunter. She did not stay long, but something must have clicked for her, because shortly afterwards Lovie decided to make Chicago her permanent home and, as well as leading her own band, the Blues Serenaders, she also acted as musical director for several Chicago hotspots, including the Gem, Joyland and Monogram theatres. At the Monogram Lovie and her band accompanied many major acts, and it was there that Ink Williams first heard the 37-year-old Gertrude 'Ma' Rainey. Before the year was out he would bring Ma to Paramount to cut her first sides, again accompanied by Lovie Austin.

Even though audiences had been listening to queer blues songs being performed in vaudeville, in tent shows, in bordellos and in other live settings for well over a decade, the first recordings did not take place until the beginning of 1923, in New York.

Heterosexual audiences had been treated to smut on record since at least the 1890s. The Edison company had made dozens of cylinder recordings of blue jokes and salacious stories, and up until the turn of the century it was not unusual for bars, cafés and private clubs in some of America's big cities to offer their patrons opportunity to listen to these recordings. Throughout the decade, US Postal Inspector Anthony Comstock and the Society for the Suppression of Vice investigated instances of indecent material being broadcast in phonograph booths throughout New York, and in 1899 he succeeded in securing a ban on the distribution and airing, either in public or in private, of recorded material which used profanity or sexually explicit language. Anyone attempting to circumnavigate that ban could face criminal prosecution, and many of the recordings made by Edison and others were destroyed, lost forever.

Despite the crackdown, comedy songs remained popular throughout the first decades of the 20th century, and lyrics would often use innuendo and double entendres to suggest illicit sex: early examples include Harry von Tilzer (born Aaron Gumbinsky) and Arthur Lamb's 'A Bird in a Gilded Cage' (1900), which was originally about a kept woman until Von Tilzer insisted that Lamb make it clear in the lyric that the 'bird' in question was married; 'I Love, I Love, I

Love My Wife – But Oh! You Kid!', recorded by Arthur Collins in 1909; and Irving Berlin's 1911 hit 'Everybody's Doing It Now'. 'I Love, I Love, I Love My Wife – But Oh! You Kid!' (again co-written by Von Tilzer, who had clearly gotten over his prudishness) began a fashion for songs about adultery. Church leaders, including prominent evangelist Billy Sunday, protested this wave of permissiveness in song, but 'I Love, I Love, I Love My Wife...' was a huge hit, and the song was parodied endlessly: Berlin appropriated the title for a line in his own 'My Wife's Gone to the Country – Hurrah! Hurrah!'.

By the time jazz and blues came to be recorded audiences were accustomed to hearing sex and sexuality discussed in song. And, like those early smutty Edison cylinders, these recordings were not made to be played on the radio but to be played in the privacy of your home, or in bars and juke joints. Heterosexual relationships had been celebrated – or, more usually, complained of as the source of the singer's woes – in blues recordings from the off, but it would be three years before anyone dared to record anything remotely queer.

In February 1923, exactly three years after Mamie Smith made her debut recording for Okeh in New York, Alberta Hunter recorded 'Someone Else Will Take Your Place' for Paramount in the same city. She was accompanied on the recording not by Lovie Austin, but by pianist Fletcher Henderson, the same man who had played piano on her Black Swan debut. Henderson, whose association with Black Swan and Paramount stemmed from his working as a song demonstrator with the Pace and Handy Music Company, had spent eight months on the road with Ethel Waters and the Black Swan Troubadours, and had been with her when she made her fateful trip south in February 1922.

Paramount had only introduced a dedicated race records line a few months earlier, in fact Alberta's 'Don't Pan Me' (backed with 'Daddy Blues') was the first release in its '12000' race records series, in August 1922. If Alberta had been unhappy with the way she was promoted at Black Swan, she had no such issues with Paramount, who plugged her endlessly as 'a sensation: America's supreme Blues singer'.[16] The company was owned by United Phonographs, a subsidiary of the Wisconsin Chair Company. Established principally to help promote their own Vista brand phonographs, despite being recorded in New

York (and, later, Chicago), the discs were manufactured alongside the furniture and phonographs in their factory in Port Washington, Wisconsin, just a few miles outside Milwaukee. The wording on the record labels, and the advertising the company took out in the Black press may have made it look as if Paramount operated their state-of-the-art New York Recording Laboratories, Inc. in the heart of the Big Apple, but the 'laboratory' was just another corner of the Port Washington factory. When Paramount did open their own New York studio, in 1923, it was basic at best: one room in a Manhattan office block, but it was there that Alberta recorded 'Someone Else Will Take Your Place', with Henderson and his studio band.

'Someone Else Will Take Your Place' was written by Black vaudeville performer Robert Maurice Warfield (often erroneously credited as David Warfield), who also composed songs for early classic blues singers Ida Cox and Edmonia Henderson. Singer and composer John 'J' Rosamond Johnson introduced a song called 'Someone Else Will Take Your Place' in November 1922 when he played Pennsylvania's Majestic Ballroom, accompanied by his band the Inimitable Five, but that was probably a different song, as Warfield did not register copyright in his composition until after Alberta Hunter had made her recording.

Known professionally as 'Popo' Warfield, the Chicago-based songwriter, one half of the song and dance act Sims and Warfield, was born in Kentucky in 1890, and although he was married (and apparently providing financial support for his mother and several elder siblings), he certainly seems to have had more than a passing association with the queer blues community. Having copyrighted his first song, 'Prison Spider Blues' in 1919, the following year he wrote a song entitled 'Rock Me in Your Arms, Sweet Daddy'. Sims and Warfield had featured with the *Puss Puss Burlesque Show*, but by late 1922, after a failed attempt to get their own company off the ground, they had split, and Warfield was appearing at the Grand in Chicago as part of a cast of forty in the musical revue *That Gets It*, assisting with the staging of the musical numbers.

Of course, it is not unusual for a jobbing songwriter to write in character, or to compose something from the perspective of the singer, be they male or female. It is equally common for a male or female vocalist to sing a song originally written to be performed by a singer of the opposite sex, and there are hundreds of examples of what queer music archivist J. D. Doyle calls 'cross vocals', songs that were, 'for example, intended to be sung by a woman but are instead sung by a man, keeping the pronouns intact'. This was done, he explains, because, 'Music publishers had a stranglehold on the rights to their catalogues. Singers could not change a word, so it was not uncommon for a man to seemingly sing a song to a man, or a woman to a woman. The public [then]... did not really pay attention to any gay connotations.'[17]

'Alexander (Don't You Love Your Baby No More?)', a song written by the seemingly ubiquitous Harry von Tilzer and Andrew Sterling, is clearly sung from a woman's perspective yet it was first recorded in 1904 by male novelty song singer Bob Roberts. But in 'Someone Else Will Take Your Place', although Alberta is singing a song written by a man about a woman, some of the lines, especially 'With my dainty figure and my baby stare' are clearly sung from a female perspective. The lyrics are not overtly queer, but knowing what we know about Alberta's own sexual preferences, and that throughout the song she refers to the person leaving her as her 'pretty baby' (a nod, possibly, to her association with Tony Jackson's song of the same name), adds a certain frisson and because of this, 'Someone Else Will Take Your Place' takes on a very different tone when sung by a woman rather than by its male author. Alberta's insistence that there were five or six other women lining up to fill her shoes should her 'pretty baby' leave, gives the song a distinctly queer edge, and at no point in the recording does Alberta make it clear if her love interest is male or female. In 1924 Edmonia Henderson would record Warfield's 'Worried 'Bout Him Blues', which again takes on a very different meaning when you realise that a man is writing about being abandoned by his 'daddy' for another lover. In March 1925, Warfield re-established his double act with Joe Sims, touring the States with their show *Plantation Days*: the following year he would record two Lovie Austin tunes, duetting with singer Biddy Paige (who had previously recorded as Lillian Goodner), for Vocalion. Warfield died in 1943, aged 52.

In the same month that Alberta recorded 'Someone Else Will Take Your Place', Bessie Smith made her first commercially available recordings. 1923 was going to be a big year for Bessie; after false starts with Emerson, Black Swan and Okeh, she was finally signed and recorded her first session for Columbia on 15 February, shortly afterwards issuing 'Down Hearted Blues' (a cover of the song co-written by Alberta Hunter and Lovie Austin) backed with 'Gulf Coast Blues', with Bessie listed on the label as 'comedienne'. It was also the year she met her second husband, Jack Gee.

Significantly, although not released at the time, she also recorded nine takes of ''Tain't Nobody's Biz-ness If I Do', a decidedly queer blues song, with music by Porter Grainger and words by Everett Robbins, which had first been performed by Alberta Hunter at Chicago's Dreamland Café, and which Bessie would re-record, with more successful results, two months later. Grainger does not play on the recordings, but pianist and hustler Clarence Williams, does: unbeknown to Bessie, Williams had pulled a fast one, signing the singer to a personal contract with him rather than having her sign direct to Columbia, and pocketing half of her recording fees. A few months later, once Bessie had discovered this deception, she had the new man in her life sort things out, and although she would cover songs composed by, or at least credited to Williams, the two would not appear on disc together again for several years. Bessie did not like the fact that her lack of education left her open to being duped, and she resolved to improve her reading and writing skills, which she did to such an extent that within a couple of years she was confidently corresponding with suppliers, tradespeople and others.

'Down Hearted Blues' would sell over a quarter of a million copies in its first six months, some way off the 780,000 units Alberta Hunter would claim that the record had sold, but still a phenomenal figure for a race record; its popularity inspired a copycat recording from singer Edna Hicks, who later that year would also cut several sides with Porter Grainger. Hicks's own career was cut short by a freak accident: holding a candle, she set fire to herself while helping her husband fill his car with gasoline.

The first recording of ''Tain't Nobody's Biz-ness If I Do' had been issued in January 1923 by Pathé. With vocals by Anna Meyers and backing from New York-based jazz quintet the Original Memphis Five, the disc was marketed as a 'Negro vocal record', even though the phrase 'race records' had been around since the middle of 1921, used by Okeh for their 'original race records' series, the first of which was jazz singer Daisy Martin's 'Play 'Em For Mama, Sing 'Em For Me', recorded in April and issued that July. Although credited to Porter Grainger, songs with similar themes and lyrics to "Tain't Nobody's Biz-ness If I Do' had been around for a number of years; in 1909 Eber Carl (E. C) Perrow was travelling the South, collecting folk songs and spirituals for a series of articles later published in *The Journal of American Folk-Lore*. He listed two songs, 'Some of These Days' and 'With a Chicken on my Back', both of which had similar choruses. Grainger's song had originally been part of the score to a musical, *Seven o'Hearts*, and when it first appeared, in 1922, the song was classified as a 'comedy fox-trot',[18] with newspapers labouring under the misapprehension that their readers would have little idea what a 'blues' song was.

As well as working as a pianist on jazz and blues recordings, including on sides for Viola McCoy, since his arrival in New York in April 1920, Grainger had quickly established himself in the city as a songwriter of note. By the time "Tain't Nobody's Biz-ness...' appeared in the shops, he had paired up with Donald Heywood to write many of the songs for a new musical revue, the *Creole Follies* – which opened at the Lafayette in Harlem in May 1922, and shortly afterwards signed on to work as a staff writer for a publishing house run by Clarence Williams, a man he had first encountered when both were in Chicago, and the same man who had attempted to screw Bessie over. Among the recording artists working for Williams was Tom Waller and his Band, its leader shortly to become better known as 'Fats' Waller. Williams's office was based in the Gaiety building, at 1547 Broadway, where other Black entrepreneurs – including W. C. Handy and Handy's former partner Harry Pace – also had offices. As well as running his own publishing house, Williams was also working as a local talent scout, producer and performer for Okeh Records at the time. Grainger and Williams would become good friends, with Grainger acting as best man when Williams married blues singer Eva Taylor.

In September 1922, *Dumb Luck*, 'a musical comedy in two acts and twelve scenes', opened at the Lyceum Theatre, Stamford. Not only were the songs to this new musical written by Grainger and Heywood, but the cast of the show included both Alberta Hunter and Ethel Waters, along with Waters' girlfriend Ethel Williams and Hunter's main squeeze, Lottie Tyler. The cast also included Dickie Wells, later to run a nightclub known as the Theatrical Grill in Harlem, and the orchestra was led by Bob Ricketts, who would soon become Grainger's partner. The show was reviewed in *Billboard*, 23 September 1922 by J. A. Jackson, who noted that, 'If there is to be a successor to "Shuffle Along" this show proves its right to the chance to a Broadway showing.' Jackson was wrong: the show was lousy, the promotor ran out of money, and the cast were left stranded when the production folded after just two days on the road. The failure of *Dumb Luck* caused further friction between Alberta Hunter and Ethel Waters: the Two Ethels sprang for train tickets for themselves to take them back to New York, leaving Alberta to sort not just herself and Lottie out but the rest of the entire crew. When, on 28 September 1922, the Two Ethels were both injured when a car they were travelling in crashed into a bakery truck in Boston, Alberta may well have felt that fate had lent a hand. Waters and Williams were travelling with their friend Florence Deuson (at the time, all three women were appearing at the Arlington Theatre in *Oh! Joy!*), and driver Andrew Fashitt was the only one of the quartet to escape injury.

Despite the failure of *Dumb Luck*, Grainger's star was firmly in the ascendant, and as well as his success on stage, within weeks of the Anna Meyers version of ''Tain't Nobody's Biz-ness...' appearing, competing versions by Lena Wilson (on Victor, with Grainger on piano), and Mandy Lee with Ladd's Black Aces (on Gennett) were also in the stores. In June, Bessie Smith's cover, which Columbia advertised alongside other 'special "blues" releases', hit the streets, and the following month a piano roll, aping the Smith arrangement, was being advertised for sale. Soon yet more covers followed, including one by the Tennessee Ten (on Victor) and another from Clarence Williams' Blue Five (for Okeh), a band that featured up-and-coming jazz superstars Sidney Bechet and Louis Armstrong. The song's popularity with jazz and blues musicians would lead to it becoming one of the first blues standards. It was also covered by Fats Waller in 1941: Waller had played piano on one of the earliest recordings of the song, by Sara Martin (on Okeh), released in the same week as Anna Meyers' version.

But there was little time to celebrate this success. In February 1923, Grainger teamed with another songwriter, Robert W. 'Bob' Ricketts, former musical director of the Dixieland Troubadours, and wrote the 'Laughin' Cryin' Blues' for New York's Zipf Music, a song that was quickly recorded by Sarah Martin for Okeh, and Amanda Brown (a pseudonym used by Viola McCoy, accompanied by Grainger on piano), and that in turn was followed by an instrumental version issued by Ted Claire and his Snappy Bits Band for Gennett. The following month Viola McCoy would release a different recording of the same song under her own name, again accompanied by Grainger and recorded at the same session as the Amanda Brown version, on Gennett. Fats Waller would perform a solo version of the song for piano roll that same year. Soon Grainger and Ricketts were sharing an apartment, at 2347 Seventh Avenue (now renamed Adam Clayton Powell Jr Boulevard, a few blocks north of Central Park), and although Grainger always strived to keep his homosexual life private, rumours soon spread that the two men were, in fact, romantically involved. They would not share a home for long: by September Grainger had found himself a new wife, blues singer Ethel Finnie. Finnie recorded several sides for Emerson and Ajax written, and often accompanied by, Grainger, and the two appeared regularly on radio. Grainger's homosexuality was always going to put a strain on his marriage, and the couple split temporarily while Ethel was pregnant with Porter's child, a girl they named Portia. Grainger's private life may have been somewhat complicated, but he remained close to Ricketts, and they would continue to work together until Ricketts's death in 1936.

With so much money pouring in, Grainger and his new partner established their own publishing company, initially called Grainger and Ricketts but shortly afterwards dubbed Rainbow Music Publishing, with their own office in the Gaiety building. Grainger and Ricketts were soon being referred to as the kings of the blues composers, and they would consolidate this reputation with the publication, in 1926, of their instruction manual *How to Play and Sing the Blues Like the Phonograph and Stage Artists*, a book that offered such sage advice to the novice performer as, 'If one can temporarily play the role of the oppressed or the depressed, injecting into his or her rendition a spirit of hopeful prayer, the effect will be more natural and successful... "Blues" are sung or played most effectively in a crooning or subdued style. Without the necessary moan, croon or slur, no blues number is properly sung.'[19]

The words to ''Tain't Nobody's Biz-ness If I Do' have a distinctly queer and sadomasochistic quality, and would be unusual no matter who sang them. In Meyers' original, she sings the line, 'I won't call no copper if I'm beat up by my poppa'; by the time Bessie records her version, she had added or, possibly, reinstated an extra couplet, 'I'd rather my man would hit me / Than to jump a-right up and quit me'. Billie Holiday (occasionally referred to by those with inside knowledge as Mister Holiday) recorded a big band version in 1949 which used both lines.

''Tain't Nobody's Biz-ness...' has become a standard, but not everyone who performs the song sings the original lyrics, as multi-award-winning blues singer and songwriter Gaye Adegbalola explains: '[Saffire] recorded that: it's just a great song. But what we did was take out lines that we did not believe in, like "If I'm beat up by my papa, I swear I won't call no copper...". We would never sing that. If that was me I'd be calling the cops straight away! I have performed it lots in my white tails, and I will just make up verses as I go along to different people in the audience. You see me in a white tuxedo because it's as close as I could get to bugle bead gowns. There's a kind of [pansy craze star] Gladys Bentley look, but she was more of what I would call a Drag King and that's not where I was coming from... I was more Marlene Dietrich... I had a swagger about me that could pull the girls!'[20]

Were Grainger and Ricketts writing from experience? It was a theme that Grainger – and Bessie – would return to. In 1928, while Grainger was acting as Bessie's pianist, he presented her with the song 'Yes Indeed He Do', another of his compositions that glorified domestic violence: 'When I ask him where he's been he grabs a rocking chair / Then he knocks me down and says, "It's just a little love lick, dear"' and 'If he beats me or mistreats me, what is that to you?' There may have been a slight misogynistic streak in Grainger, but it is equally possible that he himself enjoyed a bit of rough.

'If you look at people like Joni Mitchell, Dusty Springfield or Kate Bush, they wanted to talk about their relationships from a woman's perspective,' says civil rights activist Ted Brown. 'But because most songs were written by men with a male perspective, they had a battle; you know the old thing where a man does it he's being strong, but if a woman does it she's being difficult? Now, Ma Rainey and Bessie Smith, and people like that, who would have had parents or grandparents who had been slaves, were making their statements both as female artists and as Black people in a very white-orientated world. They were very aware of the oppression that their forebears had suffered. Also, often Black music was not allowed on the radio, so that gave them more freedom to be sexually explicit.'[21]

Bessie's recording was another smash, bought in the hundreds of thousands. When she was appearing on a T.O.B.A. tour, with her regular piano player Irvin Johns, the streets around the Frolic Theatre in Birmingham, Alabama, were blocked, and 'hundreds and hundreds [were] unable to gain entrance to this performance'. Others on the bill took full advantage, leaving the stage to walk around the audience selling sheet music copies of the songs Bessie performed, and although reviewer Billy Chambers thought this 'non-professional', her performance 'received heavy applause, leaving the house in a riot'.[22] A few weeks later, T.O.B.A. president Milton Starr noted that Bessie was 'breaking house records at the Bijou in Nashville', and when she returned to the Frolic in September, presumably to satiate the hundreds left out in the cold the last time she was in town, Chambers reported that, 'The record singer broke her own record as a drawing card... The audience virtually declined to accept the final curtain, so pleased were they.'[23] Music shops gave away sepia-toned prints of Bessie to customers purchasing her records, and her own promotional appearances in stores caused mini-riots in the streets outside as thousands attempted to cram themselves through the doors.

But not everyone was as enamoured, nor prepared to celebrate the good fortune of blues singers like Bessie. Abel, reviewing one of her 1923 recordings, the Lovie Austin tune 'Bleeding Heart Blues', in the *New York Clipper*, dismissed her material as 'barbaric' and complained that the 'only thing distinctive about the general run of these lyric blues is how many different ways the writers can derive to say the same thing about their runaway daddies or mammas...', although he did deign to pass on faint praise for the singer herself, 'a blues yodeler [who] possesses a minor crooning quality that fits the woeful ditties perfectly'.[24] Perhaps unsurprisingly he was equally unmoved by her next release, 'Yodling Blues' [sic]: 'there must be a market for this sort of stuff else Columbia wouldn't market for numbers by the Smith-Henderson combination this month, but its appeal must be limited to a minority.'[25]

# 9

# Bessie Gets Married and Britain Gets the Blues

*'It used to be thought that homosexuality existed only among idiots
and imbeciles and the lowest class of degenerates. This of course
has been shown to be an error. On the contrary, some of the world's
greatest poets and artists are now known to have been homosexual.'* [1]

For Alberta, Bessie and Porter, it must have seemed as if the streets
of New York were paved with gold. Not only that, but as creative
artists they were shown respect by their peers and the public, even
if those running the industry held Black talent in less regard. Alberta
and Lottie were seen together at first-night parties; Porter Grainger too
was a regular at such events, hobnobbing it with his new friends in
his expensive clothes. Alberta was a hit at the whites-only Hollywood
Inn on Broadway, and soon she and Porter (and Mrs Porter Grainger,
Ethel Finnie) would be drawing rave reviews for their regular radio
appearances together. But other LGBTQ people were having a tougher
time. In an effort to enforce prohibition, the police began a crackdown
on illicit drinking dens, and in Greenwich Village underground queer
haunts were targeted. On 5 February 1923, the *New York Times* reported
that:

Every tearoom and cabaret in the village was visited yesterday morning by Deputy Inspector Joseph A. Howard and Captain Edward J. Dempsey of the Charles Street Station, and a party of ten detectives. Detectives Joseph Massie and Dewey Hughes of the Special Service Squad were at the Black Parrot Tea Shoppe Hobo-Hemia, 46 Charles Street, to witness what they had been informed would be a 'circus.' They arrested what they thought were five women and eight men. It developed later, however, that one of the 'women' was a man, Harry Bernhammer, 21 years old, living at 36 Hackensack Avenue, West Hoboken, N.J. He is familiarly known in the Village as 'Ruby,' according to the police. The charge against him is disorderly conduct for giving what the police termed an indecent dance.[2]

On 5 May 1923 Okeh Records took out a full-page advertisement in the *Chicago Defender*, a rarity in that, for possibly the first time, a newspaper included a full-page advertisement which exclusively featured records by Black artists. Showcasing acts including Mamie Smith and her Jazz Hounds, and W. C. Handy's Orchestra, Okeh also sent copies of the advert to music stores around the country to display in their windows. Adverts for jazz and blues records had become commonplace in the Black press, but the white-run media was less receptive. In May 1923 entertainment industry magazine, the *New York Clipper*, dismissed Alberta as a 'jazz dancer'[3] when mentioning the fact that she had joined the cast of the musical *How Come*, despite her being a highly successful recording artist whose discs were selling in their tens of thousands. Taking on the role originally played by Bessie Smith, Black newspaper the *Afro-American* put her photograph on the front page, and hailed her as a 'New Broadway star'.[4]

The blues – and the women who performed them – continued to be in great demand, and in June 1923 Lucille Bogan (occasionally listed on her releases as Lucile Bogan, and born on 1 April 1897 in Amory, Mississippi) signed to Okeh; she does not appear in the 5 May advert, but is mentioned in a full-page ad that appeared in *Talking Machine World*, 15 August, and she had her first two Okeh releases listed in the same issue. Very little is known about Bogan's personal life outside of her heterosexual relationships. There have been claims that she was a free-spirited bisexual who may have earned a living as a sex worker before she became a recording artist. Certainly, many of her own compositions feature uninhibited descriptions of sex. But it would be a few years before she would record her first obviously queer song, the self-penned 'Women Won't Need No Men', a direct antecedent to her better known 'B.D. Woman's Blues'.

She made her first recording – 'Pawn Shop Blues' – in a makeshift studio on Nassau Street in Atlanta, Georgia, around 14 June 1923: the first blues recordings made outside of Chicago or New York. Immediately afterwards she was summoned to New York, where she put down four sides, covering Alberta Hunter and Lovie Austin's 'Chirpin' the Blues', backed with the Porter Grainger-Bob Ricketts song 'Triflin' Blues (Daddy, Don't You Trifle on Me)' for her first release by the company, which was in the shops less than four weeks after that first session. By coincidence, Viola McCoy had recorded the very same coupling (under the pseudonym Amanda Brown), with Grainger on piano for Columbia just weeks earlier. McCoy had previously recorded 'Triflin' Blues' for Gennett, under her own name. Bogan's earlier Atlanta recording was used for her third (and last) Okeh release, backed with another song recorded at the same session, by local singer Fannie Goosby.

Bogan's recordings are markedly different from the majority of her contemporaries. Her voice is weary, rough and weather-beaten, and lacking in the professional skills picked up by singers like Bessie Smith and Ma Rainey during their years on the road, or by Alberta and Ethel in the cafés and in theatres where they honed their art. Her Okeh releases were well advertised but could not have done well for the company, as there would be a four-year gap before she would record again.

While the record companies were busying themselves signing anyone and everyone who could carry a blues number, or who at least looked as if they could, on 7 June 1923, Bessie Smith married security guard Jack Gee. The couple had not known each other long, and Columbia's Frank Walker, then acting as her de facto manager and booking agent, warned her against the union, but Bessie was obstinate and knew her own mind. It would not be long before Gee usurped

Walker, forcefully taking over the management of her fast-rising career. Walker would always claim that he signed Bessie to the company some six years after he first heard her perform, in a gin mill in Selma, but she had to extradite herself from her personal contract with Clarence Williams first. Walker tried to keep her on a straight path, insisting that she put some of her earnings away as Bessie was known to spend money as soon as it was in her hand. Bessie reluctantly agreed, but once she discovered that Walker was sitting on $75,000 of her earnings she insisted he hand it over, spending the lot in days. The money was not entirely wasted: Bessie paid for a house in Philadelphia for her and Jack, and their adopted son Jack Junior, and she offered to bring her family out from Chattanooga to share in her success. Jack, however, was totally inept as a manager, spending Bessie's money on flashy cars and fast women (he was not much of a drinker, unlike his spouse, who had a taste for rough liquor) and despite the distrust on both sides, Walker would continue to book many of Bessie's dates for her.

The marriage to Jack was tempestuous, and marked by infidelities on both sides: Jack had an eye for the ladies, and Bessie liked both women and men. This was not her first marriage: in Hamilton County, Ohio, on 4 January 1921, Bessie wed a fellow entertainer, a man called Earl Love. They met while working in Atlantic City, and at the time of applying for their marriage license, both were living at separate boarding houses on Carlisle Avenue (with Earl living just a few doors away from the Empress Theatre), and both listed their occupations as 'performer'. Love had been married previously, and had a child which lived with Love's widowed mother. Within twelve months, Bessie would be a widow herself.

Bessie had little opportunity to celebrate her new marriage. The demand on her time, and on that of other singers, was insatiable, and just two days after she and Jack were joined in holy wedlock it was reported that Clara Smith who, outside of Ma, was seen as Bessie's main rival, had also been awarded a recording contract, this time with Okeh in New York. The newspaper, the *Pittsburgh Courier*, got it wrong though: ten days earlier Clara had walked into the studios of Columbia – the very same company that Bessie was recording for – and made her first recordings, six takes of a ponderous song called 'I Got Everything a Woman Needs', and five of 'Every Woman's Blues', accompanied by a listless Fletcher Henderson on piano. Both songs were written by Stanley Miller, Clara's regular pianist, who would go on to compose a number of her records. The same story reported that Clara's husband, Will Graham, had decided to abandon their double act and had 'bought a cleaning and pressing business with a bootblack stand, employing two boys'.[5] Graham and Smith's marriage was a turbulent one, hardly surprising when Clara was sleeping with other women, and at the beginning of August Graham would be found in the back room of a house on Broadway with three bullet holes in him, along with a .38 calibre revolver and a letter addressed to Clara, care of 328 West 59th Street.

A fortnight after her own marriage, Bessie was off on a ten-week tour of southern states, sponsored by Columbia Records: she played the 81 for a week, including a midnight show for whites only, and at each appearance the theatre was at capacity; local record stores did a roaring trade in Bessie Smith discs (one enterprising store, the Ludden and Bates Piano Company, set up shop at the theatre 'and cashed in in every way possible'[6]), and one of her 81 shows was broadcast live by radio station WSB. Within weeks Columbia representatives were claiming that they were enjoying 'phenomenal sales of their records of Bessie Smith... the purchases have been made by both white and colored people, and the number of purchasers have been about equally divided between the races'.[7] In Baltimore a 'Bessie Smith Week' was held by record retailers to celebrate the star's astonishing success.

No sooner had the tour ended than, in September 1923, over seven days, Bessie was rushed off to New York where she took part in at least four recording sessions, the first of which yielded three takes of a song called 'Jail-House Blues', with its authorship credited initially to Clarence Williams, although it should have been credited to Smith herself: later releases give them co-authorship. Covered (in 1929) by Mamie Smith, with Porter Grainger on piano, the song's lyric alludes to bisexuality, with Bessie singing about sex with both a woman and with a male jail warden. Its opening verse, with the lines, 'Thirty days in jail with my back turned to the wall / Look here, Mister Jail-keeper, put another gal in my stall', suggest that the singer has been sexually abused while in prison, presumably by the warden or guards, and that now she wants another woman in the cell with her, either to take her place from the constant demands on her body, or to share her own intimate nights with. In the third verse, Bessie again refers to unwanted sex with the staff of the jail, 'You better stop your man from ticklin' me under my chin.'

Sex was big business in US prisons, and newspapers had been reporting on an epidemic of same-sex vice within the system for some time. In 1915 Thomas Mott Osborne, the warden of the notorious Sing Sing prison, was indicted on 'charges of perjury, mismanagement and immorality', not only amongst the inmates of the establishment, but that, 'he himself is guilty of unlawful and unnatural acts with five convicts... thereby rendering himself incapable of commanding respect, esteem and confidence of the inmates of said prison and rendering himself incapable of maintaining discipline.'[8]

Campaigning socialist publication the *Appeal to Reason* alerted its readers to the fact that 'Sex perversion is common in all prisons... It is not "nice" to discuss, or "refined" to contemplate, but it is an ugly fact nevertheless that homosexuality exists in all prisons.' Writer Kate Richards O'Hare, editor of another socialist paper, the *National Rip-Saw*, explained that vice was not only rife, but that prison governors and warders were making a tidy penny by turning a blind eye to the practice, and that, 'in the cases of young and unprotected girls', sex was 'actually demanded and enforced'[9] by older female inmates and prison staff.

Ninety years after Bessie recorded her version, British trio the Vinyl Closet issued their cover on the album *Pink, Black and Blues*. Led by veteran LGBTQ and Black civil rights activist Ted Brown, and featuring musicians Brett Lock and Chris Houston, the album featured covers of a dozen LGBTQ-themed blues songs as well as a couple of rock 'n' roll standards with queer associations. Says Brown:

> Brett and Chris are two white musicians from South Africa, and one of the reasons that they came to Britain is that they had been thrown out of their own country because they had been part of the anti-apartheid movement. They were very happy to

be involved in a project that was mainly about Black music. I knew that there had been revolutionary Black music of all kinds and that much of it was hidden, but I was a little surprised at how blatant some of the sexual terminology was, and to a certain extent I was surprised that people were so upfront about their sexuality. I expected that, when we came across these records, that the artists would be hinting at their sexuality rather than stating it as blatantly as they do.

I was genuinely surprised: I did not know that there were that many songs... and then to find that musicians such as Louis Armstrong had been involved, to discover that these songs were not simply being recorded by off-the-wall nutcases, but that top musicians were involved. That lead us to looking more into the music of New Orleans and all of those places, and how that lead on to rock 'n' roll.[10]

LGBTQ artists did not limit themselves to performing (or composing) the blues. Playing in Chicago in 1923, jazz orchestra Sammy Stewart and his Singing Syncopators (alternatively billed as Sammy Stewart and his Knights of Syncopation), was the first Black jazz orchestra to play Gershwin's *Rhapsody in Blue* in its entirety. Led by homosexual pianist Stewart, a man infamous for having turned down Louis Armstrong just as the young Satchmo was starting to make a name for himself, the band had started out, in Columbus, Ohio, as Sammy Stewart's Six Piece Colored Orchestra and had quickly built a solid reputation as a dance band of note, filling ballrooms and concert halls and on at least one occasion almost starting a riot as people rushed onto the dancefloor.

After a year playing at the Ritz in Detroit, where they were rated as 'one of the finest dance orchestras Detroit has yet heard',[11] the outfit moved to Chicago, where they began at the New Entertainer's Café, on East 35th Street, before winning a lucrative residency at Leo Salkin's Sunset Café, where local musicians including Jelly Roll Morton would often sit in with the band. Stewart and his jazz orchestra were regularly heard on radio, via the airwaves of KYW Chicago, and in 1925 Stewart made his first recording, the instrumental 'Copenhagen' (written by Charlie Davis) for the Puritan record company. 'The Sunset was the

biggest black and tan club west of New York,' recalled café manager
Joe Glaser, who would go on to manage Louis Armstrong. '[We] had
the cream of the black and tan shows, and there wasn't a big name
in coloured show business that didn't work for me at one time or
another. I spent more money for my shows than the Cotton Club.
Why, I once hired a band out of Columbus, Ohio – Sammy Stewart –
for thirty six hundred a week. But Sammy was a bad boy. He would
have been one of the biggest names in the business today if he didn't
go wrong.'[12]

Glaser's issue appears to have been with Stewart's sexuality: others
who worked with him insist that Stewart was an honest man who only
hired the best musicians, although he was rather fond of the bottle.
Drummer Harry Dial told jazz historian Ralph Gulliver that, 'The only
reason I can think of Joe Glaser saying he was bad was the fact that he
was a homo, but Chicago was full of them and it was commonplace.'
'I'm afraid it was true,' confirmed Roy Butler, 'although there was
never anything going on between him and any of his men, there
were enough stories leaking out to suggest that this was indeed so.
He was always outwardly correct and took girls to dances, etc., but I
think this was only to mislead. This could have indirectly affected his
career, and kept him from achieving his maximum potential, because
people thought different in those days. It was certainly unfortunate
because he had progressive ideas when dance music had no particular
direction. I'm also sorry because he gave me my first big break.' Bill
Stewart, a member of Sammy's band, felt that there was more than
just this behind Glaser's remarks. 'I believe the fact that Joe Glaser
couldn't dictate to Sammy Stewart as he pleased, with reference to
contracts and conditions (Glaser had a reputation around Chicago
in this respect) motivated the remark that "Sammy was a bad boy".
I have to admit that Sammy was stubborn as hell, and probably to
his own detriment much of the time. Also I believe Sammy was a
homosexual, but in all my years working with him I couldn't swear
to it, he was that discreet.'[13] Stewart would make further recordings
during the 1920s, including an instrumental version of 'My Man Rocks
Me' for Paramount and eight sides for Brunswick in Chicago in 1928,
and would go on to become one of the first Black musicians to join the

prestigious American Guild of Pipe Organists. He died at his home in New York, in August 1960.

In 1923 the Blues hopped across the pond. As early as September 1916, London-based Black seven-piece the Ciro's Club Coon Orchestra (originally from New York and known there as Dan Kildare's Clef Club Orchestra) had recorded a version of W. C. Handy's 'St. Louis Blues', but now New York dance teacher Morry M. Blake left his West 71st Street studio behind him, decamped to London and began to introduce Britain to the Blues-trot, 'a new dance... which is known as "Blues" in Paris and America. It is after the style of the fox-trot, and danced to fox-trot music. "Blues" music, however, is written in the same measure as the familiar fox-trot, but has a different strain. Ballroom fox-trots are played at about forty-eight bars to the minute, "Blues" should be played at thirty-five.'[14] Blake penned a few paragraphs on the new dance, and US-born, London-based pianist Joseph Gealblatt (who had Anglicised his name to Joseph George Gilbert) wrote a new song, 'The Blues-Trot Blues' to accompany this new fad which, as Blake himself wrote, 'embodies all of the characteristics of the original Darkie "Blues", and is a striking illustration of the specific difference between a "Blues" and a fox-trot'.[15] Gilbert's usual metier was in composing novelty songs, including 'Me and Jane in a Plane', 'When You Played the Organ And I Sang the Rosary' and 'Annie, You're Just Like My Mammy'.

Newspaper columnists argued about the steps involved (was it little more than a slower version of the foxtrot? Was there even a dedicated, recognisable dance at all?), but suddenly every dance school from Dublin to Doncaster was offering lessons in the 'blues dance', and carnivals, fairs and dancehalls were being serenaded by 'authentic' blues orchestras, including Madame Kettle's Southern Blues Dance Band, whose only association with the south was in that they came from the coastal town of Worthing in Sussex, and London's Cuban Blues Dance Band, whose career extended into the 1930s. Jack Hylton, Britain's top bandleader, recorded an instrumental version of the 'Blues-Trot Blues' as a follow-up to their recent cover of the Ager-Yellen tune 'Louisville Lou (The Vampin' Lady) Blues', and among the first batch of Blues-related releases from Columbia's British imprint was an instrumental cover of Porter Grainger's "Tain't Nobody's Business If I Do',* recorded by the Savoy Havana Band. Dozens of similar acts recorded instrumental blues numbers, emphasising the British record industries' belief that the blues was nothing more than a passing fancy with rewards to be reaped before it went out of fashion, like so many other fads enjoyed by Britain's 'bright young things'.

Part of the reason that this craze took hold and hung around for longer than many dance trends was that this new slow blues dance had found royal favour. The then Prince of Wales, the future King Edward VIII and his brother, Prince George, the Duke of Kent, were huge fans, said to be 'so fond of it that they make special requests for it at every ball they attend'. The pair so loved the dance that they scandalised polite society when they 'were caught introducing a slow "blues" kind of movement into a foxtrot'.[16] The brothers were bisexual, and often indiscreet: George was rumoured to have had affairs with, among many others, writer Cecil Roberts and with playwright and composer Noël Coward. 'We had a little dalliance,' Coward would later tell biographer Michael Thornton. 'It didn't last long. We were both very young at the time. He was absolutely enchanting and I never stopped loving him.'[17] Coward, who was inconsolable after Prince George's death, the result of a military air crash in 1942, also jumped on the blues-trot craze, penning the song 'Russian Blues' in 1923, which again was recorded by Jack Hylton and His Orchestra.

It was more than the music and the dance that made it across the pond, the performers were cleaning up too. Sophie Tucker proved a big hit when she performed in London in 1922, and she would continue to be popular: her 1926 recording of 'Some of These Days' sold over a million copies in Britain, an unprecedented number at that time, and she gave her final performance in Britain more than forty years after her London debut. She was so popular in Britain that when The Beatles starred at the Royal Variety Performance in November 1963, the entire audience understood Paul McCartney jokily introducing the song

---

* The spelling of the song's title would change frequently: this is how it appears on the label of the British 10-inch release.

132

'Till There Was You' as once having 'been recorded by our favourite American group, Sophie Tucker'.* Paul Robeson made his British debut in 1922, appearing in the play *Taboo*, and returned three years later to star in Eugene O'Neill's *The Emperor Jones*. In 1919 US jazz band the Southern Syncopated Orchestra – which at one point included Sidney Bechet among their members – made their first tour of Britain and Ireland: two years later, nine members of the outfit perished when their ship sank off the Scottish coast.

Black performers had been appearing on stage in Europe for some time, but more often than not as an exotic attraction, exemplified when Bert Williams, George Walker and the cast of *In Dahomey* performed in London. *In Dahomey* had been a sensation: shortly after its British debut, in April 1903, up-market monthly *The Tatler* even featured leading lady Aida Overton Walker demonstrating the cake walk to its readers, and Bert Williams was being hailed as a star on both sides of the Atlantic. Following its London season, the show embarked on a year-long tour of the provinces and of Ireland. Yet despite its box-office success, Black performers in Britain were often treated with disdain. Although reviews for the musical were uniformly excellent, columnists could not resist using phrases such as 'a black faced nigger of a despondent frame of mind' to describe Williams, who despite being West Indian appeared in blackface, or describing the revue patronisingly as 'an evening with the coons.'[18] At the Hippodrome, on Charing Cross Road, a blackmail racket perpetrated against LGBTQ cast and crew was exposed after two of the Black victims were assaulted in the street by the Hippodrome's hairdresser George Douglas, described by police as, 'The associate of a gang of thieves [who] made the lives of the coloured men there unpleasant by demanding money from them under threats of personal violence.'[19] However, attitudes towards the actors changed dramatically after the entire cast was invited to give a performance in front of King Edward VII at Buckingham Palace on 23 June 1903. From that night on Williams and Walker, and the other named players in the

---

\*   Despite what McCartney may have said from the stage of the Prince of Wales Theatre in London, Tucker never recorded 'Till There Was You'.

revue, were treated less as curiosities and more as star entertainers. The cast enjoyed performing in London, with one columnist noting that the 'whole company play London with a spirit which the "nigger comedian" is not encouraged to show in the States'.[20]

Alongside a passion for blues and jazz music, and for African American artists, the fashion for effeminacy found that it too was not limited to the big cities of America. Karyl Norman, one of America's leading female impersonators, had already proved a hit in Britain when he toured the country in 1921 and, like their US counterparts, voices in the British press were soon raising their concerns that the new wave of permissiveness that had followed the end of the war was leading to a society overrun with sexual switch-hitters. Harley Street physician Jane Walker complained that the British male was 'a soft, degenerate, spat-wearing, cigarette-smoking mollycoddle... and a great deal more that is even worse. He is, in fact, a mass of effeminate habits, the very antithesis of his sturdy forbears'.[21]

Britain's affection for jazz and blues came at an inopportune time, and although Black performers might have claimed that they were getting a better deal in Europe, where audiences were more receptive and segregation – although often imposed in venues – was less prevalent, this was not always the case. Less than five years after the end of the First World War, many British musicians and variety hall performers were struggling to find work, and venues were fighting to fill seats. Around a million young men had died as a result of the conflict – either in battle or later, from their wounds – and the Spanish Flu epidemic which coincided with the end of the war saw off another 250,000 potential audience members. The influx of Black American artists at such a volatile time stirred up racial tension and caused Members of Parliament to ask questions in the House of Commons about the validity of work permits given to performers.

Albert Voyce, chair of the Variety Artistes Federation (which, in 1966 would merge with the actors' union, Equity) was one of the many voices complaining about British artists being overlooked in favour of this imported talent, while revealing that segregation was still being practiced in certain venues. 'We vigorously protest against the importation of aliens "en bloc", and coloured ones at that; more so when there are so many hundreds of British white men and women entertainers unemployed,' he told the *Era*. 'We contend there is no demand for an all-coloured performance when English men and women entertainers are starving.'[22] Shortly afterwards he expanded on this, telling reporters that, 'I think it would be a disgrace if permission were granted to exploit imported black men and women in this way, while hundreds of talented British artists are on the verge of want for lack of engagements. We have no objections to American artists coming to England. In fact, 90 per cent of those who come here join our federation and are welcome. There are also in England Negro turns, most respectable and most decent, who behave themselves and keep their place. But we view with the greatest apprehension a cabaret where black artists would actually mix with the white folk at the tables.'[23] Voyce's attitude was based, in part at least, on the 'misbehaviour' of some of the cast and chorus of *In Dahomey*, and on the arrest and subsequent incarceration of an actor appearing in *Uncle Tom's Cabin* for stabbing a man in self-defence.

In response to his concerns over Black artists fraternising with white patrons, the venue in question, the Empire, announced that it would erect a rail to stop Black musicians leaving the stage. The Musicians' Union also raised their concerns. 'There are something like two thousand of our members out of work,' said an official, 'many of them due to the introduction of American Negro bands, now in favour with certain dance clubs. British musicians could play quite as well.'[24] Visiting Black artists would continue to experience bigotry in British venues, and segregation was not limited to US theatres. In 1930, despite his huge success in *Othello* at the Savoy Theatre in London, where he took twenty curtain calls on his debut, Paul Robeson and his friends were embarrassed when he was refused a seat in the stalls at another production. Management would allow him to sit in a private box with his party, but not in the front stalls with white patrons.

While Britain was getting a taste for the blues, back in Chicago Ink Williams was desperate to add to his roster of female blues singers... and the one name he wanted was the woman who had been filling tent shows and theatres for close on two decades, Gertrude 'Ma' Rainey.

135

When she arrived in Chicago in late 1923 to appear at the Monogram Theatre, Williams made his move, and that December, Ma made her debut recordings for Paramount. The company had no studio of its own in the city at that point: Williams worked out of a small office on South State Street and recordings were made at either the Marsh Recording Laboratories or the Rodeheaver studio, both on Wabash Avenue. During that session she immediately made it clear where her sexual preferences lay, cutting a song that obliquely references sex between two lesbian or bisexual women.

It had taken a while to persuade her to come into the studio, and by the time she did Bessie, Clara, and Mamie Smith, Alberta Hunter, Ethel Waters, Lucille Bogan, Lucille Hegamin and Viola McCoy – pretty much all of the women classic blues singers – had already been there, done that. Following her own recorded debut, Bessie's fame had grown so quickly that, while appearing at the Globe Theatre in Detroit, 'Thousands of people were turned away [and] eight policemen were required to maintain order at the entrance of the theatre.'[25]

But that was not through lack of trying: like Bessie Smith, she had been sought out by various record companies, but she was too busy to take time out to visit Paramount's Chicago offices. Had the record companies earned a reputation for playing fair with Black artists her attitude may have been different, but why waste her valuable time with this poorly paid fancy when she had been doing quite nicely touring with her own troupe, known variously as Madam Rainey's Gold Beauties[26] or Madam Rainey's Southern Beauties,[27] and was already recognised as a major box-office draw. In 1922 she renamed that outfit the Broadway Strutters and, breaking away from the T.O.B.A. circuit temporarily, they joined the John T. Wortham company that March. Wortham's Joyland fair toured extensively throughout 1922, with Ma managing a sideshow, dubbed Dixieland, where she and her company of 'fourteen of the best negro [sic] performers in the United States'[28] held court.

Referred to variously as 'Madame Rainey', 'the Prima Donna of Dixieland', and the 'Million-Dollar Highbrow'[29] – Wortham billed his star attraction as 'Madam Rainey, the Million Dollar Blues singer', and boasted that 'her Broadway Strutters [are] the very best colored performers that time and money could put together. This is not an old plantation show like one generally sees but an up-to-date musical show.'[30] Ma's repertoire included popular hits of the day, such as 'Stingaree Blues', which New Orleans-based singer Esther Bigeou had recorded for Okeh in November 1921, and that Alberta Hunter would cover the following year. In late 1922, in a show of generosity, when two members of the Strutters decided to marry Ma dipped into her own pocket to pay for the wedding reception, although she insisted that the wedding take place on stage for the entertainment of the audience. With the tent shows closed for the season, the Broadway Strutters began 1923 in theatres, with Wortham 'emphatically declaring that the Madam Rainey company would be with his attractions next year'.[31] Wortham knew he had a huge draw in Ma Rainey and was keen to keep her and her troupe under contract, leaving her no opportunity to record before the end of the touring season.

Keen to catch up with her rivals, Williams had Ma record eight sides accompanied by Lovie Austin and Her Blues Serenaders, a grand name for a three-piece band featuring Tommy Ladnier and Jimmy O'Bryant, who had both previously played on sessions for Alberta Hunter. First into the stores was the coupling of 'Bo-Weavil Blues', a traditional blues song which is given authorship to Rainey, and Thomas Dorsey's 'Last Minute Blues'. The disc was credited to Madame 'Ma' Rainey, immediately establishing her credentials as the preeminent blues woman: in their 1924 catalogue, Paramount boasted that she was, 'The only Blues singer of the Race elevated to the title of "Madame".' On 12 December, Ma signed the rights to her own compositions recorded at these sessions to the Chicago Music Publishing Company, controlled by Ink Williams on behalf of Paramount.

Ma recorded at least two extant versions of 'Bo-Weavil Blues', one of which was issued on disc in April 1924. The song features the lines 'I don't want no man to put no sugar in my tea / I don't want no man to put no sugar in my tea / Some of them are so evil, I'm 'fraid they might poison me.' If Ma has decided that she doesn't need a man to bring her sugar, maybe she would like a woman to do it instead, especially as, in the song's coda, she states that she is 'gettin' tired of sleeping by myself'. The song was covered the following year by Bessie Smith

137

(coupled with another Ma Rainey original, 'Moonshine Blues') but with the lines altered to 'I don't want no sugar put into my tea', losing any potential lesbian references.

Ink Williams was keen to get Ma back out on the road, to help promote her recordings. He called his friend, pianist Thomas A. Dorsey, and asked him if he could put together a touring band for his latest signing. Dorsey recalled seeing her when he was a child, and of how he had marvelled at her performance while he was selling bottles of carbonated drinks at the 81 in Atlanta, but despite her already recording his compositions, this was the first time he met her properly. 'I travelled with her almost four years... I went to her home in Columbus, Georgia. I knew her folk and her brothers and things like that. [She was] lovely. She paid the help. Other blues singers, the musicians would start for 'em, but they'd quit and go somewhere else, and they might not get paid.'[32]

Pianist Billie Pierce, then still a teenager, recalled meeting both Ma and Bessie early in her career:

[Around 1923] I started with Billy Mack and his traveling show out of New Orleans. That was Mack's Merry Makers. We traveled and worked lots of places and little towns in Florida and Louisiana. I worked two weeks for Bessie Smith before that, at the Belmont Theater in Pensacola, that's when Clarence Williams, her pianist, was taken sick. Bessie Smith was good too – she was a good entertainer. She wanted me to go but I didn't care to travel then. I was too young to hit the road. Then I worked with Mama Rainey as a chorus girl – I was just a chorus girl with Mama Rainey, I didn't play piano for her or nothin'. Only thing I can tell you about Mama Rainey was – she had a real good voice; a heavy gross voice for the blues and everybody liked her singing.[33]

Ma's trombone player, Al Wynn, recalled that:

Ma was a wonderful person to work with – very lovable disposition. She was always doing nice things and taking everyone as if they were her own kids because at that time we were very young.

138

And contrary to what most people believe – Mother – Ma Rainey wasn't old at that time although she was well known and well established because she started so young, she was a child prodigy in her time. She enjoyed doing pleasant things and the people were very nice to her all over the country and we were making nice salary for the time. She had started as a young girl and I had the pleasure of meeting her mother and her grandmother who were still living at the time and going to her home in Columbus, Georgia. They were very active and remarkable people. Ma Rainey was rather heavy – she wasn't attractive at all, but what she lacked in looks she made up in personality and sweetness – her heart was so big it made her beautiful in the eyesight of everyone that got to know her.[34]

# 10

# Peachtree Man Blues

*'Especially vulnerable was the hermaphrodite who has the
characteristics of both sexes – female breasts and male genitals.
With the characteristic combination of pithiness and pitilessness
that labelled a legless man a "Halfy," the hermaphrodite was
known as "Peaches" or "Peach Tree".*[1] – Paul Oliver

From a lowly start during the very earliest days of theatre, when all roles on the stage were filled by men[*], by the 1920s, female impersonators – including Julian Eltinge, Bert Savoy, Francis Renault, Karyl Norman and Andrew Tribble – had become major stars, cast in Hollywood films, filling theatres, performing in front of crowned heads of state and garnering hundreds of column inches in newspapers and magazines as their public feverishly lapped up their exploits. During the late Victorian era and early 20th century, especially in Britain, there had been a fashion for male impersonators too, with artists such as Vesta Tilley becoming an international sensation, and the scandalous Annie Hindle, the 'first out-and-out "male impersonator" New York's

---

[*] In Britain, women were banned from the stage until the 1660s; up until that point all female roles were played by men.

stage had ever seen',[2] who arrived in America from Hertfordshire in England in the 1860s. By 1870 Hindle, who had been appearing on stage in male attire since they were a child, was being billed throughout the States as the 'Great Annie Hindle' and was being compared to William Lingard, a female impersonator who had made his own US stage debut just two years earlier.

In 1886 Hindle caused a national outrage when they married 'a pretty little brunette of 25'[3] named Annie Ryan, and had female impersonator Gilbert Sarony act as best man. Five years later the pair were in the press again, following Ryan's death, profiled in a rather vivid – and, for the time, surprisingly sympathetic – description of the funeral service: 'Here she was a mourner by the side of her dead – that dead a pretty woman, and in life the lawful wife of the woman who now shed tears over her coffin. The wife of a woman! The expression sounds absurd, yet it is absolutely, literally correct. Annie Ryan, the wife, was dead and Annie Hindle, the husband, was burying her. No stage romance is this, no fable of grotesque, but simply proof anew that truth is indeed stranger than fiction.'[4] The two had lived openly as a married couple (a solemnised priest, the Reverend E. H. Brooks, had performed the ceremony), in a community where, 'The neighbors respected them. The outer world did not disturb them with their gossip.'[5] In June 1892, Hindle was married again to a Louise Spangehl. Again, a serving minister conducted the ceremony – this time the Reverend G. C. Baldwin of Troy, in New York state – and, as they had for their previous marriage – Hindle told the Baptist minister that they were in fact a man, Charles Edward Hindle.

In Black vaudeville several women would make a name for themselves by characterising men, including Dorothy Paxton, a blues singer and male impersonator known as 'The only girl baritone in Chicago', Kitty Dover, whose career lasted well into the 1930s and included appearances with the Marx Brothers and Karyl Norman, and Lillyn Brown (the second wife of the great-great-great uncle of Meghan, Duchess of Sussex) who led her own band, the Jazz-Bo Syncopators. Brown recorded 'Bad-Land Blues' for Emerson in 1921, a song that takes on a distinctly queer edge when you realise that she is singing in character as a man, and is threatening retribution on the cad who

141

stole Brown's gal. The flip side, Tom Delaney's 'Jazz-Me Blues' features Brown singing the line 'It sounds so peculiar because the music's queer'.

Perhaps the most famous of these was the bisexual Gladys Smith, who in the second half of the 1920s would marry comedian Jimmie Ferguson (star of the *Chocolate Dandies*) and, as Gladys Ferguson, become the lover (according to contemporary gossip) of Bessie Smith. Black female impersonator Jake Collins was touring as early as 1900 with white-run circus Tony Ashton's Olympic Show, and Leroy Bland was featured with Mahara's Minstrels, the troupe led by W. C. Handy.

Some of these early drag kings and queens became huge stars. Eltinge, whose 'illusions' were much more feminine than the stereotypical harridans and pantomime dames, the style adopted by Andrew Tribble and comedian Bert Savoy, even had his own line of cosmetics and a national monthly magazine. Born William J. Dalton in Newtonville, Massachusetts in 1881, Eltinge began performing on stage in female roles before he was a teenager but was severely punished by his father for his girlish ways, which led to young Billy doing his best to cover up his sexuality: he once declared that 'I am not gay, I just like pearls', and his publicity boasted about the number of fistfights he had been involved in. However, encouraged by his mother he continued to pursue a career on the stage. He made his Broadway debut in 1904, and two years later, while touring in Europe, he was invited to perform for King Edward VII at Windsor Castle. He appeared on the big screen with Rudolph Valentino, made several silent comedies, and had a Broadway theatre named after him.

Eltinge's fanbase grew: he appeared on stage in musicals, wrote songs (he had his own trial session for Victor in 1913, recording a demo version of his stage hit 'The Leader of the Suffragettes'), and built his own, antique-filled Hollywood mansion, Villa Capistrano, where the confirmed bachelor lived with his mother and entertained extravagantly. In 1908 it was announced that Julian was to wed Eva Tanguay, a Canadian singer and actor billed as 'The girl who made vaudeville famous' (and a major influence on Mae West), and although they would not officially marry, the pair held a mock ceremony, exchanging rings with Eva dressed in traditional male formal attire and Julian as the blushing bride.

His principal rival was Karyl Norman, who began his stage career in 1911 and was billed as the 'Creole Fashion Plate', although wags and snippy critics (and Groucho Marx, according to his brother Harpo) would refer to him as the 'queer old fashion plate'. Like Eltinge, Norman was known for his lavish gowns, most of which were made for him by his devoted mother, and he was equally keen to quash any gossip about his sexuality. Again, like Eltinge he had an international following, but although Eltinge had become famous outside of the States for his many film appearances, Karyl Norman had travelled to and performed extensively in Europe. In Britain in 1921 he confounded critics, who genuinely believed that Miss Karyl Norman was indeed a 'pretty Creole revue actress'.[6] Norman too talked of marriage in the press and, in 1922, was briefly engaged to acrobat and male impersonator Ruth Budd. Actor Fifi D'Orsay, who appeared with him in the *Greenwich Village Follies* in 1924, said that Norman was, 'Marvellous. He was a great performer and I loved him. Karyl Norman was a wonderful guy, beloved and respected by everybody, although he was a gay boy, and for the gay boys in those days it was harder for them than it is today.'[7] Norman was a fine singer and a keen songwriter, and although he would not record himself, several other acts covered his songs. Bert Savoy's performance style was a million miles away from the more feminine impersonations of Julian Eltinge or Karyl Norman, appearing on stage as part of a comedy double act in a costume far more dowdy than those Norman and Eltinge boasted of spending thousands of dollars on, but he did leave us with a brace of recordings, made with his stage partner Jay Brennan, 'You Must Come Over' and 'You Don't Know the Half of It', issued by Vocalion in 1923. Mae West's 'come up and see me' catchphrase is reputed to have been based on Savoy's own 'you must come over'. Savoy's character was the 'tart with a heart', a red-haired, wisecracking former sex worker whose stock-in-trade was comic tales told at the expense of her friend Margie – a schtick used by camp comics and female impersonators ever since.

Savoy died in a freak accident in June 1923, when he was struck by lightning on Long Island, killing him and his companion, singer and dancer Jack Vincent, instantly; his last words were reported to be

'Mercy, ain't Miss God cutting up something awful?' His body remained unclaimed by relatives, and it was left to his stage partner Jay Brennan to organise the funeral, which was attended by more than 1,500 people, with police deployed to manage the crowd. At the time of his death, it was reported that Savoy and Brennan had been earning $1,500 a week. Columnist O. O. McIntyre called Savoy 'The gayest of female impersonators', and stated that his passing affected Broadway so badly that 'it was as though the same electric bolt that killed Savoy had stunned the street'.[8] Although devastated by his loss, Brennan would attempt to rebuild his career with a new partner, Stanley Rogers, who 'assumed the clothing, voice and mannerisms of Savoy',[9] but without the same success.

One of those at Savoy's funeral, perhaps the most controversial of all of these early drag stars, was Francis Renault, born Antonio Auriemma in Naples in 1893. Renault began his career on stage as a boy soprano, before becoming 'Auriema' when he was still in his teens, when he first wore the fabulous gowns he became famous for. Unlike the ever-so-manly Eltinge, Renault (or Auriema) would wear these stunning creations – complete with beaded headdresses – in the street in towns where he was appearing, which he claimed that he did to drum up publicity for his performances. Unsurprisingly this tactic led to his being arrested several times.

Edward Russell, a contemporary of Eltinge, Tribble, Norman, Renault and Savoy, who appeared in drag as 'The famous Evelyn Russell' and whose speciality was an impersonation of Eltinge's former fiancée Eva Tanguay, recalled that, 'We were treated as artists and ladies... We used to carry on with all the stars. We dated millionaires and all that but it was all under cover, you had to be in those days.'[10] But it was not all hi-jinks and lavish lifestyles: Russell recalled that blackface singer Al Jolson was unfriendly, 'He never liked any of the girls and wouldn't fool with us,' and the threat of arrest was never far away. 'Once upstate, we all did five days because we were on the corner with one of the girls who didn't like to wear wigs. She had let her hair grow a little. We weren't carrying on, just standing there. It was rough sometimes... The only time we got into trouble was when we worked the stags. They would raid us. One time they even got the piano player too. But they were fun. The fellows loved us. It was not what we did but how we did it, know what I mean?'[11]

All of these performers can be seen as antecedents of today's drag kings and queens, but outside of the theatre or concert hall, in the circus, the sideshow and the freak exhibit, alongside sword swallowers, snake handlers, bearded ladies and sundry performing animals, a far more peculiar act was dragging the curious off the streets and through the flap in the canvas. In 1860, P. T. Barnum added Miss Dora Dawson, the 'double voiced singer', who possessed a 'deep and powerful tenor and sweet and delicate soprano voice', to his latest venture, America's first public aquarium. Billing her as 'half man, half woman',[12] Barnum dressed Dora in an outfit that made her appear as 'a fashionably costumed gentleman' on one side, but 'an elegantly dressed lady'[13] when she turned around. It was a simple illusion, but one that would be used to great effect by others for decades to follow. Dawson became one of the star attractions of Barnum's Aquarial Gardens in Boston, and after leaving his employ she continued to find work in vaudeville for many years.

Dora Dawson set the standard for those that followed. The half man, half woman would appear on stage with their costume split down the middle, head to toe: one side would be half of a fashionable evening gown or cocktail dress, the other something more manly, anything from a tuxedo to a Tarzan-style loincloth. The 'female' side of their body was shaved, plucked and wore elaborate make-up, while the 'male' side would make an ostentatious show of muscles and body hair.

From the mid-1890s, the exotically monikered Lalah Coolah was a major drawing card on the touring circuit: 'He, she or it has been viewed by great crowds,' the *Pittsburgh Commercial Gazette* reported, 'And all say it is a wonder. His dual features – the combination of the sexes – is so plainly marked that the most skeptikal [sic] observer frankly yields the palm to the man Venus.'[14] In Boston, the following year, while on a tour of dime museums, fairs and nickelodeons, customers were able to witness the spectacle of 'this remarkable human freak' exchanging marriage vows with 'a young lady from Newark, N.J.',[15] although the paying guests at their wedding would have had no idea that Lalah and his bride were pulling the same stunt at pretty much every venue they appeared at. Sadly, in 1898 the pair's son died in infancy, but with bread to put on the table Lalah was soon back out on the road, this time without his wife, and continued appearing in museums, fairs and carnival sideshows until well into the 1920s. Called 'The Creator's strangest marvel', Lalah's publicity claimed that, 'ever since the birth of this strange being scientists have been amazed when brought into contact with it... the very wisest of doctors have been nonplussed and dumbfounded.'[16]

Albert Alberta, 'Perhaps the most unsolvable, the most unfathomable of all the freaks of Mother Nature', was a major attraction on Coney Island in the late 1920s:

The half man, half woman, featured with 'A Night at Coney Island,' the big side-show vaudeville attraction which is now at Loew's Hillside theatre. Temperamental, frequently morose, sometimes it will be Alberta who predominates, and then this strange freak will wrap a rich silk negligee about It, display that shorter and finely shaped leg and foot in its high-heeled shoe, and take to knitting and sewing. And then again It is Albert who holds sway, and the moods of the athlete, the man, will break forth. An hermaphrodite, Albert-Alberta is also an enigma, put into this world for some strange reason, perhaps, and living its days until the span is completed.[17]

Albert Alberta Karas, often billed as the 'European Enigma', claimed to have been born in France in November 1899, the first of six children, and named Alberta at birth. According to their own biography, which appeared in a four-page programme distributed at their stage shows, they were:

Brought up as a girl, and mingled with girls at school and at play with no idea as to what was taking place within my body. At the age of ten years and eight months or thereabouts, the left side of my body was growing out of proportion to the right side. My mother became alarmed and called the family physician.

146

A thorough examination disclosed that I was developing the characteristics and form of a female in and on the left side of my body, while the right side was developing the characteristics and form of a male.

The biography stated that the youngest of their siblings, Albert, was also 'double sexed, yet he possesses all other outward appearances of a handsome athletic young man... He has a manly voice, he dresses and mingles with men, loves men's sports, etc. but it seems that Mother Nature in this case is again at work and that my brother Albert is destined to some day be called my sister Alberta. As a matter of fact he is today the only boy able to nurse a baby.' Albert Alberta, Albert (the one who was not yet called Alberta) and their troupe toured extensively, initially as part of the revue *A Night at Coney Island*, along with sword swallowers, snake charmers, human skeletons and Henry the Spider Boy, and later as 'the Original Albert Alberta Sex Family', filling theatres around the country and wowing audiences.

Plenty of similar artists would follow in their stiletto steps, including Leo-Leora, Freda-Fred, George-Ette 'The double bodied Venus', and Gene and Eugene, but Karas was not what they claimed to be, and it is doubtful that any of the other members of the troupe were true hermaphrodites either. Karas was, in fact, a female impersonator named Harry Caro who, it is said, fashioned his one female 'breast' from a bag filled with birdseed. Despite the fakery, Albert Alberta would continue to find work until well into the 1940s, finishing out their career at Hubert's Museum (better known as Hubert's Flea Circus), on New York's 42nd Street, where other acts included Lady Olga the bearded lady, and a strange, hook-nosed ukulele player called Larry Love, who would later find fame as Tiny Tim.

Genuine hermaphrodites were rare, but not unheard of, in show business. In 1875 an un-named hermaphrodite was working as a fortune teller in a French café in Greenfield, Massachusetts, but the half man, half woman who exhibited themselves at Baltimore's Dime Museum two years later was more than likely another man with one shaved leg and a birdseed breast. The audience at the Wonderland Theatre in Scranton, Pennsylvania, got more than they bargained for when they

147

paid their five cents to see Gus Richards, the half man, half woman who played there alongside Serpentello the contortionist, Mellini the magician and the 'live rooster orchestra', and Richards attacked his pianist because he 'did not play the music right'.[18]

For decades now, people have been asking questions about the sexuality and gender identity of Guilford 'Peachtree' Payne, one of the most enigmatic and obscure of all the queer blues performers. 'Peachtree' issued just one record during his career, and he would have been forgotten if not for musicians like blues guitarist Mike Bloomfield, or music historian J. D. Doyle, curator of the Queer Music Heritage website, showing an interest in his story.

Born on 4 August 1882, in Madison, Indiana, Horace Gilford Payne's mother, Margaret Stapp (also known as Margera and Margerite), was unwed and just 17 years old when her son was born: at the end of October she married the child's father, 23-year-old Gilford Payne. Throughout their lives both father and son would have to contend with people misspelling their name, although 'Gilford', without a 'u' is the version bestowed officially, and the one that was used on Peachtree's draft card and in his signature. Two years later Margaret gave birth to their first daughter, Sophia. A few days after his 7th birthday, young Horace's parents presented him with a baby brother, Charles, and in 1891 a second daughter, Goldy, was added to the burgeoning clan. A third son, who was never named, was born in 1892 and died shortly after his first birthday: his grave is unmarked and he is simply listed on cemetery records as 'Infant Payne'. Sister Evadore (Eva) came along in March 1897, completing the family.

In 1898, and still only 15, Gilford Payne Junior joined the predominantly African American 48th US Volunteer Infantry. He served during that year's Spanish-American War, a conflict in which around 2,500 American men died – the vast majority not as the result of being injured by the enemy, but from the ravages of disease. That conflict led directly to the Philippine-American War, in which around 18,000 combatants were killed and up to 1,000,000 Filipino civilians lost their lives, many through famine and disease. At some point Gilford was injured. There is no explanation of what ailment he suffered, apart from the mention of a 'scar on right elbow' on his World War Two draft card – more a distinguishing mark than a debilitating disfigurement. The same document confirms that he was in receipt of a disability pension as a result of his involvement in the Spanish-American War, but service records show that he had not lost any limbs, did not suffer from a lack of mobility and nor did he suffer from any facial disfigurement. Had Gilford Junior suffered the kind of injury that might later lead to his earning a reputation as a hermaphrodite? Injuries sustained by combatants during the First World War lead directly to New Zealand-born surgeon Harold Gillies pioneering the use of reconstructive plastic surgery, but at the time that Gilford Payne was invalided out of the service, there was no such treatment available for whatever the injury was.

Payne's father, Gilford Senior, died in 1905: a firefighter employed at Madison's electric light station, he 'fell dead of heat penetration during a heatwave[19]': a post-mortem later discovered that Gilford Senior had been living with heart disease, and the heat had brought about a heart attack. At some point before the end of the decade, Horace Gilford Payne married Mollie Bell, a Kentucky-born washerwoman, and the pair set up home at 314 North 11th Street, Terre Haute, Indiana.

It is not known how or when the younger Gilford Payne began to supplement his meagre disability allowance by playing the blues, but by 1914 he was playing the piano in Ben Murry's café, on the corner of Cherry and North Third streets in Terre Haute, and by the spring of 1920 he was on the road. Billed as 'The champion of all Blues Chirpers',[20] an epithet more usually awarded to a female singer, it is possible that Payne also worked as a female impersonator: on 25 March an artist using the name 'Peachtree' appeared on the stage of Chicago's Dreamland Café alongside a line-up that included singer Ollie Powers, eccentric dancer Willie Coret, a display of tango dancing, and Chaplin impersonator John Higgins. The acts had come together to provide entertainment for a party given in honour of Broadway Jimmey, 'one of the world's foremost eccentric dancers' and a member of the cast of the musical revue, *See-Saw*.

Payne made his only recordings, for Okeh in Chicago, on 25 October 1923, making him one of the earliest male African American

149

singers to record and release a blues number, doing so before Papa Charlie Jackson and Daddy Stovepipe, whose debut releases were both recorded and issued in 1924, and a month before Sylvester Weaver recorded 'Guitar Blues' and 'Guitar Rag' for Okeh, the first record from a male blues guitarist. It would be another two years before the introduction of electrical recording made it possible to catch the essence of male folk blues and Delta blues singers such as Robert Johnson and Blind Lemon Jefferson, and for the first half of the 1920s, record companies had invested all of their time and efforts into signing female singers, especially those with vaudeville experience who knew how to project, an ability that gave them the edge when it came to the basic, and archaic, studio set-up. The only Black men who had recorded blues vocals had been stage stars like Bert Williams, jazz singers, or comedians such as Charles Anderson, who recorded a version of 'Baby Seals Blues' under the title 'Sing 'Em Blues' at around the same time as Payne recorded his two songs. Anderson was 'a very good female impersonator'[21] according to Ethel Waters, who often appeared as a mammy on stage, as well as a gifted yodeller who had appeared on the same bill as Bessie Smith on several occasions. 'Baby Seals Blues' was written as a duet and Anderson had been singing the song, in character as a mammy, on stage for more than a decade, yet he missed an opportunity to showcase his range by only singing the male part for the recording. That being said, a number of times during 'Sing 'Em Blues' Anderson goes into a high falsetto, and his later recordings demonstrate both his incredible range and control: on the 1924 release 'Yodle Song – Coo Coo' [sic], he sustains a high note for thirty seconds without drawing breath. Anderson had also been the first Black man to sing the vocal version of W. C. Handy's great hit 'St. Louis Blues', and had impressed the young Ethel Waters so much that she wrote to Handy for permission to perform the song when she joined the Braxton and Nugent troupe.

Within a few weeks, Okeh issued 'You Don't Worry My Mind', backed with 'Peachtree Man Blues', with the singer credited on the label as Guilford (Peachtree) Payne. Payne was accompanied on both recordings by bandleader and pianist Eddie Heywood, who had also accompanied Charles Anderson on his debut. Heywood had played piano at the 81 Theatre in Atlanta for over a decade, and it was in Atlanta, in June 1923, that he had accompanied Lucille Bogan on her recording of his own composition 'The Pawn Shop Blues', the first blues recording made outside of Chicago or New York. His son, Eddie Heywood Junior, would later play with Billie Holiday.

Both compositions were credited to Guilford Payne, and copyright in 'You Don't Worry My Mind' was registered on 12 November 1923. On both sides of the disc Payne handles the lead vocals, interspersing them with short bursts of female impersonation and the occasional falsetto trill that would put Little Richard – or Charles Anderson – to shame. On 'You Don't Worry My Mind' he only employs his female voice for one line, but 'Peachtree Man Blues' is almost a duet, with Peachtree taking male and female adult roles, just as Frankie 'Half-Pint' Jaxon would do, as well as impersonating children's voices on one verse.

The erotic aspects of the peach – its voluptuous shape like a pert backside or a buxom cleavage, and its juicy flesh – have been providing songwriters with the perfect metaphor for sexuality for decades, and there's not a lot in the lyrics of 'Peachtree Man Blues' to mark it out as particularly queer on first listen. But, as blues guitarist Artie 'The Cat' Renkel explained, 'Peach-tree was a common term for a hermaphrodite in the deep south and still is... That was before the age of sex-change operations and stuff, and some of these guys made a living as transvestite prostitutes. Hey, to each his own, you know?'[22] Several writers, researchers and musicians have claimed that Peachtree was a hermaphrodite, including LGBTQ historian St Sukie de la Croix, who states in his book *Chicago Whispers* that Peachtree was 'a man gifted with women's breasts (peaches) and male genitals'.

In his book *Blues Fell This Morning*, blues historian Paul Oliver states that, 'Especially vulnerable was the hermaphrodite who has the characteristics of both sexes – female breasts and male genitals... The hermaphrodite was known as "Peaches" or "Peach Tree." This abnormality produces complex emotions and passions that could not easily be controlled, and in the teeming communities of the Black Belts it could not be kept private. Such a victim of chance, "Peach Tree" Payne, sang of his troubles, imitating the voices with a rare facility that his state had accorded him.'[23] It's a story that is often told, but any hard evidence to back this up has been lost in the mists of time, if indeed it ever existed. All of the tales about Peachtree's gender stem back to this one quote, which first appeared in 1960, when Payne was still alive. It is unlikely that he was aware that he was being written about, but that is something we can never know.

By 1930 Payne had a split from Mollie, had taken on a second wife, Ethel, a school teacher, and had moved to Detroit: the couple were still together ten years later. Although Peachtree Payne would not release another record, he continued to perform (on the 1930 census he's listed as a musician working on the radio), singing and playing piano for many years afterwards.

With few genuine hermaphrodites on the ground, the history of vaudeville and of circus tent freak shows is littered with fakes, including Josephine Joseph, who pattered her career after Albert Alberta and who starred in Tod Browning's era-defining horror film, *Freaks*, released in 1932.

Two years before she appeared on the big screen, she had been drummed out of England after she and her husband, George Wass (who also acted as her manager) were taken to court and charged after it was claimed that they 'knowingly by false pretences did cause certain money to be paid by certain persons unknown for admission to an exhibition called Josephine-Joseph, with intent to cheat and defraud.'[24] The police brought the case 'to protect the gullible public'.

'She might be without breast on one side, but that does not make her half-woman, half-man,' said police superintendent Hannan, of the Blackpool police, 'as breasts can be removed by operation and muscles can be developed by physical exercise. The only person who could be called half-woman half-man is hermaphrodite.' His colleague, Inspector Elliott, who went to see Josephine at Blackpool's Central Beach, reported that the 'woman's right leg was bare, and she was wearing a sandal on the right foot; she was wearing a black stocking on the left leg and a lady's shoe on the left foot. The hair was brushed from the right side to the left, giving the appearance that it was cut short the right side. The right side represented a male and the other a female.' Wass introduced her to the paying public as 'Josephine Joseph, half-woman, half-man, brother and sister in one body,' telling the audience that her 'breast on the right side was like that of man and the left like that of a female. He said there was a difference in the eyebrows, and that one side of the skull was larger than the other. He also said that one of her arms was longer than the other, adding: 'There is no artificial padding used; what you have seen, ladies and gentlemen, is the work of the Almighty.'[25] Waas asked his wife (born Antoinette Sambor) to tell her enraptured audience about how she felt, and she replied, in a masculine voice, 'At times I feel like a man, but act like a woman.' Switching to a more feminine voice, Josephine added, 'At other times, I feel like a woman and act like a man.'[26] Josephine escaped prosecution, but George Waas – who had been offered the opportunity to have his wife examined by a court-appointed physician – was fined £25 and announced, 'that he would give the show up and leave the country'.[27]

Superintendent Hannan and his men were clearly on a crusade to rid the seaside resort of undesirables. Just two weeks before George and Josephine were in court, Hannan prosecuted another fake hermaphrodite, Robert Arthur Cox, for conspiring to defraud the public. The 22-year-old Cox, of Rugby, had also been plying his trade in Blackpool as a hermaphrodite named Phil-Phyllis. When the police raided the amusement arcade where Phil-Phyllis was appearing, they found that:

> The left side of Cox's body, which he represented as that of a woman, was covered with lingerie from the shoulder, and on the left foot was a lady's shoe. His right side, which he represented as that of a man, was bare, and wore a man's shoe on his right foot. He had a band round his head, a quantity of hair protruding from the left side. Cox, in his remarks to the people, said that he was 22 years of age, and was born in America... His abnormality was first discovered when he was boy. When he died, his body would not buried or cremated, for it had already been sold to the American Research Hospital.[28]

The local police insisted that they, 'offered no objection whatever to freak shows where there was genuine abnormality of nature, but the contention here was that this was sham, a deliberate dressing of a man to appear if he was physically half man and half woman.'[29]

By November of that year Cox (using the name Robert St John) was back at work, this time in Hull, working the circuit as Senora-Senorita. Like Albert Alberta, Cox and his manager handed out pamphlets that included a fictional biography of Senora-Senorita, alongside a brief history of hermaphrodites. Posters outside the sideshow booth announced to passers-by that Cox was 'The talk of six countries' and asked, 'Is it brother and sister in one body?' Once customers had handed over the threepenny entrance fee they were allowed to enter the booth, where they would see him 'exhibited on the platform. He exhibited to them that part of his limbs had the development of a man and part the development of a woman. He then said, "This is a genuine show, not a fake," and that he was prepared to be examined by a medical man or a midwife.'[30] Despite once again being prosecuted for fraud, obtaining money under false pretences and for indecent representation, Cox and his manager were exonerated of all charges.

Peachtree Payne liked a drink, and was often arrested as a result of his drunken behaviour. In March 1948 he was found guilty of damaging two cars whilst drunk, presumably whilst driving under the influence of alcohol. Two years later Payne was drinking at the Phoenician Club in Terre Haute when he became embroiled in an argument with fellow drinker Edward Williams, who drew a .41 revolver on Peachtree and threatened to shoot him. Williams, who was accompanied by a 15-year-old girl, drove off at 80 miles an hour, with police in pursuit; he was later charged with intoxication, driving while intoxicated and carrying a concealed weapon.

In October 1965, now aged 83, Horace Gilford Payne moved into a care home for former servicemen, the Indiana State Soldiers Home, in Lafayette. He continued to sing and play, often performing for the residents of the home. Three years later he was 'adopted' by members of the American Legion Auxiliary; Peachtree had long been a supporter of the local Legion, playing at their annual dinners and celebratory events from the late 1940s onwards. Although this was a mostly honorary position, he was no doubt pleased to learn that he would be receiving the occasional small financial gift from Legion members. Sadly, Gilford Payne did not have much opportunity to enjoy this honour; he died less than five months later, in February 1969, leaving a niece and a nephew but no children of his own from either of his marriages.

Ten years after Peachtree's death, in an interview with *Guitar Player* magazine, blues guitarist Mike Bloomfield touched on his own association with queer blues, while discussing his recording of the Memphis Willie Borum song 'Bad Girl Blues', which he issued under the title 'Women Loving Each Other': 'That's an old song, man, from the '30s, I think. It was written by a guy who's still alive. I told the record company to give him credit on the liner for the song, but something happened – there was some reason why he wasn't credited. His name is William Borem [*sic*] ... Maybe I couldn't get away with it. Maybe it is offensive. I don't know. But it's one of the tunes about lesbianism that I really like.' 'Bad Girl Blues', with its opening line 'Women lovin' each other, man, they don't think about no man', was recorded by Memphis Willie Borum in 1961 – he had originally recorded the song at a session for Vocalion in 1934, but that was never issued. Johnny Winter would also record 'Bad Girl Blues' in 1986.

'There's a ton of them,' Bloomfield continued. 'And there's old songs about transvestites, about transsexuality, about hermaphrodites – actual songs by hermaphrodites, blues about them. There's a guy named Guilford "Peachtree" Payne who had breasts and a penis and made records about that... As a matter of fact on the song "Peach Tree Man" that's where I got the title.'[31] Bloomfield liked the tale of Peachtree Payne so much that, in 1978, he wrote his own song, 'Peach Tree Man', about 'a friend of his named Stanley who was a transvestite who fell in love with Michael,' according to his producer, Norman Dayron. 'Peachtree means something – it's like a double-entendre for somebody who's both male and female. Michael called people like that "overts." He made up that word. He just loved people who were overts. So he came up with this phrase, "overt from the peachtree land."'[32]

155

# 11

# In Harlem's Araby

*'Effeminate man and masculine women are an abomination, and a blot upon the face of the earth.'*[1] – Madame Qui Vive

In January 1924 scandal sheet *Broadway Brevities and Society Gossip* began a monthly serial entitled 'Nights in Fairyland', which intended to expose the LGBTQ hangouts of Manhattan, and specifically Greenwich Village. As was usual with *Brevities*, people and venues were, more often than not, referred to in vague terms, editor Stephen G. Clow and his team no doubt hoping that anyone who recognised themselves or their business in the column would happily pay substantial hush money to prevent further, damaging, revelations. Canadian-born Clow, who previously ran vanity publishing house the Broadway Publishing Company, took over ownership of *Broadway Brevities* in 1917, approximately a year after the first issue had been let loose. It was not the first publication of its kind, but the unique mix of tittle-tattle and portrait photos of leading actors brought it a loyal readership and a certain notoriety. Clow and his team ingratiated themselves with New York's finest, attending opening nights and parties and gathering gossip for the magazine by paying hard-up chorus girls and backstage crew a few dollars for anything they could use. The magazine's speciality was insinuation: the character of one virtually anonymous young man, named only as Berkeley C- S-, was described as being 'just a tiny dash of Spanish lavender and plain Semitic added... oh well, boys will be boys.'[2] According to its own advertising, *Broadway Brevities* contained 'all the inside low down on everybody prominent along the Great White Way,'[3] and although Clow and his team would be careful not to name anyone who might sue, they made it obvious to all but the most casual observer of the cinema and theatre scene of the day exactly who they were writing about.

By the beginning of the twentieth century, Broadway was being described as the 'gay white way'. Although this euphemism originally referred to the hundreds of brilliant white lights that illuminated the theatre district, the phrase was soon gleefully adopted by LGBTQ people whose work or leisure activities brought them in close proximity to the area. In 1907, theatrical impresarios the Shubert brothers debuted their musical, *The Gay White Way,* and although the brothers themselves were careful not to put openly LGBTQ people on stage, they were more than happy to employ queer talent behind the curtains. Their star name, Al Jolson, employed fellow entertainer Frank 'Pansy' Holmes as his valet and personal secretary, and many of the camp mannerisms Jolson used on stage (and, later, on screen) were modelled on Holmes. Jolson carried a lot of weight with the Shubert company, and he often insisted that Pansy was given roles in productions in which 'Jolie' starred, such as *Dancing Around* (1915), *Robinson Crusoe Jr.* (1917), *Sinbad* (1918) and *Bombo* (1921). Pansy also had bit-parts in several of Jolson's movies. Sadly, Pansy – who knew 'practically everything of importance to Jolson'[4] and spent more than three decades in his employ, often signing Jolson's cheques and correspondence – was a terrible gossip, and Jolson fired his old retainer after he started spreading rumours about the state of his employer's health, telling friends during one bout of sickness that 'she won't last the night'. Jolson's 1934 movie *Wonder Bar*, one of the last pre-Code movies made, features a delicious little joke involving two handsome men dancing together, entirely at odds with the Motion Picture Production Code's instruction that 'Pictures shall not infer that low forms of sex relationship are the accepted or common thing.'

Stephen Clow had a gift for being in the wrong place at the wrong time. In 1921 he just happened to be in the apartment of a young actor and nascent screenwriter, Zelda Crosby, when the police arrived. Crosby had been taken to hospital where, three days later she would be pronounced dead, having taken an overdose of barbiturates and morphine after a brief affair with an unnamed millionaire movie producer, and the police wanted to know what information Clow had. The *Los Angeles Examiner* would later report that, 'All-important evidence had been suppressed. This evidence, it is said, consisted mainly of tell-tale letters and the condition of the apartment in which Miss Crosby was found unconscious. It was reported that the letters had been stolen from the room and that her acquaintances from the moving picture colony had hastily rearranged the room after Miss Crosby had been removed to Bellevue hospital.'[5] Soon rumours were flying around of people having been paid off, of 'an intimate friend of the dead girl' who 'received $25,000 to supress the facts regarding her romance', and of 'a theatrical publication' whose 'edition soon disappeared from the streets in some strange manner'.[6] Another publication reported on how, 'One young man – a journalist hanging on the ragged edge of decency, stated that he had some inside facts and intended to bring the whole thing out in a grand jury investigation. But he never got to the grand jury and the whole thing was suddenly hushed up.'[7] The journalist in question was Steven Clow, accused in the press of withholding 'facts relating to the suicide of Zelda Crosby',[8] a woman known as the 'girl with the face too pretty to be filmed'.[9]

LGBTQ people were always in Clow's sight: he considered them an easy way to make money as no star of stage or screen would want their adoring public to know about their private sexual proclivities, and there were plenty of stories in the press about Zelda's close friendships with young women and the wild parties she hosted for her showbiz friends, although 'only once was it necessary to call a policeman',[10] her housekeeper claimed. None of that mattered to Clow, who filled the pages of *Brevities* with scandalous gossip, tales of Hollywood excess and thinly veiled attacks on the members of the entertainment industry's queer community. Clow thought nothing of insinuating that actor John Barrymore was a homosexual with a taste for sailors when the magazine asked, 'What is the inspiration Jack Barrymore has found on the lower city wharves?', or of suggesting that Vincent Astor, heir to one of America's wealthiest families, bought 'his lipsticks in Chinatown'.[11]

Clow was not the only one to notice that the prohibition-hit venues in New York were becoming a little more fruity in an aim to attract more business. In Lower Manhattan, on the corner of Chinatown, Frenchie Lavelle ran his ballroom and restaurant, famous for the camp singing waiters who would mince about between the tables, carrying food and drink while singing along with the band and exchanging wisecracks. 'The singing waiters were artists in their way', wrote O. O. McIntyre in his syndicated column *New York Day By Day*. 'About the tables they walked, punctuating their songs with cries and gibes such as "she's only a bird – draw two in the dark – in a gilded ca-a-age! A mug of ale – a pitiful – two whiskies out of a dollar – sight to see".' Frenchie Lavelle's was a place where 'all New York went slumming... Swells from the avenue. College boys and girls. Married men with the yoke off for the night. Sailors. gangsters. Old men thrilling to folly. Chunky guerrillas. And effeminate men.'[12] McIntyre claimed that Lavelle 'had police protection and could do as he pleased,' and during the years of prohibition (and beyond) it was not unusual for bars, restaurants and nightclubs to pay protection money to either gangsters or the police... or both. Lavelle's singing waiters were caricatured in the 1932 film *Call Her Savage* and, according to McIntyre, two of the waiters went on to have highly successful careers in music publishing.

Jackie Rogers, a lesbian car thief known in the village as the Prince of Wales because of her resemblance to the future king, was one of the few people given opportunity to write about Greenwich Village in less scandalous tones. In a series of articles for the *Daily News*, she called it 'The dearest and most picturesque place in New York', and said that living among the residents of the Village had 'nothing to do with my wicket exploits except that it was there I met the girl for whose sake I took the first car'. Jackie wrote of:

The effeminate men, the masculine women – I will trot them out in their colorful garb and show what fine and lovable people many of them really are. I will describe the queer Village places where true Bohemians gather – not the jazzy little cabarets frequented by uptown flappers and their youthful escorts. To those tinkling places the real Villager seldom goes...

I met a different class of people than I had ever known in college or in business. I shall never forget my introduction to that new phase of existence. It was in a famous restaurant which was much written about. A periodical regaled its readers with detailed accounts of these 'Nights in fairyland'. Some of my readers will read this with a smile as they recall the sudden increased popularity that the already famous restaurant enjoyed after that so-called exposure. I went there in company with my girl chum, Jean C-. I had always dressed in tailored fashion and my chum was delightfully sweet and feminine. We were greeted as if everyone had known us all our lives. At this place I was shocked when some of the so-called men produced powder puffs and began refurbishing their complexions.[13]

New York was rife with bars and cafés catering for lesbian women and gay men, and many attracted the attention of the authorities as well as the columnists of *Broadway Brevities*. In 1923 police closed The Jungle, a Greenwich village tearoom, 'because of the character of some of the effeminate men who packed it nightly'. Although it remained unrecorded, a popular song in the clubs of New York was 'The Greenwich Village Epic', otherwise known as 'Way Down South in Greenwich Village'. Originally credited to George Baker and Bobby Edwards, the song had been around since at least 1913, but by 1926 it had acquired several new verses penned by Clement Wood, one of which ended, 'Here the modernest complexes / And the intermediate sexes / Fairyland's not far from Washington Square.'

In the same month that Clow began his *Nights in Fairyland* column, Clara Smith recorded a new song from Porter Grainger and Bob Ricketts, 'I Don't Love Nobody (So I Don't Have No Blues)' which, because of Clara's immense popularity, was immediately covered by a number of other blues singers, including Virginia Liston, Edna Hicks and Lena Wilson. The lyrics are about a woman using a man to get what she wants, and closely mirror Clara's own situation when she sings, 'I don't love nobody, I want the world to know / When I'm with a fellow, it's simply for making a show / I keep a fellow spending 'til his money's gone / And tell him that he's nothing but a pure greenhorn.' Clara's version also adds the couplet, 'I let a fella take me all around the town / And if he asks to kiss me, I will knock him down...' Clara would record a number of sexually charged blues songs written (and often accompanied) by Grainger, including his own 'Jelly Look What You Done Done', and 'He's Mine, All Mine', written by Grainger using the pseudonym Jimmy Foster.

In early 1925 Bessie and Jack were enjoying some time apart from each other. Usually when Jack was not around Bessie took full advantage of the opportunity, partying all night and drinking her favoured rough alcohol, and this would be no exception. She had recently been joined on tour by her niece Ruby Walker (Ruby began working with Bessie as a wardrobe mistress but soon graduated to dancer and comedian), and that February, accompanied by Ruby, she attended the annual Hamilton Lodge drag ball at the Rockland Palace in Harlem. Whenever Jack was about Bessie tended to steer clear of the wild life, but with him out of the picture temporarily she wanted to party. Bessie was coming down from a personal high, having witnessed crowds so big that they stopped the traffic outside the theatres she performed in, with hundreds of disappointed fans unable to secure a ticket to one of her shows. In Pittsburgh, 'thousands of people were turned away, and those who did attend actually stormed the theatre'.[14] Life was quite literally a riot and Fred Longshaw, formerly the leader of Brownie's Panama Serenaders but now leading Bessie's own touring band, had been a witness to the madness. Over the next month Bessie would cut twelve sides for Columbia, all featuring Longshaw, and the pair would continue to work together sporadically for the rest of her recording career.

The Hamilton Lodge masquerade balls had been running since the end of the 1860s, and had long enjoyed a reputation for allowing LGBTQ people of all races to intermingle, but following the end of the First World War, their popularity exploded, and they became a huge pull for Harlem's glitterati, many who came to marvel at the costumes and outrageous antics of the LGBTQ attendees. By the end of the 1920s more than 7,000 people would pack into the Rockland Palace each year, where stars including Tallulah Bankhead, Ethel Waters and Bessie Smith were 'cramming the boxes... by the thousands watching sex perverts prance around with sex-perverted minds'.[15] Other groups attempted to organise their own masked balls; an association of Harlem barbers held their own annual 'mask ball and carnival' that was popular with local musicians and theatre folk – several of the cast and crew of *Shuffle Along* were seen enjoying themselves at their November 1921 ball, held at the Manhattan casino – but none would ever come close to attracting the kind of numbers that the Hamilton Lodge balls regularly pulled in.

'We got back to New York in time to go to the faggot's ball,' Ruby told Chris Albertson. 'All the faggots were there showing their glamour, some women wished they could look as good, with their false titties and wigs, high heel shoes, evening gowns and jewelry, they were beautiful sights to see. To see them, dancing with a man, you would say, "Look at that man dancing with a beautiful woman," and he had his dick strapped down so tight, that it looked like a fat pussy instead of a dick.'[16] In Jack's absence, Bessie had been dating Longshaw, but they had a fight and went to the ball that night separately. These huge events would not escape the attention of Clow and his *Brevities* columnists, who lambasted the Rockland Palace balls as 'a display of brazen sexual oddity that cannot be equalled anywhere in the country. Crowds of spectators gather to witness the horrible orgies of the perverted... Appearances are deceiving. Most of the "women" in attendance at the orgies are men in disguise. A majority of the people wearing tuxedoes are female.'[17] The *New York Age* used slightly less salty language describing the Rockland Palace balls to its readership, but the message was clear: this was not a place for respectable, God-fearing straight folk.

Ye Fairies Ball is an abomination put on annually by the Hamilton Lodge and suckers and morons pack the Rockland Palace by the thousands to watch and mingle with fairies, fagots [*sic*], pansies – you know, funny men who are women in all but form. In England they'd be in jail, but in America they glorify them... Honest folks, I spent an hour in the damn place and when I finished looking at these hideosities [*sic*], I had to take my girl (the real one that I brought) out into the middle of Eighth Avenue and go into the kiss that sends you to sleep and wakes you up married, just to bring the masculine blood back to my veins and a bass note back in my tonsils.[18]

The annual masquerade ball hosted by the Hamilton Lodge would continue to be well-attended, and each year thousands of 'men dressed in feminine attire' and 'terpsichoreans of dubious sex' would turn up in their finery. Once the entertainment stopped, these same men 'clambered into high priced automobiles and taxis and hied to the Yeah Man night club on Seventh Ave. There they proceeded to make whoopie in grand fashion while their male escorts and admirers stood off appraisingly and smiled.'[19] The Hamilton Lodge ball was the most obvious expression of drag culture at that time, and a forerunner to the LGBTQ ballroom scene that developed in New York from the 1970s onwards, but it was not the only place where men dressed as women, women dressed as men and people of all sexual persuasions were allowed the freedom to express themselves. In Washington D.C., William Dorsey Swann, a Black former slave and his boyfriend Pierce Lafayette, a messenger who worked in a pensions office, were hosting more intimate drag balls of their own. Swann was often in trouble with the police and on 31 December 1895, he was arrested for hosting 'a "drag" for the benefit of his white friends'. Unfortunately for the authorities they arrived before the New Year's Eve party was in full swing, and the best they could do was confiscate the 'liquid refreshments, which consisted of beer, wines of various kinds and the most expensive champagne',[20] and arrest a number of the men in attendance as vagrants, the charge often levied at prostitutes. Incidentally, only the Black attendees were arrested (including 'James Frazier, a member of the entertaining party'); the white men present 'were summoned as witnesses'. The following January Swann and Lafayette were both taken into custody after police 'raided a "drag" given by a party of whites and blacks... Prof. Gardner sat at the piano while those who gave the "drag" danced with their "invited guests." Two of the male dancers were naked.' In the melee, a number of those attending managed to escape, but the authorities managed to snare 'five of them, who gave feminine names at the station house' and who were 'attired in silks and satins of brightest colors'.[21]

Swann had been arrested in April 1888 in a similar raid. That time he had been dressed as the queen of the ball, and he attempted to fend off the officers pouring into the third-story residence while others escaped:

The queen stood in an attitude of royal defiance. Her arms hung by her side. On her head was a black wig. The long, white buttoned kid gloves reached up almost to the shoulders and the (he) queen seemed bursting with rage. The ten-foot trail to her low-cut and short-sleeved white silk dress, with the lace overdress, stood out its full length, and appeared spread for a full reception, but different from that met with. At length 'her majesty' recovered speech, and, advancing her right foot, which was encased in a gold-embroidered black slipper, she said, with a haughty air, 'You is no gem'men'. The officer made a grab for the queen, but the touch was too much for the royal one, and she fought the policeman's approach and arrest. They had it rough and tumble in the room, and by the time it ended 'the queen' was considerable of a wreck, pretty thoroughly disrobed, and as she (he) was brought to the light there had been a great transformation, and 'the queen' of white satin loveliness proved to be a lightly built man.[22]

By 1925 there were 175,000 Black Americans living in Harlem, and many of them were struggling financially. Unscrupulous landlords would charge Black families as much as double what their white tenants paid, leaving some with little option but to hold rent parties to make ends meet. With the average Black worker earning $25 a week and rent in the area often as much as $15 a room, the easiest way to raise extra funds was to invite people over to parties where, for the price of admission, the booze would flow freely, 'dancing in its worst form [was] indulged in',[23] and sex was there for the asking. Advertised by word of mouth, or by printed card (usually offering a 'whist party' or some such) left on noticeboards, in doorways and apartment house mail boxes, Harlem's rent parties could be dangerous affairs. A combination of cheap booze and sex often lead to violence, and on several occasions people were beaten, shot or stabbed. In November 1926, at a lesbian party in the Columbus Hill area, two women got into a fight over the affections of a third woman, Clara, known to her friends as 'Big Ben', her 'name coming from her unusual size and from her inclination to ape the masculine in dress and manner, and particularly in her attention to other women'. Big Ben was not at the party, however the other two women, Reba Stothoff (at whose apartment the rent party was taking place) and Louise Wright, got into a fight which led to Reba grabbing a bread knife. Louise tried to leave, but Reba grabbed hold of her by the hair, yanked her head back and drew the knife across the unfortunate woman's throat, 'cutting the head almost off. Death was practically instantaneous.'[24]

Dancer Mabel Hampton recalled visiting a buffet flat (or 'pay party' as she termed it) in Harlem at around the same time. 'This girl, she had four rooms in the basement, and she gave parties all the time... We'd buy up all the food – chicken, and different vegetables, and salads and things, and potato salad – and I'd chip in with them you know 'cause I'd bring my girlfriends in, you know... You pay a couple of dollars. You buy your drinks and meet other women and dance and had fun... Sometimes there would be twelve or fourteen – maybe less and maybe more.'[25] Mabel revealed that most of the women there were Black, and most were dressed in their street clothes:

Most of them wore suits [jackets with skirts, rather than trousers]... Very seldom did any of them have slacks or anything like that because they had to come through the street. Of course, if they were in a car, they wore the slacks, but then five or six of them would be in the car and come with their slacks on. And most of them had short hair. And most of them was good-lookin' women too... There was single and couples because the girls just come and bring [a friend] – the bulldykers used to come and bring their women with them, you know. And you wasn't supposed to jive over there [but] they danced up a breeze. They did the Charleston – they did a little bit of everything... The music was records. They were all records.[26]

And those records were essential in helping blues spread from the tent show and vaudeville circuit into peoples' homes.

Porter Grainger was no stranger to Harlem's more bohemian ways, and along with two men he met in the offices of publisher Clarence Williams – Jo Trent (who would later work with Grainger and Bob Ricketts on the stage musical *Honey*) and a teenage piano playing prodigy called Thomas Waller – he wrote 'In Harlem's Araby', a song influenced by the popularity of the 1921 composition 'The Sheik of Araby', which itself was inspired by the enormous success of the Rudolph Valentino film *The Sheik* that same year. Best known as an instrumental, in April 1924 the duo of Waller and Grainger recorded a vocal version of the song, issued on Ajax Records under Grainger's name, with Grainger affecting an exceptionally camp vocal as he satirised the bright young things of the Harlem Renaissance.

The original authorship of 'In Harlem's Araby' is somewhat confused. Several instrumental versions (for example, the one by the Dixie Devils, first issued in 1929) list Grainger as the sole composer, suggesting that the lyrics came entirely from Waller and Trent, but a 1950s copyright renewal notice has no mention of Grainger at all. New York native Waller was still just 19 years old when the recording was made, and although the printed lyrics are credited to Trent, some of the words that made it into the song but that do not appear on the printed score seem to have come straight from Grainger's personal experience, as they do not appear in other vocal versions. Grainger's vocal version of 'In Harlem's Araby' takes the listener on an audio tour of the district, promising the curious that, 'Friends you ain't seen nothing yet / There ain't a place where you can get / A thrill like Harlem late at night.' Grainger guides his eager sightseers through cafés, drinking establishments, dance halls, rent parties, and the meaning of lines such as:

> They've got women just like men
> 'Cause they act-a like brothers
> It's hard to get along with them
> So I speak for the others
> In Harlem's Araby
> You can't tell 'G' from 'B'...

...would be clearly understood by his Manhattan socialite friends, as well as the less urbane folk of Harlem and Greenwich Village, as the inability to distinguish the girls from the boys.

Thomas 'Fats' Waller would go on to be one of the most important and innovative musicians and composers of the jazz era, and he would later insist that he played on recordings made by Bessie Smith before she signed to Columbia.[27] The claim was made before Bessie's death, when she could easily have denied or disproved it. His first credited recordings were made, for Okeh, in late 1922, while both Waller and Grainger were working for Clarence Williams, but could Fats have played piano for the Empress of the Blues on those long-lost Emerson recordings, or on her failed auditions for Black Swan or Okeh, made when he was just 17? All three companies, like Waller himself, were based in New York, so it is not impossible that he was in some way involved with Bessie early on in her recording career, and he enjoyed more than a passing acquaintance with her. One of his favourite party pieces was an imitation of Bessie, as described by actor Slim Thompson: 'The men put on the girls' clothes and the girls wore the men's clothes. Art Tatum put on a dress and broke it up, doing an imitation of Mary Lou Williams. Not to be outdone, Fats was dressed as Bessie Smith and really killed us, singing "See See Rider". In the midst of the song, Fats stopped and said "Boy, I'm really riding, and Mary Lou you're not doin' so bad with the keys!"[28] Fats would record with both Ethel Waters and Alberta Hunter, and Bessie would record Waller compositions, but the two would not work together during her time at Columbia.

Irrespective of any involvement with the young piano maestro Tom Waller, Bessie's star continued to rise, and any news of her would guarantee a few extra thousand copies of a newspaper being sold. Papers fought over the rights to reprint images and, better still, gain a short quote or an interview from the great singing sensation. Most, if not all of these were clearly made up, either by theatre managers, members of Bessie's own entourage or by the newspaper men themselves. In March 1924, beneath a photograph of a beaming Bessie, the star described exactly why she thought audiences identified with her material. The blues, she explained, are not 'funny' songs, 'The modern songs are greatly modified, but the original blues songs are deep, emotional melodies, bespeaking a troubled heart.'[29] It's highly doubtful that Bessie, whose favourite phrases were, 'I ain't never heard of such shit' and 'kiss my black ass', used a word like 'bespeaking' in her entire life.

By the end of 1925, Bessie Smith was being talked about in the pages of trade magazine *Variety* as being the biggest draw in Black theatre, with 'a half dozen of the best informed colored men and women in the show business' claiming that she was earning $800 a week, 'not including her takings from record making', however the same article had her making up to $1,000 per recording and working for Ajax Records, a company that had closed its doors in August that year, just a year or so after Grainger and Waller issued their version of 'In Harlem's Araby'. It also claimed that Bessie was 'a woman who has never played in a white house in her life',[30] which was completely untrue. Bessie may have been happy with her position as Black theatre's biggest draw, but Ethel Waters was less so. At the Plantation, near Times Square, she was being upstaged and outshone by Josephine Baker.

Ethel's career should have been at its height but, keen to capitalise on her stardom, she made a series of costly mistakes. Now, like both Bessie and Ma, the proud owner of her own train carriage, in April 1925 she began negotiating a new contract with Columbia Records 'that, if concluded, will provide her with more advertising than has ever been accorded to a colored woman artist',[31] something that would have pleased her no end. A couple of weeks later Ethel and her friend, fellow performer and erstwhile manager Earl Dancer, signed a lucrative three-year deal with white touring circuit Keith-Albee. It was a move Ethel later regretted. Prior to a performance for an all-white audience in Chicago earlier that year, Ethel had given concert performances exclusively to Black patrons, and the racism she faced playing white theatres was worse than any she had experienced up until then. On hearing of the deal struck by Dancer – owner of Harlem's Golden Gate Club – on Ethel's behalf, hoofer Bill 'Bojangles' Robinson demanded that his own contract be extended: 'he insisted that his prestige must be preserved,' wrote J. A. 'Billboard' Jackson in his syndicated column. 'A five year contract would be the least that he could accept and maintain his dignity – and he got just that.'[32]

Following her featured role in *Shuffle Along*, Josephine's star had been in the ascendant. Back in February 1924, it had been announced that Noble Sissle and Eubie Blake's next production would be a musical revue entitled *Chocolate Dandies*. When it debuted the following month in Pittsburgh, the revue was now titled *In Bamville*, and starred Sissle and Blake alongside a 'big cast and chorus of 125 European and American colored artists',[33] including a young chorine called Josephine Baker. According to the press, Baker had been plucked from obscurity to join the cast of Sissle and Blake's new show and, if those same newspaper reports were to be believed, Noble Sissle had discovered her personally while she was giving a performance, with other students, in her home town of St Louis. This official version of the discovery of the 'elongated, double-jointed, dancing comedienne' completely ignored Clara Smith's role in Josephine's rise to stardom, as well as the fact that Baker had spent the best part of a year, from August 1922 onwards, in the chorus of Sissle and Blake's massively successful *Shuffle Along* – not that it would have bothered too many people at the time, including Josephine herself.

By the end of July, *In Bamville* had reverted to the name *Chocolate Dandies*, and Josephine and the crew were about to head off to New York. Opening at the Colonial Theatre on Broadway on 1 September, Josephine was the breakout star of the show, which played New York through until the end of November before going off on tour, and she was singled out for her performance: 'The Baker woman as an eccentric comedienne is a whirlwind and one of the greatest hits of the night.'[34] *Variety* noted that, 'At least two of the chorus scored hits with dancing specialties. In particular a sort of colored Charlotte Greenwood* caught the house. She is Josephine Baker... an eccentric dancing comedienne, affecting a regulation boy's haircut, with her locks plastered so that she appears to have satin hair.'[35] 'It isn't often

---

\* Greenwood was a popular dancer and actor whose career on stage and screen lasted for forty-five years. Tall and limber, she was known as the 'only woman in the world who could kick a giraffe in the eye'.

that a chorus girl has an opportunity to make a hit in a musical show, but there is one chorus girl' wrote another reviewer, '...who in the language of the Rialto is a "riot". Miss Baker is tall, slight of figure and long of limb. She seems as pliable as a rubber band... her gyrations are comic to the last degree.'[36]

Despite good press, and the show's role in popularising a new dance, the Charleston (audiences were initially introduced to the Charleston the previous October, when the all-Black musical revue *Runnin' Wild*, which included two songs by Porter Grainger and Jo Trent, debuted on Broadway), *Chocolate Dandies* was not a success. Production costs were prohibitively high and by the late summer of 1925 Baker was appearing at the Plantation, a nightclub within Broadway's Winter Garden complex, where Ethel Waters was headlining. The floor show at the Plantation, *Tan Town Topics*, was staged twice a night, at midnight and again at 2.15 a.m., with the second show noted for featuring more risqué songs and a less restrained performance from the chorus girls. 'Ethel Waters is featured but is outdistanced by Josephine Baker, and Miss Baker's name isn't even spelled in capitals,' a reviewer for *Variety* marvelled. 'A couple of youths from Chicago said that Ethel has absorbed "too much class" since playing around the middle west. Whatever it is the girl does not live up to the inside boosting of the colored show folk who think highly of her as a performer,' he continued, although grudgingly admitting that, 'Miss Waters has two good numbers, one a dandy and of which she might make more.' The article also noted that Josephine seemed rather enamoured with dancer Bessie Allison: 'From the sidelines it looked as if the Misses Baker and Allison were more pally than any of the principals.'[37] A different unnamed reviewer, writing in the *Afro-American*, called *Tan Town Topics* 'one of the best floor shows ever staged in town', adding 'Josephine Baker is a riot.'[38]

After four years of playing in the shadows, Josephine Baker was on her way to becoming a bone fide star, and if she and Bessie Allison had been close, their friendship was about to be brought to an abrupt end, for the following month Baker was sailing across the Atlantic and heading to France. In 1929 Bessie Allison, then a dancer in the chorus line at the Cotton Club, would marry Charles Buchanan, director of the Savoy Ballroom. She developed an interest in politics, and went on to become the first African American woman elected to the New York state legislature, representing Harlem and championing civil rights.

Following the success African American artists had already enjoyed in Britain, the rest of Europe was opening up to Black artists, and the gangly dancer who pulled funny faces would emerge as a world-class superstar on the stage of the Théâtre des Champs-Elysées' with Caroline Dudley's *La Revue Nègre*. Dudley, a white socialite and would-be theatre impresario, had originally wanted Ethel Waters to head the then-unnamed troupe, but Ethel wanted too much money: $500 a week. Her avarice gave Josephine's career the boost it needed, and turned the chorine into a superstar. Other important and influential artists would also get their big break in *La Revue Nègre*, including horn player Sidney Bechet, and Paris would take Baker and Bechet to its heart, with both becoming huge stars in France. London, Paris and Berlin swung to the sounds of blues and jazz, and following Baker's success, a significant number of Black American stars made the trip across the ocean to perform in the UK and Europe.

Actors and singers still playing to segregated audiences or forced to use the tradesman's entrance to gain access to their own stage back home were, rightfully, being accorded celebrity status in Europe. Florence Mills became a huge star when *Blackbirds* played in London in 1927, and that same year bisexual pianist Leslie 'Hutch' Hutchinson, a former lover of Cole Porter who had made his first recordings in New York in 1923, became a sensation while playing at the Café de Paris in London's West End, and was quickly signed to the British branch of Brunswick Records. The following January, two months after the untimely death of Florence Mills, stars including Josephine Baker, Alberta Hunter and Noble Sissle appeared on stage together at the London Pavilion in a benefit in her honour, helping to raise £1,000 for a charity to aid victims of the recent London flood. According to Hunter, 'We went to Europe because we were recognized and given a chance. In Europe they had your name up in lights. People in the United States would not give us that chance.'[39]

Josephine was a sensation, and *La Revue Nègre* was feted as, 'The most amazing synthesis of modern music and dancing that has yet been seen... As for Josephine Baker, she is a mimic, a singer, a dancer, who

171

is perpetually surprising. What is perhaps chiefly to be remarked is the manner in which exotic effect is added to exotic effect, with a sureness of execution, an attention to detail, a sense of ensemble, without flaw, without the smallest deviation from the minutely regulated design. Here is virtuosity indeed.'[40] Other publications agreed: 'I have watched most of the freakish dancers who have exhibited strange antics on the Paris stage during the past few years,' wrote René in *The Bystander* magazine, 'but none of them has come within megaphone distance of Miss Josephine Baker, the whooping whirligig of this fantastic troupe. As husky as she is dusky there must be nearly six feet in length of Josephine and there is nothing out of harmony about her proportions – she dances just the sort of inspirited capers that ought to go with jazz music, but, in addition, she can introduce enough contortions to make even a treble jointed contortionist feel envious... Judged by the standard on which she ought to be judged, Josephine Baker is probably the finest jazz dancer in the world.'[41]

## 12

# Million Dollar Blues

*'The blues are our own, and they originated not from religious hymns as many people think, but from the feeling of sorrow and oppression born with the darkey. Any religious Negro can sing a spiritual, but it takes a good one to sing the blues.'*[1] – Ethel Waters

In Chicago, in August 1924, Ma Rainey made the first recording of a song which is rightly recognised as one of the most notorious queer-themed records of all time, the dirty blues standard 'Shave 'Em Dry Blues'. The phrase 'shave 'em dry' refers to rough, aggressive sex, with someone taken by surprise, without any foreplay or, in the case of anal sex, without any form of lubrication, and although Ma's recording is primarily about rough heterosexual sex, the lyrics make several allusions to lesbianism. Much of the song's action takes place on State Street in Chicago where, Ma insists, many of the women are wearing men's 'brogan shoes'* and acting 'like a man'. Ma's version gives co-authorship to Ma and to Henry Jackson, although it had existed in

---

* Although they are often confused with them, brogans were quite different from the shoes we recognise as brogues today. Brogans would not have had the distinctive punched leather tooling, but were more basic and utilitarian, similar to an ankle boot and cheaply made from untreated leather.

173

some form or another for many years, and had been a staple of her act long before she began her recording career.

Like Alberta, Bessie, Ethel and all of the others, Ma's earliest recordings were made by her and her band performing live in a studio, the music captured by a large horn and transferred onto wax, but this archaic way of recording was about to change. Back in 1920, the Bell Telephone Company and its subsidiary, Western Electric, had started to experiment with electrical recording, using microphones to capture performances rather than those unwieldy acoustic horns. At the same time a sound engineer in Chicago, Orlando Marsh, was also trialling a system of recording using microphones. After Bell received a patent for the process, they licensed it to Columbia, in New York, and Victor in New Jersey, in 1924: the age of electrical recordings had begun. Papa Charlie Jackson would record a version the following spring, with the song's title truncated to simply 'Shave 'Em Dry', and disc's label now crediting the co-author of the song as W. Jackson. Papa Charlie's version is lyrically similar to Ma Rainey's, although he amends a couplet in the opening verse from 'There's one thing I don't understand / Why a good-looking woman likes a workin' man', to 'Why a knock-kneed woman likes a bow-legged man.'

Other versions, and similar songs derived from 'Shave 'Em Dry Blues', would be recorded over the following decade, including an infamous re-reading by Lucille Bogan, under the name Bessie Jackson.

Bogan recorded two distinctly different versions of the song, in 1933 and 1935, and these recordings bear little resemblance to Ma's version. Rainey's recording hints at bisexuality; although primarily singing about heterosexual copulation, she also mentions butch women cruising State Street, at that time one of Chicago's busiest thoroughfares, with classy restaurants, department stores and theatres, and suggests, at the very end of the song, that she would rather be at home entertaining a woman friend. Bogan's sexually explicit version, recorded on 19 March 1933, was not issued by her record company as it was recorded for private use, along with a second, equally raunchy song 'Till the Cows Come Home'. Although dubs were made and copies distributed on the black market, it finally saw the light of day on the 1968 compilation *Screening the Blues*; 'Till the Cows Come Home' would not see an official release until 2004. This version is filled with crude sexual imagery, in fact, it is nothing short of obscene, from the opening couplet, 'I've got nipples on my titties big as the end of my thumb / I've got something between my legs gonna make a dead man cum', a line that clearly influenced The Rolling Stones' 1981 hit 'Start Me Up', to the final verse, where Lucille sings about how her 'cock [in Southern Black slang at that time the word meant vagina, not penis] is made of brass', and that she is more than happy to be paid for sex. It has been suggested that Bogan was not familiar with the obscene lyrics possibly penned by her pianist Walter Roland, and that her joyful, abandoned performance came about in part because she was surprised at their vulgarity. Roland also recorded a version of the song, with different but equally blue lyrics, and throughout that take Bogan can be heard laughing and encouraging her piano player to 'play them dogs, boy'. These versions of the song are probably the closest we have to its original form, sung in bawdy houses and bars long before Ma Rainey cut her take. Hokum singer Lil Johnson recorded a song called 'New Shave 'Em Dry' in 1936 which has none of the sexual imagery of the Bogan/Jackson version.

Born in Birmingham, Alabama in April 1897 (as Lucille Anderson; although other sources cite Amory, Mississippi as her birthplace, her birth state is recorded as Alabama on the 1940 US census), Bogan began her recording career in Atlanta, in June 1923. Following a tip from a local distributor, Okeh's Ralph Peer had come to town in search of new Black talent, setting up a makeshift recording studio in an empty loft on Nassau Street. Bogan was one of the handful of artists that Peer recorded on that trip (he also recorded white hillbilly musician Fiddlin' John Carson), cutting one song, 'Pawn Shop Blues', which would later be coupled with 'Grievous Blues' by vaudeville singer Fannie Goosby, but before that could hit the stores Bogan was called to New York, where she recorded her first full session for Okeh that same month. Although 'Pawn Shop Blues' has gone down in music history as the first race record to have been recorded outside of New York and Chicago, it was not Bogan's first release: three months before that disc appeared, Okeh issued 'Don't Mean You No Good Blues' backed with 'Lonesome Daddy Blues', both sides written by Bogan and Henry Callens, and both recorded at that first New York session, where she also recorded a cover of the Alberta Hunter-Lovie Austin song 'Chirpin' the Blues'. 'Pawn Shop Blues' would end up being her third and final release for the label.

Married in her late teens to railway fireman Nazareth Bogan (the pair had a son, also called Nazareth, and she inherited a stepdaughter from her husband's first marriage), unlike the majority of classic blues singers Lucille had limited – if any – stage experience, although it appears that she had been singing in juke joints or barrelhouses before she walked into that loft on Nassau Street and was offered a recording contract. Her Okeh releases did not sell as well as the company had hoped; her contract was not renewed and Bogan would not record again until 1927, after she moved with her husband and their son to Chicago, and signed first with Paramount and then Brunswick. In 1930, and still living in Chicago, she wrote and recorded a song about prostitution, 'They Ain't Walkin' No More', better known by its proper title (censored at the time for obvious reasons) 'Tricks Ain't Walkin' No More'. Around 1931 she decided – possibly encouraged by her record company – to change her professional name from Lucille Bogan to Bessie Jackson ('Sloppy Drunk Blues' was issued by Brunswick, credited to Bogan, in 1930; the same recording was issued one year later, on the Perfect label, credited to Jackson), presumably because, like many of the classic blues singers, she was finding it harder to find work. Altering her name might have helped her bypass any prejudice engendered by using her real name, but it also gave her the opportunity to record for other companies and double her earnings. It is also possible that she was trying to pass herself off as another singer: a different Bessie Jackson had been busy in vaudeville, performing 'coon songs' solo, and comedy sketches with a partner, James Brown, throughout the first two decades of the 20th century. And should anyone confuse Bessie Jackson with Bessie Smith that could only be to Jackson/Bogan's advantage.

Although many of the blues singers of the classic era recorded sexually explicit songs, these made up just a small portion of their overall output. You could quite rightfully claim that many of the queer jazz and blues numbers that were recorded over this period simply reflected the fashions of the times, and there are plenty of examples

176

of (assumedly) heterosexual artists and acts recording LGBTQ-themed songs as well: 'Masculine Woman, Feminine Men', 'Let's All Be Fairies', 'He's So Unusual' and the like. Although little for certain is known of her life, a significant percentage of Lucille Bogan's recorded canon is made up of raunchy numbers, and songs with controversial themes such as prostitution, lesbianism, drug addiction, bootlegging ('Whiskey Selling Woman') and domestic abuse. The fact that most of her songs were written (or adapted) by her has led many researchers to assume that she must have been singing from experience, and although there is no evidence outside of her lyrics (songs including 'Barbecue Bess', 'My Georgia Grind' and her cover of Charlie McFadden's 'Groceries on the Shelf' contain thinly veiled references to selling sex) it has often been suggested that Bogan was a sex worker as well as a singer, songwriter and recording artist with more than 100 sides under her belt. The claims originated from gossip that circulated among musicians in Birmingham, while others who knew her (or claim to have known of her) have suggested that she had strong ties to Birmingham's Black criminal fraternity.

The newspapers branded Ma 'One of the greatest warblers of those haunting melodies which have taken the country by storm.'[2] In October 1924 Paramount brought her to New York and over the course of an intensive two-day session she and her band recorded seven released sides, including one of her best-known songs, 'See See Rider Blues', accompanied by musicians including Louis Armstrong and Fletcher Henderson. Ma was a big influence on Armstrong, as her friend Thomas Fulbright – an actor who occasionally played camp or female roles on stage – would later note: 'His facial expression; his singing; his very stage presence were all vivid reminders of Ma... He is as near to being a perfect description of Ma Rainey as one can give. He sounds like her and when he opens his mouth and stretches his lips across his teeth in that certain way, he even looks like her... As well as being a wonderful musician, singer and performer, Louis is also a very shrewd mimic into the bargain.'[3]

Although she would record the vast majority of her material in Chicago, Ma was no stranger to New York; she attended a further recording session in the city in December 1925, recording eight sides for Paramount, and she appeared on stage at Harlem's Lincoln Theatre on at least two occasions. During October and November 1924, while on tour throughout the North, she was also regularly broadcasting live on radio, with her new band the Georgia Jazz Hounds. At her performances a huge Paramount-brand gramophone would dominate the stage: a young girl would come out with an oversized disc and place it on the turntable. Her live band would strike up and Ma could be heard to sing the first few bars of the song as if she were actually inside the cabinet of the record player... which, of course, she was. Suddenly the doors beneath the turntable would fly open and Ma, in her finest dress, her gold necklaces flashing in the lights, would step forward to finish the song to rapturous applause.

All of those years of travelling meant that Ma knew how to put on a show. She had watched her husband wow an audience as he stepped out of a cardboard and canvas airship and danced onto the stage, and she had seen the gimmicks that Alberta Hunter and Bessie Smith employed. Banjo player Danny Barker, who played with musicians including Sidney Bechet, Cab Calloway and Jelly Roll Morton, recalled how her show would open with the announcement: 'And now I bring to you the sensation of the age, the fabulous Ma Rainey!' Barker remembered how, 'The curtain opened up and there was a big phonograph machine made out of plastic or wood, a big folding contraption, and she opened this door... they opened up the door and there was Ma Rainey, like she was stepping out of a cathedral, and she came out singing, "He May Be Your Man (But He Comes to See Me Sometimes)" [a 1922 hit for Trixie Smith on Black Swan], or one of them blues. And she stepped down, and there she was, brought to you right out of the Victrola.'[4] Writing in the *Chicago Defender*, Bob Hayes described a similar scene, witnessed in early 1926, when the audience had heard Ma, 'singing as only the "mother of the blues" can sing, but unseen until she steps from a big Paramount talking machine. Oh boy! What a flash Ma does make in her gorgeous gowns, backed by her Georgia jazz band, one of the best five-piece bands heard here in a long time.'[5] Ma always went over well in Chicago. The Scribe, writing in the *Chicago Defender*, reported on Ma's sell-out performance in the city in December 1925, and brought readers' attention to the talents of her adopted son: 'Ma Rainey, mother of the blues, stood her admirers out in car tracks last Monday night at this house. As usual, she sang – or I meant to say moaned – the blues into the hearts of her listeners and registered a decided hit. Little Rainey Jr., danced and sang fine for a little chap, and her jazz band, led by [Thomas] Dorsey, played good numbers and seemed to please.'[6]

Ma loved her jewels, her gold and her finery. To her these things were tangible symbols of her success. 'Her gowns were very elaborate for the gowns of the day,' her trombone player, Al Wynn, revealed. 'They had rhinestone bits and jewellery – oh she was a fanatic for jewellery – all kinds of diamonds and gold pieces were still in vogue and she had any number of necklaces made up of twenty and fifty dollar gold pieces. She had a fabulous collection of diamonds and jewellery most of which she couldn't afford to wear in the streets but she would wear them in the theater.'[7] She was not too concerned where these baubles came from, and in late 1924, while appearing at the Lincoln Theatre in Pittsburgh, she purchased what was claimed at the time to be $25,000 worth of trinkets including 'a bejewelled brooch, which twinkled brightly when she threw back her head in song; a set of diamond drops which shot fire from her ears... And brilliant bracelets which sparkled with every gesture.'[8] Unsurprisingly the bangles and brooches turned out to have been stolen. She had purchased them – at a fraction of their true value – in Nashville from failed actor turned cat burglar, Allen Derrick. Ma had form here: in August 1919, while travelling with Tolliver's Smart Set, she appeared in court to give evidence in the trial of another burglar, Will Cunningham, causing uproar in the court when she and other witnesses turned proceedings into a comedy performance.

Jazz pianist Mary Lou Williams saw Ma and her band at the show in Pittsburgh. 'The fabulous Ma Rainey came into a little theater on Wiley Avenue,' she later recalled.

Some of the older kids and I slipped downtown to hear the woman who had made blues history. Ma was loaded with real diamonds – in her ears, around her neck, in a tiara on her head. Both hands were full of rocks, too; her hair was wild and she had

179

gold teeth. What a sight! To me, as a kid, the whole thing looked and sounded weird. When the engagement ended, and Ma had quit the scene, rumor had it that the jewelry was bought hot and that Ma was picked up and made to disgorge – losing all the loot she had paid for the stuff.[9]

The police followed Ma to Cleveland and arrested her on stage, bringing her show to an abrupt end, and took her under armed guard back to Nashville. Al Wynn, who was in her band at the time, told Paul Oliver that 'The authorities got on her and gave her a hard way to go until she could prove that everything was bought legitimate,'[10] which they clearly were not. A Ma-less act, led by Thomas Dorsey, carried on to their next booking, in Pennsylvania, where Dorsey had a lookalike, bedecked in Ma's stage costume, stand in for her. Within seconds of the fake Ma stepping from the Victrola the game was up, with the audience shouting 'That ain't no Ma Rainey', and throwing missiles at the stage. Dorsey and the band – and the fake Ma Rainey – were forced to beat a hasty retreat and the theatre had to issue refunds to ticketholders.

In 1925, Stephen G. Clow, publisher of *Broadway Brevities*, was sent to prison for six years, and fined $6,000, after being found guilty of blackmail and of using the mail to defraud. *Broadway Brevities*' head of advertising sales, Andrew Brown (whose partner, Lillian Lorraine, was formerly the mistress of Florenz Ziegfeld, one of Clow's victims), was given a two-year sentence, and the publishing company was fined $11,000. Celebrities from the theatre world testified that they had paid the magazine for advertisements in order to stop scandalous stories being published within its pages: a similar magazine, *Town Topics*, had pulled a comparable stunt two decades earlier, and Clow always maintained that it was Brown's idea, not his, to use blackmail. John Lloyd, advertising manager for filmmaker D. W. Griffith, testified in court that he had bought $600 worth of advertising from Clow's team after they threatened to print stories concerning a young actor (an unnamed Clarine Seymour) who had died in unusual circumstances while filming Griffith's 1920 Lillian Gish vehicle *Way Down East*. Actor and speakeasy owner Texas Guinan, subpoenaed to appear before the court, refused to speak out against Clow. The editor would later claim that Guinan showed 'phenomenal loyalty to me when the dark days came',[11] and for some time before Clow was pulled into court, fearing for his safety, he had been seen around New York accompanied by his bodyguard, Gentleman Jack O'Brien, a former welterweight champion, vaudeville performer and chess master.

Gay playwright Sam Shipman was one of the few people to speak out about Clow's crooked ways in court. The September 1923 issue of *Broadway Brevities* contained a slanderous article, 'Schnitzel Sam on the Pan', about Shipman and claiming that Clow had come up with the title for Shipman's biggest success, *East is West*. '"Broadway Brevities" has gone after most of the well-known figures on the Great White Way,' he told the court. 'Generally they were attacked on the emotional side – some chance friendship, perhaps entirely innocent, made the subject of slimy inferences. With me they were forced to pursue a different method because they had nothing "on" me.' Shipman admitted to loaning money to Clow, money that was never returned, before finally realising that Clow 'had been shaking me down when he asked for these loans. He evidently thought they were hush money. After that I refused to give him more money and the succeeding issues of the magazine contained hints that I was a plagiarist.'[12]

That same year weekly scandal sheet the *Hotel Tattler* had changed its name to the *Inter-State Tattler* in an effort to avoid a $10,000 libel case brought against it by a Harlem real estate broker. On 7 February 1925, 'Town Tattle', the showbiz gossip column of the already gossipy *Inter-State Tattler*, featured the barely disguised revelation that Bessie was conducting an affair with male impersonator Gladys Ferguson, warning the latter that: 'Gladys, if you don't keep away from B., G. is going to do a little convincing that he is her husband. Aren't you capable of finding some unexplored land "all alone"?' The B was Bessie and the G her violent, revolver-carrying husband Jack Gee. For some reason, again and again writers have repeated the falsehood that Gladys Ferguson was Gladys Bentley, but the two women were entirely different people, and there is no evidence to suggest that Bessie ever had an affair with the tuxedo-wearing, piano-playing host of Harlem hot spots including the Clam House and Connie's Inn, next door to the Lafayette Theatre, which would later become the Ubangi Club. Ferguson was born, as Gladys Smith, in South Carolina, picking up the surname Ferguson when she married comedian Jimmie Ferguson; Bentley was born and raised in Philadelphia. Bentley was a big, buxom woman, whereas Ferguson was petite, and could easily pass for a boy or a young man. Bessie liked her girls small and light-skinned, or 'high yellow': she had an affair with the 'world's greatest woman buck dancer',[13] Carrie Nugent, who was part of Bessie's touring show in 1923 and 1924. Her other great love, Lillian Simpson was, like Nugent and Ferguson, a svelte dancer and chorus girl that Bessie fell for and included in her show.

Carrie Nugent was acquainted with Ethel Waters. The two women first met back in 1917, on Hallowe'en night at Jack's Rathskeller, when Waters was first spotted and offered a chance to join professional vaudeville act Braxton and Nugent (not the same Nugent, incidentally; probably not even related). Waters, then just starting out, was naturally in awe of the supremely talented Carrie Nugent, who was already a star or, as Ethel described her, a 'sensational Negro tap dancer who'd hoofed her way around the world and been admired and acclaimed everywhere.'[14] Nugent, who had been on stage most of her life either as a solo attraction or part of the double acts including Gulfport and Nugent and Winn and Nugent, had been a star of the Black vaudeville circuit, was previously a member of Billy Kersands' Minstrels and the Alabama Minstrels, who had also included Ma Rainey in their number, but if Ma had an affair with Carrie before Carrie began carrying on with Bessie, we will never know. Feted as a 'champion woman buck and wing dancer', as early as 1912 Nugent had been acclaimed in the press as the 'holder of numerous medals' who had 'appeared in some of the leading music halls of Paris, the Alhambra in London, and in fact all over Europe',[15] and although she does not appear by name in any of those places, she may well have been a child performer in any number of touring shows: Edwardian Britain had a taste for African American entertainers, and Black singer and dancer Belle Davis moved to London in 1901 and brought her 'pickaninnies', all still children under 10, with her, before she moved on to Paris, where she would act as choreographer for *La Revue Nègre*, the show that would later make Josephine Baker an international star. However, by January 1924 Carrie Nugent was becoming a bit long in the tooth for a dancer, and had been reduced from headlining to appearing alongside Bessie and her pianist, Irving Johns, on a bill that also included Fox and Williams, the latter a one-legged dancer, as little more than a dancing distraction for audiences as Bessie belted out 'Gulf Coast Blues'.

From March 1925 Bessie Smith was on a tour of T.O.B.A. theatres, usually playing a week in each one, accompanied by a full show featuring up to twenty performers. Like Ma, Bessie also liked to show off her wealth, and it was one such display that almost brought the tour to an end before it had begun. On a return visit to her home town of Chattanooga, on 22 February 1925, Bessie was attacked on the street at knifepoint. The attack, by a man called Buck Hodge, was reported in the press as a bungled attempt to relieve her of her jewellery. The singer, booked to appear at the African American owned and run Liberty Theatre, was wounded on Foster Street, near to the home of Lizzie Catholic, a woman who identified herself as Bessie's sister, but was more likely a close friend. Catholic was constantly in trouble with the local police and was arrested several times after being found drunk on the streets of Chattanooga brandishing a weapon, looking for a fight.

Earlier that day, Hodge had made drunken advances towards Bessie's niece Ruby at a party where – despite prohibition – everyone had been drinking heavily. Hodge was less than happy when his sloppy overtures towards Ruby were thwarted by her aunt. The stabbing was less an attempt at a jewellery heist, more an act of drunken revenge. Bessie was rushed to the nearby Erlanger Hospital, where she made such a fuss that the staff reluctantly let her leave after treating her wound. Luckily the gash she sustained was not serious, and she was able to continue with her scheduled dates. Hodge was found guilty of assault and sent to White Oak prison, near Chicago. In September 1930, Hodge was one of a group of fourteen men who escaped from White Oak after cutting a hole in the wall of their dormitory, although Bessie's assailant was back behind bars within twenty-four hours. According to Ruby, a short time afterwards Hodge was jumped in a Chattanooga pool room and took such a beating that he died from his injuries.

After playing the Frolic Theatre in Bessemer, Alabama on 16 March 1925, Bessie then paid a return visit to her old haunt, Atlanta's 81 Theatre, before moving on to the Douglass Theatre in Macon, Georgia, the Lyric in New Orleans, and the Palace, in Memphis, Tennessee. Bessie would, naturally, go on last, performing half a dozen or so songs, with priority usually given to her latest Columbia release. After her tour she went back to New York for more recordings, laying down two sides with Fletcher Henderson's Hot Six, including a cover of the W. C. Handy song 'The Yellow Dog Blues', on 6 May. But trouble seemed to be following Bessie. Starting out in summer 1925 under their own canvas, her *Harlem Frolics* show toured extensively, with Bessie and her troupe ferried from city to city in her own Pullman carriage. There was prestige to be gained by touring with Bessie, but the days were long and the pay poor: comedy act Toliver and Harris were initially part of the *Harlem Frolics* line-up, but after an argument over unpaid reimbursement for their train tickets, an enraged Bessie threw a piano stool at Tolliver and the pair left before one of them was badly injured. Aware that a no-show on their part could damage their reputation with theatre owners, the duo wrote a letter to Charles Henry Douglass, owner of T.O.B.A.-circuit Douglass Theatre in Macon, Georgia, telling him that, 'We don't know what she may tell you, so we want to be square and that is why we are writing you,' and telling Douglass that they were 'Hoping to play you in the near future.'[16]

Back in October 1923, and no doubt egged on by a record company keen to exploit the misnomer that the two women were sisters, Bessie and Clara Smith recorded a pair of duets, 'Far Away Blues' and 'I'm Going Back to My Used to Be'. It would be another two years before Columbia would again bring the two women into the studio together: on 1 September 1925 Clara and Bessie recorded two further songs, 'Down Old Georgia Way' and 'My Man Blues', at the Columbia studios in New York. The latter of the two tracks appeared on the flipside of Bessie's next disc, 'Nobody's Blues But Mine', but sadly for their fans, 'Down Old Georgia Way' appears to have been lost. It would be the last time the two great blues stars would record together, because shortly after this session the women, up to this point friendly rivals, had a major falling out.

Sometime around October, both were present at a party held in New York, and both women had been drinking heavily. Although details are sketchy, at some point an argument erupted, quite possibly over another woman, and fists flew. Bessie quickly overpowered Clara and 'beat the daylights out of'[17] her. The two women were due to appear at a show, promoted as a 'blues night', at Harlem's New Star Casino, but Bessie refused to go on, and they would never work together again. Yet they would appear together on disc, after a fashion: that same month, October 1925, Ethel Waters co-wrote and recorded 'Maybe Not At All' for Columbia, a fun side on which she imitates both Bessie and Clara. At the same time, Clara Smith was playing the Elmore Theatre, Pittsburgh, supported by several acts including the Andrew Tribble Duo. There are no further mentions of Tribble performing using this name for his act: could he have roped in his estranged wife for the week-long booking, or was he working with an unnamed straight man? The adverts for the engagement have Clara listed as an 'Okeh Record Star', when she recorded exclusively for Columbia, so it is hardly a reliable source of information. Clara, who at some point seems to have adopted a daughter she named Willie Lee, described as 'a smaller edition of the mother, and who may succeed to the mantle worn by her illustrious mother'[18], married for a second time. In March 1926, she wed Charles 'Two Sides' Wesley, a former player with baseball team the Birmingham Black Barons – one of the founding eight teams of the Negro Southern League – and the Memphis Red Sox, who was now part of the management team of the Atlantic Black Crackers. It clearly was not a good fit for Wesley, born in Montgomery, Alabama in 1896, for the following year he was back playing for the Memphis Red Sox, and he would continue playing for various teams for the rest of the decade.

For a while the couple lived in an apartment within a large brick house, seemingly owned by Clara's aunt, in Harlem. Clara called Charles 'Tootie'; their apartment, which took over most of one floor of number 18, West 130th Street, was stuffed with furniture, and photographs of Clara and her family, but as Carl Van Vechten, a frequent visitor, recalled, Clara 'always seemed to be short of money'[19]: on one such visit, Van Vechten walked in on a rent party that the singer was hosting. At the same time, Porter Grainger – no longer living with his wife – was sharing an apartment on the same block (at 2, West 130th Street) with composer, author and choreographer Frederick C. 'Freddie' Johnson, his co-author on the Bessie Smith hit 'Sing Sing Prison Blues'. In 1925, when Grainger first moved in, there were some twenty-five apartments, ranging in size, across the six floors of the building, and the Grainger/Johnson residence, apartment 2, was a one-bedroom flat. On 6 June the Oklahoma-set musical *Lucky Sambo* – written by Grainger and Johnson – debuted at the Colonial Theatre, Brooklyn. The pair began writing the musical as *Aces and Queens*, in 1923, before first changing the title to *Oil Scandals* (initial try-outs featured blues singer Monette Moore in the cast) but after extensively retooling the work it relaunched in June 1925 as *Lucky Sambo*. As well as writing and producing, Johnson and Grainger both appeared in the show, Grainger as a songwriter with the improbable name Hitt Keys, and the cast included Tim Moore, who would go on to star as Kingfish in the televised version of the *Amos 'n' Andy Show*. An immediate hit, the show was even reviewed by Britain's theatrical bible, *The Stage*.

By August, an extensively remodelled version of *Lucky Sambo* was on tour, without Grainger, Johnson or Moore in the cast, but with Gertrude Saunders, Bessie Smith's rival for the affections of Jack Gee, added in an attempt to bring audiences in. Despite unfavourable comparisons to *Shuffle Along*, the reviewer from *Variety* particularly liked the show, and singled out the jail scene as 'the funniest thing of its kind seen in burlesque in a decade'.[20] *Billboard* reviewed the show no less than four times over the next year, telling its readers that the show was 'in a class by itself, a company of colored entertainers par excellence, who will please any and all patrons of this type of theatrical entertainment'.[21] Johnson and Grainger would continue to work together, writing the musical *Cottontime*, which debuted in Cleveland on Easter Monday 1926, but by the end of that summer Grainger was working with Leigh Whipper, former actor and theatre manager turned writer and producer; together they would write most of the dialogue and several comedy sketches for Broadway's annual *Vanities* revue, which opened on 24 August. Fred Johnson left the apartment on West

130th Street, leaving Grainger to reside there alone, paying $50 a month in rent.

The *Harlem Frolics* tour continued without Tolliver and Harris, and by the middle of the following year the revue was playing mostly in theatres, on occasion with Bessie's brother Clarence joining the cast as comedian and acting as stage manager. In May 1926 they were in Tennessee, by July they were in North Carolina, and they continued on until they got to Georgia in November. Everywhere they went the show was praised for being 'one of the best colored shows in the country',[22] with 'pretty girls, clever comedy and snappy music'.[23] For much of the time, Bessie shared her bed with a pretty young dancer in her chorus, Lillian Simpson, but the two women were discreet, and she was banished to the crew quarters when Jack decided to make an appearance, which he would do sporadically to check on his wife, collect the takings and make a show of handing out the payroll. During one of his occasional visits, while the troupe was gathered in their railway carriages, waiting to move on to the next destination, Bessie discovered that Jack had been sleeping with one of her chorus girls. A furious Mrs Gee charged off to the carriage where her band and chorus were resting, found the girl in question, beat her senseless and threw her and her belongings off the carriage and onto the railroad tracks. Fired up, she then stormed off to find her errant husband. She did not find Jack, but she did find his gun. Looking out of the window, she saw him, standing over the sobbing girl. Bessie aimed the pistol and fired a shot in their direction. '"You no good two-timing bastard," she shouted, waving the gun in the air. "I couldn't even go to New York and record without you fuckin' around with these damn chorus bitches. Well, I'm gonna make you remember me today."'[24] With that, she aimed another shot at them, which sent Jack on his way. Bessie jumped down from the carriage and raced after him, emptying the gun. 'She was shooting at him with his own gun,' Ruby told Chris Albertson. 'Bessie was shooting at Jack and she never shot him once! They say that she didn't try hard enough! We left him in that town.'[25]

Although they had been married for less than three years, Bessie had already had enough of Jack's philandering ways. True, Jack had turned a blind eye to Bessie's own sexual shenanigans when she was on tour, but he demanded absolute fealty from her whenever he was around, even though he was working his way through the chorus girls whenever her back was turned. She had even recorded several sides apparently written or co-written by Jack, despite the fact that her husband had no musical training or experience, including the hit 'Women's Trouble Blues', issued in March 1925; it is most likely that Bessie had written these songs herself and gifted the scant royalties to her husband as a sop. One woman in the *Harlem Frolics* troupe he would not have bothered was Boula Lee, a singer and dancer married to Bessie's musical director, Bill Woods, but who was apparently completely open about her own attraction to other women.

Boula was causing trouble. She had developed a crush on Ruby, and one of the other girls in the touring act, Bessie's own girlfriend Lillian Simpson, suggested to Ruby that she should encourage her, as the younger woman did not know what she was missing. That was a huge mistake: Boula was possessive, and a real catfight broke out backstage one night, after Boula misread the interaction between Ruby and another girl. Boula ended up scratching Ruby's face, and an incensed Bessie waded in, separating the two women and making them swear to keep this quiet, as Jack had sent message that he was returning to the fold that evening. For protecting Ruby from her uncle's wrath, Bessie made her swear not to tell him about her own affair with Lillian. When Jack questioned Ruby about how she had managed to scratch her face, Boula's husband blurted out that, 'It was one of them bulldykers who's after Ruby.' 'What do you mean, one of them? It was your wife!' Bessie shouted.[26]

Whatever bloom there had been on their marriage had all but faded by the time that Bessie began her affair with Lillian Simpson, and with Jack so often out of the picture, Bessie took full advantage of the situation. At a party around Christmastime, Bessie decided to make eggnog but left the milk out of the recipe and everyone ended up very drunk. It was then that Bessie told Ruby that she had her eye on Lillian: 'I like that gal,' she said. Ruby assumed that her aunt meant no more than she thought Lillian was a good dancer. 'No, I don't mean that... I'll tell her myself, 'cause you don't know nothin', child.'[27] Moments later,

Bessie led Lillian away from the room. Ruby, who was sharing a room with Lillian at their lodgings, was not especially surprised when she awoke the following morning to find Lillian had not slept in her own bed.

Lillian had been a schoolmate of Ruby's, and her mother had once been Bessie's wardrobe mistress. She had heard stories from Ruby and her mother of touring the country, playing to packed theatres, and she imagined that a career on the stage would not only add some glamour to her life but provide her with financial independence. When she was just 16 years old, Ruby brought her in to meet her aunt Bessie: Ruby had taught Lillian a few basic dance steps and, although Bessie really had no need for another dancer, she felt obliged to help her out. It certainly helped that Lillian was a real looker.

But Bessie's affair with Lillian would be short-lived. Lillian quickly assumed that sleeping with the boss meant that she would be afforded special privileges, or that she could get away with being less than one hundred per cent professional, but Bessie made a clear distinction between work and play. Lillian wanted all of the benefits of sleeping with Bessie, but none of the responsibility. When the tour reached St Louis, and with Jack once again absent, the pair resumed their affair. However, an emboldened Lillian felt it was her turn to call the shots. When Bessie crept up behind her one evening to plant a kiss on her, she recoiled. With Ruby watching, the younger woman told Bessie 'Don't play around with me like that.' An incensed Bessie snapped back, 'The hell with you, bitch! I got twelve women on this show and I can have one every night if I want it. Don't you feel so important, and don't you say another word to me while you're on this show, or I'll send you home bag and baggage.' Three nights later, after being given the cold shoulder by Bessie, on the evening of 13 January 1927, Lillian attempted suicide, trying to gas herself in her room.

After pushing a note under the locked door, Lillian had blocked any gaps in the window, turned on the gas and placed her head in the oven. Luckily the suicide note was found by another member of the chorus who brought it to Bessie. Bessie raced to the room – the same one Lillian had been sharing with Ruby – and broke down the door; the landlord of the house could not open the window and so smashed the glass. Lillian was still breathing, just, and Bessie took her to a local hospital.

Lillian recovered and the pair recommenced their affair, but Lillian was petrified of what Jack Gee might do to her if he found out about them, and a few weeks later, on 5 February in Detroit, she left the *Harlem Frolics* company for the last time. Bessie made no attempt to persuade her to stay.

# 13

# Sissies, Freaks, 'Half-Pint' and The Hokum Boys

*'I had not meant to dwell so long on the spiritual. There is a more recent development that is just as important. It is the comic negro song... I mean the raw, rough comic song of the true American negro, sung by his own singer.'[1]* – Herman Petzer

The evening following Lillian Simpson's departure, Bessie visited a buffet flat in St Louis, organised by a local friend of hers, and watched enthralled as two men performed a queer sex act on each other. In May 1925 Bessie recorded her self-written song, 'Soft Pedal Blues', which, without going into explicit detail, described some of the shenanigans at a buffet flat; she would also sing about rent parties in 1931, in one of her final recordings for Columbia, another of her own compositions, 'Safety Mama'.

At that time St Louis did not have a defined LGBTQ area, although the neighbourhood around Olive Street had become synonymous with lesbian and gay nightlife long before the city's first gay bar, Dante's Inferno, opened there (3516 Olive Street) in the mid-1930s. Previously known as The Wedge, Dante's Inferno specialised in drag acts – including old vaudevillian Doral Mack – and when it first opened employed a female 'Mistress of Ceremonies', singer Nina Lee. In April 1936, Miss Lee attempted to poison herself whilst in the depths of depression. She was discovered, unconscious, on the doorstep of her friend, musician Irvin Green, who rushed her to hospital.

Josephine Baker's friend, chorus girl Hazel Valentine (often misnamed as Helen Valentine) ran a buffet flat on 140th Street – in the 'Jungle Alley' part of New York – known locally as the Daisy Chain, where sex acts of all kinds took place. The name was apt: the phrase 'daisy chain' is slang for a group sexual activity, where the participants serve as active and passive partners to different people simultaneously. In 1929 Fats Waller, who used the venue as his own personal pick-up joint and once boasted that the Daisy Chain was 'heaven on earth for a poor sinner like me',[2] wrote a tune, 'Valentine's Stomp' dedicated to Hazel, and in January 1937, at his orchestra's first Decca session, Count Basie recorded his own composition, 'Swinging at the Daisy Chain'.

The so-called 'roaring twenties', a period of massive growth and prosperity, saw a huge increase in lawlessness across the States, much of it prompted by the imposition of prohibition, and by the middle of the decade criminality relating to the black market in booze had reached epidemic proportions in cities such as New York and Chicago. An estimated 1,300 gangs brought terror to the streets of the Windy City, and many of these hoodlums were cash-rich, with bulging wallets full of the profits from the city's bootlegging and protection rackets, and from illegal gambling clubs run by men such as the notorious Al Capone. That money, in turn, was being used to pay off local police and politicians.

The city's seemingly lawless night life provided perfect fodder for newspaper and magazine reporters on the lookout for scandal, and in 1926, *Variety* reported on the anarchic scenes that would meet anyone visiting the city's busy 'black and tan' nightspots, specifically the Plantation – a street-level café on the corner of 35th and Calumet streets, just a few blocks away from the notorious Stroll and said to be controlled by Capone – and the Sunset, at 315 East 35th Street, a former car repair garage, which had been converted into a small dancehall and which was managed by Joe Glaser, the same man who would go on to manage Louis Armstrong.

'Of the two the Sunset is the better, although located just across the street from the Plantation,' *Variety*'s cabarets correspondent, Hal, reported.

Grand avenue and 35th street is the heart of Chicago's spacious black belt, thickly populated. The black and tan resort is their paradise. Here they may parade their clothes, mingle with the white element that doesn't seem to care, and rub elbows companionably with daring youngsters and portly commercial men who loudly explain that they are there slumming. The dusky patrons are but a small percentage of the trade. The real business is carried on with sophisticated high school youngsters, cynical office clerks, and effusive representatives of produce houses, who seem to relish the carefree atmosphere. Stags are abundant. Outside the cabarets Negroes loiter in doorways, eager to supply you with any variety of liquor. They ask $3 a pint for gin, but will consent to a lower price after bargaining. Their first asking for 'bonded' whisky is $8, and that also can be lowered. If you are a stag they will talk furtively of 'women'.

All employees and entertainers, with the exception of the manager, are colored. Entering you are confronted by a ticket booth housing a white toothed belle, who explains that a cover charge is paid admittance. Fifty cents admits you on week days and $1 at other times. Ringside tables carry 'Reserved' cards for a majority of fictitious names. 'Browns' and 'Smiths' are in abundance. The Plantation is decorated as attractively as many of the loop cafés, with a predominating scheme of red. The plantation atmosphere is carried out with picket fences. Alcoholic exhilaration is practically unanimous among the patrons. At intervals during the early morning a high-school girl will become hysterical and plead with a glitter-eyed youngster to take her home. The mammoth King Oliver and his 10 musicians provide the music. If you haven't heard Oliver and his boys you haven't heard real jazz. It is loud, wailing and pulsating. You dance calmly for a while, trying to fight it, and then you succumb completely, as King makes his trumpet talk personally to you –

193

and the trumpet doesn't usually say nice things. Hip dancing is carried on wholesaledly [*sic*] between the customers. Native jazz has no conscience.

A regular floor show, supplied entirely by colored entertainers, is at the Plantation. Dancing is carried on at a whirlwind pace: singing loud and rather coarse. There are eight chorus girls, some looking almost white. They execute five ensemble numbers. Included among the principals are Marion Harrison, Laura Elliott, Naomi Hunter, Norman Astwood, Billy Ledman, Mordechai Wells, and Joyner and Phillips. They work before the girls in a gypsy number strut, Russian stomp and Charleston. Costumes are attractive and the numbers are executed with the traditional colored finesse. To say that the entertainers throw themselves wholeheartedly into their work is saying nothing new about colored performers. The principals and the chorus girls seem to enjoy it even more than the paying patrons. Were it not for the arrogant, penny-snatching management the Plantation could be one of the worthwhile night places for slumming parties.

The management apparently does not realize nor care that the white patron is openly insulted; that white women are not safe, and that show people in particular seemed to be picked out for insult. Show people originally 'made' this café and were spenders; but this is a thing of the past now, as they have been impressed with the knowledge that they are not safe. Although the Plantation café makes a great play for white trade and the performers, the performer is laying himself open to unpleasant publicity and trouble by being in attendance. Ginger ale, $1.25.[3]

Hal's description is vivid, but makes no mention of the number of LGBTQ artists appearing in, or patrons regularly using, Chicago's black and tans, nor of the upsurge in drag as both entertainment and a way of life. At that time, Chicago was at the epicentre of queer nightlife, and living and playing in the city was providing inspiration for a number of queer artists, including Ma Rainey who, in June 1926, accompanied by a band that included a musical saw player, recorded a song that told of how she had come home, after enjoying a couple of nights of freedom in the dancehalls, to find her man sleeping with another man, a passive, effeminate character known as Miss Kate; her own composition, 'Sissy Blues':

I dreamed last night I was far from harm
Woke this morning found my man in a sissy's arms
Hello, Central, it's 'bout to run me wild
Can I get that number, or will I have to wait a while?
Some are young, some are old
My man says sissy's got good jelly roll
My man got a sissy, his name is Miss Kate
He shook that thing like jelly on a plate
Now all the people ask me why I'm all alone
A sissy shook that thing and took my man from home.

The use of a musical saw adds an otherworldly, ghostly feel to a song whose lyrics confirm that sexual fluidity – if not exactly accepted – was understood and, to an extent, tolerated in certain circles. As performance artist Sarah Kilborne, who features the song in her stage show *The Lavender Blues: The Story of Queer Music Before World War II*, explains: "Sissy Blues" challenges our assumptions of the past. Ma Rainey recorded "Sissy Blues" in 1926, years before any male recording artist laid down a version of a sissy-themed song, she was the first musical artist to sing about a male same-sex affair that paired a so-called "normal" or masculine-identified man with a "sissy" or effeminate male partner. When I introduce the song to audiences, I explain that back when the song was recorded a man could have sex with another man and still be considered "normal" as long as during the sexual encounter he performed the masculine role. In "Sissy Blues", the protagonist's two-timing man has been seduced by the feminine wiles of another; it just so happens his new partner is anatomically male. "Sissy Blues" is about a classic heartache – a woman losing her man to another lover – but the meaning of "lover" is given a decided twist. It's an outrageously modern song.'[4]

Ma's timing was impeccable; in 1925 American songwriter Edgar Leslie (who wrote the lyrics to 'For Me and My Gal') and his Italian-born, piano-playing partner James V. Monaco (co-author of the standard 'You Made Me Love You (I Didn't Want to Do It)') had penned the comedy song 'Masculine Women! Feminine Men!'. The song was recorded by a number of acts during 1926 and 1927, including Billy Murray, Irving Kaufman (under the pseudonym Frank Harris), the Six Jumping Jacks, British lesbian comedian Gwen Farrar (one-time girlfriend of actor Tallulah Bankhead, who, in 1931, issued the clearly suggestive 'If I Had a Girl Like You' from the musical *Wonder Bar*) and Merritt Brunies and his Friars Inn Orchestra, causing a sensation on both sides of the Atlantic, with lyrics about gender-fluid men and women, and even a verse about how the Prince of Wales liked to wear women's clothing: in 1936 comedian Judd Rees would go further still, issuing the single 'The King's a Queen at Heart', which not only poked fun at the incumbent monarch's sexuality, but was also the first record issued to use the word 'homosexual'.

Shortly after 'Sissy Blues' hit the stores, on 29 September 1926 *The Captive*, a play by Édouard Bourdet (originally titled *La Prisonnière*) which had been a huge hit in Europe, made its debut at the Empire Theatre in New York. One of the first Broadway plays to deal with lesbianism, *The Captive* caused a scandal and, although it was a huge hit with audiences, it was shut down after 160 performances.

Before the play had finished its run, on 31 January 1927 *The Drag*, which was promoted as being 'a male *Captive*' and 'a homosexual comedy drama'[5] was staged in Bridgeport, Connecticut, having been denied the opportunity to open in New York. Penned by Mae West under the name Jane Mast, the cast of *The Drag* was made up principally of gay men, performers that West knew personally and others from clubs in Greenwich Village. The casting choices she made were payback in part to early drag pioneers Julian Eltinge and Bert Savoy, both credited with being influences on West's stage persona.

West had been performing on stage for almost twenty years when *The Drag* debuted, and had made her first appearance on Broadway in 1911. With the lead female role initially promised to her sister Beverly (replaced, by the time the play was staged, by Emily Francis), rehearsals for *The Drag* took place late at night and in secrecy, after West had finished performing in her hit show *Sex*. *Sex* had been an enormous success

196

and had turned West's career around. After years on the slide, during which she had been appearing in small vaudeville houses and burlesque revues, *Sex* – which she wrote, produced and directed and in which she played brothel madame Margy Lamont – made her a star. Advertising for the show included a warning to potential patrons that 'if you cannot stand excitement see your doctor' before occupying their seat. Although critics panned the show – *Billboard* called it 'poorly written, poorly acted, horribly staged' and the 'cheapest, most vulgar, low "show" to have dared to open in New York this year' – audiences loved it.

Described by *Variety* as 'a rare orgy indulged in by a certain set'[6] and a 'sex perversion exposition' in which the producer allows the actors 'to cavort and carry on as they like',[7] although *The Drag* was a major hit, earning West $30,000 on its opening night alone, it was criticised for its portrayal of homosexuality, especially in its final act, where most of the action takes place at a drag ball. The Society for the Prevention of Vice warned the producers that if the play continued, all Broadway productions that season would be censored. New York's police commissioner sent officers to the opening night, who recommended that *The Drag* be banned from New York, and Broadway producers, fearful of enforced censorship, banded together to denounce the play. Despite an invitation-only performance held at midnight at Daly's Theatre, 1221 Broadway (the same theatre at which Mae was appearing in *Sex*), *The Drag* would not open in New York.

A little over a week later, on 9 February, the police raided productions of *The Captive*, *Sex*, and *The Virgin Man*, which had been adapted from the hit British farce *The Three Birds* and now incorporated themes of homosexuality and lesbianism. West – along with other members of the cast of *Sex* – was tried and found guilty of staging an obscene production, sentenced to ten days in jail and fined $5,000. Although *The Drag* would never make it to Broadway, in 1928 West recycled much of the material for a new play, *The Pleasure Man*. Once again, the police forced *The Pleasure Man* to close within its opening week, and West, plus her cast and crew, including a number of female impersonators, was arrested.

She was hardly the first taboo-breaking actor to have been persecuted by New York's morals police. In April 1900 actor and

197

director Olga Nethersole was tried for violating public decency after she attempted to stage a play titled *Sapho* in the city. Miss Nethersole was found not guilty of bringing disrepute to the New York stage, and the same was true of Mae. A lengthy trial, characterised by rampant homophobia, ended after the jury failed to reach a decision. All charges were dismissed, and the notoriety only helped boost Mae's box-office cachet; shortly afterwards she was off to Hollywood, and international fame.

It was a good time to be in Hollywood: the town's LGBTQ scene had been developing for some time and by the mid-1920s was fully established. In Hollywood, pianist and songwriter Stoughton Fletcher III, known professionally as Bruz Fletcher, had been building up a reputation for his witty songs for several years, although he would not record until 1934: his song 'Lei From Hawaii', dripping in double entendres, was a hit with many of the sophisticates of the era, including gay actor Monty Woolley, who was said to have sent copies of the disc to his friends. Bruz lived openly with his boyfriend, artist Casey Roberts, and the two were occasionally featured in the society columns of the day.

While *The Drag* was wowing audiences and upsetting critics, back in Chicago in April 1927 blues singer Bert 'Snake-Root' Hatton walked into a recording studio and put down his only two known sides, 'Down in Black Bottom' and 'Freakish Rider Blues', issued in September that year by Vocalion. Hatton, the son of a Methodist minister, had been performing in his home town of Topeka, Kansas, since his early teens. He was something of a minor star locally, where apparently 'young and old have been thrilled by his wonderful tenor as he has sung his way into the hearts of the people',[8] and he was even being referred to as 'Topeka's second Bert Williams',[9] high praise indeed when Williams had been hailed by the *New York Dramatic Mirror* as 'one of the great comedians of the world'.[10] By 1926 he was singing and performing comedy with the Smart Set, and for a number of years he was regularly featured on WMBS radio in Pennsylvania as a 'mammy singer'.

The lyrics and tune to 'Freakish Rider Blues' were written by Hatton. The word 'freakish' referring to either an effeminate man or a masculine woman, was a common phrase in the bars and speakeasies of Harlem, and its use soon spread to other cities. Back in the mid to late 19th century, the term 'freakish man' had been used to refer to an eccentric or peculiar-acting fellow; pianist and composer Ignacy Jan Paderewski, with his unkempt mop of fiery red hair, was referred to in the US press as a 'wholly freakish-looking man',[11] and the word or phrase continued to be applied to anyone whose appearance did not conform to the norms of Victorian society and, as clothes styles became more outlandish, the word was often used to denote any type of clothing, from hats to spats, that stood out from the ordinary. 'Ride', as a slang term for sexual intercourse, has been in use for centuries, appearing in print as early as 1692 in John Dryden's translations of the satires of the Roman poet Juvenal.

Like several other songs, notably Bessie Smith's 'Jail-House Blues', Hatton's lyrics playfully jump between same-sex and heterosexual relationships, and after being approached by a 'freakish' man attempting to pass as a woman in the first verse the singer spends most of the rest of the song trying to establish his manliness, insisting that he likes 'pigmeat' (young girls), preferably those who are already in relationships: 'Every time you catch me rooting / I'm rooting in some hog man's bag.' Two months after Hatton recorded 'Freakish Rider Blues', and again in Chicago, in June 1927 Lucille Bogan recorded 'Women Won't Need No Men' later issued as the flip side to her Paramount Records release 'War Time Man Blues'. An early, self-penned song about female emancipation, and about how a woman does not need to rely on the support of a man to get on in life, Bogan's lyric includes a verse that begins, 'Coming a time, women ain't going to need no men / Coming a time, women ain't going to need no men', a line that Willie Barker would lift for his 1929 recording 'Crooked Woman Blues' and that Bogan herself would later employ (as Bessie Jackson) on her better-known 'B.D. Woman's Blues' in 1935.

The sexual innuendo and slang used by Hatton provide an early recorded example of hokum blues – bawdy, comedic songs with roots stretching back to the minstrel shows of the mid to late 1800s. In the years immediately following the First World War, as the demand for race records began to grow, hokum songs and singers grew in popularity. Hokum blues poked fun at the times, with songs about drinking and gambling, rent parties and all manner of sexual practices and preferences, and compositions such as 'Pin in Your Cushion' and 'Banana in Your Fruit Basket' made little effort at subtlety to disguise the true meaning behind the lyrics. Critic Kennard Williams was not a fan: 'The production of blues seems to have reached its peak of suggestiveness if one is to form a conclusion from some of the titles and monotonous repetitions of the music that accompanies the titles,' he wrote in 1925. 'Several years ago this type of song was a novelty, and in the hands of the veteran Handy was a pleasant contrast to the nauseating vaporings of today. All of the suggestion in the world seems to have been dug up for the entertainment of those who care for this class of music.' Williams singled out Bessie Smith's lesbian-themed 'Jail-House Blues' as one of the prime examples of this decline in standards, going on to state that:

> Like slang, and thieves' jargon, many of the versions of the blues were conceived for the brothers of the underworld, and should have been kept in the same association. Some shrewd vaudeville performer found that a gullible public would swallow this the same as any other 'hokum', used them in theaters and hence their transfer to records. The production of this style of modern version of the blues as well as the market for this class of composition is obvious. Manufacturers find the sale profitable and the tastes of the purchasers is evident. As long as these songs are confined to the 'barrelhouse' cabarets and private homes they are not a matter for public criticism, but when they reach the stage of the theater they are justly open to censure. The damage done by them is irreparable.

Williams claimed that the writers of hokum blues songs were, 'No less traitors than was Benedict Arnold. Plastic minds and susceptible adult ones need protection from the modern blues. It is to the credit of legitimate musicians that they have refused to use their talents to the discredit of their race.'[12]

A number of well-known jazz and blues musicians were more than happy to bring such discredit, and the undisputed King and Queen of the genre was the diminutive singer, dancer and orchestra leader Frankie 'Half-Pint' Jaxon.

Frank Devera Jackson was born in Montgomery, Alabama, on 3 February 1895 (according to his 1917 draft card, and confirmed by Frankie himself during an interview with Bill Miller, publisher of the *Australian Jazz Quarterly*), but he was orphaned before the century was out and, along with his sister Rosa, was raised by cousins in Kansas City, Missouri; Frankie's First World War draft card lists his place of birth, erroneously, as Kansas City. Frankie and Rosa attended Attucks School, which had opened in 1905 to serve students from Kansas City's Black community; the school was named after Crispus Attucks, a Black American killed by British soldiers in the Boston Massacre of 1770. Employed in a barber shop by day, Frankie began his performing career around 1910, working as a dancer and singer in cafés, movie theatres and bars in Kansas City before landing a job with the Henry McDaniel company (McDaniel was the father of Hattie McDaniel, the first African American actor to win an Oscar, for her portrayal of Mammy in *Gone with the Wind*) travelling with the show throughout Texas, where his vocal range and flamboyant manner established him as a crowd favourite. A gifted dancer, actor and singer, he often teamed up with other hoofers, including Alabama-born comedian Gallie De Gaston, who would later work with Louis Armstrong in Chicago and with Gladys Bentley in New York, and tour Britain in the revue *Blackbirds of 1936*. Both De Gaston and Jackson (as he was still known) would occasionally switch things up by wearing female attire for their comedy numbers. For a short period after the team of Gaston and Jackson split, Frankie worked with Bessie Smith's former partner, Wayne 'Buzzin'' Burton, but by the spring of 1916, after a short stop in Harlem, Frankie had begun appearing regularly as a musician in Atlantic City, taking a break to serve in the military when the US joined the First World War.

Leaving the army a sergeant, he resumed his work as a musician and performer. Now going by the name Frankie 'Half-Pint' Jaxon – a nickname he earned in the army because he stood no taller than 5 ft

2 in – he returned to Atlantic City where he held down a residency at the Paradise Café. For the next few years, Frankie's work routine would stay reasonably fixed: winter would be spent working in either Philadelphia or Chicago (where he shared a bill with Sammy Stewart and his Knights of Syncopation), but from March or April until September he would be in Atlantic City. At the Paradise Café he worked with many of the stars of the day, including Ethel Waters, and became friendly with Bessie Smith, offering her advice on staging. Here Frankie would again perform in drag, alongside his partner Helen Lee: 'Sometimes she would impersonate me in the type of clothes I wore, and I would do the opposite with her in a finale, dressed as she would as a female,'[13] he revealed. Although prohibition was enforced nationally in 1920, the resort of Atlantic City was one of the few places in the country that people could still get a drink; former sheriff of New Jersey, Enoch 'Nucky' Johnson, made it plain when he told the press that, 'We have whisky, wine, women, song and slot machines. I won't deny it and I won't apologize for it. If the majority of the people didn't want them they wouldn't be profitable and they would not exist. The fact that they do exist proves to me that the people want them.'[14] As a result, the regular tourist season quickly extended for the full twelve months of the year, and the club became hugely popular with white audiences who loved the heady mixture of booze and music.

During the first half of the 1920s the Paradise Café was constantly targeted by anti-drink campaigners, desperate to find a reason to close the place down, and the venue was forced to shut its doors on several occasions by the local authorities after outbreaks of drunkenness and violence, although the owner, David Abrahms, and his business partners always seemed to find a loophole and would reopen the establishment within days. It certainly helped that the powerful 'Nucky' Johnson, now head of the Republican Party locally, was a crook who was tight with leading underground figures including Al Capone, and was taking a cut from the sale of illicit liquor and backhanders from bar and brothel owners. Like Capone, Johnson would eventually be jailed for tax evasion.

Although he would continue to work sporadically in Atlantic City, Frankie soon moved to Chicago, where he worked at the Sunset Café,

315–317 East 35th Street, with Carl Dickerson's Novelty Orchestra. Frankie was a popular draw: he sang with many of the top jazz and blues bands that passed through the city, and also performed regularly with Joe 'King' Oliver at the nearby Plantation Café (at 338 East 35th Street). By the end of 1922 Jaxon was not only singing at the Sunset Café, he had risen to the rank of assistant cabaret director at the club, leading him to work with other LGBTQ performers including Ethel Waters and his old friend Bessie Smith. He spent some time on the road with former burlesque star Mae Dix and her ten-piece Chicago Harmonaders, although sharing a stage with Fred's Pigs (a trained pig act) or providing the entertainment to picture house audiences before the main film was screened was not Frankie's idea of fun.

In 1926 Jaxon took on a job heading the cabaret at the West End Hotel, in St Louis, Missouri, where, that April, he was caught up in a raid. The West End Hotel was targeted by police because it had a reputation as a place where 'white persons and Negroes were associating' and where 'white girls had been seen staggering out at late hours',[15] and despite the authorities' meagre haul of just two gin rickeys, forty-three people were arrested, thirty-six of them white, for violating the 'dry law'. The following month, while still in St Louis, he made his first recordings, for the Okeh label: the comedy number 'Hannah Fell in Love with My Piano' is credited to Frankie Jackson, tenor with piano by local musician De Lloyd Barnes. De Lloyd Barnes recorded several sides for Okeh that year, accompanying blues singer Victoria Spivey and others, but would not record again after 1926.

Shortly after making that recording, Jaxon returned to Chicago. He initially appeared, as a dancer rather than a singer and bandleader, at the Grand Theatre, performing novelty dances – including the then-current craze, the Valencia – for producer Norman Thomas, but he very quickly landed himself a plum job, as director of entertainment at the Dreamland Café, on South State Street, another venue that thought little of breaking prohibition. The South Side's illicit booze racket was now run by the notorious gangster Al Capone, who took over control after his former boss, Johnny Torrio, retired following an attempt on his life by his enemies on the North Side of the city. Capone was in league with Chicago's corrupt mayor, William Hale Thompson, and much of its police force. At the height of the illicit booze wars, in July 1926, the Plantation was bombed while approximately 100 people were inside. The following March the Plantation, closed for refurbishment, was the victim of an arson attack, with damage put at $50,000.

When not working in Chicago, Frankie Jaxon was back on the train to Atlantic City, singing with Charlie Johnson's Paradise Ten orchestra, the house band at Small's Paradise. Johnson's band was featured on radio from 1927, but would never have been able to broadcast or record their version of 'The Boy in the Boat', with Frankie ad-libbing vocals so obscene that they would have to be toned down before George Hannah finally committed the song to shellac in 1930. That year Frankie headlined at the Apollo Theater, producing and starring in his own show, where he was described as 'a fine singer, genuine talented actor and a natural born dancer'.[16] Also in 1927 Jaxon recorded one of his most famous songs, 'Willie the Weeper' (itself based on the much earlier 'Willie the Chimney Sweeper'), the tale of a drug-fuelled nightmare that became the basis for Cab Calloway's 1931 hit 'Minnie the Moocher'.

In October 1928 he began recording with Tampa Red's Hokum Jug Band for Vocalion, whose line-up included Ma Rainey's accompanist Thomas A. Dorsey. Dorsey had only recently returned to making music after suffering a nervous breakdown, and he would soon abandon secular music altogether in favour of the church. Over a short period (1928–31) many sides were recorded by a band called The Hokum Boys (or similar), a generic catch-all used by a revolving set of musicians, and an early example of the studio-based group. Piano player Alexander Robinson, and his wife Aletha Dickerson, herself an accomplished pianist who also worked as secretary to 'Ink' Williams at Paramount (the couple became the de facto heads of Paramount's race records department following Williams's departure), was usually involved somewhere, even if he had simply arranged the session, and many of the musicians recording under this epithet had already recorded or had successful careers as jazz or blues sidesmen, using their own names. Because of this, the line-up of The Hokum Boys changed with almost every disc they issued, and nicknames or pseudonyms were often used. Dorsey became Georgia Tom, and recorded with a number of hokum groups. He recorded versions of the song 'Somebody's Been Using

That Thing', featuring lyrics about a man 'who puts paint and powder on his face' and 'women who walked and talked like men', with both The Hokum Boys (for Paramount), and with Tampa Red and Bobby Robinson and the Famous Hokum Boys (for ARC), a band that included Big Bill Broonzy. Dorsey later recalled, in an interview for *Living Blues* magazine, that these bands were pulled together purely to record, and often at short notice. 'That was for records, recording... We'd throw a recording bunch together in 30 minutes. We'd just call, if you could get hold to him, say "Well, we gon' rehearse here. We gon' rehearse at such-and-such a time. Come on, we want you in the band."'[17] Remuneration was basic: maybe $15 or $25 a session, and few if any of the players saw any royalties from the sales of the discs, but when you could get a decent meal for thirty or forty cents, and the musicians you worked with could knock out four sides in a couple of hours, it was easy money.

Just to confuse the issue further, there were at least two different comedy double acts working at the same time using the name 'The Hokum Boys'. On one Vocalion release, the 1929 recording 'Kunjine Baby', the trio of Tampa Red, Georgia Tom and Frankie Jaxon are given a new name, the Black Hill Billies, the appellation bestowed by the record label, not the members of the band themselves. 'Somebody's Been Using That Thing' was first recorded by Al Miller and His Market Street Boys, for Brunswick, in March 1929; a version issued by Milton Brown and His Brownies (Decca, 1936) has a verse about 'two old maids in a folding bed', but without the verses used by The Hokum Boys. Dorsey was a busy man: at the same time as he was recording with Jaxon, he was still acting as Ma Rainey's pianist and bandleader, playing on the majority of her 1928 recordings, including 'Prove It On Me Blues'.

Although the disc released from Jaxon's first session with Tampa Red's Hokum Jug Band featured the decidedly heterosexual 'It's Tight Like That' on the A-side (Tampa Red and Georgia Tom issued a different version of the song simultaneously), the flip contained the decidedly queer 'How Long How Long Blues'. On their version of the Leroy Carr-penned song, Jaxon plays the parts of both a kept woman and her 'daddy'... and it's pretty obvious on first listening that Frankie is not enquiring about the length of time before he sees his lover again, but about the length of something else entirely. Frankie makes no attempt to sing any of Carr's original lyrics, instead the song quite literally reaches its climax with Frankie simulating an orgasm.

In April 1929, during their third session, the band recorded the definitive version of the obscene queer blues standard 'My Daddy Rocks Me (With One Steady Roll)'. Written by J. Berni Barbour (1881–1936), and originally recorded in 1922 for Black Swan by Trixie Smith and the Jazzmasters as 'My Man Rocks Me (With One Steady Roll)', the song is widely recognised as the first to pair the words 'rock' and 'roll' in a sexual context. It was later covered by the Southern Quartet (aka the Southern Negro Quartette) in September 1924, although their version – a mix of barbershop and proto-doo-wop – altered the lyric to 'My baby rocks me...', much more acceptable for the four-man vocal act. The song was also recorded by Harold Ortli and His Ohio State Collegians with vocals by Clarence Buck in February 1925 for Okeh (recorded in Ohio), and by Charles Creath's Jazz-O-Maniacs with Floyd Campbell (again for Okeh) in March 1925, with Campbell once again opting to change the lyrics to 'My baby rocks me...', thereby denuding the song of any homosexual content.

Jaxon's version of 'My Daddy Rocks Me...' makes no such nod to decorum. It is, quite frankly, obscene. Adopting a high-pitched girlish voice, the moans and howls that permeate the recording are Frankie once again faking an orgasm to the point of climax, and doing it rather well. Known for occasionally performing in drag, and for a show-stopping performance where he would duet with himself singing both the male and female vocal parts on the song 'I'm Gonna Dance Wit De Guy Wot Brung Me' (which Jaxon recorded in Chicago in 1927 for Gennett), at their next session, in July 1929, Frankie would once again adopt the role of a woman when he sang the Shelton Brooks number 'I Wonder Where My Easy Rider's Gone', a song popularised by Sophie Tucker. That same month, at the next session Frankie led for Vocalion, this time with Georgia Tom but not Tampa Red, he recorded 'Operation Blues', a song that would remain officially unreleased, but that would appear on at least two different 'under the counter' labels in the 1930s as 'Is Doctor Eazet In?', credited to Painless Doc. Dorsey plays the role of the doctor on this recording, with Jaxon his female patient ('don't get fresh doctor, I'm a married woman... oh! what's that you got there doctor? What's that you got a-holding in your hands? That's nothing but my tool, honey...').

That particular recording was a difficult one for Dorsey to be involved in, as he did not consider himself a comedian and was uncomfortable in the role, and he had also recently had his religious beliefs reawakened, something that would soon lead to his ditching the blues altogether for more sacred music. Those issues aside, Dorsey enjoyed working with Jaxon. 'He was quite a jolly guy and nice to get along with. And he was up to it, too. He knew his way around. He knew all the big nightclubs and cabarets and so forth and so on... Frankie was a guy, he could talk a lot before the crowd about what he wanted to talk about, he never told nobody much about himself.'[18]

For the first half of the 1930s Jaxon, whose sides were also issued on the Supertone label under the pseudonyms Cotton Thomas and Jelly Roll Hunter (a fully intentional, knowing double entendre), could be heard on Chicago's WJJD radio station six nights a week with his own band The Hot Shots (the band also held down a residency at the city's Capitol Theatre), in a fifteen-minute live programme sponsored by the Midwest Drug Company of Philadelphia. The show's theme tune, 'Fan It' became a local hit, and for a short while Frankie was a major celebrity in the East of the country, with promotional fans and even a Jaxon jigsaw, advertised as the first ever produced of a radio artist. In promoting the show, Frankie's bosses insisted that:

One man sent him a bill for $7.50 the other day, saying that's what it cost him to have his radio cabinet refinished after one of Frankie's broadcasts. It seems that the radio got so hot, it cracked the varnish on the cabinet. One woman keeps her radio in the refrigerator when his program is on, another one fries her bacon, and a farmer in Indiana puts his set in the barn so that he can save on his heating bill.

The solution, they suggested, was simple: 'get yourself a five cent fan and Fan It!' Woody Herman and His Woodchoppers would cover the song almost a decade later for Decca.

The year 1933 was a big one for Frankie and his band, with a week-long residency in Chicago's Palace Theatre in July and being employed to entertain at the Streets of Paris, a temporary village that was built as part of the Chicago World's Fair. Here, for a 25-cent entry fee, visitors could enjoy an approximation of Parisian café society and for a further $7.50 they could attend a grand ball with entertainment from 'The hottest jazz band at the exposition', led by Frankie Jaxon with 'his clarinet, his baton and his yodelling'.[19] In June 1935, Frankie performed at the opening of Chicago's refurbished Mid-Night Club; the Black-owned club, on Green Bay Road, was well-known for acting as the base of Howard Redding, who was operating an illegal bookie operation. The club had been closed following a series of raids, one of which saw seven armed gangsters, several brandishing sub-machine guns, force patrons to lie face down on the floor while they raided the bar and offices for cash; they took just $155 from the club, but a further $760 from the pocket of Redding himself. That same year pianist Cassino Simpson was sent to the Illinois State Hospital for Mental Diseases, after attempting to kill Frankie. It's probably no coincidence that Jaxon's fifteen-minute radio show was taken off the air soon after: a contemporary newspaper item reported in vague terms about 'other rumors'[20] surrounding Frankie's absence from the airwaves but did not go into any detail. Cassino had been a member of the Hot Shots, and the pair had recorded together in 1933, but Simpson was already having mental health issues, and he would spend the rest of his life in the institution.

Jaxon's last recording sessions took place between 1937 and 1940, for Decca in New York and Chicago, but his influence on other performers continued to be heard. Cab Calloway owed much of his act to Frankie, as did other bandleaders, and in October 1936 a band known as the Harlem Hamfats – who would back Frankie up on three sessions in 1937 and 1938 – recorded 'The Garbage Man', a jazz tune with one of the vocalists (possibly trumpet player Herb Morand, who also takes the writer's credit for the song, or the band's leader, Papa Charlie McCoy) imitating a woman in the style of Frankie Jaxon or Billy Banks on the opening verse:

Knock knock, 'Who's there?'
Stick out your cans, this here's the garbage, garbage man.
'Can you take it?' Yeah man! Yeah man!
Stick out your cans, here comes the garbage man...

'When we were researching that one, so many people would tell us that their grandmother sang it to them,' laughs musician Brett Houston-Lock. 'That's how hidden the meaning was. They would not have known that it was based on a dance craze in gay clubs.'[21] It seems that those innocent grandparents were also unaware that the 'cans' that Morand wanted them to stick out were buttocks. Although they were called the Harlem Hamfats the studio-based band, which also featured Charlie McCoy's brother Joe, were based in Chicago, where they recorded the majority of their sides. Eight years later jazz quartet the Four Aces (a different band to the white vocal quartet, popular in the 1950s) recorded a version of the song, very clearly based on Herb Morand's original but with new, suitably risqué lyrics by group member George Smith.

In December 1938, still in New York, Jaxon appeared on Broadway as Buddy in the Black musical comedy *Policy Kings*; despite good reviews for his own performance, the story of a Harlem numbers racket failed to click with audiences, with the curtain of the Nora Bayes Theatre coming down for the last time on 8 January. In 1941 Frankie retired from show business for good. Times – and tastes – were changing, and many of the stars of the twenties and thirties were suffering from the combined onslaught of the Depression, the repeal of prohibition, the massive growth in demand for the cinema and, inevitably, the Second World War. Jaxon once again reverted to his given surname of Jackson and took a job with the military at the Pentagon in Washington, D.C. The following year, aged 47, he married for possibly the second time to Eunice Eleanor Miller: the 1930 census had him living in Chicago with a different wife, Evelyn, and two lodgers. Still working for the army, Frankie relocated to Los Angeles sometime around 1944, and although little is known about his last years, he spent some time as a residential patient at the Brentwood Neuropsychiatric Hospital, an establishment that specialised in the treatment of service veterans

209

with mental health issues. He died in the Veterans Administration Hospital, in West Los Angeles on 15 May 1953 (his death certificate lists his wife's name as Sirnader Jackson; she is also named as Jaxon's wife in the *Australian Jazz Quarterly* interview from 1948), and was buried with military honours (and a new birthdate of 3 March 1897) at the Veterans Administration Cemetery in Los Angeles.

By the time of his death, Frankie had been out of the industry for thirteen years, but he helped pave the way for the next big thing. Rock 'n' roll was just around the corner, a style of pop music that almost certainly took its name from suggestive songs such as 'My Daddy Rocks Me (With One Steady Roll)', a song that he had helped popularise. In a serendipitous twist, one of the first uses of the phrase 'rock and roll' to refer to rhythmic music was in a 1945 *Billboard* review for a Woody Herman recording – the same man who had covered Frankie's 'Fan It' twice.

# He Just Don't Appeal to Me

*'...the greatest Negro artist [Robeson] has ever heard is a vast, golden skinned raucous voiced woman called Bessie Smith, "Queen of the Blues," whose songs make up in wit and artistry what they may lack in strict propriety.*[1]

On 7 August 1927, Alberta Hunter and her girlfriend Lottie Tyler left New York for an extended working holiday in Europe: Alberta had dates to fulfil in France and Lottie, now independently wealthy following the death of her uncle Bert, decided to go along. However, by the end of October Lottie was back on board ship and heading home, after telling Alberta that she had fallen in love with another woman. Alberta would not have had much time to mourn the end of their relationship; she had been booked to play in Monte Carlo and, in January, would be off to London. The two women had made no pretence at being exclusive during their time together, and would stay close long after this particular parting of the ways. In 1929 the pair, along with Langston Hughes and Carl Van Vechten, made the gossip columns when they were spotted together at a Paul Robeson recital at Carnegie Hall, and whenever Alberta was in town she lived with Lottie at the latter's New York home, an apartment at 400 West 152nd Street, Upper Manhattan.

Alberta would have been very much aware that she was following in Josephine Baker's stiletto-heeled footsteps. News of Baker's success in Paris had filled plenty of column inches back in the States, and she was about to become an even bigger sensation with her appearance in the French film *La Sirène des Tropiques* (Siren of the Tropics), which played throughout Europe to great acclaim before making its way to the United States, where it debuted in 1929. For that US version, Joe Jordan was employed to write a score for the otherwise silent movie, and he brought Porter Grainger in to provide lyrics to two songs, 'Love for a Day' and 'Josephine, My Tropic Queen'. The score, the rights to which were purchased by Irving Berlin, was recorded by Joe Jordan's Sharps and Flats, featuring members of Duke Ellington's and Fletcher Henderson's orchestras, and issued on discs to be played alongside the film – a primitive form of synchronised sound that was used heavily in the early years of sound pictures. Jordan and Grainger became the first Black Americans to compose an entire film score.

While Alberta was establishing herself in Europe, back in New York in September 1927, during a two-day session that yielded four new recordings, Bessie Smith, accompanied by Porter Grainger on piano, performed on a cover of Eddie Green's composition 'A Good Man Is Hard to Find', a song that Alberta had been including in her own cabaret act for almost a decade.

Born in Baltimore in 1891, Green started out on stage as a comedian while still a juvenile but by the mid-1910s had graduated to songwriting; he later went on to star in *Amos 'n' Andy* on radio. Written in 1917, and copyrighted by Pace and Handy in the summer of 1918, when America's involvement in the First World War was at its height, 'A Good Man Is Hard to Find' was initially sold as piano rolls and sheet music before, in 1919, it was recorded by white singer Marion Harris for Victor. Although Harris performs the song in a ragtime/jazz style, the lyrics contain the line, 'now the blues have overtaken me / since my lovin' man has gone away', and according to Green's daughter Elva, her father had consciously 'written in a bluesy style, probably so that it would better relate to the general public'.[2]

Marion Harris had been a big star in the years immediately before Bessie began her recording career, issuing her first jazz and blues sides for Victor in 1916 and appearing with the Ziegfeld Follies. Although she was white, the press made the most of her roots to stake her claim as the first white jazz singer: 'Heralded as the queen of all "Blues" singers, and the greatest singer of popular songs... Like most Southern children, she had a colored mammy, from whom she learned to sing darky melodies.'[3] The song became more widely known, however, after it was picked up by Sophie Tucker, who included it in her act at the 400 Club, at Reisenweber's café in New York, one of the first establishments in the city to feature live jazz bands. 'When an accomplished artist like Sophie Tucker takes up a song and makes it a success,' wrote *Billboard*, 'It's a foregone conclusion that the song has merit... The fact that Miss Tucker has selected A Good Man Is Hard To Find is conclusive proof that Miss Tucker has confidence in Pace and Handy's big song success.'[4] So great a hit was she, that the 400 Club was renamed the Sophie Tucker Room. Other blues singers would also record versions of the song, including Victoria Spivey (for Okeh in 1928), and Alberta Hunter on her 1980 comeback album *Amtrak Blues*. In 1941, Alberta claimed that '"A Good Man is Hard to Find" was one of my specialties. I taught it to Sophie Tucker who has featured it ever since.'[5] However, in a series of interviews she gave for the book *Alberta Hunter: A Celebration in Blues*, she changed her tune, admitting that Sophie learned how to sing the song like Alberta by having her pianist spy on Alberta's performance.

Smith's recording was issued at the end of October 1927, just days after her next Columbia session. This time Grainger would not appear on the recording, but it is entirely possible that one of the two songs she performed that day was written about him: Bessie knew that Grainger was homosexual, and often poked fun at his 'dicty' ways although Bessie's biographer Chris Albertson, suggests that a terrified Grainger was bedded by Bessie on more than one occasion.

Composed by Bessie herself, 'Foolish Man Blues' features Fletcher Henderson on piano rather than Grainger. In the song, Bessie sings, 'There's two things got me puzzled, there's two things I can't understand / That's a mannish actin' woman and a skippin', twistin', woman actin' man.' The following year bisexual Black author Claude McKay quoted from the song in his novel *Home to Harlem*: 'And there is two things

213

in Harlem I don't understan' / It is a bulldyking woman and a faggoty man.' The publication of McKay's novel had been announced in July 1927, several months before Bessie recorded the song, however the book did not reach the shelves until March 1928. Did McKay make a late alteration to his manuscript, or had he perhaps heard Bessie perform the song live sometime before she recorded it? It is far more likely that both he and Bessie were simply adapting the opening lines to Ma Rainey's 1924 hit 'Shave 'Em Dry Blues': 'There's one thing I don't understand / Why a good-looking woman likes a workin' man.' Bessie's lyric was honest: she always showed a preference for femme female partners, and was unlikely to have shared her bed with a 'mannish actin' woman'.

Porter Grainger had been one of Bessie's more ardent supporters and faithful sidemen, despite Ruby claiming that 'she put many grey hairs on Porter's head', performing on more than a dozen tunes with the singer between 1924 and 1928, composing or co-writing a half-dozen more, and writing a musical revue, *Mississippi Days*, for her. He was also no slouch at self-promotion, and when the opportunity arose for him to take Bessie to a party full of influential people, including some of his Harlem Renaissance friends, he jumped at the chance. On 11 (or 12) April, while Bessie was appearing at the Lafayette, Porter Grainger took Bessie and her niece Ruby to a party thrown by Carl Van Vechten, at his West 55th Street Manhattan apartment. Van Vechten was a long-time fan, so it's hardly surprising that, when he ran into Grainger in town in late February and discovered Bessie was to be in New York that spring, he would entreat Grainger to bring her over to his place.

She was uncomfortable at the party: having made a grand entrance swathed in silks and furs, she proceeded to get drunk, but she gave a performance, accompanied by the loyal, eager-to-impress Grainger. 'Porter Grainger brought her to my apartment on West Fifty-fifth Street,' Van Vechten would later write,

Fania Marinoff and I were throwing a party. George Gershwin was there and Marguerite d'Alverez and Constance Collier, possibly Adele Astaire. The drawing room was well filled with sophisticated listeners. Before she could sing, Bessie wanted a drink. She asked for a glass of straight gin, and with one gulp she downed a glass holding nearly a pint. Then, with a burning cigarette depending from one corner of her mouth, she got down to the blues, really down to 'em, with Porter at the piano. I am quite certain that anybody who was present that night will never forget it. This was no actress; no imitator of a woman's woes; there was no pretence. It was the real thing – a woman cutting her heart open with a knife until it was exposed for us all to see, so that we suffered as she suffered, exposed with a rhythmic ferocity, indeed, which could hardly be borne. In my own experience, this was Bessie Smith's greatest performance.[6]

Gershwin was just as enamoured as Van Vechten was of 'brilliant Negro artists such as Bessie Smith, who was one of the few people for whom George would desert the piano to hear. He was not a little impressed, too, by her ability to down a stiff jolt of gin before she sang the blues.'[7] Van Vechten had all of her recordings and had seen her perform on Thanksgiving Day 1925, at the Orpheum Theatre in Newark, New Jersey, later writing an effusive review for the January edition of *Vanity Fair*, but when it came to New York's critics he was one of the few that fell for Bessie's voice. The rare reviews that her records were afforded in the *New York Clipper* were almost always scathing, dismissing her as a 'blues yodeler [who] possesses a minor crooning quality',[8] and whose 'appeal must be limited to a minority'.[9] In fairness to the critics, her early releases suffered from the archaic recording system: once she began making electrical recordings (the first of which were issued by Columbia in 1926) the true majesty of her voice shone through.

Van Vechten wrote about Bessie in another feature for *Vanity Fair*, an article entitled 'Negro "Blues" Singers', that appeared in the March 1926 edition of the magazine. The article is patronising, and introduced with a paragraph from Van Vechten's editor that dismissed New York's interest in African American talent as a seasonal fad, but for the first time a queer writer had published an appreciation of three queer blues singers: Bessie, Clara Smith (of whom he was equally infatuated), and Ethel Waters. Van Vechten's prose is, as was usual for him and for the times, florid and demeaning, yet he successfully described the experience of seeing Bessie live, shows how her audience would hang off her every word, and gives some insight into just how powerful her stage presence was. He wrote that he considered Ethel Waters the best blues singer, not just of the three women he sketched, but 'superior to any other woman stage singer of her race',[10] and that Clara was 'more of an artist than Bessie', but it is his description of Bessie that takes up more than half the article. He may think her as 'crude and primitive', but he continues that 'she represents the true folk-spirit of the race'.[11]

Van Vechten's turn of phrase may appear anachronistic and condescending, but through his articles for *Vanity Fair* he introduced the magazine's readers to such important figures in the Harlem Renaissance as the queer Black writers Langston Hughes and Countee Cullen, to blues and jazz musicians including Bessie, Clara and Ethel, and to many other key Black artists. Hughes, one of Van Vechten's closest friends, had become acquainted with Bessie the previous summer, while she was appearing in Macon, Georgia, but the drinks party at his home in April 1928 would be Van Vechten's first opportunity to spend time with the Empress in the flesh.

Perhaps someone at the party told Bessie about the article. Perhaps she had been drinking on an empty stomach. Maybe she was just sick of these ofays (derogatory Black slang for a white person) looking down at her, but by the time she finished her turn, Bessie was roaring drunk. When time came to leave, Bessie pushed Van Vechten's Russian-born wife, Fania Marinoff, to the floor as the hostess attempted to kiss her guest goodbye. Marinoff, a diminutive actor who often found her efforts on stage lambasted by Stephen Clow in the pages of *Broadway Brevities*, had married Van Vechten despite knowing that he was homosexual. She made the move from Broadway bit-part player to screen actor in the same year that they married, 1914.

'Get the fuck away from me!', the singer screamed at the prostrate Marinoff. 'I never heard of such shit.' As Ruby recounted to Chris Albertson, 'Bessie was good and drunk when she finished her last song, so Porter came over to me and said, "Let's get her out of here quick, before she shows her ass." We got her coat on her and got her to the front door when all of a sudden this woman comes out of nowhere.

"Miss Smith, you're not leaving without kissing me goodbye," she said...
Poor Porter, he would have done anything to be with that crowd, but
now Bessie had done shown her ass to all them people. I felt so sorry
for him.'[12] Grainger was mortified, but once Bessie had recovered her
composure, and gotten over her hangover, she would gleefully tell her
friends about what transpired that night, laughing as she regaled them
with imitations of Grainger, Van Vechten, Marinoff and others present.
'"Shit," she exclaimed, "you should have seen them ofays lookin' at me
like I was some kind of singin' monkey!"'[13] Smith clearly forgave the
Van Vechtens, or they forgave her, for in 1936 she sat for Carl as he
took a series of photographic portraits of her.

Wild and exciting, you took your life in your hands when you dared
to step through the doors of a New York club. Patrons and performers
were targets for violence: Floyd Mitchell, a member of the four-piece
band that supplied the music for basement dive the Black Bottom (on
East Fourth Street) was hospitalised in November 1930 after a fight
broke out between rival gangs and a bullet hit him while the band were
on stage. Despite featuring Black performers, having Black waiting staff
and being frequented by Harlem's Black glitterati, many of the most
successful clubs, including Connie's Inn (which had previously been
known as the Shuffle Inn and would later become the Ubangi Club),
the Cotton Club (where Duke Ellington led the house band and Louis
Armstrong could be seen night after night) and Small's Paradise, still
practiced segregation of sorts, with the best tables reserved for their
white patrons. The segregation enforced by New York's nightclubs
would encourage one Cotton Club visitor, Barney Josephson, to launch
his own club: when it opened in December 1938 the Café Society
became the first nightclub in Greenwich Village to actively eschew
segregation, with Josephson stating that, 'I wanted a club where blacks
and whites worked together behind the footlights and sat together out
front. There wasn't, so far as I know, a place like that in New York or in
the whole country... One thing that bugged me about the Cotton Club
was that blacks were limited to the back one-third of the club, behind
columns and partitions. It infuriated me that even in their own ghetto
they had to take this.'[14] George Immerman, co-owner (with his brother

Connie) of Connie's Inn, insisted that at his venue at least, 'white and black fraternize, enjoying their nocturnal pleasures jointly without the slightest friction'.[15]

> There is generally one period during the night, about the time for the first review [sic], when all ringside seats are filled with whites while the Negro patrons fill the seats just behind. As the night wears away, however, and the whites begin to leave, the waiters 'usher' the incoming colored patrons to the seats left vacant at the ringside when the second review generally takes place... The Cotton Club is popular as a place in which whites 'do Harlem'. While prohibition agents swoop down on some of the places occasionally and look under the tables for wet goods, there is certainly no dearth of stimulants in the night clubs. You are supposed to bring it on the hip, but an obliging attendant can supply you if you make the right sign... But the real wicked places in New York are not the night cubs. If you really want to dip into the real Sodom and Gomorrah of the big city, have some knowing 'cabby' take you to one of those private clubs, generally some place hidden within the privacy of a residence. There your entertainment may include pajama-clad women, exceedingly low lights and plenty to drink. If you are 'intelligentsia minded' or like 'atmosphere' you can also feed your sex-starved soul with a dip into one of those little private affairs where white and Negro friends get together.[16]

This fraternisation was not limited to the patrons. One of the other regular stars of Connie's Inn was Gertrude 'Baby' Cox, best known for performing the scat solo on Duke Ellington's 1928 hit 'The Mooche'. Cox was the daughter of Jimmy Cox, a comedian and songwriter known as the Black Charlie Chaplin, and author of the blues standard 'Nobody Knows You When You're Down and Out', recorded by Bessie Smith in May 1929, and later covered by a whole new generation of blues fans, including Dave van Ronk, Janis Joplin and Eric Clapton.

Known as 'Baby' since joining her parents' vaudeville act as a child, and celebrated as the 'smallest colored coon shouter in the world',[17] she had toured with blues singer Bessie Brown (in 1922), and worked on stage with Butterbeans and Susie before – in 1929 – taking on a role in Connie's Inn's annual revue, *Hot Chocolates*, alongside Fats Waller. *Hot Chocolates*, 'a fast, savagely Negro show of a far from negligible Fahrenheit',[18] had a long and difficult gestation, originating with the Plantation's 1925 show *Tan Town Topics*, which had starred Ethel Waters and Josephine Baker, but it proved to be hugely popular with audiences. Including Waller's massive hit 'Ain't Misbehavin'', after a successful season at Connie's Inn, Waller, Cox and an ensemble cast that at various times included Louis Armstrong and Cabell 'Cab' Calloway, took the show on the road. Baby would also appear in revivals of the show in 1934 and 1935, alongside singer Myra Johnson, who was advertised as the 'only rival of Ethel Waters'.[19]

Sometime around 1928 Baby had married her second husband, Herbie Cowens, drummer with a Harlem-based jazz orchestra led by trombone player Doc Crawford (the orchestra, with Cowens still on board, would later be taken over by Lucky Millinder). The marriage was doomed from the start: Cowens was a flamboyant man who, the writers of the *Chicago Whip* had decided, must be a homosexual, as instead of cohabiting with his wife and his stepson, he instead chose to live in 'bachelor quarters' where he 'fed his three pampered poodles German crackers and cream'.[20] That would have been fine, and would not necessarily have raised any eyebrows had not Baby decided to embark on an affair with 19-year-old Bobby Johnson, who worked with Baby at Connie's Inn. It was only then that the world discovered that Baby had given birth to a second son, who she claimed was Herbie's despite his having been conceived and born while the two were living apart.

Harlem's clubs, inns and cafés continued to benefit from prohibition, as owners and promoters fought each other to bring the most outrageous – and most crowd-pleasing – act to their venue. At the Clam House, or Gladys's Clam House as it became known to the locals, Gladys Bentley sat at the piano and would belt out the Kokomo Arnold song 'Sissy Man Blues' along with bawdy versions of the hits of the day. 'So adept was she at this art that she could take the most tender ballad and convert it into a new low with her filthy lyrics. In fact, some of these lyrics would be so rank that the house lady would look on in despair while Gladys, not content with merely singing them herself... would encourage the paying guests to join in on the chorus which they did willingly. At this stage, it was just a matter of time before the house got raided.'[21] The Clam House was tiny, with just eight tables, yet stars including Beatrice Lillie (close friends with Britain's two biggest pansy craze stars, Noël Coward and Douglas Byng) and Tallulah Bankhead were regulars, and the place was always packed: 'The name Gladys is synonymous with Clam House. The two cannot be successfully separated. At least, that's the opinion of many Wall Street and Broadway celebrities who flock there nightly to hear Gladys pound her favorite tunes and do de do her most primitive melodies.'[22] Writer and former suffragette Blair Niles would draw a barely fictionalised portrait of Gladys and the Clam House in her gay-themed 1931 novel, *Strange Brother*.

Born in Philadelphia in 1907, 'the eldest of four children of a poor family',[23] Gladys knew she was 'different' from an early age, stealing her brother's clothes and wearing them to school when she was just 9 years old: 'I soon began to feel more comfortable in boys clothes than in dresses... the teachers sent me home to put on dresses several times', but despite this, and the 'fun poked at me by schoolmates who followed me in the street',[24] she stubbornly persisted, developed a crush on one of her female teachers and was dragged to various doctors by her parents in search of a cure for their peculiar child. She once told her friend, Los Angeles-based musician Phil Moore, that during her mid-teens she enjoyed a three-year incestuous relationship with her younger sister, a troubled girl who later killed herself by jumping out of a window on the second floor of the family home. Gladys blamed herself for this tragedy, and she was hospitalised for several months following the trauma, believing that she was possessed by the devil. Not long afterwards, and still only 16, she was out of the house and on her way to New York.

Gladys began performing in the mid-1920s under the pseudonym Bobbie Minton, before reverting to her given name. Her first stop in Harlem was the Mad House: the pianist had left to tour Europe with the cast of *Blackbirds* and they needed a replacement immediately. Although they had expected a male keyboard player, the management reluctantly gave Gladys a trial, and she proved to be an immediate hit – in more ways than one. She accepted the job for $35 a week, but was such an instant success than she was soon being paid $125 a week. Lesbian activist Mabel Hampton recalled meeting her at the Lafayette around that time. 'She was a brown-skinned woman, and she dressed boyish all the time, and she'd fight up a breeze... She was kind of heavy-set and kind of heavy-voiced, and by the time she got through beatin' the women, the men didn't bother her. See, 'cause she knocked the hell out of the women. Oh, she bruisified [sic] them if they looked at somebody else and she wanted them...'[25]

From there she went on to a club called Mexico's and then to the Clam House, where she consolidated her reputation as a 'sensational playing and singing entertainer'.[26] Writing in his autobiography Langston Hughes, one of the leading gay writers of the Harlem Renaissance, described her as, 'something worth discovering in those days... For two or three amazing years, Miss Bentley sat, and played a big piano all night long, literally all night, without stopping – singing songs like "The St. James Infirmary," from ten in the evening until dawn, with scarcely a break between the notes, sliding from one song to another, with a powerful and continuous underbeat of jungle rhythm. Miss Bentley was an amazing exhibition of musical energy – a large, dark, masculine lady, whose feet pounded the floor while her fingers pounded the keyboard – a perfect piece of African sculpture, animated by her own rhythm.'[27]

She recorded her first sides for Okeh in August 1928, 'Ground Hog Blues' backed with 'Worried Blues' (she later claimed to have cut eight sides in all at this session, and was paid a total of $400), returning three weeks later to cut 'How Long – How Long Blues' (a faithful rendition of the Leroy Carr original, with no reference to Frankie Jaxon's indecent take on the song) and 'Moanful Wailin' Blues', but despite performing some of the most outrageous lyrics heard in Harlem, she would not record anything like the sexually charged songs cut by Bessie Smith, Ma Rainey or Lucille Bogan until she moved to Los Angeles in the late 1930s, when she would record (sometimes uncredited) a number of her more risqué cabaret numbers for a succession of small companies.

At the same time, lesbian comedian Jackie Mabley was well on the way to becoming a star. She began to make a name for herself in the early 1920s, initially on the T.O.B.A. circuit before hitting the big time in New York, appearing at venues including Connie's Inn (in October 1925) and the Cotton Club, and by 1927 was playing the Lafayette and Lyric theatres, infamous for being part of the 'Chitlin' Circuit', a loose aggregation of Black-owned and run venues (mostly; the Lafayette was run by a white man, Frank Schiffman, notorious for mistreating and underpaying his Black talent), many of which were also part of T.O.B.A. It was on a T.O.B.A. tour that Jackie witnessed an horrific act of racist violence from the window of a train carriage: 'We were going in a Jim Crow car,' she told the *Washington Post*. 'Don't care how many Blacks there were, you still had to go Jim Crow – and we were travelling from Dallas to San Antone [*sic*]. And the train stops in Paris, Texas, and I look out and see this man tied to a stake. They were gonna burn him. So I pulled down that shade...'[28]

Born Loretta Mary Aiken in North Carolina in 1894, Mabley was one of twelve children (some stories suggest she was one of sixteen), and her father Jim owned the town grocery store. Of mixed black, Cherokee, and Irish heritage, her great-grandmother, Harriet Smith, had been a slave. By the time she was 13 she had two children, both the result of rape and both given up for adoption. To escape this hellish existence, a 14-year-old Loretta found her way to Cleveland, and then to Pittsburgh, where she performed on a professional stage for the first time; she had hoped to find work as a dancer, but being pregnant once again, she was given a small role in a comedy called *The Rich Aunt from Utah*. Soon afterwards, her fledgling comedy act was noticed by Black vaudeville stars Butterbeans and Susie. Following their advice she found herself an agent and a new name that, she would later reveal, was taken from an old boyfriend and adopted, as one of her many brothers objected to his sister earning a living in the theatre. 'My eldest brother was the cause of me changing my name,' she would later reveal. 'He told me I was a disgrace to the Aiken name, because I was on stage. I told him I wasn't doing nothing but working, but they used to think that stage women wasn't nothing but prostitutes.'[29]

Unlike many of her contemporaries, Mabley enjoyed touring the Chitlin' Circuit, as she explained in a 1961 interview: 'There was a circuit called the T.O.B.A. which was the greatest thing and should be today, because it taught young people how to be entertainers... [Today] there is no training ground, these children might make a record or something and they throw them out on the stage... they go out there and they don't even know how to walk on it.'[30]

Openly lesbian (Jackie 'came out' in 1921, decades before the phrase was in use), she often hosted all-woman parties at her home in Greenwich Village, as Mabel Hampton recalled: 'I didn't have to go to the bars because I would go to the women's houses, like, Jackie Mabley. We would have a big party, and all the girls from the show – all the girls from this place or that, she had all the women there.'[31]

While Gladys Bentley and Jackie Mabley were making a name for themselves in New York, back in Chicago Ma Rainey recorded the most outrageous, obvious and autobiographic queer blues song committed to disc so far – and for many years afterwards – the classic 'Prove It On Me Blues'. On this session, Ma was accompanied by her Tub Jug Washboard Band, which featured many of the same musicians that had recorded as part of the Hokum Jug Band with Frankie Jaxon, including Tampa Red and Thomas 'Georgia Tom' Dorsey. 'Prove It On Me Blues' was recorded on 12 June 1928 and the lyrics were inspired, at least in part, by an event that had taken place in the first half of 1925, when a women-only party given by Ma had been raided by the police, and the semi-naked singer was arrested trying to escape, clutching a dress far too small to be hers. Legend has it that Bessie Smith came down to the police cells the following day and paid the fine which allowed Ma to be released. Although author credit on the disc is given to Ma, she appears to have been adapting a song, 'They Say I Do It But Nobody Caught Me', co-written by Charles Booker, that had already been recorded twice (in December 1926, accompanied by Duke Ellington, and January 1927), by Gussie Alexander for Okeh Records, although both of those versions would remain unreleased and are now lost.

'Prove It On Me Blues' is bold, bawdy and explicit, a song in which Ma proudly boasts about her lifestyle, and in which she refuses to accept polite society's bigoted view of women like her. It is a record that can still shock today, and it remains popular with LGBTQ singers. 'By the time I came to record "Prove It On Me Blues",' says blues singer Gaye Adegbalola, 'I had read the life stories, I'd heard the rumours, I had read the newspapers by the time I recorded that. I had been a professional for twenty years at that point, and I knew the whole history of it, but I was not yet comfortable enough with myself to fully come out... that would take another ten years.'[32]

The previous year, Ma had released 'Don't Fish in My Sea', one of several songs on which she shares authorship credits with Bessie Smith (all were recorded in November and December 1926), in which she swears off men altogether after being left on her own by another despicable cheating, no-good man. Now, with 'Prove It On Me Blues', she makes it plain that her sexual preference is for women. The song starts with her having a row with a girlfriend, a woman who she is so stuck on that she 'Follows everywhere she goes', and it goes on to state that she, 'Went out last night with a crowd of my friends / They must have been women, 'cause I don't like no men.' Later in the song Ma sings about how she prefers to dress in male clothing and that she can, 'Talk to the girls just like any old man.' To cap it all, the advertising that appeared in the Black press feature a caricature of Ma, dressed in a tweed three-piece and trilby, chatting to two glamorous, femme women while a Chicago cop approaches from the other side of the street, his nightstick raised, preparing to make an arrest.

For decades now, people have suggested that Ma recorded another lesbian-themed song at around the same time. 'When something is put on the internet, it seems to take on a life of its own,' says queer music archivist J. D. Doyle. 'Like the myth that Ma Rainey recorded "Bull Diker's Dream".' Despite many sources claiming otherwise, at no point in her career did Ma record a version of this sexually explicit song, originally composed around 1890 by Jesse Pickett but often miscredited to John 'Jack the Bear' Wilson. That's not to say that she did not perform the song: several different sets of lyrics exist for it, and it would not be difficult to imagine Ma singing them after hours to a private audience, or perhaps at a buffet flat or rent party: 'She was always ready for a ball,' one anonymous musician told jazz magazine the *Record Changer* in 1955. 'She was full of life.'[33] Most of the recordings of the song that do exist are – because of the bawdy nature of the lyrics – instrumentals, including two recordings by pianist James P. Johnson, who accompanied Bessie Smith on a number of sessions between 1927 and 30. In 1977, almost four decades after Ma recorded her version of 'Prove It On Me Blues', out-lesbian singer Teresa Trull issued her take, on the Olivia Records album *Lesbian Concentrate*.

Within weeks of Ma recording 'Prove It On Me Blues', in Atlanta, Georgia, Wayman 'Sloppy' Henry recorded a song, 'Say I Do It', for Okeh Records. Like Ma, Henry claimed that he had written the song himself, yet the tune, chorus and many of the lyrics are either lifted from or influenced by either Ma's version of the song or Charles Booker's 'They Say I Do It But Nobody Caught Me', and it is probable that 'Prove It On Me Blues' existed in one form or another – probably as a barrelhouse song – before either Gussie Alexander, Ma Rainey or Sloppy Henry recorded it. Although Henry recorded it in August 1928, his version of the song would not be issued until the following year, backed with another self-composed tune, 'Some Sweet Rainy Day'.

If Ma's version was explicitly lesbian, then Henry's was the most overt song yet released about a gay male couple. Ma's lyrics are playful and leave the listener to make up his or her own mind just as to what Ma is enjoying with her lady friends, whereas Sloppy Henry's are much more obvious, detailing the homosexual relationship between two Baltimore men, a male prostitute named Pete and his boyfriend, Moses.

Moses and Pete lived on Greenwillow Street in northwest Baltimore
Pete run with Mose 'cause he powdered his nose and even wore ladies' hose
Two could be seen running hand in hand in all kinds of weather
'Til the neighbours, they began to signify 'bout the birds that flock together
Mose he began to sigh, Pete yelled out his reply
Say I do it, ain't nobody seed me, they sure got to prove it 'bout me...

225

Just in case anyone missed the point, later in the chorus Pete admits that, 'It's true I use a powder puff and has a shiny face / I wears a red necktie 'cause I think it suits my taste.' For decades, stretching back to the late Victorian era, colourful accessories had been used as a signal by homosexual men to identify each other, such as a green carnation worn in the lapel which had been popularised by Oscar Wilde – and gay men in New York had keenly adopted a fashion for green suits and red neckties in the early decades of the 20th century.

There can be no doubt that Porter Grainger had been embarrassed by Bessie's drunken shenanigans at the Van Vechtens'; he was a keen networker, constantly making useful connections within New York's creative circles and joining many clubs and fraternal organisations, but luckily most of those present seemed to laugh it off, preferring to remember the night for Bessie's dazzling performance rather than for her alcohol-fuelled exhibition. As a rule, Harlem's LGBTQ crowd looked after its own, and when one of their better-known members was apprehended for breaking the law it came as a shock. In 1928 Augustus Granville Dill, business manager of the NAACP's monthly magazine *The Crisis*, and a champion of Harlem's Black artists, was arrested for soliciting in a public lavatory. His friends may have rallied around, but his boss, Harlem Renaissance heavyweight W. E. B. du Bois, fired him. At the time, du Bois claimed that his decision was motivated by finance rather than the arrest, but years later he would admit that he had struggled to deal with this 'new and undreamed aspect of sex', as 'I had before that time no conception of homosexuality. I had never understood the tragedy of an Oscar Wilde,' and he had since 'spent heavy days regretting my act'.[34]

Grainger may have been upset by Bessie showing him up in front of his influential friends, and by the news of Dill's arrest, but he had to shake it off. He had work to do. In January 1929, Grainger played piano for Clara Smith as she recorded her version of 'It's Tight Like That', written and originally recorded by Hudson Whittaker (Tampa Red) and Thomas 'Georgia Tom' Dorsey the previous October, and that was soon followed by a session for singer Bessie Brown, her penultimate recording session for Brunswick in New York, who recorded Grainger's own composition 'He Just Don't Appeal to Me'. The song was released in March 1929, backed with another Grainger composition, 'Song from a Cotton Field', written (in 1927) about the hard, back-breaking work of an itinerant cotton picker. Although she would not record the song, Ma would often close her shows with a performance of 'It's Tight Like That', featuring the whole cast of her revue.

Born in Marysville, Ohio, in 1899, vaudeville singer Bessie Brown, also known as 'The Original' Bessie Brown to distinguish her from another singer of the same name (who recorded with her husband, George W. Williams, for Columbia from 1923 onwards), only had a short recording career, issuing around twenty sides between November 1925 and April 1929 for Banner, Vocalion and Brunswick, as well as recording several more under pseudonyms including Sadie Green and Caroline Lee. Bessie's father took off when she was just an infant, and her mother soon remarried, leaving the child in the care of her maternal grandparents. By the age of 16 Bessie was married herself and had a child on the way, although she would divorce her husband three years later. Taking her daughter, Helen, with her, Bessie Brown moved to Chicago, to find work as a singer. With her deep, booming voice and excellent diction, she also found work on stage as a male impersonator. By 1920 she had remarried, to a gentleman named Clarence Bookam Shaw, and moved to Cleveland, where she would retain a family home for more than twenty years.

She also appeared in variety shows, including the *Moonshine Revue*, *The Whirl of Joy* and *Dark-Town Frolics*, and on the stage as a cabaret performer, primarily on the East Coast. She recorded in both New York and Chicago, and was backed by some of the best musicians working in blues at the time, including Clarence Williams, Fletcher Henderson and, of course, Porter Grainger.

On 'Song from a Cotton Field', Grainger writes about how, 'All my life, I've been makin' it / All my life, white folks taking it'; he had previously recorded his own solo version for Okeh, one of the very few instances of Grainger singing and playing his own compositions, and it had also been covered by Duke Ellington, as an instrumental, retitled 'Song of the Cotton Field'. Grainger's version is much bluesier than the Bessie Brown recording.

227

However, 'He Just Don't Appeal to Me' is a very different song, about an effeminate man who is somewhat wanting where it counts. The protagonist of the song is described by Miss Brown as 'long and tall, he looks just like a fashion plate', meaning that he dressed immaculately, looking for all the world like a male model who had stepped straight out of a magazine illustration. The term 'fashion plate' was also used pejoratively to describe effete or foppish men, especially after female impersonator Karyl Norman adopted the stage nickname 'The Creole Fashion Plate', and in contemporary press reports it was often noted that Grainger himself was a fastidious dresser. Is he describing himself? It would not be the first time that one of his songs appeared to contain an autobiographical element.

In 'He Just Don't Appeal to Me', Bessie Brown (or Porter Grainger) complains that, despite her man having 'Loving, he-man ways' he simply 'Ain't got what I need / For he just don't appeal to me / And I'm not satisfied...' and goes on to berate him because, 'He lacks a little something that he just ain't got'. British actor and singer Julie Covington covered the song on her 1971 debut album *The Beautiful Changes*, accompanied by a New Orleans-style traditional jazz backing. It must have seemed as if the time was right to reintroduce this four-decades-old tune to the record-buying public: the previous two years had seen several songs about cross-dressing characters – including The Beatles' 'Get Back' and The Kinks' 'Lola' – score with the public, and the following year Lou Reed's Bowie-produced opus *Transformer* would be dominated by queer-themed songs, including the classic 'Walk on the Wild Side,' a song about trans women.

# 15

# It's Dirty but Good

*'You don't sing* [the blues] *to feel better. You sing 'cause that's a way of understanding life.'*[1] – Ma Rainey

In less than five years, Ma Rainey recorded ninety-four sides for Paramount, but she would not make another recording for the company – or for anyone – after October 1928.

Many sources claim that, after her final session for the label, Paramount terminated her contract, deciding that her style of blues was no longer fashionable. With a global depression about to get its grip on the United States and radio in the ascendent, it is true that people were not buying her recordings in anything like the number they had been just a few years earlier: the reality was that no one was selling in the massive numbers they had previously. However, if Paramount did indeed terminate her contract, then the decision was sudden and unexpected. Just a few months earlier they had still been investing in full-page advertisements for Ma's records, and she was still a major live draw, commanding $350 a week on the T.O.B.A. circuit alone, better than almost anyone apart from her friend Bessie Smith. When not playing T.O.B.A. time, Ma and her thirty-nine-member-strong troupe – travelling from town to town in Ma's own bus – booked their own dates, demanding a minimum of fifty per cent of the box office (the same cut she was now getting from T.O.B.A.-arranged dates) and insisting on a cash advance for advertising materials. And theatre owners were happy to pay it.

It seems unlikely that Paramount would have given her the boot for being out of fashion, although tastes – especially in and around New York – were changing. New York was overrun with vaudeville acts trying to make it big, so much so that by the beginning of 1929 agents were imploring singers, dancers and comedians to avoid travelling to the metropolis: a letter issued by the Keith's circuit told hopefuls that 'acts playing out of Chicago, Detroit or elsewhere are better off than the hundreds now around New York and laying off'.[2] Male singers now dominated the blues field, and more effort was being put into finding feel-good, hokum style-blues than replicating the weary, troubled songs Ma specialised in. Some new female voices were given a chance to shine, but companies lost interest quickly if their efforts did not immediately click with the public. Columbia hoped that 'Down on Pennsylvania Avenue', recorded by Georgia-born singer Bertha Idaho on 25 May 1929, would find favour with the citizens of Baltimore and the sophisticates of New York, but she was dropped after recording just four sides. Written by Tom Delaney – whose songs were also recorded by Bessie Smith (1923's 'Sinful Blues', often erroneously credited to Perry Bradford), Ma Rainey (in 1924 Rainey co-wrote 'Southbound Blues' with Delaney), Ethel Waters (who recorded 'The Down Home Blues' in 1921), Clara Smith and Alberta Hunter (who both recorded versions of his song 'Nobody Knows the Way I Feel This Mornin'' in 1925) – 'Down on Pennsylvania Avenue' tells about a street in Baltimore where 'some freakish sights you will surely see / You can't tell the he's from the she's' in the cabarets and nightclubs. That particular line referenced the Porter Grainger co-composition 'In Harlem's Araby', rather apt when you consider that, at the time of the recording, Pennsylvania Avenue bisected the area south of Druid Hill Park, which was known as Baltimore's Harlem, and was where the majority of the city's 120,000 Black residents lived. By the 1940s Pennsylvania Avenue would become firmly established as Baltimore's main destination for Black entertainment, and today the area is a thriving and vibrant African American cultural centre.

Although Columbia only saw fit to offer Bertha Idaho two sessions to prove her worth, in May 1928 and May 1929, she continued working on stage and on radio. In 1928, she starred in a touring review, *Mississippi Steppers*, and in late 1929 was starring in *The Georgia Peaches*, with 'a galaxy of pretty girls and funny comedians'.[3] Three of the four songs she recorded were written by Delaney, who began living with Idaho after the death of his first wife, Pearl, in 1928; by 1932 the couple were living in Baltimore and could be heard on the local airwaves. Around the same time that Idaho was signed to Columbia, the company began working with a raunchy Texan-born singer named Mary Dixon, who had previously issued one single on Vocalion. The lyrics of 'All Around Mama' – recorded just four weeks after 'Down on Pennsylvania Avenue' – bear a thematic similarity, with Dixon singing of how, 'I met a man, was a butler / When he spoke I ran / Was too mannish for a woman / Too girlish for a man.' Dixon's recording career spanned just fifteen months: her first recording, 'Dusky Stevedore' was made on 30 July 1928, her last, 'Daddy You're a Low-Down Man' in October 1929. There is no suggestion that either singers Idaho and Dixon, or songwriters Tom Delaney and Henry Cole (the composer of 'All Around Mama', who would also write for both Bessie and Clara Smith), were queer, but both of these songs demonstrate the same awareness of the blurring of gender identity as 'Masculine Women, Feminine Men' and many other similar songs.

As the public's demand for ever more outrageously camp entertainment continued unabated, record labels scoured the country for songwriters and performers to satiate the demand. Producer Sam Ayo recalled how 'when the portable stations came through' he could record an artist 'in Dallas or San Antonio or some such place like it. A portable station was actually the old wax deals.' He would 'get the hotel rooms and drape them up to make them soundproof, and actually arranged to record in the various hotel rooms'.[4]

One such recording, 'Dirty Dozen', was recorded at the Peabody Hotel in Memphis, Tennessee on 22 September 1929. The singer, credited on the disc as Speckled Red, was born Rufus Perryman, in Hampton, Georgia in October 1892. Perryman's song, and its many descendants, took its name from a word game, traditionally played by young African American boys, in which the players take turns to insult each other's relatives, especially their mothers: the first boy unable to ignore the barrage of insults and lose his temper is the loser. According to Jelly Roll Morton, the line 'Your momma do the lawdy-lawd' was originally 'your momma don't wear no drawers...', but its roots go back further still, to a poem used in African American churches in the mid-1800s used to drill information from the Bible into the heads of illiterate children. Perryman later described its origins to Paul Oliver, telling him that, 'They used to have a word they say, "playin' the dozens". It was talking dirty you know; the boys be together and they'd try and out-talk one and the other till one feller would holler "you put me in the dozens" because he couldn't think of no more to say. So I made a kind of a song out of the words and I called it The Dirty Dozens. But they was real bad words you see; I was playing in one of them turpentine jukes where it didn't matter. Anything I said there was all right in there you see. I had to clean it up for the record but it meaned the same thing but it was a different attitude.'[5] Perryman may have claimed that he cleaned up the lyrics, but the recorded version of the song retained its queer heart:

> I like your mama and your sister too
> I did like your daddy, but your daddy wouldn't do
> Met your daddy on the corner the other day
> You know by that, that he was funny that way.

Perryman, the older brother of Willie Lee Perryman (aka Piano Red and Doctor Feelgood), earned the name Speckled Red as he was albino, his face covered in freckles. He recorded the song several times, as well as derivatives including 'Dirty Dozen Number 2' (covered in June 1930 by Tampa Red, with Georgia Tom Dorsey on piano), 'Dirty Dozen Number 3' and 'New Dirty Dozen'. He was a self-taught pianist who played very much in the barrelhouse style, a precursor to boogie-woogie and rock 'n' roll, and themes from 'Dirty Dozen' can be clearly heard in the playing of several big stars of the 1950s, including Chuck Berry. In 1930, female guitarist and vocalist

Memphis Minnie recorded a version, dubbed 'The New Dirty Dozens', with an identical tune but different lyrics with no LGBTQ content, and the guitar motif in Berry's hit 'Carol' is clearly related to the riff played by Memphis Minnie.

Cover versions of 'Dirty Dozen' popped up like weeds in a flower bed: shortly after Perryman's recording appeared other versions were on the market by harmonica player Jed Davenport and His Beale Street Jug Band (an instrumental, recorded in Memphis in January 1930), by Leroy Carr and Scrapper Blackwell (recorded in Chicago in January 1930, and issued by Brunswick) and by Lonnie Johnson with Spencer Williams (recorded in New York, on 7 February 1930, for Okeh), as well as the one recorded by Memphis Minnie. The recording by Carr and Blackwell retained the 'queer' subtext, and the recording by Johnson and Williams uses an almost identical lyric to the one used by Carr and Blackwell.

Former Chicago bootlegger Kokomo Arnold – a huge influence on iconic bluesman Robert Johnson, and a musician who played in tent shows with both Ma Rainey and Bessie Smith – recorded a version in 1935, for Decca, issued as 'The Twelves (The Dirty Dozen)' with an almost verbatim version of the 'queer' verse. On this release, recorded in Chicago on 18 January 1935, the composer credit is given to 'Woods', although the Speckled Red version has Perryman credited as composer. Frankie 'Half-Pint' Jaxon recorded a version of 'The Dirty Dozen' (with the Harlem Hamfats) for Decca in March 1937, retaining the tune and the chorus of the original, but with different lyrics for the verses. In Jaxon's version, the 'queer' verse becomes, 'I like your kitty and your doggie too / But I found out that your doggie wouldn't do / I saw your little kitty on the street the other day / I found out he was funny that way.'

Three days before he recorded 'The Twelves', Arnold laid down his most infamous recording, his own composition 'Sissy Man Blues', with the composer accompanying himself on guitar. 'Sissy Man Blues' would later be covered by Pinewood Tom (real name Josh White) accompanied by guitar and jazz piano, by George Noble on Vocalion and by Connie McLean's Rhythm Boys for Decca in New York in April 1936.

Lord, I woke up this mornin' with my pork grindin' business in my
 hand
Says I woke up this morning with my pork grindin' business in my
 hand
Lord, if you can't send me no woman, please send me some sissy
 man.

McLean's version is markedly different to the other three interpretations, but all four retain the line 'Lord, if you can't send me no woman, please send me some sissy man.' McLean's jazz interpretation introduces a new verse, with the unnamed vocalist (possibly guitarist Ludovic Brown or McLean himself) singing that he is 'going up to the Daisy Chain, see if I can find my good gal over there', a reference to the pansy craze-era club run by Josephine Baker's friend Hazel Valentine, and popular with LGBTQ Harlemites. The sissy caricature would remain popular with blues singers; Louis Powell only recorded two sides, for Vocalion in New York in March 1938, one of which was his version of 'Sissy', a song composed by Irving Kahal, Louis Panico and Jack Fascinato. 'Sissy' proved a popular tune: it had already been recorded as an instrumental by the Ted Weems Orchestra before Powell cut his version, and was covered one week later by Frank Dailey and His Stop and Go Orchestra, with vocals by Ann Seton. Electric organ player Vernon Geyer also recorded a version in Texas in May that year, again as an instrumental. Singer Frank Crumit, best known for his novelty songs, recorded 'Sissy' for Decca in New York on 17 March; on the same day the Milt Herth Trio, featuring Willie 'The Lion' Smith on piano, recorded their version of the song.

Unlike the Dailey, Herth and Crumit versions, which all play down the LGBTQ aspect of the song in the vocal refrain, Powell's version expands on its queerness, with the vocalist adding a camp spoken-word introduction in which he appears to be impersonating the late drag artist Bert Savoy: 'We're all sissies and we must get together... Oh dear, dear me. You could never fool me, honey, you're just another sissy.' Arnold himself had first-hand experience of Chicago's queer nightlife, and in 1937 he spent several months performing alongside female impersonator Luzetta Hall at Doc Jennings' 33rd Stret Café.

'"Sissy Man Blues" is a song about a straight man in prison who can't get a women,' LGBTQ activist Ted Brown explains, 'So he would be happy with a sissy man!' Brown says that it was a compilation CD featuring this song that inspired him to team up with South African musicians Brett Lock and Chris Houston for their own queer blues performances.

'He had a CD of these bawdy blues songs,' Brett adds. 'It was interesting that there were so may quite openly gay songs from so early on, and yet mainstream enough that they were actually recorded. That was kind of the spark of it, and from that we started to do some research about those particular artists, and then discovered lots more.'

'We had a copy of the *Sissy Man Blues* compilation, but the sound quality on some of those songs was so poor that we felt compelled to do a recording ourselves,' adds Brown. 'People were assuming that up until Stonewall there had not been any LGBTQ music, and that was a big motivation for us, to cancel out that invisibility. We were there and we were expressing ourselves, and we wanted to get these songs back out there, to prove that we were there, the LGBTQ community was there and expressing themselves in fairly open and positive ways. I can't think of one of these songs that is regretful or remorseful about people's sexuality, particularly things like 'B.D. Woman's Blues', or 'Prove it On Me Blues', where Ma Rainey actually says, "I don't like no men".'

'We wanted to make sure that these songs were available and to acknowledge that, certainly in the Black community back in the twenties, there had been this music that had crossed sexual boundaries. At that time Black music was considered "Race Music", and was not played on the radio, and consequently many of the artists felt free to express themselves.'

'We decided to call the album *Pink, Black and Blues* as an acknowledgement that a lot of the artists who blazed the trail were Black,' Chris explains. 'They were more or less left alone by the authorities because they were not seen as important, and in a weird way the racism of the authorities allowed them to get away with it... they didn't worry about the moral corruption of the Black community.' 'The Black record industry was entirely separate,' adds Brett. 'You had the "record industry" and the "race record industry"...' 'And that resonated with us,' Chris continues, 'As that kind of echoes the way the record industry was structured in South Africa.'[6]

As well as jazz and blues recordings, companies had been flooding the market with gospel singers, choirs, and fire and brimstone evangelists, issuing sermons on everything from the dangers of tobacco and alcohol to the evils of sexual permissiveness. In early 1930, the Reverend J. M. Gates issued one of his intense sermons on Okeh, titled 'Manish Women'. Recorded 16 December 1929 in New Orleans, the call-and-response sermon is a blues in all but name, with no instrumentation, but with many of the lines sung by Gates and selected members of his congregation. Gates was as incensed by women who 'try to walk and talk like a man' as with 'men who try to walk and talk like a woman'. Manish women, the good Reverend explained, 'will rob and steal like men', and were 'getting everywhere... in the pool house, on the streets, in the little village, out in the little towns... I don't know what they going to do about them.' Gates recorded over 200 sides for companies including Victor, Paramount, Gennett and Okeh, and he often railed against what he saw as permissive women, and in his later recording 'Smoking Woman in the Streets' (and that's smoking cigarettes, as opposed to smoking hot) he also took aim at women 'trying your best to look and be as much like a man as possible'.

Ma's erstwhile label, Paramount, was slow to react to the changing tastes of its customers, but even they got in on the act in October 1930, when they issued two sides from Missouri-based singer (and, it is rumoured, female impersonator) George Hannah, 'The Boy in the Boat' and 'Freakish Blues' (also known as 'Freakish Man Blues'; Hannah recorded two further cuts, 'Alley Rat Blues' and 'Molasses Sopper Blues' at the same session). With piano accompaniment from Meade Lux Lewis, Hannah sings these uncredited compositions, although it has been suggested that this version of 'The Boy in the Boat', a party song that had been sung for decades before it was finally committed to shellac, had been penned years before by Tony 'Pretty Baby' Jackson. Hannah, whose short professional career included performances at Mary's Dreamland, a cabaret on Park Avenue, St Louis with a nightly floor show, had previously recorded for Vocalion, in St Louis in 1926, and Meade Lux Lewis would later record in Chicago for both Decca and Victor.

The phrase 'The Boy in the Boat', a slang term for the clitoris, had been in use for a number of years (the *New Partridge Dictionary of Slang and Unconventional English* has its first recorded use in 1916, but it appears to have been circulating for several decades before that), and by the mid-1920s it was a common enough term among Black musicians to find its way into several songs. According to Fats Waller's biographer Ed Kirkeby, 'One of the most frequently heard songs in the rent-party repertoire was "The Boy in the Boat," a broadly sexual song with many verses composed over the years by many singers. It was to have an important place in the career of Tom Waller, who came to use its melody as a speciality.'[7] Around 1919 Waller wrote a new tune for the words, and that eventually became 'Squeeze Me', a tune covered by Willie 'The Lion' Smith in 1939.

In September 1928, Charlie Johnson and His Paradise Band Jazz Orchestra issued an instrumental called 'The Boy in the Boat' on the Victor label, an entirely different tune to the one popularised by Waller and Hannah (authorship was claimed by Johnson himself), but no doubt based on the same slang phrase, as around the same time as the recording session took place (19 September 1928), Frankie 'Half-Pint' Jaxon was performing a lewd version of the song with Johnson's Paradise Ten in Atlantic City. RCA imprint Bluebird issued an alternate version of the tune, from the same recording session, a decade later, this time credited to Charlie Johnson's Orchestra. Jaxon and Johnson would record together, in Chicago in 1930, but sadly would never cut their version of 'The Boy in the Boat'.

Hannah's version includes explicit lesbian references, especially in the verse:

When you see two women walking hand in hand
Just look 'em over and try to understand
They'll go to these parties, have the lights down low
Only those parties where women can go
You think I'm lying – just ask Tack Ann

237

Took many a broad from many a man
Face is still wrinkled an' his breath smells like soap
I'm still talkin' bout that boy in the boat...

The Tack Ann that Hannah was referring to was a notorious petty criminal, 'Tack' Annie Williams, a pickpocket who hung around the bordellos and black and tans of Chicago's Bronzeville district, and a character Alberta Hunter – who knew her when she worked at the Iowa Club in Chicago in the mid-1910s – once described as, 'The ugliest woman who ever breathed a breath of life. She looked like a horse with a hat on. It was a sin to put a woman on earth as ugly as Tack Annie. But she was clever...'[8]

The final verse of Hannah's version deals specifically with the plight of women left to look after their own needs once their men had gone off to fight in the war.

Ever since the year tootie two
Lotta these dames had nothin' to do
Uncle Sam thought he'd give 'em a fightin' chance
Packed up all the men and sent 'em on to France
Sent them over there for the Germans to hunt
Left the women at home to try out all their new stunts
His face is all wrinkled an' his breath smells like soap
I'm talkin' bout that boy in the boat.

When Paramount reissued the single after the war, reviewer Bucklin Moon noted that the songs constituted 'some of the dirtiest lyrics ever put into the grooves of a record', calling Hannah 'A race singer of dubious merit.'[9] 'It's a phrase that has been used for all of my life,' says Gaye Adegbalola. 'These are phrases whose meaning are very clear in the Black community... in the Black community everybody knew what the "Boy in the Boat" was, what "Sugar in the Bowl" meant... all those phrases.'[10]

Years later, a former Paramount executive revealed to jazz historian Charles Edward Smith that the reason the company decided not to continue working with Ma was that 'her down home material had gone out of fashion'. If the people in the know at Paramount were indeed keeping an eye on the changing fashions, then that hardly explains why the label issued dozens of traditional blues sides in 1929, and they continued to release blues recordings throughout 1930, with discs from female singers including Clara Burston, Bessie Mae Smith, Alice Moore and, in April, even put out a pair of tunes written and recorded two years earlier by Ma herself, 'Leaving This Morning' and 'Runaway Blues'. The accepted story, of her particular brand of blues moaning no longer being what the record-buying public wanted, simply does not hold water. There has to be another reason for her not recording again after October 1928.

The Depression would hit Ma's label badly, but for some time now they – like many of the other companies – had worked out that male blues singers playing their own instruments could be more attractive financially than a singer like Ma who usually employed a band behind her, each member of which came holding his hand out expecting a cheque. In the early years of blues recording, female vocalists had been favoured partly because the primitive recording techniques were better suited to capturing a big voice with plenty of experience projecting from a stage to a theatre audience, but also because women were seen as more gullible, easier to manipulate and exploit. The advent of electrical recording made it easier to capture the thinner voices of male blues singers huddled over their guitars, but even so, the Paramount team seemed to be out of step with public demand, dropping blues duo Rufus and Ben Quillian on the cusp of releasing their breakthrough record, 'It's Dirty but Good', which instead would be picked up by Columbia and, like several other queer classics from this period, was not recorded in Chicago or New York, but in Atlanta, Georgia on 7 December 1930.

I know women that don't like men
The way they do is a crying sin
It's dirty but good, oh yes
It's dirty but good
There ain't no difference, it's just dirty but good.

The brothers, born in Gainesville, Georgia (Rufus in 1900, his younger brother in 1907), began recording in 1929 as part of the Savannah Blues Trio and the Blue Harmony Boys (issuing several sides for Paramount) before striking out as a duo and releasing a number of hokum blues sides for Columbia, all recorded in Atlanta, between 1930 and 1932. 'Most of them were kinda indecent for that day,' Ben Quillian told writer Mike Rowe in 1976. 'We were a little ahead of our time. That's about all they wanted from us was jumping little songs, "Tight Like That", "Dirty but Good", "Keep It Clean"! All kinds of funny stuff like that. We had a lot of fun, played a lot of house-parties, small dances.'[11] Rufus died in mysterious circumstances, found in the street in Atlanta with a head wound. His younger brother assumed he had run into trouble with the local police, but there was no evidence to suggest their involvement and to this day no one knows quite what happened. Self-taught, Georgia Tom Dorsey was a huge influence, as is evident on 'It's Dirty but Good', which is based on an instrumental issued in January 1929 by The Hokum Boys (Dorsey and Tampa Red), 'Selling That Stuff'.

Shifting tastes certainly affected the sales of recordings by some of the classic blues singers, but others – such as Bessie Smith – seemed either resilient or adaptable enough to cope. The end of Ma's recording career also coincided roughly with the Wall Street Crash and the beginning of the decade-long Great Depression, but America's financial institutions were not shaken to their foundations until September 1929, almost a full year after her final recording session. Moreover, in June 1929, more than six months after the company had, apparently, unceremoniously dumped her, they supplied George Thompkins, manager of the Dixie Minstrel Show (then touring with Clarence A. Wortham's carnival) with a Vitaphone system, the same sound method used for some early talking pictures, complete with a gramophone player adapted for outdoor use, to play Ma's records in an attempt to draw the crowds in to see her sideshow performance. It is true that fewer theatres were employing live talent, preferring instead to run movies for their patrons, which accelerated the demise of vaudeville, so why would a company who had terminated her contract still spend money on promoting her live

Ethel Waters in a publicity still for *On With the Show*, 1929 (Getty Images)

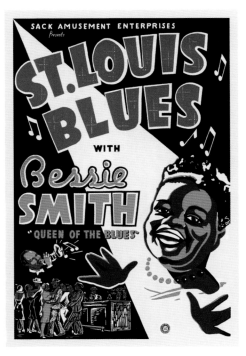

ABOVE: A poster for Bessie's one and only film, *St Louis Blues*, 1929 (Getty Images)

ABOVE: Fan It! was Frankie Half Pint Jaxon's biggest hit, used on this advertising postcard, 1929 (J.D. Doyle Archive)

ABOVE: Josephine Baker with her pet cheetah, Chiquita, 1930 (Getty Images)

ABOVE: Gladys Bentley in top hat and tails for this publicity photo, 1930 (Getty Images)

LEFT: Alberta Hunter promoting the sale of War Bonds, approx. 1944 (Getty Images)

BELOW: The floorshow at the Cotton Club, 142nd Street, 1934 (Getty Images)

LEFT: Bessie Smith photographed by Carl van Vechten, 1936 (Getty Images)

RIGHT: Gladys Bentley at the Ubangi Club, approx. 1936 (Collection of the Smithsonian National Museum of African American History and Culture)

LEFT: Ethel Waters as Hagar in the play *Mamba's Daughter*, 1939 (Getty)

BELOW: Crowds gather as more cross-dressers are arrested in New York, 1939 (Getty Images)

LEFT: Sister Rosetta Tharpe poses for a portrait in New York City, approx 1940 (Getty)

ABOVE: The aftermath of the Cafe de Paris bomb attack, in which Ken 'Snakehips' Johnson was killed, 1941 (Getty Images)

LEFT: Duke Ellington with Billie Holiday, 1945 (Getty Images)

ABOVE: Billie Holiday and Louis Armstrong in a still from the film *New Orleans*, 1946 (Getty Images)

LEFT: Jackie 'Moms' Mabley (R) and a friend backstage, 1956 (Getty Images)

RIGHT: Billie Holiday at the Newport Jazz Festival, 1957 (Getty Images)

shows? Had they, in fact, planned to continue working with her but reassessed their situation following the stock market crash?

Perhaps she was simply becoming too difficult to handle? The once sweet-natured Ma had developed into something of a diva, and her recording sessions had become increasingly fractious. She had also gained something of a reputation for failing to honour bookings: in September 1927 Milton Starr, then-president of T.O.B.A. and the owner/manager of several theatres, wrote to Ben Stein of the Douglass Theatre in Macon, Georgia, warning him that Ma, 'was billed to open at my Columbia house Thursday and my Augusta house Friday. She failed to turn up and has simply disappeared.' If she had been playing hard to get with Paramount, then she could easily be forgiven, but it seemed somewhat out of character for her to vanish for several days and let her public down: just two months earlier Paramount were boasting about how they had to drag her 'over 1,000 miles from Charlotte, N.C., camping only two nights before her arrival in Chicago, on a special trip to make new records. After her new records were completed she left immediately for Salisbury, N.Y...'[12]; hardly the actions of a company that was about to drop her from their roster. She knew that she was making money for both Paramount and T.O.B.A., and knew too that she was being taken for a ride: she may have been Paramount's biggest-selling female artist, but Black acts were paid less and seldom saw royalties, despite the fact that Ma wrote many of her own songs. She was acutely aware that her biggest pay cheque came from live performances, and that recordings had to be slotted in when she had time, not necessarily when it suited the company. The whole T.O.B.A. circuit was suffering as a result of the Depression, and by the beginning of the 1930s was effectively finished.

She was also increasingly unafraid of expressing her own sexuality. In 'Blame it on the Blues', recorded at her penultimate session for Paramount (and her last session with Georgia Tom), Ma refers to three people she is involved with: 'Can't blame my lover that held my hand, can't blame my husband, can't blame my man'. Coming just six months after she recorded 'Prove It On Me Blues', one has to assume that the 'lover' in question is a woman, but was Ma's openness about her bisexuality proving too much? It's a moot point: by 1932 the Depression would force Paramount to discontinue recording altogether, and the company closed its doors in 1935, the year after Gennett, once a leading name in record production, had gone out of business. In 1927 record sales in America had topped 104 million, but by 1932 this had dropped to a pathetic 6 million.

The big companies were struggling and, in a bid to keep the money rolling in, several introduced budget-price labels, selling 10-inch discs for around half of the price of Columbia or Paramount. Any one of these would have been happy to have Ma on their roster, but what is often overlooked about Ma (and Clara and Bessie, for that matter) is that she was a star before she began her recording career. She had two decades to hone her craft, to build an audience, before her first Paramount recording session, and she knew exactly what her crowd wanted. She may have enjoyed the whoops of delight from her audience when she burst onto the stage from the inside of a giant plywood gramophone, but it was not her records that had given her an audience, and leaving Paramount would not diminish the demand from people to see her in the flesh. Had she wished to continue recording she could easily have signed a deal with another company: Columbia or any number of smaller Black music specialists would have loved to have had the 'Mother of the Blues' on their books. Now in her mid-40s, she was tired of playing the game.

Another reason that she was forced to forgo any further recording sessions was that, for the last two years of the decade Ma was furiously busy. She may not have been content to continue slotting in recording sessions for the pittance she earned from them when she was doing very nicely, thank you, from her live performances. Ma would continue to appear at county fairs throughout the country, usually travelling with her own troupe in a gaudily painted bus that she had paid $13,000 for the previous summer, from Mack transport in Charlotte, North Carolina. Occasionally Ma appeared with the Paramount Flappers (again displaying an association with the company said to have sacked her), described as 'an all-colored minstrel [show] with 16 people',[13] and, as spring of 1929 rolled around, Ma Rainey was still on the road, appearing in tent shows as part of George Tompkins' Dixie Minstrels show, a troupe she stayed with throughout the summer. In September

– along with her Paramount Flappers – she joined a travelling fair known as the Bernardi Exposition, and toured throughout Mississippi.

Gospel and blues singer Brother John Sellers recalled seeing Ma in a tent show when he was a child, in Greenville, Mississippi:

> My Godmother she had a house there on the edge of town and a big piece of land in back of it. She used to rent out the lot to the travelling shows. See, they had shows comin' through the town all the time but 'specially in the fall, and they would pitch their tents behind the house... There was always people comin' and goin' and I was kep' busy runnin' messages and to buy things and so forth. And sometimes they'd have these blues players come in and when I was even very young I used to hear them at the barrelhouses and that give me the idea to sing too. Then when they put up the big tent I used to slip on out and watch the show – lift up the edge of the canvas. Then they used to have talent competitions sometimes and I was just a kid but I would sing too and I got quite a few prizes that way. And then I could see the show from the inside. It wasn't only blues you know, they'd have comedians and dancers and so forth like that but I always did remember the blues singers best. That's how I first heard Ma Rainey and Ida Cox. They had a stage up there with curtains and everything and then these would open and some big woman would be hollerin' there. This was with the old Rabbit Foot and Silas Green's from New Orleans minstrel shows. And of course these singers would be famous from their recordings and they'd get a big crowd – big crowd, they be packed in there like rice in a bowl.[14]

Tompkins' Dixie Minstrels toured as part of Clarence A. Wortham's carnival, with Ma giving special matinees every Saturday for children, as well as pulling them in six nights a week with her regular set. But touring with the Wortham outfit took her back to the days of playing alongside tattooed ladies (a particular speciality of the Wortham shows) and such delights as the Queer Farm Freaks ('65 very odd animals'), the Man From Mars ('he wears a number 14 hat'), Cecil the Turtle Boy and the Chinese Ghoul.

From a family of showmen, Clarence A. 'China' Wortham had once run what was then the biggest carnival on the road in the States. He died, aged just 39, from a burst appendix in September 1922, leaving an estate valued at $1 million. At the time of his death Ma had been touring, along with her Broadway Strutters, as part of his cousin John T. Wortham's travelling Dixieland Revue. Clarence Augustine Wortham, China's son, was just 13 years old when his father passed, and far too young to have taken up his mantle. Instead, following his death, China's widow Belle Wortham sold the rights to his name, alongside all of Wortham's equipment, to Fred Beckman and Barney Gerety, Wortham's manager and secretary respectively, who kept the business running until the close of the 1930 season. With the Wortham carnival nearing the end of its life, playing a sideshow after headlining theatres throughout the country may have felt like a major comedown for a star performer and major recording artist, but not for Ma. It kept her in front of an audience which adored her, and made sure that the dollars kept rolling in. It would have been far easier to settle in Chicago or New York and continue churning out blues records, but Ma was clearly enjoying life on the road, dazzling audiences from Texas and Alabama in the South to Ohio in the North with those famous gold teeth, the expensive jewellery and sparkling stage outfits. By the autumn of 1929 she had hitched her wagon alongside George Murray's Sugarfoot Minstrels, and when they quit for the season after a final performance in Hot Springs, Arkansas on 16 November 1929, Ma and her band set off on another gruelling T.O.B.A. tour.

In 1930, Ma renamed her act the Arkansas Swift Foot Minstrels, and toured the South extensively, under canvas: her band included pianist Sunnyland Slim. Rumours persist that she joined up with Bessie Smith, the pair appearing in a revue titled *Bandana Babies*, produced by Boise de Legge, a stage manager and actor who had appeared as Blair Kimball in the pioneering all-Black drama film *The Flying Ace*. Other reports state that Ma alone played with *Bandana Babies* (which took its name from a song featured in the stage revue *Blackbirds of 1928*), after she was forced to abandon her own troupe because of financial worries brought on by the Depression, and joined the Donald MacGregor Carnival, touring small Texas oil towns. Her friend, actor and female impersonator Thomas Fulbright, who Ma nicknamed 'Baby', later wrote about how her famous necklace of gold coins 'had been replaced by a poor imitation pearl one', but that she continued to 'sing her songs for her people... they would weep with her and laugh with her. Ma might not have been the most religious person but believe me, anyone who put what she did into a song must most certainly be very close to God.'[15]

# 16

# Raiding the Pansy Club

*'Love making among women is indulged in openly in night clubs. If men
can wear dresses and flirt with men, why should not women satisfy
their own passions without censure? That is the question that youth is
answering for itself. That is the price that youth is paying for repeal.'*[1]

While Ma's career was beginning to dip, Bessie's was hitting new
heights. In March 1928, accompanied by Porter Grainger on
piano and trombonist Charlie Green, she had recorded the two-part
'Empty Bed Blues', one of the most explicitly sexual records she would
make. Over the eleven verses of 'Empty Bed Blues' Bessie sings about
sex with a man who clearly knows a trick or two, a coffee-grinding,
deep-sea diving man who is so good in the sack that he leaves her
a crying, quivering mess. The record was a huge hit, boosting both
her audience numbers and her pay cheque. In an interview for Chris
Albertson, Lovie Austin remembered that, 'You could hear that record
all over the South Side.' Then working as the musical director for the
Monograph Theatre in Chicago, she told Albertson that, 'We couldn't
book her for the Monogram because she wanted too much money, and
the theatre wasn't big enough to hold half the people who wanted to hear
her. I don't think Bessie had seen such crowds since she first started
out making records.'[2] If consumers' tastes were indeed changing, and

female vocalists were no longer in vogue, there was little evidence of that here. Audiences continued to flock to her performances: touring the States later that year, in a revue entitled *Steamboat Days*, Bessie broke box-office records at the Frolic in Birmingham, Alabama.

In 1929 she starred in her first (and only) movie, a two-reeler from Radio Pictures (RKO) loosely based around W. C. Handy's hit 'St. Louis Blues', as part of an all-Black cast of seventy-five singers, musicians and dancers. The film was a huge hit, added as an extra feature in countless picture houses across the country, and despite falling into crass racial stereotypes provides us with the only known footage of Bessie. It is a shame that when the publicity department at Radio were paying for full-page advertisements in the trade press they not only neglected to feature Bessie's image but also got the name of her recording company wrong. Bessie was so pleased with the film that she turned up at the home of writer and director Dudley Murphy with a gift – a case of illicit gin.

'I was at a party given by Bessie Smith soon after her "St. Louis Blues" picture and I saw her spend $700 in one night,' her friend and contemporary, Victoria Spivey, recalled some years later. 'Bessie controlled two homes at this time. At the end of the year 1930, Bessie was so big that she had a 25 people company that was touring theatres like the Lincoln in New Orleans, the biggest theatre in New Orleans for vaudeville. Bessie's act was the thing to watch by everybody. The Lincoln was a far cry from "tumbledown theatres and leaking canvas roofs" [as it was described by Paul Oliver in his book, *Kings of Jazz: Bessie Smith*]. Bessie would have had a big laff [*sic*] and would have given out with one of her favorite curses...'[3]

Despite Bessie's popularity with audiences, she was still subject to outright hostility and racial abuse in certain sectors of both the Black and the white press. In January 1929, Ernest Varlack of the *Baltimore Afro-American,* dismissed her sell-out appearance at the Standard Theatre in Philadelphia with a scathing, but thankfully short review: 'Bissie Smith, [*sic*] who they say is a fairly well-known blues singer, is the current attraction at the Standard. Sam Davis, Bootsy Swan, Beulah Benbrow and Willie Holms are among those to be found acting – if that is what you'd call it – in this bluesetta.'[4] In May 1929 she joined the cast of the musical *Pansy* (nothing to do with the pejorative use of the word, or in any way referencing the pansy craze); Bessie's role consisted of little more than a walk-on, between acts, to sing a song while actors changed clothes and stagehands shifted scenery, but although her performance of 'If the Blues Don't Get You' was singled out for praise – many audiences thought it was the only thing in the revue worth paying for and 'she was obliged to repeat [it] until she was almost exhausted'[5] and the patrons were happy that they had their money's worth – she was dismissed by columnist Walter Winchell as 'a buxom "pickaninny"'.[6] Like Ma, Bessie could still command a crowd and still demand good money for her performances: if her style of blues singing was no longer in fashion it was only with the self-appointed sophisticates of New York who, sadly, were the very people influencing those running the industry.

Bessie and her former friend Clara were both in New York in August 1929: as Bessie finished a week at the Lincoln Theatre, Clara was opening at the Alhambra in a musical comedy entitled *Dream Girls*. Shortly afterwards she would go back out on tour, playing mainly picture houses between film screenings, with a new troupe she dubbed the Black Bottom Revue. But although Bessie was still finding plenty of work, her personal life was a mess. Tired of her husband spending so much time – and her money – on promoting his lover Gertrude Saunders, Bessie attacked her twice, and was charged with assault. Her marriage to Jack Gee ended soon afterwards, and although they would not divorce, the next few years were mired in bitter battles between the pair over Bessie's income and the upbringing of their adopted son, Jack Junior. Gee, who had been producing Bessie's successful *Steamboat Days* revue, went on to stage *A Night in Harlem*, a vehicle designed for and starring Saunders and, in a further effort to establish himself as an entrepreneur, in February 1930 he put on a revue without Bessie, *Midnite Steppers* at Atlanta's 81 Theatre, the same venue that had provided the launch pad for Bessie's own career, and at the Douglass Theatre in Macon, but by the time it reached the Koppin in Detroit the line-up had almost completely changed, Jack being entirely unsuited to nurturing a stable of temperamental performers. Despite their rift, Jack would continue to weave in and out of Bessie's life, and several of her 1930 performances were advertised as 'a Jack Gee production'.

Jack's girlfriend, Gertrude Saunders, began her recording career before Bessie, issuing her first sides for Okeh in 1921, at the same time as she was appearing in *Shuffle Along*. But she didn't click with audiences in the same way that Ma or Bessie would. That might be because her soprano voice is entirely unsuited to the two songs chosen for her initial release, Sissle and Blake's 'I'm Craving for That Kind of Love' backed with 'Daddy Won't You Please Come Home' (which, as the character Ruth Little, she sang in *Shuffle Along*), and the primitive recording system used resulted in an unpleasant, almost painful listening experience. 'Daddy Won't You Please Come Home' provides an important and early example of scat singing, and influenced the 'boop-oop-a-doop' phrase later popularised by Helen Kane, whose act was the basis for the animated superstar Betty Boop, but not long after the disc was released she was fired from *Shuffle Along,* her part taken by Florence Mills. Mills scored an enormous success in the role, and would remain a major star for the rest of her life... which, sadly, would not last long. She died in a New York hospital, on 1 November 1927, of tuberculosis, at the age of 31. Porter Grainger wrote a mawkish tribute song to her, 'She's Gone to Join the Song-birds in Heaven', which was recorded by Eva Taylor, with Grainger on piano, and issued by Okeh just weeks after her passing. The disc sold in the tens of thousands.

Gertrude Saunders would issue just two further couplings, the first combining two Maceo Pinkard numbers for Victor in 1923. Her only other release would be of two songs recorded at a session for Vocalion in 1927, where Porter Grainger accompanied the singer on a pair of songs written by Andy Razaf. Gertrude's private life was just as tempestuous as Bessie's: as well as stepping out with Jack Gee, in 1927 she went to court to obtain a restraining order against boyfriend James Evans, who viciously beat her, leaving scars and bruises on her face and body, after she ordered him to move out of her home. Later that same year she was attacked and robbed on the street in Philadelphia by a gang of five men while walking with her new beau. It's little wonder that, in 1931, Gertrude suffered a breakdown, and was forced off stage for a period.

The unquenchable fascination with what Bessie had described, in 'Foolish Man Blues' as 'a mannish actin' woman / And a skippin', twistin', woman actin' man' reached its zenith in the underground, prohibition-breaking clubs of New York (especially those in Harlem, Times Square and Greenwich Village), Chicago – where a female impersonator using the stage name Joan Crawford was camping it up at the Cozy Cabin Club (the 'oddest night club in Chicago',[7] according to their advertisements) – and other major cities around the world. Performers, including the acid-tongued Jean Malin, quickly eclipsed the male and female impersonators that had been a stage staple for decades. Suddenly the acts of Julian Eltinge and Karyl Norman – homosexual men who liked to put on a frock but would furiously deny that they were anything but one hundred per cent, red-blooded American male – were old hat. Malin brought something new to the world of LGBTQ entertainment.

Malin began his own career in drag, but it was in the spring of 1930, while acting as the tuxedoed M.C. of the Club Abbey, that he 'gave Broadway its first glimpse of pansy nightlife',[8] as Mark Hellinger of the *Syracuse Journal* put it. After appearing in male chorus lines and at the occasional drag ball, made up as Hollywood vamp Imogene Wilson, Eugene 'Jean' Malin scored his first nightclub job around 1926 at Paul and Joe's, a speakeasy on West 19th Street which had been hosting drag acts since the end of the war. Continually raided for breaking prohibition, Paul and Joe's ceased trading sometime shortly before March 1928, and Malin, whose act was attracting a lot of interest, moved to a new club, the Rubaiyat.

Malin's schtick was unique. Although he had not been averse to slipping on a frock while at Paul and Joe's, he acted as Master of Ceremonies at the Rubaiyat not in a dress but classily outfitted in white tie and tails. Although he would continue to be referred to as a female impersonator in the press, and he would appear in drag in the movie *Arizona to Broadway*, Malin appeared at the club not as a woman but as an outrageous gay man, something that had not been seen before. With a clutch of barbed catchphrases (including 'I'd rather be Spanish than mannish', later adapted as the title of the A-side to his one and only released record), Malin's act was high camp, and appeared at exactly the same time as Douglas Byng was enjoying huge success with his camp songs in London. The clamour for campery would see Byng, a

250

master of wordplay who performed scandalous songs such as 'I'm One of the Queens of England' and 'Cabaret Boys', prove a massive hit when he appeared at the Cotton Club in October 1931.

It was following the closure of the Rubaiyat that Malin took on the role that would make him famous; M.C. – referred to scathingly in the press as the Mistress of Ceremonies – at the Club Abbey, on the ground floor of the Hotel Harding, 205 West 54th Street. Opened in early 1930, the venue had previously been home to the Club Intime, run by the notorious Mary Louise 'Texas' Guinan, vaudeville star, actor and speakeasy proprietor, and the new club was run by her brother, Tommy, utilising many of the same staff. Many of the regulars from the Rubaiyat followed Malin to the Club Abbey, including Charles 'Chink' Sherman, associate of mob boss 'Lucky' Luciano, and a known drug dealer.

The Club Abbey had a reputation for putting on outrageous acts. One of their earliest turns was an African American drag performer calling himself the Black Peggy Joyce who, in March 1930, was sued by the real Peggy Joyce – an actor, dancer and former star of the Ziegfeld Follies regularly featured in the media for her flamboyant and scandalous lifestyle – for defamation. Malin's enormous success at the Club Abbey was quickly noted by others, including Karyl Norman, who were quick to adopt this new, outrageous style. Norman developed his own bitchy persona, berating members of his audience if he felt they were not paying enough attention to the stage, and before the end of the year would be fronting another New York night spot, the aptly named Pansy Club, owned by Joseph Bart. 'What was novel about Malin was that he did not bring a drag act to the club, but instead performed in elegant men's clothing, and brought with him the camp wit of the gay subculture,' explains LGBTQ historian J. D. Doyle. 'If he was heckled by men at the club, he knew how to cut them to shreds, to the delight of the crowd.'

In September 1930 the Club Calais opened on West 51st Street. Modelled on the Club Abbey, Arthur 'Rosebud' Budd was the Jean Malin-style M.C., lesbian pianist Frances Faye played the tunes and the floorshow was led by 'a lad named Jackie May, who is dressed in girl's clothing and looks better than many a lass. His favorite ditty is, "I Must

Have That Man".[9] Malin's own star continued to rise, and as well as working well into the early hours as the consummate nightclub host, he could also be seen on the stage of the Ritz Theatre, on West 48th Street, in the comedy *Sisters of the Chorus*, where, in the role of dressmaker Hubert du Frayne, he 'almost had the audience holding its sides'.[10]

It appeared as if, suddenly, New York was overrun with pansy night spots, but this fascination with camp, sophisticated humour had been building for a while. Pianist and master of the camp monologue Dwight Fisk was a sensation, and Hollywood's Bruz Fletcher began to make appearances in the city, often as accompanist to actors Leatrice Joy or Esther Ralston. Gossip columnist Bud Murray may have been exaggerating, but was not too far off the mark when he wrote that, 'A new show is in rehearsal there, headed by our dearest friend, Kitty Dover, the world's greatest male impersonator – and in the same cast is – The Creole Fashion Plate, Karyl Norman – Frances Renault – Lester Lamont and Olin Landick (all female impersonators) and the title of the show is "A Big Box of PANSIES" (Whoops).'[11] Opening in December 1930 Cyril's Café was blasted by Black-run newspaper the *Afro-American* as:

Patronized by the loco literati. This café, with its informal atmosphere, attracts the artistic group, freethinkers, communists and thrill-seeking youths from downtown. Sunday afternoon was its opening and we saw erotics, neurotics, perverts, inverts and other types of abnormalities, cavorting with wild and Wilde abandon to the patent gratification of the manager and owner, Cyril Lightbody... About two a.m., five horticultural gents came in 'in drag' as the custom of appearing in feminine finery is known. Patrons with talent were invited to perform for the pleasure of the others so Joey Coleman sang a number with David La Fontaine at the piano. Jimmy Walker played. The quartet from Lizts, [*sic*] and Correll Boyd thumped out some popular airs.[12]

The place quickly became popular with Harlem's trans community, vying for business with other enterprises including the Dishpan, the Hobby Horse and Tillie's Kitchen.

One of the liveliest haunts had been the Clam House, where people flocked to hear lesbian pianist Gladys Bentley, dressed soberly in a demure blouse and skirt, belt out risqué versions of the hits of the day and flirt outrageously with the prettiest women in her audience, while owner Big Tillie spent the evening cooking up huge batches of fried chicken in the kitchen. Despite being a big woman, Gladys's energy was boundless: 'Miss Bentley... just sits at the piano for hours and shouts songs. She plays and sings until you'd think she would drop from exhaustion. And just when you believe she has tired she gets up and dances all over the place... Miss Bentley is the life of the party and up there they tell the story of how she once got mad, picked up the piano, put it under her arm and went home.'[13] With that kind of reputation she quickly attracted the interest of Carl Van Vechten and other leading lights of the Harlem Renaissance, and now Gladys had gone upmarket, hosting at the Ubangi Club (formerly Connie's Inn), where she was 'prancing about in her cream-colored full dress suit, her hair closely chopped and slicked down into a pompadour... delivering her prize number about "Nothing now perplexes like the sexes, Because when you see them switch you can't tell which is which."'[14] The Ubangi Club, whose interior was decorated to give the room the feel of the African jungle (well, a jungle filtered through Tarzan movies) boasted singing waiters, a celebrity membership that included Ethel Waters, and a 'revue which included the famous "Male" chorus, a group of pansies',[15] who columnist Louis Sobol described as 'six simpering, mincing-stepped horticulturals [who] present a routine which the audience finds highly amusing'.[16] Soon Gladys was living in a swanky apartment complete with servants and, in 1933, allegedly married another woman in a civil ceremony in Atlantic City, a white woman at that: 'Gladys Bentley, the hefty sepe [sepian] caroler and her hotcha have parted,' Sobol reported twelve months after the event is supposed to have taken place, adding, 'They were involved in a fantastic marriage last year.'[17] 'To add to these whispers, she could be seen any day marching down Seventh Avenue attired in men's clothes and she seemed to thrive on the fact that her odd habits [were] the subject of much tongue wagging.'[18]

In the week before Christmas Karyl Norman, the famed 'Creole fashion plate', opened at the most notorious of them all, the Pansy

Club at 204 West 48th Street, in the area better known as Times Square. Formerly known as the Picardy Club, a favourite haunt of New York's bright young things, the Pansy Club was a hit with patrons but not with the press or the police, who conducted their first major raid on the venue in the early hours of 29 January 1931, shortly after the shooting at the Club Abbey. The Club Abbey had provided the venue for an attempted gangland hit on 'Chink' Sherman, which ended up with him needing hospital treatment for three bullet wounds and a dozen stab wounds. Malin and other members of the Abbey's staff were taken into custody for questioning, but surprisingly they saw very little of what transpired.

Sherman had been attacked – while the club was still full of revellers – by bootlegger Dutch Schultz, in retaliation for the murder of his best friend, a crooked Bronx policeman who often collected money for Schultz's illicit booze operation. Chink had recently acquired a financial interest in the club from mobster Owney Madden (a business associate of Legs Diamond), and Schultz blamed Sherman and his new business partners for his friend's murder – which had occurred outside what was now the Club Abbey.

Schultz's men had gone into the Abbey to cause trouble a few weeks earlier but they were outnumbered, overpowered and thrown out of the club. This time they were determined to leave their mark, and when the police arrived, shortly before dawn and shortly after Sherman had been whisked off to hospital, they found that the 'interior of the club was a spattered wreck. Broken chairs, splintered tables, bullet-pierced walls and many bloodstains led police to the belief that two gangs had translated their enmity into a free-for-all battle with revolvers, knives and fists,'[19] and, apparently, the odd chair leg too.

A few short hours after the Club Abbey shooting, the Pansy Club was raided. Although the police claimed that they were seeking out infractions of the prohibition rules, just one bottle of hootch was discovered by detectives Carberry and O'Neill. That did not matter: the club's manager, Max Bellow, was duly arrested. At the same time as the police were lining the Pansy Club's customers up against the wall, they were also raiding the Club Calais where, as the press put it, Jackie May 'leads a bevy of fellow whoops sisters'.[20] Manager Louis

Edelstein was taken into custody after two pints of liquor were found in a store room behind the bar, dragged out of the building by police to a chorus from his regulars: 'Louie's arrested for possession! Louie's arrested for possession! Let's all get arrested for possession!'[21] A few hours after the raids on the Pansy Club and the Calais, arrests were made at another speakeasy, on Manhattan's Eighth Avenue. The Club Calais was eventually closed in April 1933 by court order.

Although the authorities stated that their aim was to crack down on people ignoring prohibition, the truth was that New York's police commissioner, Edward P. Mulrooney, was tired of the trouble that the city's queer nightspots were attracting; he was determined to roll back the closing time on such clubs from 3 a.m. to 1 a.m., and he was prepared to enforce a curfew to ensure that businesses complied. Better still, Mulrooney would see to it that these venues, which he saw as 'a menace to the citizens of New York',[22] would be closed down altogether.

If not exactly free from police interference, for a number of years Harlem had been seen as at least relatively safe for LGBTQ people. But it had also become a Mecca for 'every wide-eyed tourist or New York thrill-seeker' according to an article in the *Afro-American*. 'No matter how much they know or how many places they have seen, their sophisticated education is never complete until they have been duly initiated into the mysteries of Harlem's inner circle of nightclubs, and 300 or more exclusive basement speakeasies, discovering and participating in the merry and often stimulating hilarity that has made this section of Manhattan the accepted "Capital of Jazz" and "Jungle of Joy".'[23] Harlem and Greenwich Village were celebrated as places that 'had declared war on the "color line",' taking business from venues in Broadway and forcing many clubs and theatres there to close temporarily. Broadway's club owners would act swiftly, and by September *Variety* was informing its readers about the plethora of pansy places in the area:

Reports are around that Broadway during the new season will have nite places with 'pansies' as the prime draw. Paris and Berlin have similar night resorts, with the queers attracting the lays. Greenwich Village in New York had a number of the funny spots when the Village was a phoney night sight seeing collection of joints, the Village spots died away, as only the queers eventually remained the customers and they were broke. The best entertainer in the Village joints along the pansy lines was Jean Malin.[24]

But despite what *Variety* would have its readers believe, not all European venues were succeeding. In Paris, the dancehall at Magic-City, the amusement park near the Eiffel Tower that had hosted spectacular drag balls, closed. By 1922 the mid-lent ball had 'become the recognized function for all the homosexuals (males) of Paris and they spent weeks on their costumes, many of which are of extraordinary ingenuity and beauty. The favorite mask, of course, is to disguise oneself as a woman, and it is literally true that on the floor it is almost impossible to distinguish one sex from the other.'[25] Paris was singled out for the depths of its depravity, a city where 'men dance with men' and 'pamphlets on homosexual topics are given away free in the drinking places' of the Rue de Lappe, 'reputed to be the most depraved street in Paris'.[26]

In October 1930, the musical *Brown Buddies* made its debut at Broadway's Liberty Theatre, with a cast that included famed female impersonator Andrew Tribble and dancer Bill 'Bojangles' Robinson. Bringing Tribble to the venue would have been an obvious coup for any theatre attempting to emulate the success of the city's pansy spots, but here he was cast in a male role, that of George Brown. Several of the songs that featured in *Brown Buddies* were written or co-written by Porter Grainger, and Grainger appeared on stage too. Grainger would continue his dalliance with pansy culture early the following year with a second revue, *Fast and Furious*, which debuted at Brandt's Flatbush Theatre, Brooklyn, before transferring to the New Yorker Theatre, where it was advertised as 'the 'biggest colored musical show ever produced'. Starring Tim Moore and lesbian comedian Jackie Mabley, one of Grainger's compositions was a song called 'Pansies on Parade', sung by Lee 'Boots' Marshall and written to accompany a sketch using a garden setting to parody Harlem's pansy craze clubs and infamous drag balls, and that featured four male hoofers as the 'dancing pansies'.

Despite the involvement of some stellar talent, the show ran for just seven performances over five days.

Away from Broadway, Harlem remained a major draw for thrill-seekers and star spotters. Writing in the *Pittsburgh Courier,* the New York-based Black writer, former baseball player, member of the Negro Writers Guild of New York City, and founder of the Harlem Welfare Association, Eustace 'Chappy' Gardner reported that, 'Sepia actors and actresses have made "Gay Harlem" popular in every corner of the world! ...Harlem streets swarm with white visitors daily, gazing at Harlem's conglomeration of color, gaiety and excitement. At night, crowds fill the streets, wanting to be entertained and to see the wonders they have read about and heard about. It's a thrill to them.'[27] Yet even here, 'where the ofays and their Hershey-hued, Lindy-hopping companions could get together and moan their woes in emancipated unison',[28] the police were not averse to using underhand tactics to bring order. Blues singer Trixie Smith, who sang the first recorded version of the queer blues classic 'My Daddy Rocks Me (With One Steady Roll)', was involved in a sting when she and a friend, dancer Nettie Perry, were arrested for their part in a prostitution ring, after two undercover police officers plied Trixie's tenant, Abe White, with illegally purchased gin. Trixie was charged with renting a room for immoral purposes, her eldest daughter was taken into care by the state authorities and the youngest, at that time just seven months old, was taken to Jefferson Market prison along with her mother. After spending the weekend in the slammer, Trixie was allowed out on bail.

If certain pockets of New York were proving a haven for LGBTQ tourists, the same could not be said of every other city or state. A little over 300 miles north of New York, in Vermont, police were using entrapment to weed out homosexual men and were not averse to arresting men assumed to be homosexual and finding the 'evidence' afterwards. When the case against three men 'charged with a homosexual offense' proved so flimsy, police attempted to have the same group charged with a breach of the peace, even though 'according to the testimony, the respondents did not cause any consternation or alarm, allowed no violence or tumultuous carriage and did not in any way disturb the public peace'.[29] It transpired that officers had attempted to catch the three men *in flagrante* by attending their home in disguise and taking with them a 17-year-old they knew to be homosexual and who was also known to at least two of the men. Despite the paper-thin case, two of the men were sentenced to 'not less than one year nor more than five years at the House of Correction' after the court found that 'there was little question but that the men had abnormal minds'.[30] In July 1930 female impersonator Eddie Cushenberry was arrested after a performance at the Chauffeur's Rest cabaret in Atlantic City, although he was released after the New Jersey police commissioner decided that 'there is no state or city act that prohibits a man being a woman if he wants to be.'[31] Although columnists would often write in ambiguous terms, there was little attempt to mask the disgust behind the description of one popular nightspot that appeared in the *Afro-American*:

> Harlem Inn – 12 midnight, Saturday. 'He's mine, so you might as well leave him alone, you hussy.' ...the questionable sexes gather for their nightly rendezvous... a lad, who they say is a high school boy, comes in, highly rouged, with antique ear rings dangling from his ears... he is greeted wildly and someone orders a drink... sordid stuff this, but it's true... sometimes you wonder... then again, you understand. Dancing in close embrace... the place is steaming, it's so stuffy... someone smashes a bottle on the floor... a dope fiend curls his fingers in glee. He likes to hear the sound of breaking glass... Corn whiskey, barely a day old, finds ready buvers... 'Man Found Dead of Alcoholism,' the headline reads.[32]

Yet even where tourists might encounter trouble on a daily basis, LGBTQ nightlife continued to proliferate. On 10 December 1930, *Variety* magazine ran a front-page story with the headline 'Pansy Parlors: Tough Chicago Has Epidemic of Male Butterflies'. 'World's toughest town, Chicago, is going pansy. And liking it,' the story led.

> Within the past six months some 35 new dim lit tea rooms, operated by boys who won't throw open the doors until at least two hours have been spent adjusting the drapes just so, have opened

on the near north side. The southside of Chi, always reputed to be ready for battle any minute, also has had an increase of these sort of joints. All have waitresses who are lads in girl's clothing. They are strong on the urge for single young men to sip tea in the little booths that line the walls of the spots. Men with femme companions are welcome in these joints. Likewise all have duke readers [fortune tellers]. The readers pass for femmes in the dark. Racketeers, who have made the near North Side their playground for some years, have gone strong for these boy joints in a big way. It's evidently something new for these gun-totin' lads and they are supporting them nobly for the laughs.

In Chicago, businesses may have been paying protection to hoodlums and gangsters, but in Harlem you were much more likely to be paying the local police to turn a blind eye to your activities. In late 1930 Stephanie St Claire, a French-born Black woman who was in charge of Harlem's biggest numbers racket, told a court hearing that even though she had paid more than $7,000 to police to protect her business they had singularly failed to do so.

Back in 1926 Paramount had signed Arthur Blake, a blues guitarist, blind from birth who came from Newport News, Virginia, although Paramount's own publicity material claimed he was born in Jacksonville, Florida, where he 'seems to have absorbed some of the sunny atmosphere'.[33] Blind Blake, as he was known professionally, was a master guitar player, with a distinct, fast guitar-picking style quite unlike the slide guitar prevalent in Delta blues, popularised by artists such as Robert Johnson and Son House and that, by coincidence, the first recordings of which were made that same year. Blake's first release, 'West Coast Blues', was a hit, and over the next few years he would record dozens of sides for the company. Johnson would later earn his own place in the history of queer blues when, in June 1937, he recorded 'I'm a Steady Rollin' Man', which features the couplet 'I'm a hard-workin' man, have been for many long years I know / And some creampuff's usin' my money...' Creampuff is a scornful term for a homosexual male, a man who is derided as soft-skinned and who

259

has not done a day's manual work in his life. In the song, Johnson is complaining about his woman using his money to treat one of her effeminate friends.

Blind Blake was a particular favourite of singer-songwriter Leon Redbone, who said, 'he was recording race records at the same time as Blind Lemon Jefferson, and he was just as popular. His style was more sophisticated. He didn't have quite the voice Jefferson had, but his guitar playing was more in the style of the piano players of ragtime. His guitar playing was quite intricate for what was going on at that time, the late '20's to 1932... I listened to all the things he did I could get my hands on.'[34] The public's interest, and therefore the record companies' hunger, for lavender-hued entertainment continued unabated, and in 1930, Blake recorded his queer blues classic 'Righteous Blues'. Released in January 1931, the hokum-style song contains the couplet, 'Met a funny fellow he didn't like girls, paints his face and wears his hair all curled' which is immediately followed by the singer adopting a female falsetto to sing the chorus 'and he's righteous, oh he's righteous...'.

In February 1931, after a concerted effort by local authorities, the Chateau Madrid – where Gladys Bentley had once held court – and Club Abbey were closed, and Joseph Bart, owner of the notorious Pansy Club, on West 48th Street, was being hauled through the courts on the trumped-up charge of having 'no certificate of occupancy. The law requires all cabarets to obtain such an occupancy certificate, but the statute has not been invoked generally.'[35] Jean Malin – who, in an effort to stave off gossip, had recently married Lucille Heiman, a former dancer in his revue – went from the Abbey to the Argonaut, and once again his crowd followed him. Others went to the predominantly lesbian Garden of Joy, on Lenox Avenue, which became a favourite after-hours hangout for people including singers Ethel Waters and Alberta Hunter, dancers Mabel Hampton and her friend Josephine Baker, and the poet Langston Hughes. Immortalised in a 1927 recording by the Dixieland Jug Blowers (for Victor, featuring vocals from an uncredited Elizabeth Washington), in 1921 a riot had broken out at the Garden of Joy after police tried to close the illegal gaming tables there. Press reports claimed that thirty-five police fought 'five thousand negroes',[36] including women and children for more than half an hour before order was restored, although just eleven men – three of them white – were arrested. The chief attraction of the Garden was its being an open-air cabaret on the roof of the building, with a makeshift wooden shelter to offer some protection from the weather. Close by A'Lelia Walker, the daughter of Madame C. J. Walker, the Black cosmetics queen, ran an open house and arts salon where the great and good of Harlem would party for days. A'Lelia Walker was known for her liberal attitude towards sex and sexuality, and her home became a haven for LGBTQ Harlemites, remaining so until her death in 1931. In his autobiography, Langston Hughes wrote that her death brought about 'The end of the gay times of the New Negro era in Harlem.'[37]

The original *Broadway Brevities and Society Gossip* had been forced to close in 1925, after editor Stephen G. Clow was sent to jail. Now a free man, Clow reactivated the magazine, under the name *New Broadway Brevities.* When it resurfaced, in July 1930, any effort to show deference to New York's entertainment industry had gone; *New Broadway Brevities* was interested in one thing only – gossip – and for the rest of its life would specialise in salacious stories about sex, the threat of communism and the horrors of homosexuality.

In November 1931, *New Broadway Brevities* reported on how the police in New York were fighting a losing battle against sex and drugs in the city's notorious pansy hotspots. Despite the closure of the Club Abbey and other well-known venues, there were plenty more eager to provide a home to their former patrons. Frank's Place, in Brooklyn, was raided several times, yet the club kept on reopening. Frank's Place was popular with sailors from the nearby YMCA, and 'night after night, but especially on Saturdays and Sundays, anywhere from fifty to seventy-five sailors were there, and anywhere from fifty to a hundred men and boys, with painted faces and dyed tresses, singing and dancing.' Without naming names, *Brevities* alluded to stars of Broadway frequenting the notorious club, and repeated gossip about Hollywood's homosexual elite: 'Sailors transferred from the Pacific Coast told strange and startling tales of their encounters with movie notables, especially the star who likes them "salty and sea-going". Earning thousands a week, he spends hundreds a week on the tattooed types. Brazening it out, he had himself starred in a "navy" picture... Not only does one celebrity earn huge amounts through his picture acting, he has a profitable sideline in his antique-store.'[38] The man the magazine was talking about was William 'Billy' Haines, a star of the silent era whose first talkie had been the 1929 movie *Navy Blues*. In the final years of his screen career Haines (along with his partner, Jimmie Shields), had begun to build up a small antiques and interior design business. After he was arrested in 1933 in the company of a sailor at a YMCA in Los Angeles, his time as a star was over. MGM fired him when he refused to enter into a marriage of convenience, and his absence from the screen and from Hollywood was hushed over with an enforced six-month trip to Europe. Once back in California his interior design business continued to flourish, and friends including Carole Lombard, Clark Gable and Joan Crawford saw to it that he became Tinseltown's go-to home décor expert.

By the end of the year, newspapers across the country were claiming – somewhat prematurely – that the pansy craze was over. In November Gilbert Swan, author of the syndicated column *New York Letter* boasted of how the:

> authorities have put an end to the vogue for lisping falsetto-voiced young men. Last winter any number of them were heading the floor show program of the smart places. Jean Malin was quoted and requoted by the tabloid column penners and was 'built' into the status of a town personality. Finally he opened his own night club but it didn't last. Meanwhile, word was passed around that the officials would frown on further efforts to display the cavortings of certain performers of the female impersonator type. And so another of Manhattan's oh-so-different entertainment fads disappeared overnight.[39]

The following month, O. O. McIntyre's nationally syndicated column, *New York Day by Day* eviscerated Malin, lambasting the 'Narcissus posings of the blond and oyster-white' star, calling his act 'a depravity sickening even those hailing it as innovation', and declaring that 'vaudeville and burlesque have also almost completely eliminated pansy performers'.[40] The latter comment was untrue, but McIntyre made it clear that he was not a fan of the 'loathsome antics of a Jean Malin or other pansy performers'.[41]

After a spell acting as M.C. for Broadway nightspot the Club Richman, Malin began a short season as host of Manhattan's New Lido Club, where his act featured him singing the then-current hit song 'I'd Rather Stay Home with Mickey Mouse (Than Go out with a Rat Like You)'. The New Lido Club's previous M.C. had been actor and singer Helen Morgan who, despite being married at that time, was carrying on with former chorus girl Dorothy Day. The two women had both been in the cast of *Ziegfeld's Follies of 1931*, and had become inseparable, the newspapers noting that, 'almost every night... when Helen worked at the New Lido Club, Dorothy would come around, sit in the balcony, wait for Helen to finish her stint, and then they'd make the rounds of the spots that stay open till the sun comes up.' Morgan had been in trouble with the law several times for breaking prohibition, and was plagued by alcoholism: she died in Chicago of cirrhosis of the liver in October 1941.

The acts at the New Lido Club were mixed, although the club itself was – like most clubs in New York at that time – segregated. Lois Long, columnist for the *New Yorker*, caught Malin there shortly after he began his residency. 'The show is one of those fast, noisy, suggestively-gowned things that scream Broadway. The numbers done by the colored folk (tap-dancing, voodoo stuff by the chorus, and the like) are pretty second-rate Harlem, but Mr. Jean Malin (a white boy) is the first person to make the geranium an amusing flower as far as I am concerned. I know that a lot of people think that anybody who says "Swish" in a high tenor is a shrieking wit, but I am stubborn. Mr. Malin had to win me.'[42]

Not that it would have bothered Malin much what Long or anybody else thought of his act; Tinseltown was beckoning. By the fall of 1932 he would be appearing at the Club New Yorker on Hollywood Boulevard and signing a contract with Metro Goldwyn Mayer to appear in a movie with Clark Gable and Joan Crawford. Soon he was pictured lunching at the Brown Derby, and rubbing shoulders at dinner with A-listers Marlene Dietrich and Maurice Chevalier.

Record companies continued to issue recordings of numbers that were inspired by the pansy craze, were performed by the stars of the scene, or – where possible – ticked both boxes. In April 1932 Billy Banks and His Orchestra recorded their version of 'Oh! Peter (You're So Nice)', for Brunswick. A song written almost a decade earlier, and first popularised by jazz composer Zez Confrey and His Orchestra, several prior recordings of the song exist, the majority of which are instrumentals. Banks's version, which features jazz legend Pee Wee Russell on clarinet, reinstates the lyrics to the song's chorus, leaving Banks to sing the rather unambiguous refrain:

Oh Peter you're so nice, it's paradise
When you are by my side, that's when I'm satisfied
Come on and kiss me do and hug me tight
There's nothing sweeter, Peter, Peter
Call around tonight...

Singer, dancer, bandleader and impressionist Banks was originally from Alton, Illinois, but from the late 1920s was based in Cleveland, where he was spotted by Duke Ellington's manager Irving Mills, who brought him to New York. Banks was performing in Harlem in spring 1932, at Connie's Inn and at the Lafayette (he appeared at a benefit for the poor, organised by Duke Ellington, at the Lafayette Theatre in May 1932), and he would later appear with Noble Sissle (co-creator of *Shuffle Along*) and His Orchestra. The same group, now known as Billy Banks' Rhythmakers (his outfit would also be credited as Billy Banks and the Harlem Hot Shots), also recorded 'Mean Old Bed Bug Blues' in 1932 for Vocalion, featuring Fats Waller on piano; the song had originally been recorded by Lonnie Johnson in August 1927, and was covered by Bessie Smith – this time with Porter Grainger on piano – the following month. On his version, Banks again imitates a female voice in some verses, the song becoming a duet. Some have credited the vocals to Una Mae Carlisle, but the session notes and Vocalion disc label clearly state that Banks is the only vocalist performing on the disc. Around the same time that he made these recordings he was appearing regularly on radio: two years later he would record in Chicago with Noble Sissle's International Orchestra, which also featured jazz giant Sidney Bechet.

He went on to perform at Billy Rose's Diamond Horseshoe, one of Manhattan's most opulent and successful nightclubs, in the basement of the Paramount Hotel. One of his specialities was to perform a 'duet' where he imitated both Louis Armstrong and Rose 'Chee-Chee' Murphy. In 1946 he was working at the Greenwich Village Inn, but after the end of the Second World War he found more work in Europe, performing and recording in England (with the Freddy Randall Band for Parlophone) in 1952, before moving permanently to Japan where he died in 1967.

The pansy craze suffered a fatal blow on 10 August 1933, with the death of its leading light, Jean Malin. The star had just finished his last night at the Ship Café, Venice Beach, when he and several friends, including his boyfriend Jimmy Forlenza and comedy actor Patsy Kelly, were involved in a freak accident. Kelly was an out lesbian who was surprisingly frank about her own sexuality: for years she lived openly with actor Wilma Cox, and in the 1940s she would become the lover of bisexual actor Tallulah Bankhead, herself the former lover of singer Billie Holiday. Piling into his car, Malin hit the wrong pedal and sent the vehicle backwards off the pier and into the ocean. The passengers escaped, but Malin was trapped behind the steering wheel and drowned.

Although interest in camp entertainment would limp on for a few more years, Malin's death, the Depression, and the repeal of prohibition earlier that year meant that fewer and fewer tourists were coming to Harlem. Not long after his death Malin's estranged wife was hauled up in court for running a high-class prostitution racket. The clubs that continued to offer LGBTQ acts or that were hosted by obviously queer M.C.s were overrun with hoodlums and becoming increasingly dangerous places to be. One of the few venues that continued to pack in the crowds was the 101 Ranch, situated on 139th Street. The same venue had once been the Chauffeur's Club, where Josephine Baker had worked before she hit the big time, and it is often confused with the Daisy Chain, where her close friend Hazel Valentine would hold court.

The 101's M.C. was Clarence 'Clarenz' Henderson, formerly a dancer and comedian in the double act the Henderson Brothers who, despite being married twice and having a 6-year-old daughter, Clarice, was homosexual and often performed in drag. Clarenz committed suicide by jumping from the kitchen window of his second wife's fourth-floor flat in March 1936. It was not his first attempt: he had previously tried to end it all by drinking peroxide.

Who knows what heights Jean Malin or Clarenz Henderson might have reached, had their careers not come to such tragically early conclusions. By the time they passed, the bright lights that had illuminated the pansy hotspots of New York and Chicago were already dimming, but for some of the stars of the era – including Gladys Bentley and Jackie Mabley – there were still plenty of adventures ahead.

# 17

# B.D. Women and Old Maids

*'I like to travel with my show people. You know, my people are noisy, loud and wrong, a bit uncouth, but I love them for their gaiety and naturalness, they are part of my life. Some of the dumbest people you want to meet are high up in the show business, but I love them all. I would not know what to do off stage without them.'*[1] – Ethel Waters

As the Roaring Twenties became the Threadbare Thirties, Porter Grainger was making a stab at big-screen immortality, writing *Old Man Trouble*, a musical short for Jules Bledsoe, creator of the role of Joe in the musical *Show Boat*. A single-reel short made for Columbia Pictures (at that time a distinctly separate operation from Columbia Records), the movie featured two Grainger compositions, 'Old Man Trouble' – a song heavily influenced by Bledsoe's performance of 'Old Man River' in *Show Boat* – and 'Wadin' in the Water'. Although the film lasted for just seven minutes, it received excellent reviews: 'One of the best things in its class that has yet been presented in sound shorts,'[2] enthused *Film Daily*, while the *Tampa Morning Tribune* rated it as 'outstanding'.[3] Around the same time Grainger and his second wife, blues singer Ethel Finnie, split up for the second – and final – time, and Ethel moved back to her home town, New Orleans, taking their daughter Portia with them. Turning her back on show business,

Ethel landed a job as a cook; she would eventually file for divorce in 1939. Grainger continued to pursue a career in film, and in 1930 was contracted to provide the music for a series of twelve 'talkie shorts called "The Royal Roustabouts" to be produced by the Magnaphone Picture Corporation'.[4]

Despite these early successes, Grainger's film career would not take off, but Ethel Waters would do far better for herself in the new 'talkies'. She had recently married Clyde Edward Matthews, known to his friends as 'Pretty' Matthews, and had made her first movie, singing her latest hits 'Am I Blue?' and 'Birmingham Bertha' in *On with the Show*, the first all-talking, all-colour feature-length film.* However she had been out of the country when the film hit the big screen, singing 'The low-down blues... in all the gay capitals of the old world,'[5] and scoring big at the London Palladium and at the Café de Paris near to Leicester Square (opened in 1924: there had been an earlier Café de Paris at 16 Arthur Street, WC3, advertised in the pages of the *Chicago Whip* in 1920, no doubt in the hope of reaching performers who may have been travelling to London, as a 'colored restaurant' where 'a "homey" welcome awaits you'), and missed her opportunity to capitalise on her success at home. It is unlikely that would have bothered her too much while she was enchanting audiences in Britain. 'Ethel Waters, the coloured comedienne, who comes here with a big talkie and gramophone reputation, immediately captivated Palladium audiences in her first appearance in this country. Rather tall of stature and light in hue, Miss Waters possesses an attractive personality, and in the effectiveness of the way in which she rendered her numbers must be regarded as the finest coloured artiste of her class who has visited this country since the late Florence Mills came here from America.'[6] As far as British audiences were concerned, Ethel was a major star.

Never afraid of hard work, she gave her British fans her all, but after a four-week engagement at the Café de Paris her voice was shot, and she was treated by a London-based throat specialist for laryngitis.

---

* Sadly, no colour versions of *On with the Show* survive, but black-and-white prints do exist.

Taking time off to recuperate only increased demand, and she returned to work at the end of January 1930 at an increased salary. While she was away from home, her New York friends were keen to show that she had not been forgotten, and in the same week that she was due back on stage in London Carl Van Vechten was proudly showing off a bust of Ethel he had purchased from Italian sculptor Tony Cellini.

While the Depression continued to bite, Ethel's star rose ever further skywards, and by the middle of 1931 she was starring on Broadway in Lew Leslie's *Rhapsody in Black* (former vaudeville performer Leslie was best known for staging the floor show at the Cotton Club), drawing capacity audiences. She realised, though, that many in her field had not been as lucky, and she was not about to rest on her laurels. 'I am so used to the bad side of this depression that the coming of better times will shock me like an electric bolt,' she admitted to journalist George Murphy Jr,

> Don't let anybody kid you about being carried along on Broadway. Broadway gives you the reward of hard and consistent work. You have to have the ability and the grit to stick before Broadway notices you. I don't feel that I have reached the point where I can say I am at the top, and there is no more to worry about. As long as I am in this game – and I expect to be in it the rest of my life – I expect to work hard to please my public. ...They call me the greatest colored comedienne; I don't know about that, but I do know that I have to keep on the move to give the public what they want in the way they want it.[7]

In 1933, when appearing at the Cotton Club with Duke Ellington, Ethel grabbed the attention of songwriter Irving Berlin. Berlin was so impressed with her rendition of 'Stormy Weather' – a song written specifically for Waters that has since gone on to become a recognised classic, recorded by everyone from Billie Holiday and Judy Garland to Ringo Starr and Bob Dylan – that he decided to add her to the cast of his new musical revue *As Thousands Cheer*, the first Broadway show to give an African American star equal billing with white actors. *As Thousands Cheer* was another hit, although not everyone involved was happy with the addition of a Black actor to the cast, and three of the show's stars, including gay actor Clifton Webb, a 'life long bachelor'[8] who lived with his mother and travelled with 'a pair of valuable French poodles and a valet',[9] refused to take a bow with her at the end of the show's first try-out. An incensed Berlin told the cast that there would be no bow at all unless they treated Waters with the respect she was due. Webb should have acted with more decency, especially as he had faced bigotry himself. He had been much maligned in the gossip columns, with plenty of mileage gained from his close friendships with such members of the gay glitterati as Noël Coward, Laird Cregar and Monty Woolley: sadly, racism was (and often still is) as prevalent in the LGBTQ community as in any other sector of society.

'Supper Time', one of the four numbers that Berlin gave Waters to sing in *As Thousands Cheer*, was about racial violence, inspired by a newspaper headline about a lynching in Florida, and it appeared six years before Billie Holiday would record the better-known anti-lynching song 'Strange Fruit'. Ethel pulled on her own experience, recalling the lynching that had happened while she and her band had been touring Georgia in 1922, to add gravitas, and her heartfelt performance helped to bring her to the attention of a whole new audience. On Christmas Day 1933, Noël Coward, one of the many stars satirised in the show (Waters also gave a wicked impersonation of Josephine Baker), sent Ethel a telegram, calling her performance of the song 'A subtle and beautiful moment in the theatre.'[10] A week later, pianist Pearl Wright, who accompanied Ethel on more than thirty recordings between 1925 and 1929, nominated her for the Spingarn Medal, awarded annually by NAACP for outstanding achievement by an African American. In April 1936 Eleanor Roosevelt, wife of the then-president, asked Ethel to join her in a newly formed commission, dubbed the 'anti-lynch cabinet'. Mrs Roosevelt had been actively pursuing a way to introduce an effective anti-lynching law since joining the NAACP two years earlier, work that would lead to J. Edgar Hoover spreading racist rumours about her own genetic heritage, that she was mixed race; and that would ultimately result in the Ku Klux Klan issuing a $25,000 bounty on her head. Despite her increasing fame, Ethel would continue to face a racist backlash: in March 1937, after appearing at a whites-only venue in Kansas City, she attempted to put on a special midnight show for Black patrons. Local activists organised a boycott against the Mainstreet theatre's segregation policy, and barely a handful of people turned up for the performance.

Alberta Hunter, Ethel's long-time nemesis who had enjoyed her own successes in Britain, had spent long enough on stage by now to have become wise to the crooked ways of certain venue owners. When, in October 1930, she was offered a contract by Frank Schiffman, the white manager of the Lafayette Theatre, she already knew that Schiffman was a shady dealer with a reputation for underpaying his artists. But this was a year into the Depression: things were getting tough and Alberta agreed to play the Lafayette for $250, rather than the $600 she had been getting... which itself was a fraction of the $2,700 a week she had been on when she signed with the Keith-Albee circuit in February 1929, making her the highest paid Black artist in America at that time, surpassing the earnings of Bessie Smith.

Schiffman – who in January 1934 would become co-founder of Harlem's famous Apollo Theater – had tried the same trick with dozens of artists before Alberta, with a clause in his contracts that allowed him to cut an act's fee should they fail to meet his standards: the always-savvy Alberta had her own contract drawn up, and refused to sign the one supplied by Schiffman. Still, after she had given her first performance that week, Schiffman tried to force her to accept a further $100 cut; a furious Alberta went to the press and, with the powerful Black actors' union on her side, forced Schiffman to pay her the full amount. Schiffman would not forget, and in June 1946, when Alberta was playing the Apollo, Schiffman pulled her from the line-up after just two shows, paying her a meagre $100.

Alberta may have detested Frank Schiffman, but he would help make Jackie Mabley a star. In early 1930 Mabley had been in Baltimore, on the stage of the Royal Theatre, appearing in the revue *Sidewalks of Harlem*, before coming back to New York, eventually making it to the Alhambra, in Harlem, in October. The Depression had devastated the city – by the end of 1930 there were an estimated 50,000 families in New York whose chief income earner was out of work; soup kitchens were besieged, and churches organised appeals for clothing, hats and

271

shoes – but after a tough apprenticeship, Jackie Mabley was firmly on the road to stardom. She had spent most of the preceding decade touring: mentored by comedy act Butterbeans and Susie (who in turn had learnt much of their craft during their years of touring with the likes of Ma Rainey) and playing in some of the roughest towns and venues on the Chitlin' Circuit.

Following the Alhambra she landed regular appearances at many of New York's most 'in' places, including Connie's Inn, the Cotton Club and, by 1937, at Frank Schiffman's Apollo, again appearing alongside Gladys Bentley. It was there that she picked up the nickname 'Moms' Mabley, thanks to her protective nature over many of the younger, less-experienced performers... although many who shared a dressing room with her (and her girlfriend) also referred to her as 'Mister Moms', an epithet that was partly inspired by her androgynous clothing; it was only later that she adopted the housecoat and knitted hat look for which she is best remembered. Bentley was guaranteed a sell-out audience wherever she appeared, and her fame was such that she was employed to act as the M.C. of a new club on Harlem's West 136th Street, named Gladys's Exclusive. However, in February 1933 she found herself hauled into Manhattan's Supreme Court for breach of contract: the two owners of Gladys's Exclusive claimed that they had her tied to a five-year agreement to front the club they had named after the singer, but that she had reneged on their contract, walking out to 'perform in a downtown establishment in which she was said to have a financial interest'.[11]

Bessie's personal life continued to spiral out of control. On 16 May 1931 she was arrested for being drunk and disorderly on the streets of Wheeling, West Virginia. Thrown into the slammer along with her estranged husband, when the pair were released the following morning they grabbed their belongings and headed off to Philadelphia, leaving the rest of the troupe behind, with no money and no transport. In November of that year she made her last recordings for Columbia, 'Safety Mama' and 'Need a Little Sugar in my Bowl'. The Depression, radio and changing tastes had brought an end to the era of the classic blues singers, Bessie's records were now selling in the low hundreds, rather than the tens of thousands, and Columbia terminated her contract while it still had time to run. Frank Walker, the man who had looked after her recording career and had acted as her personal manager for almost a decade – was the man tasked with breaking the news to his former star. She would not record again for two years, after John Hammond – who had first seen her perform in 1927 at the Alhambra at the height of her fame – went in search of her to cut some sides for Okeh which, in an ironic twist, had been bought out by Columbia in 1926. Hammond – who brought together, at his own expense, an all-star jazz combo to back Bessie, including Jack Teagarden, Benny Goodman and Chu Berry for the November 1933 session – would later claim that he 'discovered' Bessie after her career had hit the skids, but although it is true that she was no longer recording, like Ma Rainey she was still filling theatres and was never off the road.

In 1933 or '34 Bessie performed at the Fort Work Stock Show in Texas; also appearing was her former mentor, Ma Rainey, accompanied by a young banjo player, T-Bone Walker. 'Bessie Smith is my favorite girl blues singer. Ma Rainey could sing the blues, but she couldn't sing the blues like Bessie. They had different styles. Bessie was the queen for everybody, better than Ethel Waters. She was really great, she could sing *anything*.' Walker would recall that, by this time, Ma's once-famous good temperament had changed for good. 'Ma Rainey was a heavy set dark lady, mean as hell but she sang nice blues and she never cussed *me* out. She had a show with the Haines Carnival at the Stock Show and I played for her.'[12]

By now, in New York at least, Bessie's fame was waning: a 1933 appearance at the Lyric Theatre saw Jackie Mabley billed above the Empress of the Blues. Even so, she continued to be in demand outside of the Big Apple, and although there were rumblings about her having had her day, as far as her audience was concerned, Bessie still had plenty left to give. 'I had the wonderful privilege to be in one of Bessie's shows about 1934/35,' fellow blues singer Victoria Spivey recalled, in a letter to *Record Research* magazine. 'When I arrived at the theatre I found a fabulous show. Bessie Smith was not "selling chewing gum and candy in theatre aisles",' a claim made by Paul Oliver in his book *Kings of Jazz: Bessie Smith*. '[I] was making $100 a day for myself... It's a good bet that Bessie was topping my payroll.'[13] Spivey had an equally dim view of Ruby Walker, accusing her of being a 'lying Black bitch'[14] and disparaging many of the claims Ruby made about her aunt Bessie's life to biographer Chris Albertson. Spivey would not be the only one to criticise Ruby's words, or her intentions, with several of Bessie's acquaintances and family members suggesting Ruby was primarily interested in enlarging the importance of her own role in Bessie's story. Bessie's sister-in-law, Maude Faggins, would characterise Ruby as, 'self-obsessed, neurotic, and a liar.'[15]

Despite New York's indifference, on 16 February 1934, Bessie played a benefit at the Savoy Ballroom, New York alongside Harpo Marx, Fletcher Henderson and dozens of others for the Scottsboro Boys, a group of nine African American teenagers and young men, aged 13 to 20, accused in Alabama of having attacked a group of white teens and of raping two white women. Two years earlier Alberta Hunter had performed at a similar benefit at the Rockland Palace (home of the Hamilton Lodge drag balls), backed by Cab Calloway and his orchestra. Both shows were organised by the National Committee for the Defense of Political Prisoners , whose committee included gay Harlem Renaissance poet Countee Cullen, W. C. Handy, and writer and wit Dorothy Parker. Despite one of the alleged rape victims admitting that her story was a complete fabrication, the Scottsboro boys were found guilty, and although charges against four of the nine defendants were eventually dropped, the other five were convicted and received sentences ranging from seventy-five years to death; Clarence Norris's death sentence would be commuted to life imprisonment in 1938.

She may have given her time in aid of a good cause, but the noisy New York critics were convinced that Bessie's moment in the spotlight was up: audiences were after something more sophisticated and her appearance at the Harlem Opera House – with Don Redmon and His Band – did not even merit an encore. 'Bessie Smith is undoubtedly a good blues singer,' claimed a reviewer in the *New York Age*, 'but blues singers don't seem to rate as highly as they used to. Her reception by the audience, although warm enough, seemed to be actuated by appreciation of her personality rather than her act. Of course the usual risqué lines evoked the usual obscene howls of laughter, but she wasn't called back at all.'[16] The same week it was announced that Bessie would be among the cast of 200 of a new 'musical extravaganza' entitled *Dusk and Dawn*, written by Will Marion Cook and to be staged in Chicago that December.

By the following February, the reviewers of the *New York Age* had clearly decided that the blues were no longer suitable for the sophisticates of the metropolis. Bessie's appearance at the Apollo in Harlem was slammed by Vere E. Johns with coruscating vitriol: 'A lady announced as Bessie Smith shouted some doubtful "blues" and waved her torso around,'[17] he wrote, her performance on that hallowed stage summed up in just fifteen withering words. Despite this she was back at the Apollo in May, this time as support act to Mrs Louis Armstrong (Lil Hardin, Armstrong's second and, at that time, estranged wife) and her Kings of Rhythm Orchestra. Once again, the *New York Age* had little interest in her 'old blues singing school' style, although this time the reviewer did begrudgingly accept that Bessie was 'probably the first of her clan to modernize her style of singing',[18] suggesting that she alone of the blues-singing Smiths had kept an eye on changing tastes and fashions, incorporating up-tempo swing numbers in her set. But by August she was being dismissed in the pages of the newspaper as the 'last of the old regime of "blues singers"'.[19]

The snippy comments from the critics writing for the *New York Age* might have stung her pride, but they made little difference to booking agents and audiences and despite what her detractors may have claimed, audiences still filled the theatres. Luckily not all of the commentators hated her; the management of the Apollo continued to add Bessie to the bill, bringing her back over Christmas 1935, and some critics were impressed by her attempts to update her style. 'Bessie Smith, chanting a sort of "swing-blues" that is bluer than deepest indigo, seems to improve with age,' wrote one. 'As nimble footed as a sprightly chorine half her age, Bessie swings... In a dance tempo that brings almost as much hand clapping as her moanful and risqué songs do.'[20]

If New York's critics were wanting a new star to laud, then there was one waiting in the wings, one whose style had been honed, in part, by listening to the recordings of the great Bessie Smith. They would not have to look too far to find her either, for at that time a young torch singer who had recently taken a new stage name, Billie Holiday, was appearing at the Cotton Club, part of the cast of a floorshow that included female impersonator Miss Gertrude, dancing duo Wade and Wade and Master of Ceremonies Babe Wallace.

Born Eleanora Fagan, in Philadelphia in April 1915, she began appearing in Harlem clubs under the name Billie Halliday, the first name taken from actor Billie Dove, the second came from her father, banjo player Clarence Halliday. In 1933 she came to the attention of John Hammond, and that December, took part in her first recording session, for Columbia in New York. Early the following year her first recording, 'Riffin' the Scotch', was issued, with Miss Halliday credited as the featured vocalist with the Benny Goodman Orchestra, but before the year was out, Billie Holiday (the new surname taken from her father's stage name) would be a solo star.

The unwanted daughter of a 13-year-old mother, Sadie Fagan, Eleanora grew up in Baltimore, listening to the early recordings of Bessie Smith and Louis Armstrong. By the time she was 11 she had already dropped out of school and had been the victim of a rape, and before she had reached her 12th birthday she was working in a brothel, running errands for the women who were employed there, as she stated in her autobiography *Lady Sings the Blues*:

Alice Dean used to keep a whorehouse on the corner nearest our place, and I used to run errands for her and the girls. I was very commercial in those days. I'd never go to the store for anybody for less than a nickel or a dime. But I'd run all over for Alice and the girls, and I'd wash basins, put out the Lifebuoy soap and towels. When it came time to pay me, I used to tell her she could keep the money if she'd let me come up in her front parlor and listen to Louis Armstrong and Bessie Smith on her victrola. A victrola was a big deal in those days, and there weren't any parlors around that had one except Alice's. I spent many a wonderful hour there listening to Pops and Bessie. I remember Pops' recording of 'West End Blues' and how it used to gas me. It was the first time I ever heard anybody sing without using any words. I didn't know he was singing whatever came into his head when he forgot the lyrics. Ba-ba-ba-ba-ba-ba-ba and the rest of it had plenty of meaning for me—just as much meaning as some of the other words that I didn't always understand. But the meaning used to change, depending on how I felt. Sometimes the record would make me so sad I'd cry up a storm. Other times the same damn record would make me so happy I'd forget about how much hard-earned money the session in the parlor was costing me. Guess I'm not the only one who heard their first good jazz in a whorehouse. But I never tried to make anything of it. If I'd heard Louis and Bessie at a Girl Scout jamboree, I'd have loved it just the same. But a lot of white people first heard jazz in places like Alice Dean's, and they helped label jazz 'whorehouse music'.[21]

Two years later she and her mother were both living in Harlem, where the 14-year-old Eleanora found employment as a teenage prostitute – although she would not do so for long: both mother and daughter were arrested and imprisoned just weeks after Eleanora's 14th birthday. Within a year she would be singing in Black-run clubs, using her new name, Billie Halliday.

In a 1971 interview, Ruby Davis, who was Holiday's roommate for around six months, told journalist Linda Lipnack Kuehl that Holiday, 'had a nickname among the men. They called her Mister Billie Holiday because she was seldom seen with fellas. And I will always believe that her mother was the cause of it because she never wanted Billie to get close to any fellas. She would tell her that they were no good... just like Billie's father.' Count Basie called her 'William'; her own pianist, Carl Drinkard, told writer Donald Clarke that, 'She [had] this reputation for being a fabulous les... Lady told me, "Sure I've been to bed with women, Carl, but I was always the man".'[22]

Billie had several lesbian relationships during her life, including a high-profile one with white actor Tallulah Bankhead. The pair initially met in the 1930s, when Bankhead could often be found in the clubs of Harlem with her clique of socialite friends, but they would not become lovers for at least a decade. 'It was Billie's deep feeling and originality which moved me from the first time I heard her,'[23]

Bankhead told *Ebony* magazine in 1960. By the time they began their affair Billie had become a major star, feted by her peers and recording classics including 'God Bless the Child', 'That Ole Devil Called Love' and 'Strange Fruit', a breathtaking description of a lynching. Tallulah would often be seen at Billie's shows, and on more than one occasion she intervened in an attempt to put her messy personal life back on the rails: once, after Holiday had been arrested for drug possession, Tallulah posted bail, and on another occasion Bankhead paid for a psychiatrist after Holiday threatened to commit suicide. In 1947 when, found guilty of possession, Billie was sent to the Alderson Federal Prison Camp in West Virginia, Tallulah intervened again, pleading with FBI director J. Edgar Hoover for Billie's freedom, telling him that, 'Miss Holiday is a very great artist. She doesn't need to be confined within prison walls. What she needs is understanding, medical help and the warmth of a loving home.'[24] Sadly her intervention was of no use, and Billie served eight months. Shortly after she was released (in March 1948, her sentence cut short for good behaviour), she told *Ebony* magazine that:

I came out expecting to be allowed to go to work and to start with a clean slate and write a new chapter in my life... [But] the police have been particularly vindictive, hounding, heckling and harassing me beyond endurance. As a result of their insidious pressure I have been frowned upon and sneered at... My life has been made miserable. These people have dogged my footsteps from New York to San Francisco and all the territory in between. They have allowed me no peace. Wherever I go, they track me down and ask me nasty questions about the company I keep and my habits.[25]

By 1952, when Bankhead issued her autobiography, *Tallulah*, things had soured between the two women, and the book barely mentioned Holiday at all. Three years later, Billie was on the cusp of issuing her own autobiography, *Lady Sings the Blues*. Tallulah, who had been sent an advance copy, was not impressed with Billie's tale and threatened to sue the publishers, Doubleday, unless they removed any mention of her name. When Billie heard, she wrote to Tallulah, addressing her as 'Miss Bankhead', and telling her that:

I thought I was a friend of yours. That's why there was nothing in my book that was unfriendly to you, unkind or libellous. Because I didn't want to drag you, I tried six times last month to talk to you on the damn phone, and tell you about the book just as a matter of courtesy. That bitch you have who impersonates you kept telling me to call back and when I did, it was the same deal until I gave up. ...There are plenty of others around who remember how you carried on so you almost got me fired... If you want to get shitty, we can make it a big shitty party. We can all get funky together. I don't know whether you've got one of those dam [sic] lawyers telling you what to do or not. But I'm writing this to give you a chance to answer back quick and apologize to me and to Doubleday... Straighten up and fly right, Banky. Nobody's trying to drag you.[26]

Whatever Holiday had written about her former lover, it was expunged before the book hit the stores.

'Unless it was the records of Bessie Smith and Louis Armstrong I heard as a kid, I don't know of anybody who actually influenced my singing, then or now,' she wrote.

I always wanted Bessie's big sound and Pop's feeling. Young kids always ask me what my style is derived from and how it evolved and all that. What can I tell them? If you find a tune and it's got something to do with you, you don't have to evolve anything. You just feel it, and when you sing it other people can feel something too. With me, it's got nothing to do with working or arranging or rehearsing. Give me a song I can feel, and it's never work. There are a few songs I feel so much I can't stand to sing them, but that's something else again.[27]

While Billie was steadily becoming a celebrity, another new name was making her own attempt at stardom, only Bessie Jackson had already reached a level of fame (or, if you prefer, infamy) a decade earlier under her real name, Lucille Bogan. Over four days, between 5 and 8 March 1935, Bogan (using the name Jackson) and her piano player Walter Roland would record a number of songs, including a second version of the notorious 'Shave 'Em Dry', the song first recorded in 1924 in Chicago by Ma Rainey, and that she herself had recorded (in its best known, 'dirty' version) two years earlier. During the March 1935 sessions, the pair also cut 'B.D. Woman's Blues', one of the most outrageous, unapologetic celebrations of lesbianism ever recorded, which was issued that year as the B-side to 'Jump Steady Daddy' on both Melotone (a Brunswick subsidiary) and Banner records.

> Comin' a time, B.D. women they ain't gonna need no men
> Comin' a time, B.D. women they ain't gonna need no men
> Oh, the way they treat us is a lowdown and dirty sin
>
> B.D. women, you sure can't understand
> B.D. women, you sure can't understand
> They got a head like a sweet angel and they walk just like a natural man
>
> B.D. women, they all done learnt their plan
> B.D. women, they all done learnt their plan
> They can lay their jive just like a natural man
>
> B.D. women, B.D. women, you know they sure is rough
> B.D. women, B.D. women, you know they sure is rough
> They all drink up plenty whiskey and they sure will strut their stuff
>
> B.D. women, you know they work and make their dough
> B.D. women, you know they work and make their dough
> And when they get ready to spend it, they know they'd better go.

No songwriter or publisher is credited on the disc: the lyrics were almost certainly composed by Bogan or Roland, but they borrow the line 'comin' a time, women ain't gonna need no men' from her late 1927 Paramount release 'Women Won't Need No Men'.

After her initial sessions for Okeh, back in 1923, Lucille Bogan had continued to record under her real name, issuing the first version of the classic 'Black Angel Blues' (later recorded by Tampa Red and by B.B. King), 'Sloppy Drunk Blues', and 'Tricks Ain't Walking No More', later covered by Memphis Minnie, but by the time 'B.D. Woman's Blues' was issued, she was using the pseudonym Bessie Jackson, a name she would continue to use for the rest of her recording career.

According to civil rights group the National Black Justice Coalition, Bogan 'had a very colorful love life, and engaged in romantic liaisons with both men and women',[28] which, if it were true, would certainly help explain how she could sing a song like 'B.D. Woman's Blues' with such obvious insight into the lives of lesbian women. Monette Moore's February 1936 release 'Two Old Maids in a Folding Bed' has a lesbian theme but is delivered by its co-author Moore, a blues singer who had been friendly with Alberta Hunter and who had once acted as understudy for Ethel Waters, as a comic novelty. Several other versions of 'Two Old Maids...' would follow, including one by Billy Mitchell, by Ben Light and His Surf Club Boys, and by blues singer Sophisticated Jimmy La Rue (recorded the day after Monette Moore cut her version, and issued by Decca subsidiary Champion), most of which would incorporate lyrics from popular songs of the day in a suggestive manner: 'Two old maids in a folding bed, one turned over to the other and said / I'm coming... I'm coming...'.

Ted Brown, the singer with queer blues revival act Vinyl Closet, who recorded their own version of 'Two Old Maids...' on their 2013 album *Pink, Black and Blues*, explains that, 'We just wanted to do whatever was available, so there are songs we'd heard on the "Sissy Man Blues" compilation and a couple of others we came across by accident. We were not really choosing them on their musical merit, it didn't really matter whether we thought the songs were good or bad; for instance, I don't think that "Two Old Maids in a Folding Bed" is a great song, it's just that it's quite clearly about a lesbian relationship.'[29]

Bogan recorded several blues numbers that allude to lesbianism or bisexuality, and although the references are perhaps more oblique, there can be no mistaking that the snuff-taking protagonist of her 1934 recording 'Pig Iron Sally' is at least a man-hater, if not an out and out bull dyke, a woman who is '...evil and mean as I can be / And I ain't going to let nobody put that doggone thing on me.' She had an affair with pianist Will Ezell, but the pair split after her husband, Nazareth, threatened to begin divorce proceedings. With little work coming in, by the mid-1930s she was back in Birmingham, living once again with Nazareth, managing and performing with her son's jazz band, Bogan's Birmingham Busters: the act recorded several sides, and although she did take part in some unissued sessions after the war with the Busters, sadly Lucille did not appear on any of their releases. She would not issue any recordings after 1935. On the 1940 census, Lucille's occupation is left blank.

By 1941 her marriage to Nazareth Senior was over for good. Junior, who had been working as an elevator operator in a Birmingham department store, wanted to pursue his dreams of musical stardom, and took his wife Mary and daughter, Angeline, to Los Angeles. Lucille left her husband and, in June 1948, would join her son in Los Angeles, accompanied by the new man in her life James Spencer, who was twenty-two years her junior. Lucille Bogan died two months later, on 10 August 1948, aged 51, from coronary sclerosis. She was interred at Lincoln Memorial Park in Compton, California but, like Bessie Smith, no headstone was purchased, and her grave went unmarked for decades.

## 18

# Death Letter Blues

*'The white sisters have taken over their edge of the cut from the sepia sisters in the uptown nightclubs. Every orchestra bills a blues singer. Of course, all the songs aren't called blues today, but the gal with the husky voice and the come-on look in her eyes is booked as the blues singer.'*[1]

On 3 February 1935 Clara Smith died in Detroit's Parkside Hospital, the first hospital built specifically to cater for the city's rapidly expanding Black community. She had been appearing in the city when she was taken ill, and failed to respond to treatment. She was just 40 years old.

In her recent performances Clara had been billed as 'The Ethel Waters of burlesque',[2] quite a come down for the 'Queen of the Moaners', a woman who had been Columbia Records' second-biggest selling blues singer, a star almost as big as Bessie Smith, the acknowledged 'Empress of the Blues'. That same year, struggling to keep a show on the road to ever-dwindling returns, Gertrude Rainey finally retired from live performances. Now nearing 50, and not having recorded for more than six years, she decided to move back to her hometown, principally to care for her mother at the two-storey home she had built for her, on Columbus's Fifth Avenue.

Clara's death went by almost unnoticed, barely registering in the press. Meanwhile her former lover, Josephine Baker, was commanding headlines. From mid-December 1934 she had been starring in Paris in a restaging of Offenbach's 1875 operetta *Creole*, revealing her to be 'a dramatic actress of superior talent'.[3] Her status was confirmed by the release of her latest movie, *Zouzou* where she appeared opposite French star Jean Gabin.

Having established herself in Paris, where she was lionised as the 'world's richest Negro woman',[4] becoming friends with arts giants including Pablo Picasso and Ernest Hemingway, and recording a number of hit songs, Baker yearned to return to her homeland, and she accepted a role in the 1936 revival of the *Ziegfeld Follies*. But if she had expected to enjoy a triumphant return to the American stage, she was to be disappointed. After a decade of European stardom she came home to be faced with outright hostility, racism and a press that dismissed her as, 'a St. Louis wash woman's daughter who stepped out of a Negro burlesque show into a life of adulation and luxury... In sex appeal to jaded Europeans of the jazz-loving type, a Negro wench always has a head start. The particular tawny tint of tall and stringy Josephine Baker's bare skin stirred French pulses. But to Manhattan theatre-goers last week she was just a slightly buck-toothed young Negro woman whose figure might be matched in any night club show, whose dancing and singing could be topped practically anywhere outside France.'[5]

'No performer who has come to these shores has been the victim of such undercover resentment as Josephine Baker,' wrote columnist and future television superstar Ed Sullivan, adding that despite her reputation as a diva, many in the show's cast '...say that she treated the chorus kids better than any other principal,' and that one rainy night she generously gave up her cab for 'a group of chorus girls. "You work harder than I do," she said.'[6] French bandleader Jo Bouillon, who would become her fourth husband, explained that, 'Josephine left Paris rich, adored, famous throughout Europe. But in New York, in spite of the publicity that preceded her arrival, she was received as an uppity colored girl.'[7]

*

Away from the stage, life for America's LGBTQ community carried on much as before. Prohibition had been repealed, but that made little difference to a country in the grip of Depression. In the cities, there were plenty of opportunities to make a buck, and just as many ways to spend it. In 1936, Gladys Bentley and Jackie Mabley were performing as part of the all-Black revue at the Ubangi Club. Like many of the stars of the pansy craze, Bentley was moving away from ribald, risqué material that had packed clubs during the years of prohibition, and was tailoring her material towards a more upmarket audience. 'Gladys Bentley, who used to sing and play so tirelessly at the Clam House, has gone plumb hinkty [snobbish] in her shiny tuxedo suit and is a real night club entertainer.'[8] The change in approach was necessary: the venues that were pulling in the crowds, and paying their acts a decent wage, had been quick to respond to the changing tastes of their patrons. Ribald and racy blues belters were out, as far as New York's cosmopolitan clientele were concerned, and swing bands that featured torch singers were in. Gladys began to advertise herself as the 'brown bomber of sophisticated song', but you could still find clubs where drag acts and LGBTQ performers were the norm. On the corner of Madison Avenue and 42nd Street was Club Madame, a cellar bar where the eponymous Madame would sing every night; when Gladys was not pounding the piano at the Ubangi Club you could find her at the less salubrious King's Terrace, and there were plenty of other places should you care to search them out, including Small's Paradise, where Porter Grainger had been persuaded to write material for Detroit Red, the 'sepian mistress of ceremonies'.[9] This might have felt like a comedown for the man who, just a few months earlier, had written the intermezzo – an instrumental piece he dubbed 'Adagio Aframerique' – for Orson Welles's all-Black staging of *Macbeth* at the Lafayette, but New York's nightclub floorshows continued to provide a lucrative income for Grainger, and throughout the 1930s he wrote for cabaret revues and drag artists as well as for records and for Broadway.

Like many of his contemporaries, Grainger had to diversify: radios were replacing gramophones in the home, speakeasies were beginning to disappear, and clubs and inns freed from prohibition had to compete with each other on the strength of their floorshow alone, yet despite

285

the repeal of the anti-alcohol laws, many of Harlem's Black clubs still served cheap, illicit booze. At basement hangout the Belmont, where 'a large black man at a piano supplies the music [and] a saffron-colored girl named Jean sings and dances', a half pint of corn whisky would set you back 50 cents, and throughout Harlem 'bootleg corn and bathtub gin remain, as always, the alcoholic staples'.[10] Nearby, at a basement club known as the Theatrical Grill, 'visiting celebrities supply most of the entertainment, supplemented by a four-piece band and a tall, coal black Negro who is one of those erotic phenomena called "queens" – female impersonators. This one has assumed the name of a famous white movie star, wears a wig and an evening gown, and sings alto.'

For a time, it became fashionable for Black drag artists to adopt the name of a well-known white female actor or entertainer, such as the Sepia Mae West, Joan Crawford – a big hit as the hostess of Chicago's Cozy Cabin Inn – and so on. Several different Black singers adopted the moniker of the Sepia Mae West, including a male entertainer known alternatively as Dick Barrow and Samuel Fouche, and a girl named Mae Johnson, who appeared on stage at the Ubangi Club with Gladys Bentley; even blues singer Ida Cox was, at one point in the mid-1930s, billed by theatre owners as the 'sepia Mae West'.

'Dickie Wells' Theatrical Grill seems as raucous as usual, with the hysterical orchestra blowing its kazoos and sucking its bottles of lightning. An ex-truck driver who prefers to be known under the name of a blond movie star, sings and sways in a beaded evening gown. And customers rise and writhe to the barbaric rhythms.'[11] The pansy craze may have been all but over, but the light kept burning, albeit dimly, at the Theatrical Grill.

Despite the attempts by New York's police commissioner Edward P. Mulrooney and mayor Fiorello La Guardia to stamp out pansy culture in the metropolis, Wells, a former dancer, knew that the public loved the near-the-knuckle antics of the rowdiest of the queer entertainers, and had every intention of giving them what they wanted. The drag act in question was known as Gloria Swanson (and occasionally as the Sepia Gloria Swanson), and was famed for her obscene rewrites of popular songs of the day, not unlike Gladys Bentley, who Gloria had shared the bill with at the Ubangi Club. Originally from Atlanta, Georgia, Walter

Winston (occasionally referred to as Harry Winston) began appearing as Gloria in the drag balls of Chicago, and lived openly as a woman... and a star. Performing a smutty adaptation of the Fats Waller song 'Squeeze Me', Gloria boasted that she 'had not worn a stitch of male attire in ten years',[12] and was a leading light of the city's pansy craze.

Gloria began her professional career in skirts in the early 1920s, acting as the hostess at speakeasies such as the Book Store, and other mob-run clubs on Chicago's South Side, before the ongoing gang violence persuaded her to move to New York. But not everyone was a fan of her 'repulsive "she-male" glorifying act'.[13] In a letter to the dancer and ballet director William Chappell, British artist Edward Burra, famed for his depictions of Harlem's nightlife, described the scene:

We went to an outrageous place called the Theatrical Grill. A cellar done up to look like Napoleon's tomb and lit in such a way that all the white people look like corpses. I've never seen such faces the best gangster films are far outdone by the old original thing. The chief attracles [sic] of the cabaret was 'Gloria Swanson', a mountainous coal black nigger in a crepe de chine dress trimmed [with] sequins who rushed about screaming 'Clappy weather, just can't keep my old arse together.'

Burra, who provided Chappell with a pencil sketch of the entertainer to accompany his rather vivid description, got more than an eyeful when Gloria approached his table. The performer lifted up her dress 'disclosing a filthy dirty pair of pink silk panties; how he managed I don't know, no balls or anything else so far as I could see...'[14]

Described as, 'plump, jolly and bawdy, with a pleasant "whiskey-voice"; with his every gesture and mannerism more feminine than those of any female; his corsets pushing his plumpness into a swelling and well-modeled bosom; his chocolate-brown complexion beautiful, and his skin soft and well-cared-for,' it was noted that Gloria 'was just the sort of playmate for the fast-living element. He had the free loud camaraderie that distinguished the famous Texas Guinan. Gangsters and hoodlums, pimps and gamblers, whores and entertainers showered him with feminine gee-gaws and trappings; spoke of him as "her", and quite relegated him to the female's functions of supplying good times and entertainment.'[15]

Gloria would open her own Harlem club, at 148 West 133rd Street, in 1935, but following La Guardia's clamping down on nonconformist lifestyles she was forced into wearing male clothes when not on stage. The following year she was appearing at the Brittwood, advertised as 'Harlem's Gayest Spot',[16] where she would continue to appear until moving to the 101 Ranch in January 1938. It was reported, in March 1940, that Gloria had died in a train wreck in Little Falls but the truth is far more mundane. A lifelong heart condition finally took her the following month, with her open casket funeral – attended by more than 200 people – taking place on 30 April 1940.

Bessie Smith died at the Afro-American Hospital, in Clarksdale, Mississippi, at 11.50 a.m. on 26 September 1937. The night before, after giving what would be her final performance, she had been on her way to Memphis, to join the cast of *Broadway Rastus*, when her Packard was involved in a collision with a truck (according to her death certificate, her car drove into the parked truck) and went off the road. Her right arm was almost severed from her body in the accident, and by the time help arrived she had lost a lot of blood. She was taken into surgery, where the arm was amputated, but she would not recover from her injuries.

As usual, in their haste to get the story out, the newspapers of the day paid little attention to the facts, reporting that Bessie had been 50 years old when she died (she was, in fact, just 42), and that she had been discovered in 1917 by a Broadway agent while singing for her supper on Beale Street, rather than beginning her career some eight years earlier on the stage of the 81 in Atlanta, or earlier still treading the boards of Chattanooga's Ivory Theatre. Her passing even made the national news in Britain, musician Spike Hughes (who had seen her perform at the Lafayette) penning a column for the *Daily Herald* that ended, 'She sang her blues for the people, by the people and at the people.'[17]

Over the week following her death, more than 30,000 people attended the O.V. Catto Elks Lodge in Philadelphia to view her remains and as had so often happened during her career, people battled to gaze upon their Empress. 'As hundreds jammed every inch of space in the massive auditorium, thousands on the outside clamored, pushed and fought in an effort to get in. The throng of mourners was so great that Charles A. Upshur, who had charge of the funeral arrangements, used more than one hundred coaches in the procession.'[18] Bessie's brothers and sisters, along with Jack Gee and his relatives, attended the coffin, and floral tributes – including one from Ethel Waters – arrived from all across the United States and Europe. Jack was too tight to spring for the cost of a headstone, and although there were several attempts to raise the funds to provide a suitable tribute to stand beside Bessie's grave, nothing would be unveiled until 1970. 'My father would show up at the concerts, demand all the money and say he'd have his lawyers stop the show if he didn't get it,' Jack Junior explained to David Medina of the *New York Daily News*. 'He made enough money to buy six headstones.'[19]

Journalist and talent scout John Hammond – the man credited with having launched the recording career of Billie Holiday – penned a hasty, vastly inaccurate obituary for the December issue of *Down Beat* magazine, repeating the story that she had been discovered by Ma Rainey when Bessie was just 12 years old, and declaring that by the end of her life she had become an obese 'personification of the old southern mammy; always a smile for everyone and a song on her lips'. In the same summation, Hammond also called the whiter-than-white Carl Van Vechten – author of the controversial book *Nigger Heaven* – 'one of the first literary Negroes'.[20] In the previous month's edition of the same magazine, Hammond repeated a rumour he claimed to have heard from members of Chick Webb's band that when Bessie 'arrived at the hospital she was refused treatment because of her color'.[21] Although Hammond – who, through his involvement with the early career of Bob Dylan and his work to have the recordings of Robert Johnson reissued, was central to the folk blues revival of the early 1960s – did not state that this was fact, he gave legitimacy to a story that was reprinted shortly afterwards in newspapers including the *Pittsburgh Courier* and that is still repeated to this day.

The story of Bessie being refused admission to a whites-only hospital and therefore being left to bleed to death was corrected by

Mick Clark, of the Clark Hotel in Memphis, who wrote to the editors of the *Pittsburgh Courier* stating that the 'story that Bessie Smith was turned down at the door of a Memphis hospital was not true'.[22] Clark revealed that he had discussed the incident with members of Chick Webb's orchestra, all of whom denied ever talking to Hammond about Bessie. Yet the story continued to circulate and be reported as gospel until writer and radio DJ Chris Albertson's biography of Bessie was published in 1972. The truth was that the doctor who attended the scene and tried to dress her injuries called for an ambulance from a Black hospital, the G. T. Thomas Afro-American Hospital in Clarksdale, but by the time she arrived there was little they could do for her, and she died from her injuries.

In a 2003 interview, Albertson reiterated his frustration:

[Richard] Morgan — who was Lionel Hampton's favourite uncle — was driving Bessie's old Packard along Highway 61 in Mississippi. It was a very dark road, there were no lights on the truck, and they were upon it quickly. Morgan swerved in an attempt to avoid hitting the back of the truck, but couldn't. Because Bessie's elbow was out the window, the crash almost tore her arm off. The driver of the truck knew that something had hit him, but he kept going, driving right into Clarksdale. Right after this accident, Doctor Hugh Smith, who was on an early morning fishing trip with a friend, came upon the scene. Bessie was lying in the middle of the road, so the doctor had his friend go to a nearby house to call an ambulance. Knowing that Bessie was black, he naturally called the black hospital. In the meantime, the driver of the truck had stopped at the white hospital where he reported the accident up the road.

While all of this was going on, a small car carrying a young white couple came down the road and drove directly into the doctor's car, pushing it against the wreck of Bessie's Packard. So now there were three wrecked cars on the road. Subsequently two ambulances came, one from the white hospital and another from the black one. The white one took the couple, and the black one took Bessie. She had been bleeding very seriously internally, and they had to remove her arm. She never regained consciousness, and died around ten o'clock that morning. I interviewed Doctor Smith, who told me in great detail of Bessie's condition. He said that even if the accident had happened right in front of a Memphis hospital – which was better equipped, of course, than those in Clarksdale – it is unlikely that she would have survived.

If there was a hint of racism in those days, the black press played it up... I asked John [Hammond] how he could make such a claim without first speaking to Richard Morgan or the doctors at the hospital about this, and he was sort of embarrassed about it.[23]

Hammond was not the only man to get the story wrong: deputising for syndicated columnist Walter Winchell, on 10 October writer Louis Sobel reported that, 'The Brunswick people have been instituting a frantic search for a sepian hot-singer named Bessie Smith whose records years ago (before swing became the vogue) were heavy sellers. They wanted her to do a new series of them. Bessie will not be able to assume the assignment because she died last week – destitute!'[24] Columbia quickly announced plans to issue the *Bessie Smith Memorial Album*, six discs in a special folder bringing twelve of her greatest recordings together. Finally issued as the *Bessie Smith Album*, the collection featured contributions from many of her best-known accompanists, including Louis Armstrong, Fletcher Henderson and Coleman Hawkins... but no Porter Grainger. In November 1939, St Louis-based blues singer Booker T. Washington recorded eight sides for RCA's Bluebird imprint, one of which was his own composition, 'The Death of Bessie Smith'.

Jack Gee, and their son Jack Gee Junior, sued the National Biscuit Company (Nabisco), who owned the truck that had sent Bessie's car off the road, for $250,000. They settled for $58,000, but Junior never saw a penny of that money, his adoptive father taking every cent for himself. Over the next few years Jack Senior would exploit Bessie's legacy in any possible way, milking her estate, and her reputation, dry. At the time of her death, she had been on the cusp of a revival: although she had not recorded for several years, she was still a popular live draw – playing several return visits to the Apollo in Harlem –-

and had been working on changing her act, moving from blues to swing and from more gaudy, light-catching outfits to something more sophisticated and elegant. In February 1936 Carl Van Vechten had taken a series of photographic portraits of the Empress, and although she had put on weight she was still beautiful, dressed in silk and with her skin glowing and her eyes bright and playful; hardly the obese mammy Hammond had described. Bandleader Lionel Hampton was planning to bring her in to record vocals for him at RCA, which would have been her first session since the Hammond-helmed recordings for Okeh in November 1933, and she had recently played a sold-out sixteen-week season at Connie's Inn, which had relocated from its old spot in Harlem to Broadway, where her former accompanist Louis Armstrong now led the orchestra. But perhaps even she realised that her time in the spotlight was coming to an end: in March 1936 an article appeared in the *Chicago Defender* titled 'New York Sees Bessie Smith; Wonders Where She's Been', where Bessie looked back at her life with the wistfulness of a trouper nearing the end of the road, despite claiming that, 'I'm feeling better now than ever in my life, and I feel as though I am on the brink of new successes.'[25] Just two days later, a second columnist noted that although 'one need never worry about Bessie Smith holding her own as a blues singer', sadly the 'type of songs she featured have gone out of style'.[26]

Bessie's last resting place – officially listed as Grave No. 3, Range 12, Lot 20, Section C of the Mount Lawn cemetery in Sharon Hill – would wait thirty-three years before it was finally accorded a headstone, paid for by singer Janis Joplin and Juanita Green, of the Philadelphia NAACP, after a campaign spearheaded by the *Philadelphia Inquirer* newspaper. The stone bore the legend: 'The greatest blues singer in the world will never stop singing.' The tribute had been penned by John Hammond.

The unveiling, on 8 August 1970, was attended by fifty people, including Bob DiNardo, author of the play *Empress of the Blues* (and a friend of Jack Gee), John Hammond and Juanita Green, who explained that when she was little, she used to take part in a children's talent contest at the Lincoln Theatre, on the corner of Broad Street in Philadelphia. One day, she came off stage and saw Bessie standing in the wings. The

Empress called her over and asked her, 'Honey, you in school?' When Juanita told her that she was, Bessie replied, 'You better stay there, because you can't carry a note!' Perhaps because her own education was so minimal, Bessie understood the importance of schooling, and often berated her son, Jack Junior, when he skipped school. Juanita, who would become a successful businesswoman and the owner of several care homes, always remembered their encounter. 'She was an expert,' she recalled. 'She was the type you didn't get angry with, you just listened to. I took her at her word and I stayed in school.'[27] Sadly, the newspaper once again repeated the story that 'Bessie died because she was black', and that 'an ambulance... left Bessie on the roadside to die'.[28] Less than two months later Janis Joplin, whose vocal style owed so much to the classic blues singers of the twenties and thirties, was found dead on the floor of her motel room. Like Bessie, Janis was bisexual and liked a drink: unlike her idol, Janis was a drug user, and large quantities of both alcohol and heroin were in her system at the time of her death.

In 1975, two years after the death of his adoptive father, Jack Gee Junior, heir to what was left of Bessie Smith's estate, took Columbia Records to court, alleging non-payment of royalties for the many compilations that had appeared over the years containing the sides Bessie recorded for the company between 1923 and 1933. CBS, the parent company of the label, claimed that Bessie had been paid a flat fee for each of her recording sessions, meaning that she (and therefore her estate) had waived any rights to royalties, and that Columbia could do what it damn well pleased with her masters. Jack Junior and his team argued that Bessie had never agreed to her recordings being compiled on albums, anthologies or licensed out to other companies, and challenged Columbia to produce a contract signed by Bessie. The Smith estate also objected to a series of 1950s compilations which, 'added "echo" and other extraneous sounds to create a so-called high-fidelity effect, but which, on the contrary, significantly altered and distorted the unique singing quality on which Bessie based her artistic reputation',[29] Jack Senior had signed over all rights to Bessie's recordings to Columbia in 1940, and twelve years later sold the rights to all of her compositions to Empress Music. Columbia won the case.

Bessie's one-time mentor, Gertrude Rainey, died of heart disease due to hypertension on 22 December 1939, having outlived her protégé by a little over two years. Just two weeks earlier John Hammond had gone to seek Ma out and attempt to persuade her 'to come out of retirement and sing for the jitterbugs'.[30] That same year singer Lillie Mae Glover, who had been performing since the mid-1920s, began to use the stage name Memphis Ma Rainey, or Ma Rainey II.

Ma spent her last years in Columbus, Georgia, in the house she had built for her mother to live in. No longer performing, she instead invested in local businesses, running a couple of local theatres, the Airdrome and the Lyric. Although she would not sing for paying audiences again, her deep, soulful voice could be heard ringing out of the Friendship Baptist Church, where her brother, Thomas Pridgett Junior, was deacon. Her passing attracted so little attention from the mainstream media that months later, assuming she was still alive, the editors of *Jazz Information* magazine wrote to her. Their request was met with a letter from her brother, and resulted in the magazine printing the first (short) biography of the Mother of the Blues.

If Harlem was still considered reasonably safe for Black artists of all sexual persuasions during the 1930s, the same could not be said for the whole of New York in the years running up to the Second World War. When, in early 1937, Jay Faggen opened the Harlem Uproar House (located some way from Harlem, on the corner of 51st Street and Broadway), Porter Grainger was one of the first people he turned to, to bring authentic Black American entertainment and to provide music for a scantily clad chorus. The attractions at the Uproar House included 'Lovey Lane, [a] nude hiding behind a headdress and a sequin or two, who quivered and tossed in rhythmic abandon', and exotic dancer Abdeen Ali, 'a light brown wisp of flesh, who drew looks of sympathy while being lashed into fatal submission by the sex-crazed slave trader'.[31] Faggen owned several ballrooms and theatres, including New York City's Roseland, the Cinderella Ballroom in Chicago, and the Savoy Ballrooms in Harlem and Chicago, but when he employed Mezz Mezzrow's Disciples of Swing, a mixed race, fifteen-piece jazz orchestra, later that same year, swastikas were daubed on the outside of the Uproar House, and Mezzrow and his men were out of a job before the week was up. To all intents, the city's stranglehold on queer nightlife was over. The New York World's Fair of 1939 offered the last gasp for many of the entertainers who had managed to hang on after the pansy craze had petered out, where it was noted that the 'hangout at the Fair for the lads with the limp wrists is Balantine's, in the amusement sector'.[32]

By the mid-forties, like so many of his contemporaries, Porter Grainger's spell in the spotlight was over. It appears that his last new songs were recorded in 1939: 'Pink Slip Blues' and 'Take Him Off My Mind' by Ida Cox, 'Down in My Soul' by Ethel Waters (with Grainger on piano) and Georgia White's ''Tain't Nobody's Fault but Yours', and although people would continue to cover his greatest successes, the blues and jazz songs he had for years been noted for, and the shows he had written to great acclaim, were no longer fashionable. Although he was still feted in the press as 'one of the greatest arrangers, producers and musical score directors we have produced in the last quarter century',[33] no one wanted to hear blues singers bemoaning their drunken, violent men when people were grieving for the very real loss of their loved ones in the bloody fields of Europe, or with the Pacific Ocean seemingly on fire, and the theatres and nightclubs that had once been clamouring for his songs were closed, many of them never to reopen. After a commission to write a song for the 1940 Presidential Election, which saw Franklin D. Roosevelt win his third term in office, his next job was writing the music to a new, all-Black musical, *Mr Swing*.

He remained busy and much in demand, but like most of his contemporaries, financial returns – and fame – were diminishing. No doubt influenced by his literary friends, he became obsessed with recording and cataloguing Black folklore and folk songs, and on 17 February 1939 he presented a new revue, *Panorama of Negro Folklore* at the Alhambra, a benefit for one of Harlem's oldest charities, the Hope Day Nursery. This new work would, it was reported, encompass: 'work songs, native dances, blues, spirituals, love songs, slave songs and many legendary episodes of a race whose transition from slavery to freedom dominates its very existence.'[34] Among the cast was a young woman formerly known as Ruby Walker, now using the name Ruby Smith. Shortly afterwards he joined a newly formed society, the Crescendo Club, a social club 'formed by outstanding Negro composers, and musicians for the purpose of keeping alive the traditional folk songs and the songs of modern contemporaries',[35] and that comprised of most of the important names of the day among its membership, including W. C. Handy, Clarence Williams, Fletcher Henderson, Duke Ellington, Eubie Blake, Freddie Johnson, Donald Heywood, Noble Sissle and Count Basie.

Mainstream work still came his way, but the flood was slowing to a trickle. In February 1941 Grainger was briefly employed by Club Mimo, a new Harlem night spot on the same block as the Lafayette Theatre and the Ubangi Club, to write the music and lyrics to *Back Home in Harlem*, the twice-a-night floorshow which starred Bill 'Bojangles' Robinson – the club's owner. For the Apollo he wrote the music to a new revue, *Swinging in Society*, starring Joe Turner and Meade Lux Lewis, the pianist on George Hannah's queer classics 'The Boy in the Boat' and 'Freakish Blues'. He also composed the words and music to *Rhythm Bound*, a revue starring comedian Pigmeat Markham, which played at the Apollo after each daily screening of the new Paul Robeson film, *Proud Valley*. He continued to foster his association with the Apollo, writing a new revue based around his own blues tunes, for Willie Bryant in April 1942. In 1945, Grainger wrote the musical score to a new three-act comedy drama, *Old Shoes*, starring husband and wife burlesque team Murray Brown and Esta Borden, but shortly afterwards, with his beloved Aunt Mattie ailing, Porter Grainger decided to leave New York and move back to Pittsburgh.

Aunt Mattie, the woman he listed as his next-of-kin and who had supported him his entire life, died in January 1948. Before the year was out Grainger was dead too. He passed away on 30 October, a little over a week after his 57th birthday, officially of pneumonitis, the result of a freak accident when part of his denture broke off and got stuck in his throat. His death certificate reverted to the correct spelling of the family surname, and he was buried at Sharpsburg, Allegheny County, Pennsylvania. Not one major American newspaper made note of his passing. Two years after his death, the Universal Theatre in Hollywood staged a play entitled *Cotys Larue*, apparently based on a piece originally written for Josephine Baker in Paris, with songs by Grainger. Over the next few years his daughter, Portia, would renew copyright in around ninety of his songs and other published works.

Billie Holiday would spend the remainder of her career in and out of court, arrested multiple times in the late 1940s for possession of heroin, and after one notorious altercation with Harry Anslinger, the racist commissioner of the Federal Bureau of Narcotics – a man who was quoted as saying that 'Reefer makes darkies think they're as good as white men'[36] – was imprisoned for a year. In August 1949, just a few months after her most recent acquittal, she recorded her version of the Porter Grainger standard 'Ain't Nobody's Business If I Do', the title subtly altered to make it more palatable for the sophisticates in her audience. With a big band backing, Billie turned the song into her personal polemic, decrying those who had judged her in a new opening verse and retaining the sadomasochistic verses first used by Bessie Smith more than quarter of a century earlier. Given Holiday's own experience at the hands of violent men, the words must have stuck in her craw, or was she taking back ownership of her own life and openly defying her critics? Sadly, Grainger had not lived long enough to enjoy this revival of one of his most successful tunes.

Holiday's own life ended in New York on 17 July 1959, aged just 44. She died handcuffed to a bed in a private room in the Metropolitan Hospital, arrested while she lay dying on yet another drugs charge. Her former girlfriend, Tallulah Bankhead, sent a wreath of red roses for the casket, which was laid to rest in an unmarked grave next to her mother, although the coffin was disinterred the following year and given its own burial place. Bankhead would never publicly acknowledge herself as either lesbian or bisexual, although she did describe herself as both 'ambisextrous' and 'as pure as the driven slush'. She died in New York in 1968.

The career of one of Grainger's most recent collaborators continued to go from strength to strength. In 1943 Ethel Waters was cast in the film version of *Cabin in the Sky*, having already appeared in the stage production, along with other African American stars including Lena Horne, Louis Armstrong, Butterfly McQueen, Willie Best and Duke

Ellington, close friend and mentor to out-gay composer Billy Strayhorn, who began working with Ellington in 1938 and contributed to the score of *Cabin in the Sky*. The press soon had Alberta romantically linked to dancer Archie Savage, who appeared with Ethel on stage and in the film, but although the two were seen together in public, and featured in the gossip columns, each was acting as the other's 'beard': Savage was a homosexual and a crook, who stole more than $20,000 in cash and jewellery from Waters while he was a guest in her home. On the set of the movie, she befriended a young dancer, Joan Croomes, and opened up to her about where her true interests lay. 'She was a lesbian,' Croomes told biographer Donald Bogle. 'She told me that she was the best that ever did it. She told me that.' Once she showed Croomes a picture of herself 'dressed in men's clothes. She had on pants and a jacket, and she had short hair. "This was when I was a boy," said Ethel... She used to sit and watch me when I took a bath. I was scared of her sometimes.'[37]

Ethel Waters would continue to break barriers for Black actors and singers for the rest of her life, although after starting divorce proceedings against Pretty Matthews in April 1934 she became much more guarded about her personal life. Never again would readers of the gossip columns be treated to tales of Ethel and her lover fighting in the street or for crashing their car into a bakery truck. On 14 June 1939, Ethel Waters became the first Black woman to star in her own television programme in the United States, when *The Ethel Waters Show* aired on NBC. The hour-long broadcast featured music, skits and a short excerpt from the stage drama *Mamba's Daughters*, which Ethel had been starring in (along with Alberta Hunter) and would shortly take on tour. The programme was a huge success, welcomed by critics as 'The greatest surprise of the season',[38] and set Ethel off on a new path. In 1950 she would take on the title role of *Beulah*, becoming the first female African American actor to star in a television sitcom. She would be replaced the following year by Oscar-winning actor Hattie McDaniel, who had recorded several blues sides in the 1920s (accompanied at her first session for Okeh by Lovie Austin and her Blues Serenaders), and whose father had given Frankie 'Half-Pint' Jaxon his first break in showbiz.

Perhaps unsurprisingly the relationship between Ethel Waters and Ethel Williams was brushed under the carpet once Waters became born again. As early as 1946 Waters was complaining to the press she was having to give up working in the entertainment industry as she 'can't get hold of God in a night club' and that she found them 'too noisy and gay for religious meditation'.[39] Joining Billy Graham's crusade in 1957, Waters began to downplay Williams's importance in her life. There's no doubt that her new-found religious conviction and her new friends – especially the fervently anti-LGBTQ Graham – encouraged her to straightwash her past (a biography from 1978, *I Touched a Sparrow*, from Christian publishers Word Incorporated, does not mention Williams once). Nominated for an Academy Award in 1949 for her role in the film *Pinky*, the year after she met Graham she appeared in *The Heart is a Rebel*, a film produced by Graham's own company, World Wide Pictures.

'One of the things that was so marvellous about Ethel Waters,' said pianist Bobby Short, co-producer of the 1985 show *Stormy Weather – A Salute to Ethel Waters*, was that, 'She influenced so many people. Her respect for her songs and her eloquent dramatic sense and her impeccable diction – that's something she shared with Bessie Smith and Ma Rainey – and her enormous, enormous natural elegance, all of that influenced people. My God, without her there could have been no Ella Fitzgerald. Ella would be the first one to tell you that... Ethel Waters opened so many doors. She was the first black singer to have her own radio show, the first to star in a racially integrated Broadway show, the first to have pop songs written expressly for her. Before she came, black singers recorded black blues for all-black labels, and that was it, honey.'[40]

Waters was not the only one to attempt to clean up her past and get religion: in an era when the McCarthy witch-hunts were routing out reds under the beds and pinkos in the closet, and when the 83-year-old W. E. B. du Bois was threatened with up to five years in jail and a $10,000 fine for being a foreign agent (something he strenuously denied), the former top hat and tails-wearing drag king Gladys Bentley decided that the time was right to straighten up her act. New York's better-known pansy parlours may have closed, but there was still a demand for sophisticated, camp performers elsewhere in the country and, with nowhere left for Gladys to play in Gotham, she went first to Los Angeles (in 1938) and later to San Francisco, to take up a residency at Mona's, at 440 Broadway.

In Los Angeles, Gladys played a number of LGBTQ venues, including Joaquin's El Rancho bar. In an unpublished memoir, musician Phil Moore recalled working with Gladys in L.A.:

During our first meeting she, not too subtely [sic], informed me she was 'gay' (I didn't know what the heck that meant, except she did seem happy), and did dress and do herself up in a different manner. A manner the likes of which I'd never seen back home. Her hair was cut short in a mannish style with pointed sideburns. Further, it was slicked back and confined into a kink0dimpled pompadour, held in bondage by Murray's or Black and White pomade... Very popular with colored men who wanted to look like they had straight hair. Miss Glady's [sic] arched pencilled on eyebrows were drawn up so high on her forehead she looked like she was always saying, 'How 'bout that shit?'

...While working in New York she'd always worn a man's formal dress tails, but in L.A. (the powers that be having heard of her New York peccadillos) she was allowed to only wear a black satin swallow-tailed coat, and a skirt to match, but the overall outfit still looked like male attire. Oh yes, she had practically no neck, but somehow managed to squeeze varied fluorescent bow ties around the stiffly starched dress shirt collar right beneath her chin. A bow to show-biz, I presume. When off stage, most of the time, she only wore men's clothing...

We worked mostly 'gay' nightclubs (found out what that meant too). I'd never seen anything like this, but I soon discovered that these people were just people, good guys and bums, just like the rest of us, and a job was a job. Miss Gladys was very sweet in explaining some of the 'gay' terms to me, such as boys picking up 'trade'. 'Don't worry, Philip, if you ain't for it, ain't nobody gonna bite you.'[41]

Although it was run by a heterosexual married couple, Mona's had a reputation as a lesbian bar and, in 1942, Gladys joined such San Francisco favourites as Emily 'Butch' Minton (Gladys had used the pseudonym Bobbie Minton early on in her career) and Miss Jimmy Reynard. San Francisco had become a hotbed for pansy performers, and clubs including the Music Box and Finocchio's, which had been specialising in drag acts since 1933, were doing big business. In its first few years, Finocchio's gained a reputation as a club where patrons could openly solicit sex with many of the acts, but following a police raid in 1936 which saw ten people arrested including the owners and at least four performers, both patrons and performers became much more surreptitious, passing notes to each other via the club's waiters. Joseph Finocchio was used to trouble: he had been arrested in 1920, just a few months after prohibition had been established, for allowing booze onsite at the Columbo Café, and again in 1934 for running his own club 'in a disorderly manner'.[42]

While Gladys was forging a new career in San Francisco, other LGBTQ artists were making a name for themselves elsewhere. Sadly, one who would not share the limelight was Bruz Fletcher, whose career was cut short when he committed suicide, in February 1941, at the age of just 34. Gladys returned briefly from San Francisco to New York before once again settling in L.A. where, as the 'Brown Bomber of Gayety', she brought her brand of 'Risk-gay originality'[43] to the Doll House on Ventura Boulevard. However, she was tiring of the shenanigans taking place in the kind of venues she was still being offered work. She did not want to be remembered as a butch lesbian nightclub performer, but unlike her LGBTQ contemporaries who, when they too found religion, suddenly forgot their pasts, Gladys gained much mileage from telling her story, candidly opening up her incredible life to the readers of the two most prominent Black magazines of the day, *Jet* and *Ebony*. In 1952, in a feature printed in the latter, 'I Am a Woman Again', she told readers of how, 'For many years I have lived in a personal hell. Like a great number of lost souls I inhabited that half-shadow no-man's land which exists between the boundaries of the two sexes.' She explained about how she had, 'Violated the accepted code of morals that our world observes...' all the while, 'Weeping and wounded because I was traveling the wrong road to real love and true happiness,' something she had now found thanks to having found the right man 'who loves me unselfishly',[44] and to a course of female hormone injections.

She gave one of her final performances on the Groucho Marx television show *You Bet Your Life*, pounding out a raucous version of the classic 'Them There Eyes', a hit for Louis Armstrong, Billie Holiday, Duke Ellington and others. She became an active and devoted member of her church, the Temple of Love in Christ, and began working on a memoir, *If This Be Sin*, which promised to tell all about her experiences in the 'twilight zone of sex'.[45] Her much-publicised second marriage soon ended in divorce, and the hormone course proved to have been invented by Gladys for the sake of the magazine feature. She died, of bronchial pneumonia, in January 1960; the book was never published. She was outlived by the mother she had accused of neglecting her as a child who, in a final act of familial betrayal, ensured that both women were reunited in death, sharing the same burial plot in the Lincoln Memorial Park in Los Angeles.

Queer-identified poet and musician Shirlette Ammons's debut solo album was the 2013 release *Twilight for Gladys Bentley*. Rather than simply covering Bentley's material, Ammons saw the album as an opportunity to reinterpret the life of a woman she describes as a, 'trail-blazing blues singer and bulldagger... I wanted to create a record that uses hip-hop, the music of posturing and prowess of my day, to channel the memory of Gladys Bentley. Gladys took popular songs and replaced the lyrics with raunchy, more provocative ones. I instead wrote original tunes that conjure the same energy of rebellion and sexual liberation.' Ammons spent over a year researching Bentley's life in an effort to 'explore and reinterpret the unsung blues singer who defied sexual and gender norms while putting on one of the hippest performances in 1920s Harlem'.[46] In 2020 PBS produced a series of short films celebrating American women through history, *Unladylike 2020*. Ammons was an obvious choice for their film about the career of Gladys Bentley.

'I wasn't trying to be Gladys mentally,' she says of *Twilight for Gladys Bentley*, 'But I still was trying to tap into the role of the identity, the "butch dyke" identity, and the masculine elements of my own self that sometimes manifests as ego and certainly as a type of sexual prowess on stage.' Being able to write openly and honestly as a queer person was a game changer for Ammons; channelling Gladys Bentley gave her permission to be more assertive about her own sexuality, and in turn to become a more visible champion for LGBTQ rights in her own local community.

# 19

# Any Woman's Blues

*'Oh, these kids and rock and roll – this is just sped up rhythm and blues. I've been doing that forever.'*[1] – Sister Rosetta Tharpe

As the 1930s progressed and Europe came closer to war, it became increasingly difficult for LGBTQ people to be as open as they once had been. The rise of fascism saw a doubling down on any and all lifestyles that did not conform to the heterosexual norm, and the people who had enjoyed the sexually liberated twenties were now running scared, persecuted for exhibiting the very same traits that they had, until recently, been celebrated for.

For almost a decade before America entered into the Second World War, the press had been spreading tales of homosexual activity from deep within Hitler's ranks. In October 1932, the Communist Party USA's New York-based *Daily Worker* newspaper reported on George Bell, a member of Hitler's general staff, who had resigned from the Nazi Party after refusing the advances of Chief of Staff Ernst Röhm, a man the paper called 'a hundred per cent homosexual of the most disgusting kind', and 'one of the most notorious pederasts walking about on this earth'.[2] Bell was later murdered for 'knowing too much':[3] it transpired that he had kept a list of the men that Röhm had slept with, to use as a bargaining chip as he was in fear for his life. Röhm was executed in 1934, during the political purge that became known as the Night of the Long Knives. In an attempt to cleanse the party of the homosexual menace and suppress an uprising, in December 1934 thousands of Sturmabteilung (the dreaded SA, early Nazi storm troops) were arrested: the Nazi Party admitted to a figure of 900, but one source claimed that at least 4,000 were arrested in Berlin in one incident alone, with hundreds butchered. Hitler, it seemed, was desperate to eradicate any trace of his once-close friend, and to stem the promulgation of rumours concerning his own homosexual interests.

The rise of Hitler brought about a new wave of the demonisation of homosexuals in Europe and America. 'National socialism, Hitler's creed, was born in homosexual dives and bred in filth,'[4] announced American lecturer Frank Drake Davidson to a rapt audience of Rotary Club members, and at every chance possible it was pointed out that Hitler counted homosexuals, sexual perverts and inverts among his allies and closest friends. For decades Europe's capitals had been a bastion of LGBTQ nightlife, but the war put an end to that. Berlin's cabarets and queer spaces were closed down by Hitler's stormtroopers and the performers that did not manage to flee to freedom abroad were rounded up. Many of the brightest stars of the Weimar era would perish in Nazi concentration camps. In 1943, Eve Adams, the Jewish woman who had set up one of the States' first lesbian bars – Eve Adams' Tearoom – in Greenwich Village in 1924, was transported from her home in Poland to Auschwitz. Her girlfriend, Hella Soldner, a singer who used the stage name Norah Waren, was taken alongside her. Neither woman would be seen again. By the summer of 1940, when Paris fell to the invading Nazis, there was little in the way of LGBTQ night life left on the continent.

In Britain, gay jazz orchestra leader Ken 'Snakehips' Johnson, who lived openly with his partner Gerald Hamilton (a critic and well-connected wit, known as the 'wickedest man in Europe'), was killed along with dozens of others when a German bomb destroyed the Café de Paris, just as he was about to make his entrance. By a strange quirk of fate – or spectacular luck in being held up on his journey – gay cabaret star Douglas Byng missed being a victim of the bombing by seconds.

After appearing as a tap dancer in the 1935 British movie *Oh Daddy!*, Johnson became a sensation on the British stage, and was employed as a dancer by bandleader Leslie Thompson, then leading his band the Jamaican Aristocrats of Jazz. The partnership was short-lived: after the pair fell out Johnson took over the act, although as band member Joey Denis said, 'he knew nothing really about music... Leslie Thompson would conduct the band, and Ken would sit there, watch and listen. When the time came to conduct the band he would just wave the stick. It was more waving in the air... but he was very good at it: he learnt very quickly.'[5] The band soon changed their name to the West Indian Dance Orchestra before becoming known simply as 'Ken "Snakehips" Johnson and his Swing Orchestra'.

Advertised as 'America's latest rhythmic sensation' he had, in reality, been born in Georgetown, British Guiana (now Guyana) and had attended school in England before spending less than two years in the States, much of it in Harlem, studying dance, and touring briefly with Fletcher Henderson. Compared by some critics to Cab Calloway, others wrote that 'he not only directs his instrumentalists in an intriguing manner, but also shows himself to be a clever step dancer and a vocalist of ability',[6] and that 'his sparkle and vitality are electrifying. His feet scarcely seem to touch the stage when he goes into a tap routine, while for thrills, his acrobatic tap dance on a miniature staircase [something he had learnt in Harlem from Bill 'Bojangles' Robinson] would take a lot of beating.'[7]

Situated in a basement off Leicester Square, the Café de Paris – where Ethel Waters had proved such a hit at the end of the 1920s – was considered one of the safest venues in the city, and while other bandleaders had left London for the provinces, Snakehips and his men stayed to entertain the blitz-hit capital. At the time of the air strike Johnson, just 27 years old, was leading the 'only all-coloured band in British vaudeville'.[8] Johnson's electric guitar player, Joey Denis (real name Joe Deniz), would later recall that, 'As we started playing there was an awful thud, and all the lights went out. The ceiling fell in and the plaster came pouring down. People were yelling. A stick of bombs went right across Leicester Square, through the Café de Paris and further up to Dean Street. The next thing I remember was being in a small van which had been converted into an ambulance. Then someone came to me and said: "Joe, Ken's dead." It broke me up.'[9]

Douglas Byng, who was scheduled to appear at the Café de Paris later that night, wanted to stop off to pick up some costumes and props from his dressing room for a charity performance he was giving at Grosvenor House before his evening show at the Café. Luckily for him he arrived after the bomb had already hit, having been delayed by friends who wanted to grab a bite to eat at La Coquille, a French restaurant popular with theatre-goers and performers in St Martin's Lane. Following Johnson's death, Gerald Hamilton would carry a photograph of the bandleader with him and would always refer to him as his husband.

Across the English Channel Josephine Baker, keen to do whatever she could to help her adoptive country's war effort, joined the French military intelligence agency, the Deuxième Bureau, acting as a kind of double agent, gathering information on the Germans and their allies through officers she met at embassies and nightclubs, and passing this on to Jacques Abtey, the head of French counterintelligence. Her immense fame meant that everyone wanted to meet her, and enabled her to pass on documents and photographs – which she kept hidden in her underwear – to British agents working for the exiled leader of the Free French army, Charles de Gaulle. Later, she spent time entertaining allied troops and, although much of the work she did to help France is still being uncovered, her place in the country's heart was secured when she was awarded the Resistance Medal by the French Committee of National Liberation, the Croix de Guerre by the French military, and was named a Chevalier of the Légion d'Honneur by de Gaulle, the country's highest civil or military honour. Somehow, she still found time to have affairs with several high-profile women, including Ada 'Bricktop' Smith and the novelist Colette.

Rumours persist of an affair between Baker and the bisexual Mexican artist Frida Kahlo, who she met in Paris in 1939, but to date no hard evidence has surfaced to confirm that. However, her relationship with Bricktop is better documented, and Bricktop herself admitted to Jean-Claude Baker, one of Josephine's adopted children, that they had enjoyed a brief affair. Bricktop ran several different clubs during her tenure in Paris, frequented by the most famous names of American music and literature, including Ernest Hemingway, F. Scott Fitzgerald, Sidney Bechet, Louis Armstrong, Fats Waller, Cole Porter and, of course, Josephine Baker. Although British cabaret star Douglas Byng would be the first man to popularise Porter's hit 'Miss Otis Regrets', the song was written after Bricktop relayed the story of a lynching to Porter, and it would forever be identified with her. 'I was one of the first coloured Americans to move to Paris,' Baker told Tim Murari of *The Guardian*. 'Oh yes, Bricktop was there as well. Me and her were the only two, and we had a marvellous time. Of course, everyone who was anyone knew Bricky. And they got to know Miss Baker as well.'[10]

As popular music developed during the forties and fifties, the influence of blues music – and the queer artists that performed it – was inescapable. As blues and jazz continued to intersect and evolve, a new term, the rhythm and blues, was coined to replace the now-outmoded 'race music', and R'n'B as it became known soon had its own baby, christened rock 'n' roll, a term well known to queer blues aficionados. Many of the early stars of the R'n'B and rock 'n' roll era, including Johnnie Ray, Little Richard and Elvis Presley, owed everything to artists such as Sister Rosetta Tharpe: Chuck Berry admitted that his entire career was just 'one long Rosetta Tharpe impersonation', and Tharpe gave Richard his first break when she had the 14-year-old open for her in Macon, Georgia and encouraged him to turn professional.

In February 1941 Donald Heywood, who had worked extensively with both Porter Grainger (the duo's revue *Creole Follies* had been a big hit in 1922; their *Hot Rhythm* show ran in Times Square in 1930) and Ethel Waters (Heywood wrote several of Ethel's biggest songs), debuted his latest revue, *Tropicana*, at the Apollo in Harlem. Starring 'Sister Tharpe, the hymn-singing blues swinger',[11] the all-Black show promised its audience 'a trip from Harlem to the West Indies and back again', and had played in abridged form in several theatres before reaching the Apollo, where it was to be staged four times a day.

The bisexual singer and guitarist, who began her career two decades earlier in a travelling evangelical troupe, had been kicking up a storm around New York for a couple of years, having debuted alongside Cab Calloway at the Cotton Club in 1938, the same year that she recorded her first sides. 'Unheralded and unknown Sister Rosetta Tharpe came up from Florida to set Broadway back on its heels with her Holy Roller chants at the Cotton Club.'[12] Before the decade was out, *Down Beat* magazine was declaring that, 'Rosetta may replace the late Bessie Smith as America's foremost living exponent of the blues.'[13]

In 1946 Rosetta Tharpe began working with pianist Marie Knight: Tharpe moved in with Knight, sharing her home with her mother and children. The pair recorded together extensively over the next decade, and remained close until the late 1960s: 'I went to a program in a church in New York,' Knight recalled many years later. 'Rosetta was on the bill with Mahalia Jackson. That syncopated rhythm Rosetta played on the guitar was very unusual, but it was exciting to me. She heard me on the floor with a group of girls from the church, and she asked if I'd like to sing with her. She had been looking for a partner, and she thought our voices would go together... I stayed with her 22 years.'[14]

In the same year that Rosetta Tharpe began her relationship with Marie Knight, Jackie Mabley was guest of honour at a party thrown by Odessa Marie Madre, a Black lesbian known as the queen of Washington D.C.'s underground, and a close friend of Billie Holiday. Madre, who spent most of her adult life in and out of court (and jail) on charges relating to bootlegging, drug trafficking and prostitution, ran a half-dozen bawdy houses locally, and Jackie would often perform in them for free when she was in the area. Jackie and Odessa were close, like sisters, and when the comedian came to town to appear at the Howard Theatre, Odessa decided to throw her a party at one of her joints, the Club Madre, where Odessa 'offered liquor by the shot, numbers by the book and girls by the hour'.[15] The party, filled almost exclusively with LGBTQ people, was in full swing when the Washington police raided but, reluctant to bring the revelries to an end, Mabley simply led Madre and their friends back to the Howard, where they were able to continue their fun.

In June 1949, Odessa was arrested for possession. When this information reached Billie Holiday, she was incredulous. 'Odessa? You mean big black Odessa?', she exclaimed to the bearer of the news, according to her piano player, Carl Drinkard. 'Lady turns around to the guy as if to say how in the world did they ever get Odessa, because she never kept any stuff around. He said, "Well, look, she had a man who was a dope fiend, and she had to keep stuff around to keep him straight." So then Lady said, "What? Odessa with a man?" Because Odessa was known as a fabulous les in Washington. He says yes. She says, "A real live man, with a dick?" And I said to myself, Oh my God, I never heard a woman talk like that before. That was when my education began.'[16]

The end of the war did not mean the end of hostilities towards LGBTQ people, or of anybody seen as a threat to the American way of life. In February 1950, at the height of the Cold War, Senator Joseph McCarthy announced that he knew of more than 200 communists working in the US State Department, and alongside a nationwide purge of anyone considered to be a communist or communist sympathiser, LGBTQ people were also subjected to interrogation and incarceration – in some cases hounded to death. McCarthy's chief counsel, Roy Cohn, was himself a closeted gay man, and the pair were directly responsible for dozens of gay men losing their jobs, but the routing of LGBTQ people had been going on for some time. The House Un-American Activities Committee had been in existence for a dozen years before McCarthy made his announcement, and between 1947 and 1950, over 1,700 people who had applied for federal jobs were denied the positions due to allegations of homosexuality. Homosexuals had been banned from all branches of the US military in 1943, and even at a time when America was desperate for troops, thousands of men and women were either refused opportunity to serve their country or were discharged after their comrades were encouraged to report them. McCarthy's personal crusade was cruel and relentless, but was badly eroded when one senator, Lester C. Hunt, committed suicide after his own son was arrested for soliciting an undercover police officer in Washington, D.C. in an obvious case of entrapment.

The following year, Josephine Baker was hounded out of the States following a very public fight with Walter Winchell. Winchell, a former vaudevillian turned gossip columnist who had become one of the most revered – and feared – of the media's talking heads, was completely caught up in the 'reds under the beds' hysteria of the times. Seen as a semi-respectable Stephen G. Clow – Winchell's nationally syndicated columns were just as acidic and barbed as Clow's, but he had the clout of press baron William Randolph Hearst behind him – Winchell was also close to J. Edgar Hoover, the closeted head of the FBI, who often provided the pressman with bodyguards to stave off the ever-present threat of bodily violence against the gossip columnist. It was Hoover who convinced McCarthy to employ Roy Cohn as his chief counsel; it was believed, by several figures in the criminal underground, that Cohn was in possession of incriminating photographs of Hoover.

Josephine had been on a much-heralded trip to the States, which made more headlines for her refusal to play to segregated audiences than it did for her performances, and for the hotels that refused to give her and her white husband, orchestra leader Jo Bouillon, a room. On 16 October 1951, she went with friends, including French stage actor Roger Rico and his wife, to dine at New York's Stork Club, which for years had been Winchell's favoured hangout. The party were given a table and placed their order for food and drink, but Josephine's order was not dispatched, and the star was left hungry, thirsty and embarrassed for more than an hour. It was only when they got up to leave that her food miraculously appeared. 'One by one they came and said there was no crabmeat, there was no steak, there was no wine,' she complained to reporters following the incident. 'Then the waiters wouldn't come near us. It was just silence... It is a snub to my color, to my people.'[17] Baker threatened to sue the Stork Club for discrimination, the NAACP demanded that the police investigate the incident, and the club's management received several bomb threats. With his de facto office under threat, Winchell went to work, informing his friend Hoover that Baker was a communist who had close ties to Russia, and he produced several letters from his readers to back up his claims, one of which stated that Baker had been a guest of the Russian state in 1936 – the same time she was starring on Broadway in *Ziegfeld Follies of 1936* with Fanny Brice and Bob Hope.*

---

\* *The Ziegfeld Follies of 1936* ran from 30 January to 9 May 1936, closing when its star, Fanny Brice, fell ill. The troubled show had already been forced to close temporarily, in February, after Baker and Brice argued over billing. At the same time, Ethel Waters was being accused in the *New York Daily News* of having hounded her white co-star, Eleanor Powell, out of the Broadway show *At Home Abroad*. Both stars denied this was the case and demanded a retraction from the newspaper.

Baker accused Winchell – who was at the club at the time – of failing to step in and help, and fellow reporter Ed Sullivan, whose popularity rivalled but would soon surpass Winchell's, got in on the act, accusing Winchell of character assassination: 'I despise Walter Winchell for what he has done to Josephine Baker,' he later said. 'Instead of even once questioning the principle which Josephine Baker was upholding he started an attack on her.'[18] Winchell had been showing hostility and outright racism towards Baker for years: when she was in New York appearing in the *Ziegfeld Follies*, he had claimed that 'Josephine Baker, who was born in the Harlem jungle, now has to speak via a French interpreter.'[19]

The fracas resulted in Baker being refused an entry visa to her homeland for more than a decade. It would take the personal involvement of Bobby Kennedy to see her finally allowed to return, in order to take part in the now-famous civil rights March on Washington (co-organised by gay civil rights activist Bayard Rustin), where she delivered a rousing speech about her own struggle with discrimination immediately before Dr Martin Luther King Jr gave his impassioned 'I have a dream' address. Having no children of their own, she and Bouillon adopted twelve children from differing backgrounds and ethnicities, dubbed the 'Rainbow Tribe'. Josephine Baker gave her final performance on stage on 8 April 1975, four days before she died from a cerebral haemorrhage in hospital in Paris.

The years of relative freedom that many in the LGBTQ community had enjoyed in the years between the two wars would not be seen again for decades. LGBTQ musicians opted to stay closeted, either because they feared prosecution or because they had been convinced by their managers that any scandal around their private lives would bring their careers crashing down. This would not stop the rumour mill from talking or gossip columnists from printing scandalous allegations, and although cabaret and drag artists would continue to find work, especially in San Francisco and Las Vegas, no major artist would dare to talk openly about their sexuality until the 1970s.

The preceding decade would, however, see the concerted efforts of a number of LGBTQ rights organisations – including the Mattachine

Society and the Daughters of Bilitis – raise the public profile of LGBTQ people. Finally, following the three days of protest in and around New York's Stonewall Inn in 1969, activists across the globe began to set up new, politically aware organisations, including the Gay Liberation Front, a group whose chief aim was to encourage adherents to 'come out', to own their sexuality and talk openly and unashamedly about it. Following the lead of the Black civil rights movement, for once, LGBTQ people were commanding headlines for more than their being blackmailed or arrested.

At the same time as these activists and organisations were taking to the streets to demand their rights, a resurgence in interest in the blues had been taking place. Initially beginning in the late 1950s and early 1960s, and spearheaded in part by American folk artists, the music promulgated by Bob Dylan and his fellow enthusiasts was the folk blues of Robert Johnson and the talking blues popularised by Woodie Guthrie, rather than those artists of the 'classic blues' period, with their low down, dirty songs. When British acts including Alexis Korner and Blues Incorporated, The Rolling Stones and The Animals began to popularise electric blues they too would borrow heavily from male folk blues artists including Leadbelly, Muddy Waters and Willie Dixon. Dave van Ronk, Dylan's Greenwich Village contemporary, was one of the few to dig into the Bessie Smith songbook, but it would not be until the late 1960s, when artists like Janis Joplin began namechecking her as an influence, that the stars of Bessie and her contemporaries began to shine again. Joplin also regularly namechecked Big Mama Thornton, and Joplin's band, Big Brother and the Holding Company, covered Thornton's 'Ball and Chain' on their 1968 album *Cheap Thrills*.

Although she did not openly acknowledge it, Joplin was bisexual and had a number of relationships with women during her short life. She was also an enormous influence on the Women's Music movement, an attempt by independent female artists to establish their own touring circuit, record labels and distribution network which began in the early 1970s. Many of those artists would sing about their own lives and relationships with a candour not seen since Bessie asked her jail-keeper to 'put another gal in my stall'. Joplin's promotion of early female blues singers, and writer Chris Albertson's biography, *Bessie*, encouraged Columbia to reissue all of Bessie's available sides, making her recordings available for a whole new generation. This renewed interest in the classic blues singers came too late to reignite the careers of Ma or Bessie, and Ethel had long since eschewed the blues, but Alberta Hunter, who had retired from performing in the fifties after the death of her mother and had gone into nursing, was ready to shine once more. She had barely set foot on a stage since completing several tours for the United Service Organization (USO) to entertain the troops during the Second World War and again during the Korean War, but now in her 80s, and having retired from hospital work, she began performing and recording again, issuing a series of albums beginning with *Remember My Name* in 1978, and performing regularly at the Cookery, in Greenwich Village (owned by Barney Josephson, who in 1938 had opened the Café Society, one of the first entirely unsegregated clubs in Greenwich Village), from 1976. Shortly after she made her comeback, Alberta explained why the once again successful star had sworn off men: 'I was married once – for about a week... What do I need a husband for now? I have a nice house, a TV and a telephone. All I don't have is a big headache, and I'd get one of them the day I got another husband.'[20] She died in October 1984, aged 89.

On 31 December 1975, a group of women styling themselves the Women's Prison Concert Collective – featuring several out-lesbian singers who were at the very core of the Woman's Music movement, including Cris Williamson, Holly Near and Gwen Avery – performed for the inmates and staff of a women's jail at San Bruno, California. Early in 1976 a recording of that concert, titled *Any Woman's Blues* after the Bessie Smith song of the same name, appeared, sold to raise funds for female political prisoners.

Gwen Avery's story was not unlike that of many of the classic blues singers she idolised. Born in 1943, in Verona, Pennsylvania, her father had already left the scene before she was born, and while she was still a child her mother had abandoned her too. She spent her early years at a speakeasy run by her grandmother – set up after she borrowed a dollar from a friend to buy a bottle of wine and a pint of whisky – using the kitchen table as her stage and singing for the customers while her grandmother tended bar. With a steady, albeit small, income from the speakeasy, she gave up on school before she was 10. Life offered few prospects for an uneducated Black woman but, ironically, it was an article she saw in an issue of *Life* magazine that would give her a way out. A piece about hippies in San Francisco struck a chord: 'The city was so permissive, there were even openly gay cops. My eyes bulged out of my head onto the page. I was gone.'[21]

Not long afterwards she began singing with a rock band called Full Moon, which led to her being invited to perform at a women's music festival in Santa Cruz and to being included on *Any Woman's Blues*. The following year her song 'Sugar Mama' appeared on the compilation *Lesbian Concentrate*, issued by Olivia Records, a label run entirely by – and for – women. Tours with many of the other Olivia artists followed, but Gwen struggled, especially during the mid-eighties, when losing friends to the AIDS crisis and the death of her partner from breast cancer sapped her energies.

In 2000, along with former touring partner Linda Tillery and her new lover Emily Tincher, Gwen released her first solo album, *Sugar Mama*, featuring a re-recording of her song alongside covers of blues classics including 'Sugar in my Bowl', which Bessie Smith had recorded in 1931. That particular song also resonated with Gaye Adegbalola, and in a way it ignited her whole career in blues. 'I went to see Nina Simone live,' she explains,

> She's playing 'I Want a Little Sugar in my Bowl', and she whispers 'Bessie Smith, y'all', and the minute I heard that I went back and I checked out Bessie Smith, and I learnt about Ma Rainey, and then I learnt about Ida Cox, and all these wonderful blues women in the twenties. My girl is Alberta Hunter, you're talking about inspiration, well she was truly an inspiration. So I was back home, and I would pull out my guitar and I was learning all of these different songs at the time. I went to a club to see Ann Rabson, but she wasn't there that night. Some guy was playing but he wasn't very good, and he was taking a break and he said, 'Anybody else want to play?' And I went up and played, and the

manager happened to be there and he booked me three nights a week... Boom!

All I knew was that what they did and what they sang really resonated with me. Just to start with Nina, she opened my eyes to my blackness, because you see when we were in the South once upon a time we thought that the golden thing was to be white, so you straightened your hair to be like the whites, you wore clothes that were somewhat conservative and not African-like in appearance, and you know, so Nina with her Afro and with her African clothing and her 'don't fuck with me' attitude, it was a whole other thing, and I admired the way she did that, and then when I got into the music, oh my goodness, these women were so outspoken![22]

In 1984 Adegbalola formed a trio, Saffire, with Ann Rabson and Earlene Lewis (Lewis left the band in 1992 and was replaced by Andra Faye), who were soon signed by blues label Alligator Records. Over the next twenty-five years Saffire would tour the world, record several albums and win a number of prestigious awards. Their repertoire included a number of queer blues anthems, songs that Adegbalola still plays today. 'These songs are testimony to our resilience as a people,' she says,

A lot of listeners miss these nuances, and how the history of working-class Black women is in the blues lyrics. So I started performing songs like 'Tricks Ain't Walking', and 'Pigmeat on the Line' pigmeat is a phrase used about someone who is a whole lot younger than you are, it's taken from pygmy... you know, someone little. Then there's 'Crazy Blues', 'Yonder Come the Blues', 'the Dirty Dozens', 'Prove it On Me Blues'...

In 'Black Eyed Blues' they're singing about domestic violence, in 'Careless Love' they are singing about unwanted pregnancy... 'Down Hearted Blues': Alberta wrote that and she kept her rights, that became Bessie Smith's first recording, and here Alberta is making money. You know she don't really give a damn who recorded it! 'B.D. Woman's Blues'... what these women were talking about was just so bold. Most of them had left home. They just up and ran away from home because they couldn't stand the lives that they had, and it was just so powerful to see and to hear about how they lived with such flamboyancy. I didn't know that they were lesbians but their music sure fit me. I really admire the Black women who were out at the time.

Today we are so accustomed to hearing artists relay tales of their sex lives in vivid and shocking detail that the impact singers like Bessie and Ma had on their audience is hard to appreciate. But there is no denying that without their talent and their honesty, recording artists would not enjoy the freedom of expression that they have in the 21st century. There are plenty of LGBTQ-identified acts making music today, some of it sexy, shocking and provocative, but sex, shock and provocation have been part of popular music for over a century, and the queer acts of today owe everything to the pioneers of the art: to Bessie and to Ma, to Half-Pint and to Peachtree, to Porter Grainger and to Lucille Bogan, and to the others who went there first, as Sarah Kilborne acknowledges in her show *The Lavender Blues: The Story of Queer Music Before World War II*, which debuted in 2016. 'What strikes me repeatedly,' she says, 'Is the fact that queer women – Black and white – were at the forefront of queer music before World War II. Queer history has often been passed down as decidedly male but the history of queer music flips that narrative. Nowhere is this more apparent than with the blues. Too often the classic blues women have been marginalised or given short shrift in historical discussions of the blues; yet these Black women were among the first recording stars in American music history. Many of the most famous classic blues women had a same-sex relationship at some point. Indeed, queer Black women put the blues on the map. Perhaps it shouldn't be surprising, but I am still surprised that so many people remain unaware of the impact of queer Black women on the history of American music.'[23]

'Sex is part of life: it's one of the gifts that God gave us,' says Gaye Adegbalola. 'The blues is so much more than "My baby left me and I'm heartbroken," it's music of liberation. So when they're singing about walking it is about prostitution, or when they're singing "Black Eyed Blues" they are singing about life, and sex is a part of life... I think we should take the "dirty" stigma off of these songs.'[24]

# Bibliography

Abbott, Lynn and Doug Seroff, *The Original Blues: The Emergence of the Blues in African American Vaudeville* (University Press of Mississippi, 2017).

Albertson, Chris, *Bessie: Empress of the Blues* (Yale University Press, London, 2003).

Baker, Jean-Claude and Chris Chase, *Josephine: The Hungry Heart* (Random House, New York, 1993).

Baker, Josephine and Jo Bouillon, *Josephine* (Harper and Row, New York, 1977).

Beemyn, Brett (ed.), *Creating a Place for Ourselves: Lesbian, Gay, and Bisexual Community Histories* (Routledge, London, 1997).

Blesh, Rudi and Harriet Janis, *They All Played Ragtime: The True Story of an American Music* (Jazz Book Club, London, 1960).

Bourne, Stephen, *Elisabeth Welch: Soft Lights and Sweet Music* (The Scarecrow Press, Maryland, 2005).

Bullock, Darryl W., *David Bowie Made Me Gay: 100 Years of LGBT Music* (Duckworth, London, 2017).

Burra, Edward John and William Chappell (ed.), *Well Dearie! The Letters of Edward Burra* (Gordon Fraser, London, 1985).

Calt, Stephen, *Barrelhouse Words: A Blues Dialect Dictionary* (University of Illinois, Chicago, 2009).

Chauncey, George, *Gay New York: Gender, Urban Culture, and the Makings of the Gay Male World, 1890–1940* (Basic Books, New York, 1995).

Clarke, Donald, *Wishing on the Moon: The Life and Times of Billie Holiday* (Viking, New York, 1994).

Curry, Ramona, *Too Much of a Good Thing: Mae West as Cultural Icon* (University of Minnesota Press, 1996).

Cushing, Steve, *Blues Before Sunrise: The Radio Interviews* (University of Illinois Press, Chicago, 2010).

De La Croix, St. Sukie, *Chicago Whispers: A History of LGBT Chicago Before Stonewall* (University of Wisconsin Press, 2012).

Du Bois, W. E. B, *The Autobiography of W.E.B. du Bois* (International Publishers Co., New York, 1968).

Elledge, Jim, *The Boys of Fairy Town* (Chicago Review Press, Chicago, 2018).

Feinstein, Elaine, *Bessie Smith* (Viking, Harmondsworth, Middlesex, 1985).

Grainger, Porter and Bob Ricketts, *How to Play and Sing the Blues Like the Phonograph and Stage Artists* (Jack Mills, New York, 1926).

Grimes, Sara, *BackWaterBlues: In Search of Bessie Smith*, (Rose Island Publishing Co, Amherst, Massachusetts, 2000).

Hammond, Bryan and Patrick O'Connor, *Josephine Baker* (Johnathan Cape, London, 1988).

Handy, W. C. and Anna Bontemps (ed.), *Father of the Blues* (The Macmillan Company, New York, 1941).

Harris, Laurie Lanzen, *The Great Migration North, 1910–1970* (Omnigraphics, Inc., 2012).

Harrison, Daphne Duval, *Black Pearls: Blues Queens of the 1920s* (Rutgers University Press, New Brunswick, 1990).

Havelock Ellis, Henry *Studies in the Psychology of Sex Volume Two: Sexual Inversion* (F. A. Davis Company, Philadelphia, 1901).

Holiday, Billie, with William Dufty, *Lady Sings the Blues* (Doubleday, New York, 1956).

Hughes, Langston, *The Big Sea* (Alfred A. Knopf, New York, 1940).

Jablonski, Edward and Lawrence D. Stewart, *The Gershwin Years* (Doubleday, New York, 1973).

Jackson, Buzzy, *A Bad Woman Feeling Good: Blues and the Women Who Sing Them* (W. W. Norton and Company, New York, 2005).

Kay, Jackie, *Bessie Smith* (Absolute Press, London, 1997).

Kimball, Nell and Stephen Longstreet (ed.), *Nell Kimball: Her Life as an American Madam, by Herself* (Macmillan, New York, 1970).

Kirkeby, Ed with Duncan P. Schiedt and Sinclair Traill, *Ain't Misbehavin': The Story of Fats Waller* (Da Capo Press, New York, 1975).

Longstreet, Stephen, *Sportin' House: A History of the New Orleans Sinners and the Birth of Jazz* (Sherbourne Press, Los Angeles, 1965).

Lomax, Alan, *Mr Jelly Roll* (University of California Press, 1950).

Martin, Justin, *Rebel Souls: Walt Whitman and America's First Bohemians* (Boston: Da Capo Press, 2014).

Murphy, Gareth, *Cowboys and Indies: The Epic History of the Record Industry* (Serpent's Tail, London, 2015).

O'Meally, Robert, *Lady Day: The Many Faces of Billie Holiday* (Arcade Publishing, 1993).

O'Neal, Jim, and Amy van Single, *The Voice of the Blues: Classic Interviews from Living Blues Magazine* (Routledge, New York, 2002).

Obrecht, Jas, *Blues Guitar: The Men Who Made the Music* (GPI Books, San Francisco, 1993).

Oliver, Paul, *Blues Fell This Morning* (Cambridge University Press, Cambridge, 1990).

Oliver, Paul, *Conversation with the Blues* (Cambridge University Press, Cambridge, 1977).

Palmer, Robert, *Deep Blues* (Penguin Books USA, New York, 1982).

Scarborough, Dorothy, *On the Trail of Negro Folk-Songs* (Harvard University Press, Cambridge, Massachusetts, 1925).

Shapiro, Nat and Nat Hentoff, *Hear Me Talkin' to Ya: The Story of Jazz as Told by the Men Who Made it* (Rinehart & Co., New York, 1955).

Shipton, Alyn, *Fats Waller: The Cheerful Little Earful* (Continuum, New York, 2002).

Slide, Anthony, *The Encyclopaedia of Vaudeville* (Greenwood Press, Westport, Connecticut, 1994).

Smith, Willie 'The Lion' with George Hoefer, *Music on My Mind: The Memoirs of an American Pianist* (Doubleday & Company Inc., New York, 1964).

Southern, Eileen, *The Music of Black Americans: A History (Second Edition)* (W. W. Norton and Company, New York, 1983).

Stewart-Baxter, Derrick, *Ma Rainey and the Classic Blues Singers* (New York, Stein & Day, 1970).

Taylor, Frank C. and Gerald Cook, *Alberta Hunter: A Celebration in Blues* (McGraw Hill, New York, 1988).

Thornton, Michael, *Royal Feud: The Dark Side of the Love Story of the Century* (Simon and Schuster, New York, 1985).

Thygesen, Helge, with Mark Berresford and Russ Shor, *Black Swan: The Record Label of the Harlem Renaissance* (VJM Publications, Nottingham, 1996).

Van Vechten, Carl and Bruce Kellner (ed.) *Keep A-Inchin' Along: Selected Writings of Carl Van Vechten about Black Art and Letters* (Greenwood Press, Westport, 1979).

Van Vechten, Carl and Bruce Kellner (ed.), *The Letters of Carl Van Vechten* (Yale University Press, 1987).

Vincent, Ted, *Keep Cool: The Black Activists Who Built the Jazz Age* (Pluto Press, London, 1995).

Waller, Maurice and Anthony Calabrese, *Fats Waller* (University of Minnesota Press, Minneapolis, 2017).

Waters, Ethel with Charles Samuels, *His Eye is on the Sparrow* (Doubleday, Toronto, 1951).

Work, John W., *American Negro Songs* (Crown Publishers, New York, 1940).

# Notes

## Introduction

1 Stephen Longstreet, *Sportin' House: A History of the New Orleans Sinners and the Birth of Jazz* (Sherbourne Press, Los Angeles, 1965), p. 90.
2 Gordon Seagrove, 'Blues is Jazz and Jazz is Blues', *Chicago Tribune*, 11 July 1915.
3 '"Hot" Music Born Here, Says Blind Musician Who Played with Band that Started It', *Times-Picayune*, 3 November 1935.
4 Author interview with Chris Houston-Lock, March 2021.
5 W. C. Handy, *Father of the Blues* (Macmillan and Company, 1941), p. 74.
6 '"Blues Daddy" Puts his Program Over', *Afro-American*, 8 August 1925.
7 John W. Work, *American Negro Songs and Spirituals* (Bonanza Books, New York, 1940), pp. 32–3.
8 'Blues Mamma "Ma" Rainey Visits Us', *Afro-American*, 10 April 1926.

## Chapter 1: Leaving the South

1 'Captured the Nation's Capital', *Colored American*, 14 May 1904.
2 'They Will Travel', *Tampa Tribune*, 31 January 1900.
3 Ibid.
4 'Pioneer of Negro Vaudeville', *Colored American*, 3 August 1901.
5 'New Advertisements', *Macon Telegraph*, 6 July 1865.

6   Julian Johnson, 'Wee Scotchman's Flying Trip', *Los Angeles Sunday Times*, 2 January 1910.

7   'Andrew Tribble', *The Freeman*, 18 March 1911.

8   'At the Play Houses, *St. Joseph News-Press*, 17 February 1894.

9   'The Variety Stage', *The Referee*, 2 July 1905.

10  'At the National Capital', *The Freeman*, 17 September 1910.

11  Lester A. Walton, 'His Honor, The Barber', *New York Age*, 3 November 1910.

12  Pat Chappelle, 'Prof. Ferris is Sustained', *Colored American*, 29 June 1901.

13  'Pioneer of Negro Vaudeville', *Colored American*, 3 August 1901.

14  '"A Rabbit's Foot" Coming', *Ocala Evening Star*, 7 October 1901.

15  'They Will Travel', *Tampa Tribune*, 31 January 1900.

16  *Webster's Weekly*, North Carolina, 30 June 1904.

## Chapter 2: Ma Rainey Gets the Blues

1   Gates Thomas, *South Texas Negro Work Songs*, Texas Folklore Society, 1926, p. 155.

2   Novelty-Grand advertisement, *Fresno Morning Republican*, 17 November 1904.

3   'A Rabitt's Foot Company' [*sic*], *The Freeman*, 15 June 1907.

4   Paul Oliver, *Conversation with the Blues* (Cambridge University Press, 1977), p. 129.

5   'Street Fair Notes', *Billboard*, 9 March 1907.

6   Jim O'Neal and Amy Van Singel, *The Voice of the Blues* (Routledge, 2002), p. 13.

7   *Jazz Information*, 6 September 1940.

8   Robert Palmer, *Deep Blues* (Penguin Books USA, New York, 1982), p. 44.

9   'Blues Mamma "Ma" Rainey Visits Us', *Afro-American*, 10 April 1926.

10  'The Stage', *Indianapolis Freeman*, 20 November 1909.

11  Sandra Lieb, 'Mother of the Blues: A Study of Ma Rainey', p 18.

12  Paul Oliver, *Conversation with the Blues* (Cambridge University Press, 1977), p. 136.

13  'Memphis Blues', *Nashville Tennessean*, 26 November 1912.

14 Abbe Niles, 'Forward', *Father of the Blues* (Macmillan and Company, 1941).

15 *Overture*, American Federation of Musicians (Los Angeles), December 1955.

16 Scrip, 'Scrip's Ten Best Acts and Annual Review', *Champion Magazine*, January 1917.

17 'Jacksonville Theatrical Notes', *The Freeman*, 16 April 1910.

18 'Pat Chappell Writes From London, Eng.' [sic], *The Freeman*, 24 June 1911.

19 Ibid.

20 Chris Albertson, *Bessie*, pp. 25–6.

## Chapter 3: The Truth About Ma and Bessie

1 'Ma Rainey', *The Paramount Book of Blues*, Paramount Records, 1929.

2 William Russell, *Interview with Lovie Austin*, 25 April 1969, Hogan Jazz Archive, Tulane University.

3 Sandra R. Lieb, *Mother of the Blues: A Study of Ma Rainey* (University of Massachusetts Press, 1981), p. 54.

4 'Pekin Theatre, Memphis, Tenn.', *The Freeman* (Indianapolis), 3 September 1910.

5 'The Stage', *The Freeman*, 24 September 1910.

6 'The Stage', *The Freeman*, 1 October 1910.

7 'Arcade Theatre, Atlanta, Ga.', *The Freeman*, 5 November 1910.

8 'The Savoy Theatre, Memphis, Tenn.', *The Freeman*, 22 October 1910.

9 'The Savoy Theatre, Memphis', *The Freeman*, 12 November 1910.

10 'F. A. Barasso's Tri-State Circuit', *The Freeman*, 11 February 1911.

11 'The American Theater, Jackson, Miss.', *The Freeman*, 18 March 1911.

12 'Wizard Theatre, Norfolk, VA.', *The Freeman*, 1 April 1911.

13 Ibid.

14 'Gossip of the Stage', *The Freeman*, 9 September 1911.

15 Wayne Burton, 'The Show is a Success', *The Freeman*, 9 December 1911.

16 'Notes From the Lyre Theatre, Louisville, KY', *The Freeman*, 2 March 1912.

17 George Slaughter, 'Lyre Theater', *The Freeman*, 9 March 1912.

18 'Colored Notes', *The Lexington Leader*, 7 July 1912.

19 F. J. W. Seer, 'Globe Theater, Jacksonville, Fla.', *The Freeman*, 4 February 1911.

20 'Cincinnati Theatricals – the Pekin', *The Freeman*, 10 August 1912.

21 Lester A. Walton, 'Music and the Stage', *New York Age*, 6 June 1912.

22 J. W. Seer, 'Globe Theater, Jacksonville, Fla.', *The Freeman*, 21 January 1911.

23 Gertrude Rainey, 'Mrs. Rainey's Letter of Protest', *The Freeman*, 28 January 1911.

24 Frank C. Taylor and Gerald Cook, *Alberta Hunter: A Celebration in Blues* (McGraw-Hill, New York, 1988), p. 11.

25 Derrick Stewart-Baxter, *Ma Rainey and the Classic Blues Singers* (Stein and Day, New York, 1970), p. 42.

26 'Colored Notes', *Lexington Leader*, 3 August 1913.

27 Sandra R. Lieb, *Mother of the Blues: A Study of Ma Rainey* (University of Massachusetts Press, 1981), p. 18.

28 Alan Baker, 'Scene and Heard', *Corsair*, 18 November 1959.

29 Charles Edward Smith, 'Ma Rainey and the Minstrels', *Record Changer*, September 1955.

30 *Twin City Daily Sentinel*, 15 October 1915.

31 Al Wells, 'Alex Tolliver's Big Show', *The Freeman*, 4 March 1916.

32 'Blues Mamma "Ma" Rainey Visits Us', *Afro-American*, 10 April 1926.

33 Advertisement, *Times-Picayune*, 17 May 1919.

## Chapter 4: Alberta, Tony and the Grizzly Bear

1 Dr M. A. Majors, 'The Dancing and the Juxto-Position', *The Broad Ax*, 22 September 1923.

2 'The Negro Moves North', *Atlanta Independent*, 28 June 1923.

3 http://archive.tuskegee.edu/repository/digital-collection/lynching-information/

4 Ben Stuttgart, 'South Alarmed as Thousands Leave', *Chicago Whip*, 23 December 1922.

5 Havelock Ellis, Henry, *Studies in the Psychology of Sex Volume Two: Sexual Inversion* (F. A. Davis Company, Philadelphia, second edition, 1915), pp. 351–2.

6   Ibid.

7   'War on Hotel Lobby Dope Fiends', *The Day Book*, 26 November 1912.

8   'Second Deputy's Office Cut Off as Aid to Crime', *Chicago Tribune*, 18 June 1919.

9   'Nootbaar Bares Flagrant Vice in "Tan" cafes', *Chicago Tribune*, 16 November 1917.

10  'Cabaret Dances Tames to Stately Minuet', *Chicago Tribune*, 8 May 1916.

11  Ibid.

12  'Blues Singer Making Big N.Y. Splash at Age 82', *Daily Dispatch*, 23 February 1978.

13  Ibid.

14  Steve Cushing, *Blues Before Sunrise: the Radio Interviews* (University of Illinois Press, 2010), p. 40.

15  'Colored Man is Slashed in Face', *Rock Island Argus*, 27 May 1915.

16  Nell Kimball, Stephen Longstreet (ed.), *Nell Kimball: Her Life as an American Madam, by Herself* (Macmillan, New York, 1970).

17  Nat Shapiro and Nat Hentoff, *Hear Me Talkin' to Ya: The Story of Jazz as Told by the Men Who Made it* (Rinehart & Co., New York, 1955), p. 89.

18  Rudi Blesh and Harriet Janis, *They All Played Ragtime* (Jazz Book Club, London, 1960), p. 160.

19  Glover Compton Interview, 30 June 1959. Hogan Oral Histories collection, HJA-033, Tulane University Special Collections, Howard-Tilton Memorial Library, Tulane University, New Orleans.

20  Nat Shapiro and Nat Hentoff, *Hear Me Talkin' to Ya: The Story of Jazz as Told by the Men Who Made it* (Rinehart & Co., New York, 1955), p. 74.

21  ibid., p. 75.

22  Alan Lomax, *Mr Jelly Roll* (University of California Press, 1950), p. 45.

23  William Russell, *Interview with Lovie Austin*, 25 April 1969, Hogan Jazz Archive, Tulane University.

24  Chris Albertson, *Bessie* (revised and expanded edition, Yale University Press, New Haven, 2003), pp. 21–2.

25  'Blues Singer Making Big N.Y. Splash at Age 82', *Daily Dispatch* (Moline, Illinois), 23 February 1978.

26  'Politicians Named as Bar "Fixers"', *The Day Book*, 17 October 1916.

27  'Second Deputy's Office Cut Off as Aid to Crime', *Chicago Tribune*, 18 June 1919.

28  'New Williams Releases', *New York Clipper*, 16 August 1922.
29  'The Stage: Dreamland', *Chicago Whip*, 13 November 1920.
30  'Alberta Hunter Arrested', *Chicago Whip*, 15 December 1920.

### Chapter 5: Porter Grainger

1   'Music, Boon For Tired Nerves Says American Manufacturer', *Lancaster News Journal*, 19 July 1923.
2   'Have We A New Sex Problem Here?', *Chicago Whip*, 27 November 1920.
3   William Russell, *Interview with Lovie Austin*, 25 April 1969, Hogan Jazz Archive, Tulane University.
4   Frank C. Taylor with Gerald Cook, *Alberta Hunter: A Celebration in Blue*s (McGraw-Hill, New York, 1988), p. 66.
5   Clifford R. Shaw, *The Jack-Roller: A Delinquent Boy's Own Story* (University of Chicago Press, 1966), pp. 84–5.
6   'Long Beach Recital of Shameless Men', *Los Angeles Times*, 19 November 1914.
7   Author interview with Sarah Kilborne, December 2022.
8   'Orders Movie Trust to be Broken Up', *New York Times*, 2 October 1915.
9   'The Beautiful Vocalion Studio', advert, *New York Times*, 25 May 1919.
10  J. A. Jackson, 'A Tip To Our Songwriters', *Billboard*, 26 March 1921.
11  Scarborough, Dorothy, *On the Trail of Negro Folk-Songs* (Harvard University Press, Cambridge, Massachusetts, 1925), p. 265.
12  Willie 'The Lion' Smith and George Hoefer, *Music on my Mind: The Memoirs Of an American Pianist* (Doubleday, New York, 1964), p. 104.
13  Okeh Records advertisement, *Evening News*, 26 October 1920.
14  'Happy Lawson Makes Hit at Masonic', *Albany-Decatur Daily*, 24 November 1916.
15  'Howard Theater – Mamie Smith', *Washington Post*, 19 December 1920.
16  'Acts get Routes', *New York Clipper*, 11 May 1921.

### Chapter 6: Ethel Waters and Early Harlem

1   'The Man on the Outside', *Buffalo American*, 22 September 1921.
2   Justin Martin, *Rebel Souls: Walt Whitman and America's First Bohemians* (Da Capo Press, Boston, 2014), p. 76.

3  'Outlaws to Go', *New York Evening World*, 4 January 1892.

4  Ibid.

5  'Race Riot in New York', *Watchman and Southeron*, 1 January 1902.

6  *Clarke Courier*, 1 January 1902.

7  'Race Riot at Childersburn' [*sic*], *Weekly Democrat*, 1 January 1902.

8  'Unwise Segregation', *New York Age*, 21 February 1920.

9  'Negro Literary Renaissance', *New York Age*, 29 August 1925.

10  Joan Nestle and Deb Edel, 'Interview With Mabel Hampton, July 1986', Lesbian Herstory Archives AudioVisual Collections.

11  Mabel Hampton (interviewee) and Joan Nestle (interviewer), 'Mabel Hampton, 1988', Lesbian Herstory Archives AudioVisual Collections.

12  Steve Cushing, *Blues Before Sunrise* (University of Illinois Press, Chicago, 2010), p. 43.

13  'The Spirit of Corporation is Awakening', *Negro Star*, 21 January 1921.

14  Ethel Waters interviewed by Willie Ruff, 1974, Yale University Library.

15  'Record Co.'s Object to Colored Men Making Phonograph Records', *Voice of the People*, 26 February 1921.

16  Black Swan Records Now, *Black Dispatch*, 6 May 1921.

17  Advertisement, *California Eagle*, 17 September 1921.

18  Black Swan Records Now, *Black Dispatch*, 6 May 1921.

19  'Negro Grand Opera', *Black Dispatch*, 12 August 1921.

20  'Black Swan Artist Agrees Not to Marry Within Year', *New York Age*, 24 December 1921.

21  Ethel Waters with Charles Samuels, *His Eye is on the Sparrow* (Doubleday, Toronto, 1951), p. 1.

22  Ibid., p. 19.

23  Ibid., p. 58.

24  Ibid., p. 91.

25  Ibid.

26  Nat Shapiro and Nat Hentoff, *Hear Me Talkin' to Ya: The Story of Jazz as Told by the Men Who Made it* (Dover Books, 1966), p. 243.

27  Ethel Waters with Charles Samuels, *His Eye is on the Sparrow* (Doubleday, Toronto, 1951), p. 149.

28  Ibid., p. 150.

29  Mabel Hampton (interviewee) and Joan Nestle (interviewer), 'Mabel Hampton, 1988', Lesbian Herstory Archives AudioVisual Collections.

30  Ethel Waters with Charles Samuels, *His Eye is on the Sparrow* (Doubleday, Toronto, 1951), p. 139.

31  Stephen Bourne, *Elisabeth Welch: Soft Lights and Sweet Music* (The Scarecrow Press, Lanham, Maryland, 2005), p. 15.

32  'Noted Singer Barred From Marriage', *Chicago Whip*, 24 December 1921.

33  Ibid.

34  'Demand for Ethel Waters Record', *Talking Machine World*, 15 August 1921.

35  'Entertains Ethel Waters', *Chicago Defender*, 4 February 1922.

36  Frank C. Taylor and Gerald Cook, *Alberta Hunter: A Celebration in Blues* (McGraw-Hill, New York, 1988), p. 49.

37  Dave Peyton, 'Review: the Grand', *Chicago Whip*, 14 January 1922.

38  Dave Peyton, 'With the Actors', *Chicago Whip*, 21 January 1922.

39  'Musician is Shot From Ambush', *Chicago Whip*, 21 January 1922.

40  'Jazz Artists Quit as Ethel Waters Starts South', *Chicago Whip*, 11 February 1922.

41  Ethel Waters interviewed by Willie Ruff, 1974, Yale University Library.

42  'Ethel Waters Sings for Radio', *Chicago Whip*, 29 April 1922.

43  Fred J. Kern, 'Editorial Page', *Belleville News-Democrat*, 11 September 1923.

## Chapter 7: Clara and Josephine

1  'She is a Real Comedy Chorus Girl', *Philadelphia Inquirer*, 20 May 1923.

2  'Gossip of the Stage', *The Freeman*, 13 January 1912.

3  'Actors Responsible For Dressing Rooms', *Afro-American*, 13 December 1924.

4  Ethel Waters with Charles Samuels, *His Eye is on the Sparrow* (Doubleday, Toronto, 1951), p. 166.

5  Ibid., p. 89.

6  Ibid., p. 166.

7  Ibid., p. 166.

8  Ibid., p. 151.

9  'Small Crowd Hear Ethel Waters Co.', *Savannah Tribune*, 18 May 1922.

10  'Ethel Waters, Famous Blues Singer, Coming', *Savannah Tribune*, 4 May 1922.

11 'Small Crowd Hear Ethel Waters Co.', *Savannah Tribune*, 18 May 1922.

12 Advert for the Dixie Theatre, *Knoxville Sentinel*, 3 May 1920.

13 Tim Murari, 'Josephine Baker', *The Guardian*, 25 August 1974.

14 Jean-Claude Baker, *Josephine* (Cooper Square Press, 2001), p. 38.

15 Ibid.

16 Ibid., p. 39.

17 Frank C. Taylor and Gerald Cook, *Alberta Hunter: A Celebration in Blues* (McGraw Hill, 1988), p. 69.

18 Josephine Baker and Jo Bouillon, *Josephine* (Harper and Row, New York, 1977), p. 21.

19 Bond's Gramophone Shop advertisement, *The Tennessean*, 11 October 1923.

20 Coy Hearndon, 'Coy Cogitates', *Chicago Defender*, 27 February 1926.

21 Jean-Claude Baker and Chris Chase, *Josephine: The Hungry Heart'* (Random House, New York, 1993), pp. 63–4.

22 Bryan Hammond and Patrick O'Connor, *Josephine Baker* (Johnathan Cape, London, 1988) p. 8.

23 'She is a Real Comedy Chorus Girl', *Philadelphia Inquirer*, 20 May 1923.

24 Leo Seligsohn, 'Meeting at the Met for Josephine Baker', *Newsday*, 4 November 1976.

25 'Gertrude Saunders Gives Her Ideas About Dancing', *New York Tribune*, 26 June 1921.

26 '"The Chocolate Brown" a Musical Comedy with a Sustained Plot', *New York Age*, 23 July 1921.

27 'Race Menaced by Masculine Women and Effeminate Men, Cardinal Says', *Times Recorder*, 9 March 1920.

28 'Why Some Men are Effeminate', *Nebraska State Journal*, 13 February 1921.

29 Emily Post, 'Insists cavemen Methods Do Not Appeal to Women', *Des Moines Tribute*, 7 May 1923.

30 'Third Sex in Art? Yes, says Psychoanalyst', *New York Sunday News*, 19 February 1922.

31 'Effeminate Men', *New York Daily News*, 9 October 1921.

32 'Music Will Get to You if You Are Exhausted', *Harrisburg Telegraph*, 19 July 1923.

33 'Nosey Sees All Knows All', *Chicago Whip*, 18 December 1920.

34 'Nosey Sees All Knows All', *Chicago Whip*, 29 January 1921.

35 'Nosey Sees All Knows All', *Chicago Whip*, 1 April 1922.

36 'Nosey Sees All Knows All', *Chicago Whip*, 4 March 1922.

37 'Nosey Sees All Knows All', *Chicago Whip*, 6 November 1920.

38 Brett Beemyn (ed.), *Creating a Place For Ourselves: Lesbian, Gay, and Bisexual Community Histories* (Routledge, London, 1997), p. 126.

## Chapter 8: Bessie Makes a Record

1 'The Latest Blues by Columbia Race Stars', Columbia Records catalogue, 1927.

2 'Nosey Sees All, Knows All', *Chicago Whip*, 23 April 1921.

3 'Barrel Houses & Buffet Flats', New York Age, 4 May 1916.

4 'Buffet Flats', *New York Age*, 3 February 1910.

5 Ruby Smith interviewed by Chris Albertson, 7 February 1971.

6 'Police Can't See Vice', *Chicago Daily News*, 10 October 1913.

7 'Nosey Sees All, Knows All', *Chicago Whip*, 26 November 1921.

8 'Nosey Sees All, Knows All', *Chicago Whip*, 5 November 1921.

9 Bob Colton and Len Kunstadt, 'The Emerson Diary', *Record Research*, December 1958.

10 Letter from Alberta Hunter to Christopher Jameson, 19 April 1959.

11 Advertisement, *Birmingham Reporter*, 18 November 1922.

12 Nat Shapiro and Nat Hentoff, *Hear Me Talkin' to Ya: The Story of Jazz as Told by the Men Who Made it* (Rinehart & Co., New York, 1955), p. 247.

13 Stephen Calt, 'The Anatomy of a "Race" Label, Part Two', 78 Quarterly, Number 4, 1989.

14 Ibid.

15 'Chicago is New Center For Phonograph Records', *Pittsburgh Courier*, 29 September 1923.

16 Paramount advertisement, *Birmingham Reporter*, 10 February 1923.

17 Author interview with J. D. Doyle, November 2022.

18 'New Williams Releases', *New York Clipper*, 16 August 1922.

19 Porter Grainger and Bob Ricketts, *How to Play and Sing the Blues Like the Phonograph and Stage Artists* (Jack Mills, New York, 1926).

20 Author interview with Gaye Adegbalola, June 2021.

21 Author interview with Ted Brown, February 2021.
22 Billy Chambers, 'Chambers Review', *Pittsburgh Courier*, 28 July 1923.
23 Billy Chambers, 'Chambers Review', *Pittsburgh Courier*, 15 September 1923.
24 Abel, 'Reviews of Disks', *New York Clipper,* 17 August 1923.
25 Abel, 'Reviews of Disks', *New York Clipper,* 24 August 1923.

## Chapter 9: Bessie Gets Married and Britain Gets the Blues

1 'A Scientific Theory', *Lincoln Star*, 25 June 1923.
2 Village Raid Nets 4 Women and 9 Men, *New York Times*, 5 February 1923.
3 'About You! And You!! And You!!!', *New York Clipper*, 2 May 1923.
4 'New Broadway Star', *Afro-American*, 11 May 1923.
5 'Clara Smith is Now Recording For Okeh', *Pittsburgh Courier,* 9 June 1923.
6 'Atlanta', *Talking Machine World*, 15 July 1923.
7 'Fine Columbia Business', *Talking Machine World*, 15 August 1923.
8 'T. M. Osborne Indicted on 7 Counts', *The Sun* (New York), 29 December 1915.
9 Kate Richards O'Hare, 'Dangerous Criminals Purchase Freedom', *Appeal to Reason*, 4 September 1920.
10 Author interview with Ted Brown, February 2021.
11 'The Reel Players', *Detroit Free Press*, 5 February 1923.
12 Nat Shapiro and Nat Hentoff, *Hear Me Talkin' To Ya* (Rinehart & Co,, 1955), p. 108.
13 Ralph Gulliver, 'The Band from Columbus', *Storyville 48*, August 1973.
14 'New Dances and Music', *Birmingham Daily Gazette*, 28 July 1923.
15 'Description of the "Blues-Trot" by Morry M. Blake, Inventor of the Dance', from the sheet music to 'The Original Blues-Trot Blues', by Joseph Gilbert and Morry Blake, Lawrence Wright Music Co., 1923.
16 'Fond of the Blues', *Dundee Courier*, 3 December 1924.
17 Michael Thornton, *Royal Feud: The Dark Side of the Love Story of the Century* (Simon and Schuster, 1985), p. 397.
18 'In Dahomey', *Sporting Times*, 23 May 1903.
19 'Attack on Coloured Actors', *Daily Telegraph*, 12 January 1904.

20 'Today's London Letter', *Edinburgh Evening News*, 25 May 1903.

21 'The Lighter Side', *Nottingham Evening Post*, 24 March 1924.

22 'Sir Alfred Butt Defends Coloured Artists', *The Era*, 14 March 1923.

23 Warre B. Wells, 'Many Protests in British capital over Invasion of Colored Players', *New York Age*, 7 April 1923.

24 Ibid.

25 'The Greatest Singer of "Blues"', *Cleveland Gazette*, 3 November 1923.

26 'A List of Colored Companies', *Billboard*, 6 August 1921.

27 'The Monogram', *Chicago Whip*, 10 July 1920.

28 *Wilson Daily Democrat*, 7 June 1923.

29 'Circus and Carnival News', *Billboard*, 9 December 1922.

30 'Wortham Shows to Open Here Monday', *Corsicana Daily Sun*, 4 May 1923.

31 J. A. Jackson, 'Broadway Strutters', *Billboard*, 6 January 1923.

32 Jim O'Neal and Amy van Singel, *The Voice of the Blues: Classic Interviews from Living Blues Magazine* (Routledge, 2002), p. 13.

33 Paul Oliver, *Conversation with the Blues* (Cambridge University Press, 1977), p. 137.

34 Ibid., p. 138.

### Chapter 10: Peachtree Man Blues

1 Paul Oliver, *Blues Fell This Morning* (second edition, Cambridge University Press, 1990), p. 99.

2 'Stranger Than Fiction', *Morning News*, 29 December 1891.

3 'Wedded to a Woman', *Pittsburgh Dispatch,* 5 July 1892.

4 Stranger Than Fiction', *Morning News*, 29 December 1891.

5 Ibid.

6 'Notes From Here and There', *The Tatler*, 10 August 1921.

7 Anthony Slide, *The Encyclopaedia of Vaudeville* (Greenwood Press, Westport, Conn., 1994), p. 375.

8 O. O. McIntyre, 'New York Day By Day', 14 August 1923.

9 'The Theatre', *Time*, 29 September 1924.

10 Bebe Scarpie, 'Famous E. Russell', *Drag*, Volume 3, number 12, 1973.

11 Ibid.

12 'Omnibus', *Buffalo Weekly Express*, 4 December 1860.

13 Advertisement for Carr's Melodeon, *Buffalo Evening Post*, 16 October 1862.

14 'The Eden Musee', *Pittsburgh Commercial Gazette*, 16 March 1895.

15 'Nickelodeon', *Boston Globe*, 12 January 1896.

16 'Lalah Coolah', *Lexington Herald*, 3 August 1902.

17 'Half and Half in Freak Act at the Hillside', *Long Island Daily Press*, 9 June 1928.

18 'Half Man, Half Woman Arrested', *Wilkes Barre Record*, 25 April 1892.

19 'Death Due to Heat', *The Republic*, 21 July 1905.

20 'In the Cabarets', *Chicago Whip*, 27 March 1920.

21 Ethel Waters with Charles Samuels, *His Eye is on the Sparrow* (Doubleday, Toronto, 1951), p. 73.

22 Artie Renkle, Blindman's Blues Forum, 27 August 2005.

23 Paul Oliver, *Blues Fell This Morning* (second edition, Cambridge University Press, 1990), p. 99.

24 'American Couple Prosecuted at Blackpool', *Lancashire Evening Post*, 22 August 1930.

25 'Man-Woman Case. Josephine-Joseph of Blackpool', *Leeds Mercury*, 23 August 1930.

26 'Showman Fined', *Edinburgh Evening News*, 23 August 1930.

27 'Man-Woman Case. Josephine-Joseph of Blackpool', *Leeds Mercury*, 23 August 1930.

28 'Half Man, Half Woman', *Rugby Advertiser*, 15 August 1930.

29 'Public Tricked', *Hull Daily Mail*, 29 August 1930.

30 'The Half and Half Man-Woman', *Daily Mail*, 24 October 1930.

31 Jas Obrecht, *Blues Guitar: The Men Who Made the Music* (GPI Books, San Francisco, 1993), pp. 264–5.

32 Norman Dayron, quoted in the sleeve notes to the 2000 CD 'Knockin' Myself Out'.

## Chapter 11: In Harlem's Araby

1 Mme Qui Vive, 'Beauty', *Buffalo Evening News*, 25 March 1926.

2 *Broadway Brevities*, October 1923.

3 Advertisement, *Hot Dog Regular Fellows Monthly*, November 1922.

4 Mark Barron, 'Jolson Heading back to Broadway', *St. Louis Daily Globe-Democrat*, 16 June 1940.

5   'New York', *Los Angeles Examiner*, 21 September 1921.

6   'Her Own Tragic Fade-Out Reverses the "Happy Ending" of All Her Pretty Photoplays', *Kansas City Daily Star*, 4 September 1921.

7   'Naughty New York', *Capt. Billy's Whiz-Bang*, Volume III, Number 27, November 1921.

8   '"Hush" a Movie Scandal', *Kansas City Star*, 24 August 1921.

9   Marjorie Wilson, 'Movieland Days and Nights', *Fort Worth Record-Telegram*, 13 November 1921.

10  Ibid.

11  'Mirrors of Mayfair', *Broadway Brevities*, October 1923.

12  O. O. McIntyre, 'New York Day By Day', *Lexington Herald-Leader*, 21 February 1924.

13  Jackie Rogers, 'Girl Thief Bares Lure to Crime', *New York Daily News*, 2 November 1925.

14  'Queen Goes Big at New Lincoln', *Pittsburgh Courier*, 22 March 1924.

15  The Flying Cavalier, 'Carrying the Torch', *New York Age*, 4 March 1933.

16  Chris Albertson, *Bessie* (revised and expanded edition, York University Press, 2003), p. 84.

17  Buddy Browning, 'Fag Balls Exposed', *Brevities*, 14 March 1932.

18  The Flying Cavalier, 'Carrying the Torch', *New York Age*, 4 March 1933.

19  'Turn Out For Fag Ball in Hot Harlem', *California Eagle*, 13 March 1936.

20  'Made a Raid', *Evening Star*, 1 January 1896.

21  'Police Raid on a Dance House', *Washington Evening Star*, 15 January 1887.

22  'The Queen Raided', *National Republican*, 13 April 1888.

23  'High Rents and Overcrowding Responsible for Many of the Ills Suffered by Harlemites', *New York Age*, 11 August 1923.

24  'Women Rivals for Affection of Another Woman Battle With Knives', *New York Age*, 27 November 1926.

25  Joan Nestle interview with Mabel Hampton, 28 December 1988. Lesbian Herstory Archives AudioVisual Collections.

26  Ibid.

27  Lee Chadwick, 'Easy Going Fats & Precision Made Lunceford Send Hot Club Cats', *Down Beat*, July 1937.

28  Alyn Shipton, *Fats Waller: The Cheerful Little Earful* (Continuum, New York, 2002), p. 100.

29  '"Blues Not Funny", says Bessie Smith', *Pittsburgh Courier*, 15 March 1924.

30  'Bessie Smith Highest Salary', *Variety*, 30 December 1925.

31  J. A. 'Billboard' Jackson, 'Around New York with Billboard Jackson', *Afro-American*, 2 May 1925.

32  J. A. 'Billboard' Jackson, 'Around Harlem with Billboard Jackson, *Afro-American*, 6 June 1925.

33  'Sissle and Blake Coming to Nixon Theater', *Pittsburgh Courier*, 15 March 1924.

34  'Chocolate Dandies is Well Worth Attending', *Times-Tribune* (Scranton), 30 December 1924.

35  'The Chocolate Dandies', *Variety*, 3 September 1924.

36  'Chocolate Dandies Coming Here Soon', *Minneapolis Star*, 7 February 1925.

37  'Cabaret Reviews: Tan Town Topics', *Variety*, 19 August 1925.

38  'Tan Town Topics Great Floor Show', *Afro-American*, 29 August 1925.

39  Stephen Bourne, *Elisabeth Welch: Soft Lights and Sweet Music* (The Scarecrow Press, Lanham, Maryland, 2005), p. 32.

40  Sisley Huddleston, 'Lights of Paris', *The Sketch*, 14 October 1925.

41  René, 'Parisiana', *The Bystander*, 4 November 1925.

## Chapter 12: Million Dollar Blues

1  'Ethel's History', *Chicago Defender*, 25 December 1926.

2  'Famous Blues Artist Coming From Alabama', *Pittsburgh Courier*, 25 October 1924.

3  Thomas Fulbright, 'Ma Rainey and I', *Jazz Journal*, March 1956.

4  Danny Barker interviewed for the 1989 documentary, *Wild Women Don't Have the Blues*.

5  Bob Hayes, 'Ma Rainey's Revue', *Chicago Defender*, 13 February 1926.

6  The Scribe, 'Ma Rainey a Riot', *Chicago Defender*, 2 January 1926.

7  Paul Oliver, *Conversation with the Blues* (Cambridge University Press, 1977), p. 138.

8  'Police Take Much of Star's Charm', *Pittsburgh Daily Post*, 31 October 1924.

9  Nat Shapiro and Nat Hentoff, *Hear Me Talkin' to Ya: The Story of Jazz as Told by the Men Who Made it* (Rinehart & Co., New York, 1955), p. 248.

10  Paul Oliver, *Conversation with the Blues*, (Cambridge University Press, 1977), p. 138.

11  Stephen G. Clow, 'How I Blackmailed the Stars of Society and the Stage', *Shreveport Times*, 1 January 1928.

12  'Smashing the Broadway Blackmailers', *The Morning Call*, 15 June 1924.

13  'Next Week at the Booker Washington Theater', *St. Louis Argus*, 14 April 1916.

14  Ethel Waters with Charles Samuels, *His Eye is on the Sparrow* (Doubleday, Toronto, 1951), p. 71.

15  'Gem Theater Bill', *Lexington Herald-Leader*, 4 August 1912.

16  Letter from Tolliver and Harris to Charles Henry Douglass, 1925, courtesy of Middle Georgia Archives via Digital Library of Georgia.

17  Albertson, *Bessie*, (Yale University Press, London, 2003), p. 88.

18  'Clara Smith is No Blues Singer', *Afro-American*, 22 May 1926.

19  Carl Van Vechten (Bruce Kellner, ed.), *Keep A-Inchin' Along: Selected Writings of Carl Van Vechten about Black Art and Letters* (Greenwood Press, Westport, 1979), p. 174.

20  'Lucky Sambo', *Variety*, 21 October 1925.

21  'Lucky Sambo Review, *Billboard*, 16 January 1926.

22  Roy E. White, 'Harlem Frolics', *Atlanta Constitution*, 27 November 1926.

23  'Fine Photoplay and Classy Stage Show on Elmore Bill', *Pittsburgh Courier*, 6 April 1929.

24  Jonathan Katz, *Gay American History* (Meridian, New York, 1992), p. 78.

25  Ruby Smith, recorded interview with Chris Albertson, circa 1971

26  Jonathan Katz, *Gay American History* (Meridian, New York, 1992), p. 79.

27  Ibid., p. 78.

## Chapter 13: Sissies, Freaks, 'Half-Pint' and The Hokum Boys

1  Herman Petzer, 'Afternoons Around Akron', *Akron Beacon Journal*, 26 March 1926.

2  Maurice Waller and Anthony Calabrese, *Fats Waller* (University of Minnesota Press, 2017), p. 60.

3  Hal, 'Cabarets', *Variety*, 21 April 1926.

4   Author interview with Sarah Kilborne, December 2022.

5   'Report NY Police Frown on "Drag" at Bridgeport Bow', *Variety*, 2 February 1927.

6   '"The Drag" As Play With 40 of "Our Sex"', *Variety*, 24 November 1926.

7   '"The Drag" Opening', *Variety*, 26 January 1927.

8   'A Word of Appreciation', *Topeka Plaindealer*, 18 December 1925.

9   'An Evening of Mirth and Melody', *Topeka Plaindealer*, 21 August 1925.

10  *New York Dramatic Mirror*, 7 December 1918.

11  'Paderewski's Genius', *Fresno Morning Republican*, 8 April 1900.

12  Kennard Williams, 'The Spotlight: Stage Music', *Afro-American*, 17 October 1925.

13  William H. Miller, 'Great Little Guy: The Life and Times of Frankie "Half Pint" Jaxon', *Australian Jazz Quarterly* issue 3, December 1946.

14  'Enoch L. Johnson, Ex-Boss in Jersey. Prohibition-Era Ruler of Atlantic City, 85, Dies', *New York Times*, 10 December 1968.

15  '43 Persons Arrested in raid on Cabaret', *St. Louis Post-Dispatch*, 19 April 1926.

16  Sylvester Russell's Review, *The Pittsburgh Courier*, 19 March 1927.

17  Jim O'Neal, *The Voice of the Blues: Classic Interviews from Living Blues Magazine*, (Routledge, New York, 2002), p. 25.

18  Ibid., p. 26.

19  'Seen and Heard at the Fair', *The Chicago Defender*, 10 June 1933.

20  *California Eagle*, 4 March 1932.

21  Author interview with Brett Houston-Lock, March 2021.

## Chapter 14: He Just Don't Appeal to Me

1   Spike Hughes, 'Paul', *Daily Herald*, 4 May 1935.

2   Elva Diane Green, 'A Good Man is Hard to Find', www.unlikelystories. org

3   'The Career of Marion Harris', *Democrat and Chronicle*, 30 January 1921.

4   'A Good Man is Hard to Find', *Billboard*, 1 March 1919.

5   Onah Spencer, 'Alberta Hunter, Born on Beale Street, has Sung in 25 Countries', *Down Beat*, 1 January 1941.

6   Carl Van Vechten, 'Memories of Bessie Smith', *Jazz Record*, September 1947.

7   Edward Jablonski and Lawrence D. Stewart, 'The Gershwin Years' (Doubleday, New York, 1973), p. 143.

8   'Review of Disks', *New York Clipper*, 17 August 1923.

9   'Review of Disks', *New York Clipper*, 24 August 1923.

10  Carl Van Vechten, 'Negro "Blues" Singers', *Vanity Fair*, March 1926.

11  Ibid.

12  Chris Albertson, *Bessie*, Yale University Press, London, 2003, p. 175.

13  Ibid.

14  'Barney Josephson, Owner of Cafe Society Jazz Club, Is Dead at 86', *New York Times*, 30 September 1988.

15  'Connie's Inn Has New Floor Show', *Afro-American*, 7 February 1925.

16  'Harlem Cabarets', *Afro-American*, 20 September 1930.

17  'William's Dreamland Theater', *The Freeman*, 27 May 1916.

18  'The Theatres', *Boston Herald*, 24 December 1929.

19  'Hot Chocolates' advertisement, *Bridgeton Evening News*, 13 February 1935.

20  'Baby Cox Nabbed In "Love Nest" By Her Irate Hubby', *Chicago Whip*, 10 October 1931.

21  Wilbur Young, 'Negroes of New York: Sketches of Colorful Harlem Characters', 1939, New York Public Library.

22  'The Clam House', *Afro-American*, 1 March 1930.

23  Gladys Bentley, 'I Am a Woman Again', *Ebony*, August 1952.

24  Ibid.

25  Joan Nestle and Deb Edel, 'Interview with Mabel Hampton', tape four, July 1986, Lesbian Herstory Archives AudioVisual Collections.

26  'New Singers, New Songs with Hall Johnson Choir', *New York Age*, 22 June 1929.

27  Langston Hughes, *The Big Sea* "Part Three: When the Negro was in Vogue", (Alfred A. Knopf, 1940).

28  'Life's Been Hard on Moms Mabley', *Washington Post*, 4 October 1974.

29  Bob Terrell, 'Moms Mabley... Genuine Mountain Bred Character', *Asheville Citizen-Times*, 22 October 1971.

30  Moms Mabley interview with Studs Terkel, WFMT, 13 June 1961.

31  Joan Nestle interview with Mabel Hampton, 28 December 1988. Lesbian Herstory Archives AudioVisual Collections.

32  Author interview with Gaye Adegbalola, June 2021.

33  Charles Edward Smith, 'Ma Rainey and the Minstrels', *Record Changer*, September 1955.

34  W. E. B. du Bois, *The Autobiography of W. E. B. du Bois* (International Publishers, 1968), p. 282.

### Chapter 15: It's Dirty But Good

1  'Black Georgians in History', *The Atlanta Journal*, 24 February 1989.

2  'New Acts Advised Against Coming to N.Y.', *Afro-American*, 5 January 1929.

3  Advertisement for the Star Theatre, Annapolis, *The Evening Capital*, 11 November 1929.

4  Paul Oliver, *Conversation With the Blues* (Cambridge University Press, 1977), p. 123.

5  Ibid., p. 65.

6  Author interview with Chris Houston-Lock, March 2021.

7  Ed Kirkeby with Duncan P. Schiedt and Sinclair Traill, *Ain't Misbehavin': The Story of Fats Waller* (Da Capo Press, New York, 1975), p. 41.

8  Frank C. Taylor and Gerald Cook, *Alberta Hunter: A Celebration in Blues* (McGraw-Hill, New York, 1988), p. 29.

9  'Records Noted', *The Record Changer*, November 1949.

10  Author interview with Gaye Adegbalola, June 2021.

11  Mike Rowe, 'The Blue Harmony Boys', *Blues Unlimited 123*, January–February 1977.

12  'Sylvester Russell's Review', *Pittsburgh Courier*, 2 July 1927.

13  'Bernardi Exposition Shows', *Billboard*, 12 October 1929.

14  Paul Oliver, *Conversation with the Blues*, (Cambridge University Press, 1977), p. 128.

15  Thomas Fulbright, 'Ma Rainey and I', *Jazz Journal*, March 1956.

### Chapter 16: Raiding the Pansy Club

1  'The Pansy Craze. Is It Entertainment or Just Plain Filth?', *Afro-American*, 6 October 1934.

2  Albertson, *Bessie*, (Yale University Press, London, 2003), p. 129.

3  Victoria Spivey, 'Blues is my Business', *Record Research 44*, July 1962.

4   Ernest Varlack, 'Philadelphia Mirror', *Afro-American*, 12 January 1929.

5   'New Plays Loom', *Cincinnati Enquirer*, 26 May 1929.

6   Walter Winchell, 'Your Broadway, And Mine', *San Pedro News Pilot*, 21 May 1929.

7   Advertisement, *Chicago Defender*, 6 April 1935.

8   Mark Hellinger, 'All In A Day', *The Syracuse Journal*, 14 August 1933.

9   Sidney Skolsky, 'Behind the News', *New York Daily News*, 20 September 1930.

10  'Wisecrackers', *Brooklyn Citizen*, 21 October 1930.

11  Bud Murray, 'In Hollywood – Now', *Inside Facts of Stage and Screen*, 1 November 1930.

12  Levi Hubert, 'On Seventh Avenue', *Afro-American*, 27 December 1930.

13  *New York Daily News*, 29 March 1930.

14  'Here's What's Happening at Harlem's Famous Ubangi Club', *Afro-American*, 8 February 1936.

15  Wilbur Young, 'Negroes of New York: Sketches of Colorful Harlem Characters', Schomburg Center, New York Public Library: WPA Writers Program, 1939.

16  Louis Sobol, 'The Voice of Broadway', *Washington Times*, 9 May 1934.

17  Louis Sobol, 'The Voice of Broadway', *Washington Times*, 28 July 1934.

18  Wilbur Young, 'Negroes of New York: Sketches of Colorful Harlem Characters', 1939.

19  'Rival Gunmen "Shoot It Out" in Night Club', *Dixon Evening Telegraph*, 24 January 1931.

20  Tom Cassidy, 'Whoops Dearie! Mean Old Police raid Pansy Row', *New York Daily News*, 29 January 1931.

21  Ibid.

22  'Two Night Club Operators Held', *Brooklyn Daily News*, 29 January 1931.

23  Frank Byrd, 'Harlem Pictured as Night Life Capital of the World', *Afro-American*, 26 April 1930.

24  'Pansy Places on Broadway', *Variety*, 10 September 1930.

25  Harold E. Stearns, 'Paris Accords "Pierrot Lunaire" Mixed Welcome', *Baltimore Sun*, 23 April 1922.

26  O. O. McIntyre, 'A New Yorker Abroad', *Fort Worth Star-Telegram*, 20 March 1928.

27 Chappy Gardner, 'Actors Have Made "Gay Harlem" Popular in All Corners of the World', *Pittsburgh Courier*, 29 December 1934.

28 Frank Byrd, 'Harlem Pictured as Night Life Capital of the World', *Afro-American*, 26 April 1930.

29 'Municipal Court', *Burlington Free Press*, 11 September 1925.

30 'Preston and Murray Must Serve At Least One Year At Windsor', *Burlington Daily News*, 12 September 1925.

31 'Pansies O.K. at Shore', *Afro-American*, 5 July 1930.

32 The Rambler, 'It's Nobody's Business', *Afro-American*, 2 August 1930.

33 Blind Blake, *The Paramount Book of Blues*, Paramount, 1927.

34 Mary Campbell, 'Reluctant Leon Redbone Will Tour U.S.', *Indiana Evening Gazette*, 7 October 1978.

35 'Old Statute to Wilt Pansy Club', *New York Daily News*, 6 February 1931.

36 'Negroes Fight Police in Big Gaming Raid', *Evening World*, 27 September 1921.

37 Langston Hughes, 'The Big Sea', Alfred A. Knopf, New York, 1940.

38 'Third Sex Plague Spreads Anew!', *New Broadway Brevities*, 2 November 1931,

39 'New York Letter', *Brownsville Herald*, 24 November 1931.

40 O. O. McIntyre, 'New York Day By Day', *Reno Evening Gazette*, 17 December 1931.

41 O. O. McIntyre, 'New York Day By Day', *Burlington Daily News*, 7 January 1932.

42 Lois Long, 'Tables For Two', *The New Yorker*, 14 May 1932.

## Chapter 17: B.D. Women and Old Maids

1 George B. Murphy Jr., 'Ethel Waters Wants to Play "Scarlet Sister"', *The Advocate*, 8 August 1931.

2 'Old Man Trouble', *Film Daily*, 9 June 1929.

3 'Lucky in Love', *Tampa Morning Tribune*, 19 September 1929.

4 'Porter Grainger's New Book Finished, *Pittsburgh Courier*, 24 May 1930.

5 'Ethel Waters Opens in Chicago', *The Advocate*, 19 April 1930.

6 *The Performer*, 27 November 1929.

7 George B. Murphy Jr., 'Ethel Waters Wants to Play "Scarlet Sister"', *The Advocate*, 8 August 1931.

8  'Veteran Actor Clifton Webb Succumbs to Attack', *The Dispatch*, 14 October 1966.

9  'Mitch Woodbury Reports', *Toledo Blade*, 11 December 1940.

10  Telegram from Noël Coward to Ethel Waters, dated 25 December 1933, W. E. B. Du Bois Papers, University of Massachusetts.

11  'Seeks to Ban Songs of Gladys Bentley', *New York Amsterdam News*, 22 February 1933.

12  T-Bone Walker's Story In His Own Words, www.britishbluesarchive.org.uk

13  Victoria Spivey, 'Blues is my Business', *Record Research 44*, July 1962.

14  Sara Grimes: *BackWaterBlues: In Search of Bessie Smith*, (Rose Island Pub, Amherst, 2000) p. 50

15  Ibid. p. 233

16  S. B., 'Harlem Opera Show Weak', *New York Age*, 3 November 1934.

17  'Theatricals', *New York Age*, 23 February 1935.

18  'Theatricals', *New York Age*, 11 May 1935.

19  'Theatricals', *New York Age*, 3 August 1935.

20  Al Moses, 'Bessie Smith Still "Queen of the Blues"', *Pittsburgh Courier*, 26 December 1936.

21  Billie Holiday, *Lady Sings the Blues* (Penguin Classics, 2018), p. 6.

22  Donald Clarke, *Wishing on the Moon: The Life and Times of Billie Holiday* (Viking, New York, 1994), p. 346.

23  Allan Morrison, 'A Southerner Looks at Prejudice', *Ebony*, January 1960.

24  Ibid.

25  Billie Holiday, 'I'm Cured For Good', *Ebony*, July 1949.

26  Letter from Billie Holiday to Tallulah Bankhead, 12 January 1955.

27  Billie Holiday, *Lady Sings the Blues*, p. 33.

28  NBJC profile of Lucille Bogan, April 2018: https://beenhere.org/2018/04/02/lucille-bogan.

29  Author interview with Ted Brown, February 2021.

## Chapter 18: Death Letter Blues

1  L. N. Newberry, 'Lead Belly of Blue Danube?', *Beaumont Journal*, 16 August 1939.

2  'Two Shows Tuesday', *Columbus Evening Dispatch*, 1 January 1935.

3  'Josephine Baker Captures Paris as Dramatic Actress', *The Negro Star*, 11 January 1935.

4  O. O. McIntyre, 'New York Day By Day', *Arkansas Gazette*, 4 February 1935.

5  'The Theatre: New Plays in Manhattan', *Time*, 10 February 1936.

6  Ed Sullivan, 'Broadway', *Daily Times*, 22 January 1936.

7  Josephine Baker and Jo Bouillon, *Josephine* (Harper and Row, New York, 1977), p. 103.

8  Paul Harrison, 'In Old New York', *Indianapolis Times*, 19 January 1935.

9  Chester King, 'Around the Tables', *Brooklyn Daily Eagle*, 6 November 1936.

10  Paul Harrison, 'In New York', *Dunkirk Evening Observer*, 22 March 1934.

11  Ibid.

12  'Female Impersonators Taboo Here', *Afro-American*, 29 August 1931.

13  Augustus Austin, 'Fletcher Henderson's Band Pleases at Opera House', *New York Age*, 1 September 1934.

14  Edward John Burra, William Chappell (ed.), *Well Dearie! The Letters of Edward Burra* (Gordon Fraser, London, 1985), p. 79.

15  Richard Bruce Nugent, 'On Gloria Swanson', 15 September 1939.

16  Advertisement, *New York Amsterdam News*, 8 January 1938.

17  Spike Hughes, 'Personal Column', *Daily Herald*, 5 October 1937.

18  John A. Saunders, 'Elite of Stage World Weep at Bier of Bessie', *Pittsburgh Courier*, 9 October 1937.

19  David Medina, 'The Selling of Bessie Smith', *New York Daily News*, 21 November 1976.

20  John Hammond, 'Bessie's Voice "Full of Shoutin' & Moanin' & Prayin'" Was Powerful To The End', *Down Beat*, December 1937.

21  John Hammond, 'Did Bessie Smith Bleed To Death While Waiting For Medical Aid?', *Down Beat*, November 1937.

22  'Claims Article On Bessie Smith Untrue', *Pittsburgh Courier*, 15 January 1938.

23  Joe Maita, 'Chris Albertson, Author of Bessie', www.jerryjazzmusician.com, 22 September 2003.

24  Louis Sobel, 'Voice of Broadway', *Lexington Herald-Leader*, 10 October 1937.

25  Allan McMillan, 'New York Sees Bessie Smith; Wonders Where She's Been', *Chicago Defender*, 28 March 1936.

26  'Still Tops', *Chicago Defender*, 30 March 1936.

27  Elliot Brown, 'Bessie Smith's Grave Gets Stone, 33 Years After Death', *Philadelphia Inquirer*, 8 August 1970.

28  Ibid.

29  Dorothy Kilgallen, 'The Voice of Broadway', *New Orleans States*, 12 December 1939.

30  Briefs filed before the Third Circuit Court of Appeals: Jack Gee Jr. et al v. CBS, Inc. and Columbia Records, concerning ownership of Bessie Smith's sound recordings, 13 December 1979.

31  George Colson, 'Harlem Uproar House, N.Y.', *Billboard*, 10 April 1937.

32  Walter Winchell, On Broadway', *The Post Star*, 13 June 1939.

33  'Footlight Flickers', *The Plaindealer*, 3 February 1939.

34  'Grainger's Panorama on Feb. 17', *New York Age*, 16 February 1939.

35  'Social Snapshots', *New York Age*, 11 January 1941.

36  David E. Newton, *Marijuana: A Reference Handbook* (2nd edition, ABC-Clio, Santa Barbara, California), p. 183.

37  Donald Bogle, *Heat Wave: The Life and Career of Ethel Waters* (Harper Perennial, New York, 2012), pp. 516–7

38  'Ethel Waters Scores in Television Debut', *The Plaindealer*, 14 July 1939.

39  Theresa Hall, 'Ethel Waters Finds She Can't Get Hold of God in Nighteries', *Baltimore Afro-American,* 3 August 1946.

40  Elliott Sirkin, 'Bobby Short: Singing the Praises of Ethel Waters', *Newsday*, 27 June 1985.

41  Phil Moore, *Things I Forgot to Tell You* (unpublished autobiography manuscript), 1985-87, Indiana University Black Film Centre Archive.

42  'Manager of Raided Resort Fined $20', *San Francisco Examiner*, 5 April 1934.

43  Advert for Gladys Bentley at the Doll House, *Valley Times*, 19 December 1947.

44  Gladys Bentley, 'I Am a Woman Again', *Ebony*, August 1952.

45  'Women Who Pass For Men', *Jet*, 28 January 1954.

46  Press release for 'Twilight for Gladys Bentley', March 2013.

## Chapter 19: Any Woman's Blues

1  Bruce Warren, 'Sister Rosetta Tharpe Gets Her Day in the Rock & Roll Hall of Fame', *NPR.org*, 12 April 2018.

2  Harry Gannes, 'Inside Story of Corruption of Nazi Regime', *Daily Worker*, 7 July 1934.

3  'Torgler "Counsel" Linked to Storm Troop Chief', *Daily Worker*, 18 September 1933.

4  'Hitler System Squalid, Cruel', *Spokane Chronicle*, 20 September 1940.

5  Joe Deniz interviewed by Gerald Harper on 'And the Bands Played On', ATV 1980.

6  'The Empire', *Birmingham Gazette*, 7 September 1937.

7  'Bush Empire', *Acton Gazette*, 1 October 1937.

8  Ibid.

9  Stephen Bourne, *Fighting Proud: The Untold Story of the Gay Men Who Served in Two World Wars* (Bloomsbury Academic, London, 2019), p. 150.

10  Tim Murari, 'Josephine Baker', *The Guardian*, 25 August 1974.

11  '"Tropicana," Another New Musical, Coming To Apollo Theatre', *New York Age*, 1 March 1941.

12  Frank Marshall Davis, 'Rating the Records', *Omaha Guide*, 4 February 1939.

13  Barrelhouse Dan, 'Digging the Discs With Dan', *Down Beat*, May 1939.

14  Sleeve notes to *Let Us Get Together*, MC Records, 2007.

15  Courtland Milloy, 'The Odessa Files: The Life and Times of the Queen of Washington's Underworld', *Washington Post*, 7 May 2010.

16  Donald Clarke, *Wishing on the Moon: The Life and Times of Billie Holiday* (Viking, New York, 1994), p.345.

17  'Josephine Baker says Stork Club Prejudiced', *Troy Record*, 19 October 1951.

18  Westrook Pegler, 'As Pegler Sees It', *Park City Daily News*, 28 January 1955.

19  Walter Winchell, 'New York Newsletter', *Evening Gazette*, 6 February 1936.

20  *Jet*, 13 September 1979.

21  Aldin Vaziri, 'Gwen Avery, Passionate Singer-Songwriter and Feminist, Dies', sfgate.com, 8 February 2014.
22  Author interview with Gaye Adegbalola, June 2021.
23  Author interview with Sarah Kilborne, December 2022.
24  Author interview with Gaye Adegbalola, June 2021.

# Acknowledgements

Huge thanks to Jill Adam, Jon Robb and the team at Louder Than Words, Gaye Adegbalola, Shirlette Ammons, Ted Brown, Paul Burns, Mikel Chamizo, Sean Dickson, J. D. Doyle (curator of the Queer Music Heritage website), Debra Geddes, Dean and Andrew Griffith, Julia Halford, Brett and Chris Houston-Lock, Robin Ince, Sarah Kilborne, the Milligan family, the team at Omnibus including David Barraclough, Claire Browne, Greg Morton and David Stock, Andy Partridge and Erica Wexler, Pete Paphides, Darren Peace, the Prosser family, Ricardo Salazar, Peter Scott-Presland, Chris Smith, Richard Thomas and the team at the Laugharne Weekend, Jon Tregenna and all involved with the Penderyn Music Book Prize, Mitchell Winn, the Woodward family... and last but by no means least, Niall and the kids.

# About the Author

Darryl W. Bullock is a writer specialising in music history and LGBTQ issues. He is the author of several books, including *Pride, Pop and Politics: Music, Theatre and LGBT Activism 1970–2021*, *The Velvet Mafia: The Gay Men Who Ran the Swinging Sixties* which won the 2022 Penderyn Music Book Prize and *David Bowie Made Me Gay: 100 Years of LGBT Music*. He has also had two volumes culled from his blog and internet radio show, *The World's Worst Records*. He lives in Bristol with a dog, two cats, an incredibly patient husband and a ridiculously eclectic record collection.